Marxism and Form

TWENTIETH-CENTURY
DIALECTICAL THEORIES
OF LITERATURE

Marxism and Form

TWENTIETH-CENTURY
DIALECTICAL THEORIES
OF LITERATURE

BY FREDRIC JAMESON

PRINCETON, NEW JERSEY
PRINCETON UNIVERSITY PRESS

Copyright © 1971 by Princeton University Press
ALL RIGHTS RESERVED
L.C. Card: 71-155962
ISBN: 0-691-06204-8

Publication of this book has been aided
by a grant from the Whitney Darrow Publication Reserve Fund
of Princeton University Press

This book has been composed in Linotype Caledonia

Printed in the United States of America
by Princeton University Press, Princeton, New Jersey

Il n'existe d'ouvert à la recherche mentale que deux voies,
en tout, où bifurque notre besoin, à savoir,
l'esthétique d'une part et aussi l'économie politique.

—Mallarmé

Intelligent idealism is closer to intelligent materialism
than is unintelligent materialism.

—Lenin

CONTENTS

PREFACE

WHEN THE American reader thinks of Marxist literary criticism, I imagine that it is still the atmosphere of the 1930's which comes to mind. The burning issues of those days— anti-Nazism, the Popular Front, the relationship between literature and the labor movement, the struggle between Stalin and Trotsky, between Marxism and anarchism—generated polemics which we may think back on with nostalgia but which no longer correspond to the conditions of the world today. The criticism practiced then was of a relatively untheoretical, essentially didactic nature, destined more for use in the night school than in the graduate seminar, if I may put it that way; and has been relegated to the status of an intellectual and historical curiosity, as which, in the form of an occasional stray reprint of an essay by Plekhanov or a passing reference to Christopher Caudwell, it is presently maintained.

In recent years, however, a different kind of Marxist criticism has begun to make its presence felt upon the English-language horizon. This is what may be called—as opposed to the Soviet tradition—a relatively Hegelian kind of Marxism, which for the German countries may be traced back to the theoretical excitement of Lukács' *History and Class Consciousness* in 1923, along with the rediscovery of Marx's *Economic and Philosophical Manuscripts of 1844*; while in France it may be most conveniently dated from the Hegel revival there during the late thirties.

I would be well pleased if the chapters that follow were found useful as a general introduction to that Marxism and to some of its principal theoreticians. I have in particular tried to give a full account of some of its key works— Lukács' *Theory of the Novel* as well as his *History and Class Consciousness*, Bloch's *Hope the Principle*, Benjamin's

Origins of German Tragedy, Adorno's *Philosophy of the New Music* and *Negative Dialectics,* Sartre's *Critique of Dialectical Reason*—which have been, at worst, inaccessible to the English-language reader and, at best, little discussed here.

Even such a relatively modest and straightforward task as this is, however, a whole program in itself: for one thing, even the better-known writers such as Sartre or Lukács have never come into focus clearly in English on account of the anti-Communist bias of their commentators, or often simply on account of the absence of any genuine Marxist culture in academic circles.

Less obvious, perhaps, is the degree to which anyone presenting German and French dialectical literature is forced —either implicitly or explicitly—to take yet a third national tradition into account, I mean our own: that mixture of political liberalism, empiricism, and logical positivism which we know as Anglo-American philosophy and which is hostile at all points to the type of thinking outlined here. One cannot write for a reader formed in this tradition—one cannot even come to terms with one's own historical formation —without taking this influential conceptual opponent into account; and it is this, if you like, which makes up the tendentious part of my book, which gives it its political and philosophical cutting edge, so to speak. For the bankruptcy of the liberal tradition is as plain on the philosophical level as it is on the political: which does not mean that it has lost its prestige or ideological potency. On the contrary: the anti-speculative bias of that tradition, its emphasis on the individual fact or item at the expense of the network of relationships in which that item may be embedded, continue to encourage submission to what is by preventing its followers from making connections, and in particular from drawing the otherwise unavoidable conclusions on the political level. It is therefore time for those of us in the sphere of influence of the Anglo-American tradition to learn to think dialectically, to acquire the rudiments of a dialectical culture and the essential critical weapons which it provides. I would be gratified if this book contributed even in a small way to such a development.

What follows is, however, not philosophy but literary criticism, or at least a preparation for literary criticism. The stress Marx laid on individual works of art and the value they had for him (as for Hegel before him and Lenin after) were very far from being a matter of personality: in some way, which it is the task of Marxist theory to determine more precisely, literature plays a central role in the dialectical process. I might also add that the closed realm of literature, the experimental or laboratory situation which it constitutes, with its characteristic problems of form and content and of the relationship of superstructure to infrastructure, offers a privileged microcosm in which to observe dialectical thinking at work.

At the same time, if the chapters that follow do not present any of the rigor of technical philosophical investigation, their status as language remains ambiguous: for they are also far from being simplified introductory sketches, or journalistic surveys of the various positions and key ideas of a writer, anecdotal narratives of his situation and his relationship to the problems of his time. Not that these things are uninteresting or without their usefulness; but from my point of view, they remain on the level of sheer *opinion* only, which is to say of intellectual attitudes seized from the outside. I have felt that the dialectical method can be acquired only by a concrete working through of detail, by a sympathetic internal experience of the gradual construction of a system according to its inner necessity. Nor have I attempted to "reconcile" these various constructions in the course of presentation; rather, in a final section, I have tried to describe the process of dialectical thinking in general, and the ways in which it can deal with literature in particular.

I should say something about the difference in emphasis between the German and the French chapters. From the point of view of the nondialectical Anglo-American tradition both modes of thought are equally exciting, equally liberating, but in different ways. It is worth pointing out that in Germany dialectical thinking has always been an official, it not *the* official, philosophical tradition: only recently again, the triumph of Adorno over Heideggerian existence-philosophy marked the renewal of the schools with that tradition after the long darkness of the Hitler period.

It is for this reason, I think—because in Germany the dialectic somehow speaks in its own name—that I have ordered these chapters around the sign of Discourse itself: for in the works they deal with, as already in Hegel, dialectical thought turns out to be nothing more or less than the elaboration of dialectical sentences. To give a little of the feeling of this sense of the movement of reality as a logos, I have resorted to the very terminology of linguistic figures themselves, of tropes and rhetoric, in which the operation of dialectical thought is viewed as a process or figure; or to that of a type of presence to and decipherment of experience which may be thought of as a hermeneutical exegesis of a text.

This is, no doubt, the moment to say something about style; and whatever my reservations about stylistics as a method in itself, I remain faithful to the notion that any concrete description of a literary or philosophical phenomenon—if it is to be really complete—has an ultimate obligation to come to terms with the shape of the individual sentences themselves, to give an account of their origin and formation. I have not always, in these chapters, pushed that far.

Nowhere is the hostility of the Anglo-American tradition toward the dialectical more apparent, however, than in the widespread notion that the style of these works is obscure and cumbersome, indigestible, abstract—or, to sum it all up in a convenient catchword, *Germanic*. It can be admitted that it does not conform to the canons of clear and fluid journalistic writing taught in the schools. But what if those ideals of clarity and simplicity have come to serve a very different ideological purpose, in our present context, from the one Descartes had in mind? What if, in this period of the overproduction of printed matter and the proliferation of methods of quick reading, they were intended to speed the reader across a sentence in such a way that he can salute a readymade idea effortlessly in passing, without suspecting that real thought demands a descent into the materiality of language and a consent to time itself in the form of the sentence? In the language of Adorno—perhaps the finest dialectical intelligence, the finest stylist, of them all—density is itself a conduct of intransigence: the bristling mass of abstractions and cross-references is precisely intended to be read in situation, against the cheap facility of what surrounds it, as a warning to the reader of the price he has to pay for genuine thinking. The resolute abstractness of this style stands as an imperative to pass beyond the individual, empirical phenomenon to its meaning: abstract terminology clings to its object as a *sign* of the latter's incompleteness in itself, of its need to be replaced in the context of the totality. I cannot imagine anyone with the slightest feeling for the dialectical nature of reality remaining insensible to the purely formal pleasure of such sentences, in which the shifting of the world's gears and the unexpected contact between apparently unrelated and distant categories and objects find sudden and dramatic formulation. It is not, I would like to emphasize, a question of *taste*, any more than the validity of dialectical thinking is a question of *opinion*;

but it is also true that there can be no reply to anyone choosing to discuss the matter in those terms.

When we turn now to the French tradition, it is at once apparent that it is of a far more concrete character: France has indeed become the philosophical home of phenomenology and, with Lacan, of Freudianism, as well as of applied Marxism. For the French situation is such that dialectical thought, like psychoanalysis, has never been an official philosophy, and has thus had to express itself through an underground influence on other philosophies and other disciplines—in the form of an extracurricular Marxist culture, or by way of the Hegel revival already mentioned. So Lévi-Strauss has professed to be a Marxist, while it is incalculable to what degree Sartrean existentialism owes its enormous influence not so much to elements from Kierkegaard or Heidegger as rather to those it found in Hegel himself.

The *Critique* is, however, essentially a work of political science, and it may seem paradoxical to find it discussed at such length in a work devoted to literary criticism. In the case of dialectical thought, to be sure, one cannot indefinitely separate the political from the ideological or the cultural; Sartre's book, moreover, has the advantage of allowing us to deal directly with those realities of class and economic basis and history which were merely presupposed in the German chapters. But essentially the value of Sartre's book for a dialectical literary criticism lies in the way it poses the problem—vital for any Marxist theory—of *mediation*: How do we pass, in other words, from one level of social life to another, from the psychological to the social, indeed, from the social to the economic? What is the relationship of ideology, not to mention the work of art itself, to the more fundamental social and historical reality of groups in conflict, and how must the latter be understood if we are to be able to see cultural objects as social acts, at once disguised and transparent? Sartre's enormous book therefore yields the techniques for a genuine Marxist *hermeneutics*, techniques which we then go on to systematize in a final chapter, in which, in Derrida's expression, we "deconstruct" the basic model of a dialectical literary criticism and demonstrate its various functions.

The attempt to work out a little more precisely some of the methodological implications of a Marxist position is bound to meet with objections of various kinds. If, as Lichtheim believes, Marxism is both German and historical, i.e., over and done with as a living and developing philosophy, then what we are doing here must be something else. From the point of view of the various Marxisms themselves, however, the writers in this book run the gamut from neo-Hegelian idealism, simple revisionism, and existentialism to extreme left deviationism and ultra-Bolshevism (Merleau-Ponty's description of the later, Marxist Sartre). I myself understand revisionism as the act of making a theory comfortable and palatable by leaving out whatever calls for praxis or change, whatever is likely to be painful for the purely contemplative intellectual consumption of a middle-class public: thus the revision of Freud quietly suppresses what we may call his materialistic foundation, namely, the insistence on the plainly sexual etiology of personality disorders. Marxist revisionism since Bernstein has similarly involved the elimination of the notion of class struggle as such; and the reader will evidently have to make his own judgment as to such tendencies in the present work.

He is, however, entitled to a more complete explanation of why he should be expected to familiarize himself at such length with that remote, complex, and forbiddingly technical system which is the philosophy of Hegel. I have taken the position here that in reality Marx *includes* Hegel, but I can well understand, at the same time, that such elaborate conceptual equipment may seem disproportionate to the daily work of literary criticism and to the individual texts themselves. This is, however, to misjudge the role of literary criticism as such in the process of political education.

We may describe the rhetoric of the older Marxist criticism as *genetic* in its emphasis on historical evolution and on the emergence of capitalist institutions from the earlier feudal and tribal modes of social organization. The works of Gordon Childe provide a familiar and characteristic example of such an approach in British historiography, while in the realm of literary criticism the books of Christopher Caudwell and of Ernst Fischer, the *Aesthetik* of Lukács, may all be taken as illustrations, in their different ways, of the same basic strategy, which focuses the reader's attention on the initial differentiation of art itself as it grows apart from ritual and religion and gradually establishes itself, first as a specialized body of techniques in its own right, and finally as a business, or an antibusiness, in modern times. The ideological effect of such an approach, above and beyond the anthropological facts with which it is concerned on the literal level, is to reorder our perception of the historical present, to restructure our vision of modern society in such a way that we are able to distinguish the shape of an older collective artistic practice behind the individualism of the literary and artistic present. The notion of historical evolution is thus essentially a *form* or pretext for a new politization of our thinking, which gives us to understand what kinds of future social renewal and regeneration are available to us by allowing us a glimpse of the healthier, socially functional art of the past.

Present-day Western culture, however, no longer lends itself to such a polemical restructuration. For one thing, I doubt if there are many people left who feel that there is much either in our art or in our society itself—at least in the extreme that it has reached in the United States today—which is worth salvaging in this fashion. For another, the continuity between the present and the historical and pre-historic past on which such a demonstration depended seems to have been definitively sundered by the new modes of production and organization of postindustrial capitalism. The reality with which the Marxist criticism of the 1930's had to deal was that of a simpler Europe and America, which no longer exist. Such a world had more in common with the life forms of earlier centuries than it does with our own. To say that it was simpler is by no means to claim that it was easier as well: on the contrary! It was a world in which social conflict was sharpened and more clearly visible, a world which projected a tangible model of the antagonism of the various classes toward each other, both within the individual nation-states and on the international scene as well—a model as stark as the Popular Front or the Spanish Civil War, where people were called on to take sides and to die, which are, after all, always the most difficult things.

It is this visibility and continuity of the class model, from the daily experience in the home and on the street all the way up to total mobilization itself, which is no longer available today. Its disappearance is of course a relative and national matter. Thus France retains a class character which the Germany of the *Wirtschaftswunder* has long since lost, and this is clearly reflected in the respective emphases of the works discussed in the present book. But for the most part, and particularly in the United States, the development of postindustrial monopoly capitalism has brought with it an increasing occultation of the class structure through techniques of mystification practiced by the media and particularly by advertising in its enormous expansion since the onset of the Cold War. In existential terms, what this means is that our experience is no longer whole: we are no longer able to make any felt connection between the concerns of private life, as it follows its own

xvii

course within the walls and confines of the affluent society, and the structural projections of the system in the outside world, in the form of neocolonialism, oppression, and counterinsurgency warfare. In psychological terms, we may say that as a service economy we are henceforth so far removed from the realities of production and work on the world that we inhabit a dream world of artificial stimuli and televised experience: never in any previous civilization have the great metaphysical preoccupations, the fundamental questions of being and of the meaning of life, seemed so utterly remote and pointless.

In such a situation, within the United States itself, there is no tactical or political question which is not first and foremost theoretical, no form of action which is not inextricably entangled in the sticky cobwebs of the false and unreal culture itself, with its ideological mystification on every level. Not whether the street fighter or urban guerrilla can win against the weapons and technology of the modern state, but rather precisely where the street *is* in the superstate, and, indeed, whether the old-fashioned street as such still exists in the first place in that seamless web of marketing and automated production which makes up the new state: such are the theoretical problems of Marxism today, at least in what might be termed the overdeveloped countries.

For it is perfectly consistent with the spirit of Marxism— with the principle that thought reflects its concrete social situation—that there should exist several different Marxisms in the world of today, each answering the specific needs and problems of its own socio-economic system: thus, one corresponds to the postrevolutionary industrial countries of the socialist bloc, another—a kind of peasant Marxism—to China and Cuba and the countries of the Third World, while yet another tries to deal theoretically with the unique questions raised by monopoly capitalism in the West. It is in the context of this last, I am tempted to call it postindustrial, Marxism that the great themes of Hegel's philosophy—the relationship of part to whole, the opposition between concrete and abstract, the concept of totality, the dialectic of appearance and essence, the interaction between subject and object—are once again the order of the day. A literary criticism which wishes to be *diagnostic* as well as descriptive will ignore them only at the price of reinventing them.

La Jolla
March 1971

ACKNOWLEDGMENTS

THREE PORTIONS of this book originally appeared in *Salmagundi*: "T. W. Adorno; or, Historical Tropes," in No. 5 (Spring 1967), 3-43; "Walter Benjamin; or, Nostalgia," in Nos. 10-11 (Fall 1969 - Winter 1970), pp. 52-68; and "The Case for Georg Lukács" in No. 13 (Summer 1970), pp. 3-35. I must here express my appreciation to *Salmagundi's* editor, Robert Boyers, for his initial interest in these projects, which might otherwise never have taken the present form. Some of the ideas in the last chapter were originally expressed in the somewhat different context of "Metacommentary," *PMLA*, LXXXVI, No. 1 (January 1971), 9-18. Finally, I must thank Mrs. Linda Peterson for invaluable suggestions and expert help in preparing the manuscript.

Marxism and Form

TWENTIETH-CENTURY
DIALECTICAL THEORIES
OF LITERATURE

CHAPTER ONE

T. W. ADORNO; OR, HISTORICAL
TROPES

To whom can one present a writer whose principal subject
is the disappearance of the public? What serious justification can be made for an attempt to summarize, simplify,
make more widely accessible a work which insists relentlessly on the need for modern art and thought to be difficult,
to guard their truth and freshness by the austere demands
they make on the powers of concentration of their participants, by their refusal of all habitual response in their
attempt to reawaken numb thinking and deadened perception to a raw, wholly unfamiliar real world?

It is as though everything in the life work of T. W.
Adorno were designed to arouse and exacerbate the very
socio-economic phenomenon that it denounces: the division
of labor, the fragmentation of intellectual energies into a
host of seemingly unrelated specialized disciplines. So it is
that Adorno's critique of modern culture, one of the most
thoroughgoing and pessimistic that we possess, cannot be
conveniently scanned in a passing hour between appoint-
ments. Indeed, for reasons which we will fully appreciate
only later on, it is unavailable as a separate thesis of a general nature, for it is at one with Adorno's detailed working
through of the technical specifics of his various preoccupations: those of the professional philosopher, the Hegelian
critic of phenomenology and existentialism; of the composer
and theoretician of music, "musical adviser" to Thomas
Mann during the writing of *Doctor Faustus*; of the occasional but lifelong literary critic; and finally, of the practic-
ing sociologist, who ranged from a pioneering investigation
of anti-Semitism in the monumental *Authoritarian Personal-*

ity to a dissection of the "culture industry" (the term is his) and of so-called popular music.

But although these various and distinct fields of study have their own structures and laws, their own independent traditions, their own precise technical terminology, although they are to be thought of as something more and other than the epiphenomena, the false consciousness, that we associate with the word ideology, they nonetheless share an uneasy existence, an uncertain status, as objects afloat in the realm of culture.

Adorno's treatment of these cultural phenomena—musical styles as well as philosophical systems, the hit parade along with the nineteenth-century novel—makes it clear that they are to be understood in the context of what Marxism calls the *superstructure*. Such thinking thus recognizes an obligation to transcend the limits of specialized analysis at the same time that it respects the object's integrity as an independent entity. It presupposes a movement from the intrinsic to the extrinsic in its very structure, from the individual fact or work toward some larger socio-economic reality behind it. To put it another way, the very term superstructure already carries its own opposite within itself as an implied comparison, and through its own construction sets the problem of the relationship to the socio-economic base or *infrastructure* as the precondition for its completeness as a thought.

The sociology of culture is therefore first and foremost, I would like to suggest, a *form*: no matter what the philosophical postulates called upon to justify it, as practice and as a conceptual operation it always involves the jumping of a spark between two poles, the coming into contact of two unequal terms, of two apparently unrelated modes of being. Thus in the realm of literary criticism the sociological approach necessarily juxtaposes the individual work of art with some vaster form of social reality which is seen in one

4

way or another as its source or ontological ground, its Gestalt field, and of which the work itself comes to be thought of as a *reflection* or a *symptom*, a characteristic *manifestation* or a simple *by-product*, a *coming to consciousness* or an imaginary or symbolic *resolution*, to mention only a few of the ways in which this problematic central relationship has been conceived.

Clearly, then, a sociology of literature has its origins in the Romantic era along with the invention of history itself, for it depends on some prior theorization about the unity of the cultural field: whether the latter is thought of in terms of political regimes (the character of monarchic, as opposed to despotic or republican, society), historical periods (the classic, the medieval, the modern-romantic), the organic language of national character (the English, French, or German temperament), or in the more recent language of cultural personality or socio-economic situation (the postindustrial, the industrializing, the underdeveloped). At first, of course, this type of thinking about the arts, this dawning historicity in the realm of taste, was the property of Right and Left alike, for it has its existential origins in the very convulsions of the revolutionary period itself, and royalists like Chateaubriand were as profoundly aware of the relativity of cultures and the historicity of human experience as was Madame de Stael, whose *Literature Considered in Its Relation to Social Institutions* (1800) may stand, after Vico and Montesquieu, as the first full-blown treatise on the subject. Indeed, we shall have to concern ourselves later on in this book with the problem of distinguishing a sociological, "value-free" approach to literature, which counts the Romantics among its ancestors, from the specifically Marxist form of literary analysis to be presented here.

Once some such notion of cultural unity has been acquired, however, the two essential elements of the sociological operation—work and background—begin to interact in dialectical and indeed almost chemical fashion, and this fact of sheer interrelationship is prior to any of the conceptual categories, such as causality, reflection, or analogy, subsequently evolved to explain it. Such categories may therefore be seen as the various logical permutations or combinations of the initial model, or as the alternating visual possibilities of the Gestalt into which it is organized: the attempts of the mind, after the fact, to account for its ability to subsume two such disparate terms within the framework of a single thought.

In this context, it becomes possible to place the vexed question of determinism by social being, or by "race, moment, milieu," between parentheses, and such issues as those which seemed to oppose Marxism and the Weberians turn out to be optical illusions. For from this point of view, the Marxist analysis of a phenomenon such as Puritanism— that it is one of the ideologies of early capitalism, or in other words that it reflects and is determined by its social context —and that of Max Weber, for whom Puritanism is precisely one of the *causes* or contributing factors in the development of capitalism in the West, are essentially variations on the same model, and have far more in common with each other as *ideograms*—in which a form of consciousness is superposed against the pattern of a collective and institutional organization—than with what we may call the two-dimensional treatments of the separate elements involved, such as works on the theology of the reformers, or on changes in the structure of sixteenth-century commerce.

Such thinking is therefore marked by the will to link together in a single figure two incommensurable realities, two independent codes or systems of signs, two heterogeneous and asymmetrical terms: spirit and matter, the data of individual experience and the vaster forms of institutional society, the language of existence and that of history. Let the following passage from Adorno's *Philosophy of the New Music* stand, therefore, not so much as an implied philosophical proposition, or as a novel reinterpretation of the historical phenomena in question, but rather as a metaphorical composition, a kind of stylistic or rhetorical trope through which the new historical and dialectical consciousness, shattering the syntactic conventions of older analytical or static thought, comes to its truth in the language of events:

> It is hardly an accident that mathematical techniques in music as well as logical positivism originated in Vienna. The fondness for number games is as peculiar to the Viennese mind as the game of chess in the coffee house. There are social reasons for it. All the while intellectually productive forces in Austria were rising to the technical level characteristic of high capitalism, material forces lagged behind. The resultant unused capacity for figures became the symbolic fulfillment of the Viennese intellectual. If he wanted to take part in the actual process of material production, he had to look for a position in Imperial Germany. If he stayed home, he became a doctor or a lawyer or clung to number games as a mirage of financial power. Such is the way the Viennese intellectual tries to prove something to himself, and—bitte schön!—to everyone else as well.[1]

Psychoanalysis of the Austrian character? Object lesson in the way society resolves in the *imaginary* realm those contradictions which it cannot overcome in the real? Stylistic juxtaposition of music, symbolic logic, and financial sheets? The text under consideration is all of these things, but it is first and foremost a complete thing, I am tempted to say a poetic object. For its most characteristic connectives ("it is

[1] T. W. Adorno, *Philosophie der neuen Musik* (Frankfurt, 1958), pp. 62-63.

7

no accident that") are less signs of some syllogistic operation to perform than they are equivalents of the "just as . . . so" of the heroic simile.

Nor does the sudden exchange of energy involved really tell us anything new about either of the elements juxtaposed: indeed, we must already know what each of them is, in its own specificity, to appreciate their unexpected connection with each other. What happens is rather that for a fleeting instant we catch a glimpse of a unified world, of a universe in which discontinuous realities are nonetheless somehow implicated with each other and intertwined, no matter how remote they may at first have seemed; in which the reign of chance briefly refocuses into a network of cross-relationships wherever the eye can reach, contingency temporarily transmuted into necessity.

It is not too much to say that through such a historical form there is momentarily effected a kind of reconciliation between the realm of matter and that of spirit. For in its framework the essentially abstract character of the ideological phenomenon suddenly touches earth, takes on something of the density and significance of an act in the real world of things and material production; while there flashes across the material dimension itself a kind of transfiguration, and what had only an instant before seemed inertia and the resistance of matter, the sheer meaninglessness of historical accident—in the determining factors in Austrian development, the chance agents of geography or foreign influence—now finds itself unexpectedly spiritualized by the ideality of the objects with which it has been associated, reorganizing itself, under the pull of those mathematical systems which are its end product, into a constellation of unforeseen uniformities, into a socio-economic style which can be *named*. Thus the mind incarnates itself in order to know reality, and in return finds itself in a place of heightened intelligibility.

It is, however, one of the most basic lessons of dialectical method that the potentialities for development of a given mode of thought lie predetermined and, as it were, foreordained within the very structure of the initial terms themselves, and reflect the characteristics of its point of departure. The limits on any large-scale projection of the sociological figure here described are therefore implicit in the nature of the objects synthesized. Like wit, the Adorno trope drew its force from the instantaneity of the perception involved,[2] and it is only too clear that to juxtapose against its historical background a cultural item understood in an isolated, atomistic way—whether it be an individual work, a new technique or theory, even something as vast as a new movement understood as a separate entity, or a period style detached from its historical continuum—is to ensure the construction of a model that cannot but be static.

Thus the full-scale study of superstructures, the construc-

[2] This should not, however, be taken as evidence for the presence of two alternating and imperfectly assimilated modes of dialectical thought in Adorno's own work. There, on the contrary, an almost physical cause may be said to account for the structural peculiarity of the text in question, which is neither more nor less than a complete *footnote*: and the abundance, as well as the stylistic and philosophical quality, of the footnotes to *Philosophie der neuen Musik* is itself "no accident" and has symptomatic value. The footnote in this context may indeed be thought of as a small but autonomous *form*, with its own inner laws and conventions and its own determinate relationship to the larger form which governs it—something on the order of the moral of a fable or the various types of digressions which flourished within the nineteenth-century novel. In the present instance, the footnote as a lyrical form allows Adorno a momentary release from the inexorable logic of the material under study in the main text, permitting him to shift to other dimensions, to the infrastructure as well as to the wider horizons of historical speculation. The very limits of the footnote (it must be short, it must be complete) allow the release of intellectual energies, in that they serve as a check on a speculative tendency that might otherwise run wild, on what we will later describe as the proliferation of "theories of history." The footnote as such, therefore, designates a moment in which systematic philosophizing and the empirical study of concrete phenomena are both false in themselves; in which living thought, squeezed out from between them, pursues its fitful existence in the small print at the bottom of the page.

9

tion of the historical trope, not to lyrical but rather to extended and epic proportions, presupposes a transcendence of the atomistic nature of the cultural term: it is essentially the difference between the juxtaposition of an individual novel against its socio-economic background, and the *history* of the novel seen against this same background. In effect, at this point a relationship which was that of form to background, of point to field, gives place to the superposition of two fields, two series, two continua; the language of causality gives way to that of analogy or homology, of parallelism. Now the construction of the microcosm, of the cultural continuum—whether it be the formal history of costume or of religious movements, the fate of stylistic conventions or the rise and fall of epistemology as a philosophical issue—will include the analogy with the socioeconomic macrocosm or infrastructure as an implied comparison in its very structure, permitting us to transfer the terminology of the latter to the former in ways that are often very revealing. Thus it turns out that as a marketable commodity on the spiritual level, the nineteenth-century novel may also be said to have known its version of a stage of "primitive accumulation of capital": the names of Scott and Balzac may be associated with this initial stockpiling of social and anecdotal raw material for processing and ultimate transformation into marketable, that is to say *narratable*, shapes and forms.

At the same time, inasmuch as the cultural is far less complex than the economic, it may serve as a useful introduction to the real on a reduced, simplified scale. Thus Engels spoke of Balzac's "complete history of French society from which, even in economic details (for instance, the rearrangement of real and personal property after the Revolution) I have learned more than from all the professed historians, economists, and statisticians of the period together."[3] Traditionally, indeed, Marxist literary criticism has furnished a convenient introduction both to the subtleties of the dialectical method and to the complexities of Marxist social and economic doctrine. But what Engels learned from the content, a modern Marxist literary criticism ought to be able to demonstrate at work within the form itself: so it is the model that now helps us to read the bewildering and massive substance of the real of which it began by being the projection.

I

THE IDEAL material for a full-scale demonstration of such historical models would no doubt be drawn from spheres as distant from everyday life as possible: non-Euclidean geometry, for example, or the various logical worlds of science fiction, in which our own universe is reduplicated at an experimental level. Illustrations derived from the history of the visual arts or from the development of mathematics are thus more useful for our purposes than the more representational modes of literature or philosophy. For in dialectical treatments of the latter, there tends to take place a kind of slippage from form into content which cannot but blur the methodological points to be made.

Thus our characterization of Balzac's primitive accumulation of raw material above was intended to function on a formal level, to underscore a parallel between two formal processes. Yet the analogy is complicated by the fact that Balzac's raw material, his *content*, happens to be precisely that primitive accumulation of capital with which we compared the form: for the origins of the first businesses and the first fortunes are among the archetypal stories he has to tell. As a model, therefore, literature is not so useful as the

[3] Marx and Engels, *Über Kunst und Literatur* (Berlin, 1953), p. 122.

more abstract arts, and the parallels with developments in the novel will in what follows be underlined as *analogies* to the central model to be presented, rather than as historical projections in their own right.

Yet even the specialized is sometimes taken for granted, even highly sophisticated techniques can come to seem natural in the general indistinction of everyday life. So it turns out that to assess the full originality of Adorno's historical vision, we must try to bring a new unfamiliarity to some of the social phenomena we are accustomed to take for granted: to stare, for instance, with the eyes of a foreigner at the row upon row of people in formal clothing, seated without stirring within their armchairs, each seemingly without contact with his neighbors, yet at the same time strangely divorced from any immediate visual spectacle, the eyes occasionally closed as in powerful concentration, occasionally scanning with idle distraction the distant cornices of the hall itself. For such a spectator it is not at once clear that there is any meaningful relationship between this peculiar behavior and the bewildering tissue of instrumental noises that seems to provide a kind of background for it, like Arab musicians playing behind their curtain. What is taken for granted by us is not apparent to such an outsider, namely that the event around which the concert hall is itself established consists precisely of attention to that stream of sound patterns entering in at the ear, to the organized and meaningful succession of a nonverbal sign-system, as to a kind of purely instrumental speech.

For Western polyphonic music is "unnatural" precisely to the degree to which it has no institutional equivalent in any other culture. Though it has its origins in ritual, though its earliest forms are not essentially distinct from the dance and chant, the pure monody of other cultures, Western music in its most characteristic forms has severed its ties with those primitive musical activities in which the musical substance, still involved in concrete life and social reality, may be said to have remained representational, to have preserved something like a content. There is no longer a mere difference in degree, but rather an absolute one in kind, between the older, functional music and this, which has developed an autonomy of its own, has acquired the status of an event in its own right, and requires its participants to suspend their other activities in the exercise of some alert but nonverbal mental capacity which had never been used before, with the conviction that something real is taking place during fifteen or twenty minutes of practical immobility. It is as if a new sense had been invented (for the active, interpretive concentration which marks such listening is as distinct from ordinary hearing as is mathematical language from ordinary speech), as if a new organ had been developed, a new type of perception formed. What is particularly noteworthy is the poverty of the materials from which such new perception has been fashioned; for the ear is the most archaic of the senses, and instrumental sounds are far more abstract and inexpressive than words or visual symbols. Yet in one of those paradoxical reversals that characterize the dialectical process, it is precisely this primitive, *regressive* starting point that determines the development of the most complex of the arts.

Finally, we must observe that inasmuch as Western music is not natural but historical, inasmuch as its development depends so intensely upon the history and development of our own culture, it is mortal as well, and has it in it to die as a genuine activity, to vanish when it has served its purpose and when that social need which it once answered has ceased to exist. The fact that the production of so-called classical records has become a big business in the present day should not make us lose sight of the privileged relationship between the golden age of Western music and a Central Europe in which a significant proportion of the collectivity performed music and knew it from the inside, in a qualitatively different fashion from the passive consumers of our own time. In much the same way such a genre as the epistolary novel loses its very reason for being and its social as well as linguistic basis in a period when letter writing is no longer an important everyday activity and an institutionalized form of communication. So also certain types of lyric poetry vanish from cultures in which conversation and verbal expression are colorless and without life, lacking in any capacity for those twin forms of expansion which are eloquence or figuration.

So it is that Western music at the very outset marks itself off from the culture as a whole, reconstitutes itself as a self-contained and autonomous sphere at distance from the everyday social life of the period and developing, as it were, parallel to it. Not only does music thereby acquire an internal history of its own, but it also begins to duplicate on a smaller scale all the structures and levels of the social and economic macrocosm itself, and displays its own internal dialectic, its own producers and consumers, its own infrastructure.

In it, for instance, as in the larger world of business and industry, we find a tiny history of inventions and machines, what might be called the engineering dimension of musical history: that of the instruments themselves, which stand in the same ambiguous relationship of cause and effect to the development of the works and forms as do their technological equivalents (the steam engine) in the world of history at large (the industrial revolution). They arrive on the scene with a kind of symbolic fitness: "it is not for nothing that the newly soulful tone of the violin counts among the great innovations of the age of Descartes."[4] Throughout its long ascendancy, indeed, the violin preserves this close identification with the emergence of individual subjectivity

---

[4] T. W. Adorno, *Versuch über Wagner* (Frankfurt, 1952), p. 8.

14

on the stage of philosophical thought. It remains a privileged medium for the expression of the emotions and demands of the lyrical subject, and the violin concerto, much like the *Bildungsroman*, stands as the vehicle for individual lyric heroics, while in other forms the massed orchestral strings conventionally represent the welling up of subjective feeling and of protest against the necessities of the objective universe. By the same token, when composers begin to suppress the singing violin tone and to orchestrate without strings or to transform the stringed instrument into a plucked, almost percussive device (as in the "ugly" pizzicati, the strummings and "weird" falsetto effects of Schoenberg), what happens to the violin is to be taken as a sign of the determination to express what crushes the individual, to pass from the sentimentalization of individual distress to a new, postindividualistic framework.

In a similar way, the rise of the saxophone, in that commercial music which replaces the older folk art of the masses, has symbolic value: for with it vibration, the oscillation back and forth in place, supersedes the soaring of the violin as an embodiment of subjective excitement in the modern age, and a metallic sound, all pipes and valves, yet "sexually ambivalent" to the degree to which it "mediates between brass and woodwinds" ("being materially related to the former, while it remains woodwind in its mode of performance"),[5] replaces the living warmth of the older instrument, which expressed life, where the newer one merely simulates it.

And if musical forms evolve in response to their public (church and salon music being little by little supplanted by middle-class spectator forms), so also they are influenced by the changing social functions of their performers as well. Wagner, himself a great conductor, for the first time undertakes to compose music in which the role of the virtuoso

[5] T. W. Adorno, *Moments musicaux* (Frankfurt, 1964), p. 123.

15

conductor is foreseen and built into the structure of the score. As in parliamentary demagoguery, the listening masses submit to the conductor with a kind of hypnotized fascination. The quality of their listening deteriorates; they lose that autonomy of judgment and intensity of concentration which the earlier generations of the triumphant middle class brought to their practice of the art. Thus they are increasingly unable to follow anything as thoroughly organized as a Beethoven sonata, and instead of the theme and variations with its development and resolution in time, Wagner offers them something cruder and easier to grasp: the repetition of easily recognizable themes not unlike advertising slogans, "fatefully" underlined for the listener's benefit by the dictatorial gesture of the conductor.

At the same time, the development of the leitmotif must be understood in terms of the autonomous dialectic of the musical tradition itself, as one of the stages in that slow working out of musical laws and of the possibilities inherent in the musical raw material. From this point of view, the Wagnerian theme, with its rigidity and its nondeveloping character, must be seen as a regression from the themes of Beethoven, which were functionally inseparable from their context. If there is for music something like a "heresy of paraphrase"—in the brutal wrenching of melody or theme from a texture in which alone it has its reason for being— then it must be added that such a practice finds its initial stimulus not so much in the caprice or formal ignorance of the individual listener as in the deeper equivalence—or cleavage—between form and content in the very structure of the work itself.

For Beethoven the sonata represented a complex solution to the problem of musical identity and musical change. The characteristics of the form—the dispatching of the theme to the most distant and unexpected keys (in order that it may return, this time with a kind of finality, to its point of

16

origin), the thoroughgoing metamorphoses it is made to undergo in variation after variation (in order to demonstrate the more surely its identity with itself)—are at one with the very establishment of the tonal system itself, for they amount to a concrete reenactment before the listener of tonality as a self-evident law, reconfirmed through the form.

For Wagner, however, the problem is that of setting up a relationship between leitmotifs which cannot be varied in the old sense, for it is now the leitmotif rather than the basic key of the composition which is the element of permanence. To make a virtue of necessity: the expression fixes the very essence of the dialectical process at the same time that it defines Wagner's freedom with respect to the historical situation. In order to devise a constructional principle capable of dealing with the archaic and cumbersome phenomenon of static repetition, Wagner finds himself obliged to invent something which bears in itself the seeds of the most advanced and progressive of future musical techniques. To be sure, the manner in which the sheer vertical sonority of the Wagnerian orchestra edges up or down the half-tones separating the various leitmotifs from each other must ultimately complete the destruction of the sonata form and of the tonality on which it is based. Yet at the same time this new *chromaticism* points, even beyond atonality, toward the future resystematization of the twelve-tone row, and may thus serve as an object lesson in the way in which the historically new is generated out of the contradictions of a particular situation and moment, and as an illustration of the function, in dialectical analyses, of such terms as *progressive* and *regressive*, by means of which elements of a given complex are distinguished only in order to reidentify them the more surely in their inseparability and to make possible a differential perception of the place of a given moment in the historical continuum.

The Wagnerian invention of chromaticism, therefore, as an example of development within an autonomous system, offers a small-scale model of the changes we might expect to find in the macrocosm of socio-economic history itself. So it is, for instance, that the economic backwardness of nineteenth-century Germany was responsible for the failure of the attempts to develop parliamentary government which is-isued from the Revolution of 1848, and led to that notorious and fateful separation between German nationalism and the more progressive Western-style democratic aspirations of the middle classes. Thus socio-economic backwardness resulted in political authoritarianism; yet inasmuch as the latter was able to stimulate industrial development far more effectively than parliamentary regimes elsewhere, the initial lag ultimately results in a dialectical leap which leaves Germany abreast of its greatest rival in production by the end of the nineteenth century, and in possession of the newest industrial plant in Europe.

And what obtains in the infrastructure yields an analogy for developments in the other arts as well. I choose more or less at random from the history of the novel the example of Proust, where an initial predilection for the essay as a mode of discourse combines with an initial predisposition to the long static scene as an existential experience of the present to produce an unexpected organizational innovation: for Proust expands his formal scene to the point where the essay-style digressions and disquisitions may be intercalated in succession with as little disruption as might be produced by the change of subject or of conversation partner in the course of a long afternoon reception. Meanwhile the scenes themselves, as immense as they are, are now reconnected by *topic*, in much the same static fashion in which the essay preselected its subject matter: by means of the hours of the day or the stops on a train, or ultimately indeed, by the very geographical identity of the Swann and

Guermantes ways themselves. Yet the result of this rather static organization, initially determined by a storytelling *deficiency* in the Proustian imagination, is a more complex rendering of the passage of time than had hitherto been possible in conventional linear narration.

For Adorno, therefore, the names of the artists stand as so many moments in the history of the form, as so many lived unities between situation and invention, between contradiction and that determinate resolution from which new contradictions spring. A whole vision of the movement of modern history is built implicitly into the lens through which we watch the progression of music from Beethoven to Schoenberg and Stravinsky. In particular, these two final figures illustrate what is for Adorno an exemplary, archetypal opposition, standing as the twin symbolic possibilities of twentieth-century creation—as the very prototypes, indeed, above and beyond art itself, of the alternatives remaining to thought and action in a henceforth totalitarian universe. It is therefore to his influential and seminal study of these two figures, under the title of *Philosophy of the New Music,* that we now turn.

II

IT HAS often been pointed out that the increasing tempo of artistic change since Romanticism and the conquest of power by the middle classes involves a modification of the functional value of the new within the artistic process.[6] Novelty is now felt to be not a relatively secondary and *natural* by-product, but rather an end to be pursued in its own right. Now knowledge of the innovations of the past furnishes a new kind of stimulus for the construction of the individual works themselves, so that technical revolutions

[6] See, for example, Renato Poggioli's *Theory of the Avant-Garde* (Cambridge, Mass., 1968).

such as that of Schoenberg must henceforth be read on two levels: not only as one more moment in that gradual and autonomous evolution of material which has characterized the whole history of music, but also, and above all, as an object lesson in a peculiarly modern phenomenon: the attempt to think your way, through sheer formal invention, into the very future of history itself.

The evolution of musical sound may therefore initially be understood against the background of the aging of musical effects in general, which have as it were their own inner life, know their moment of maturation, and suffer debility and ultimately a kind of natural death. The common triad, for instance, struck the ear of its earliest listeners with an intensity which it will never again possess; and for us such sounds, which were originally heard in the context of a polyphonic system and as the triumph of tonal harmony over it, are henceforth nothing but insipid consonance in a world in which the cause of harmony has long since been won and its initial audacities long since become commonplace.

In much the same way we can speak of something like a progress in the history of writing: one which, however, is less a matter of individual stylistic innovation than of the habits of the reading public, to be gauged against the sheer quantity of words with which a given historical environment is saturated. It is clear, for instance, that a few bare names and plain nouns, a minimum of description, had a suggestive value for the readers of earlier centuries that they now no longer possess in that overexposure to language which is characteristic of our own time. Thus style resembles the Red Queen, developing ever more complicated mechanisms in order to sustain the power to say the same thing; and in the commercial universe of late capitalism the serious writer is obliged to reawaken the reader's numbed sense of the concrete through the administration of linguistic shocks, by restructuring the overfamiliar or by appealing to those deeper layers of the physiological which alone retain a kind of fitful *unnamed* intensity.

In the musical realm, of course, the problem of the intensity of effects at a given historical moment may be described in positive or negative terms, inasmuch as the continuing value of a given system of consonance is at one with the effects of the dissonances that obtain within it as well. Yet these effects, as Adorno shows us, largely transcend the musical scheme of things, to the degree to which dissonance as such has symbolic social value, comparable to "the role which the concept of the unconscious plays throughout the history of middle-class *ratio*." The transgression of the consonant therefore functions "from the very outset as the disguised representation of everything that has had to be sacrificed to the taboo of order. It substitutes for the censored instinctual drive, and includes, as tension, a libidinal moment as well, in its lament over enforced renunciation."[7] Thus the Wagnerian diminished seventh at its inception expressed unresolved pain and sexual longing, the yearning for ultimate release as well as the refusal to be reabsorbed into bland order; yet having grown familiar and tolerable over the years, it now stands as a mere period sign of feeling or emotiveness, as a manner rather than a concrete experience of negation.

Such absorption and accommodation of repressed material has of course always been one of the social functions of art; yet at the time of Wagner it undergoes a modification not unrelated to the shift in the role of innovation described above. For where in the past dissonance had existed only in order to confirm and ratify more strongly the positive tonal order on which it depended, now its character as "self-glorifying subjectivity" and as protest "against the social instance and its normative laws" tends

---

[7] *Philosophie der neuen Musik*, p. 147.

to become an end in itself. "All energy is now invested in dissonance; by comparison the individual resolutions become ever thinner, mere optional decor or restorative asseveration. Tension becomes the fundamental organizing principle to the degree that the negation of the negation, the utter canceling out of the debt of each dissonance, is as in some gigantic credit system indefinitely postponed."[8] In a later chapter, we shall see that this phenomenon is to be seen against the background of that vaster repression of the negative in present-day society of which Adorno's colleague Herbert Marcuse is the leading theoretician. It manifests itself in the literary realm by the increasingly antisocial character of the greatest works, and by the accompanying attempt on the part of society to reabsorb and neutralize the impulses they release. Thus in *Beyond Culture* Lionel Trilling has underscored the contradiction between the institutionalization of such modern "classics" by the American university and the profoundly subversive spirit of the works themselves, which originate in a refusal and a negation of just such institutionalization in the first place.

That the work of Schoenberg is deeply marked by this situation may be judged by the disproportionate place of both positive and negative in it: absolute freedom, violent liberation from harmonic constraint in what may be called his expressionistic or atonal period; and renewed order, the self-imposed rigidities of the twelve-tone system, which involves compulsions far beyond anything dreamed of in that tonal order which Schoenberg first abolished and then replaced. Yet both moments can in the long run be understood only in the context of the concrete historical situation: in the light of that regression of hearing in the modern world in general, where, bathed in the very element of debased sound and canned music from one corner to the other of the civilized universe, we tend to adjust our perceptions

[8] *Versuch über Wagner*, p. 67.

to the level of their object, with the resultant deterioration in that ability to listen with which the composer must work.

So it is that we now hear not the notes themselves, but only their atmosphere, which becomes itself symbolic for us: the soothing or piquant character of the music, its blueness or sweetness, is felt as a signal for the release of the appropriate conventionalized reactions. The musical composition becomes mere psychological stimulus or conditioning, as in those airports or supermarkets where the customer is aurally tranquilized. The musical accompaniment has moreover become intimately linked in our minds with the advertising of products, and continues, in both "popular" and "classical" music alike, to function as such long after the advertisement is over: at this point the sounds *advertise* composer or performer and stand as *signs* for the pleasure about to be derived from the product, so that the work of art sinks to the level of consumers' goods in general. Compare in this regard the subliminal role of music in the movies, as a means of guiding our "consumption" of the plot, with the relationship of score to narrative in opera as an art form. And when, after this, we recall the high technical quality of present-day commercial composition in general, we begin to understand the destructive effect of such background music on the inherited concert repertoire, vast portions of which are eroded and emptied of their intrinsic vitality without our so much as realizing that it had ever been otherwise.

In this situation, therefore, the new in the older sense is not enough: art no longer has to do with a change in taste resulting from the succession of the generations alone, but with one intensified and raised to the second power by a new commercial exploitation of artistic techniques in every facet of our culture. The new music must come to terms not only with our hearing, as did the old, but with our non-hearing as well. Hence concrete music, which seeks to transform the unconscious contents of our daily perceptual life, the unheard aural stress of the industrial city, into a conscious object of perception. Hence the willed "ugliness" of modern music in general, as if, in this state of pathological hebetude and insensibility, only the painful remained as a spur to perception.

The parallel with language is only too clear, and it is enough to evoke the fad for rapid reading and the habitual conscious or unconscious skimming of newspaper and advertising slogans, for us to understand the deeper social reasons for the stubborn insistence of modern poetry on the materiality and density of language, on words felt not as transparency but rather as things in themselves. So also in the realm of philosophy the bristling jargon of seemingly private languages is to be evaluated against the advertising copybook recommendations of "clarity" as the essence of "good writing": whereas the latter seeks to hurry the reader past his own received ideas, difficulty is inscribed in the former as the sign of the effort which must be made to think real thoughts.

It is not only our hearing that is affected, but also the works themselves. In strict correlation with our own fitful attention, our lowered capacity for concentration, our absentmindedness and general distraction, the work of art suffers distortion, is broken down and fetishized. The whole comes to be replaced by the part, and instead of perceiving music as an organized structure, we are content to hear it while doing something else just as long as we can salute the principal melodies and themes in passing. What was once a complete and continuous discourse has become an indistinguishable blur intermittently illuminated by vulgar theme songs, motifs that have crystallized into objects and tokens, like clichés in speech. Our emotion comes to be magically invested in these entities: they are the source of a purely subjective pathos which has nothing to do with the original, integral work itself, but which is rather a result of its disintegration and of the absence of any whole response. No wonder, therefore, that modern music is so unmelodious, so resolutely unlyrical, so suspicious of the illusions of individual subjectivity and of the song in which it is supposed to affirm itself.

It is this breakdown of extended form in general to which the expressionistic music of Schoenberg is a memorial: a reaction against the idea of the completed work of art, a refusal of the very possibility of the self-sufficient masterpiece existing in and for itself. With the disappearance of the organizational value of the form as a whole the surface of the work is shattered and no longer presents an unbroken and homogeneous appearance (*Schein*), no longer stands complete and suspended, as it were, over against the world, but rather falls into it, becoming one object among others. Thus the musical work loses its most fundamental precondition: that autonomous time in which the themes live as in an element of their own, in which they were able to develop according to their own internal laws in that thorough interaction with each other, that leisurely drawing out of all the formal consequences known to aesthetics as *Spiel*. The shattering of the tonal framework frees the individual notes themselves from whatever had previously given them meaning; for the note, essentially a neutral and nonsignifying element like the phoneme in speech, derived its functional value as an intention—whether as consonance or dissonance, continuation in a given key or modulation toward some new one—from the overall system itself. So in tonality the mind held a kind of musical past and future together, whereas in the new atonal universe the note exists only insofar as it is part and parcel of a musical statement in the present. The new form must remain almost physically in touch with all of its components at any given moment: atonality is a kind of musical nominalism.

Now, therefore, the part has become the whole, and the themes become the music itself, which is over when they are over; so that the works shrink alarmingly and the revolutionary piano pieces that make up Opus 23 last only a few seconds apiece, each contained in a scant page of sheet music. (And in this context, the next step would seem to be single notes, and then silence: thus Webern may be seen as the logical completion of this tendency in early Schoenberg.) Hence the term expressionism, for where the motifs involved no longer find a formal justification within the larger relational system of the work itself they are obliged to be somehow *self-justifying*: pure expression, as autonomous and intelligible as a cry, an instant bounded by the limits of the mind's capacity to hold a single thought together. Such a situation places new stress on both listener and composer alike: for each of these works reinvents all of music within itself, like a speech each sentence of which would involve the simultaneous recreation of a new grammar to govern it.

And what holds for the form is visible on the level of *content* as well. One of the most striking features of Schoenberg's early music is undoubtedly that *fin de siècle* neurosis style which he shares with the other Austrian artists of his period, and through which his world seems so profoundly akin to that of Freud. The thinly disguised sexual longing of *Verklaerte Nacht* or *Gurre-Lieder*, the monodrama of female hysteria (*Erwartung*), lead little by little to a new flood of unconscious material. "This is no longer the mimesis of passions, but rather the undisguised registration through the musical medium of bodily impulses from the unconscious, of shocks and traumas which assault the taboos of the form inasmuch as the latter attempt to impose their censorship on such impulses, to rationalize them and to transpose them into images. Thus Schoenberg's formal innovations were intimately related to the changes in the

26

things expressed, and helped the new reality of the latter to break through to consciousness. The first atonal works are transcripts, in the sense of the dream transcripts of psychoanalysis. . . . The scars of such a revolution in expression are, however, those blots and specks which as emissaries of the id resist the conscious will of the artist in both painting and music alike, which mar the surface and can as little be cleansed away by later conscious correction as the bloodstains in fairy tales. Real suffering has left them behind in the work of art as a sign that it no longer recognizes the latter's autonomy."[9]

Thus the work of art, during the expressionistic period, would seem to be reduced to the status of testimony and symptom, of charts, graphs, X-ray plates. Yet what if the Freudian raw material (now thought of not so much as the elements of theory or scientific hypothesis, but rather as a peculiar type of content in its own right: dreams, slips of the tongue, fixations, traumas, the Oedipal situation, the death wish) were itself but a sign or symptom of some vaster historical transformation? In this context, the Freudian topology of the mental functions may be seen as the return of a new type of allegorical vision and as the disintegration of the autonomous subject, of the cogito or self-governing consciousness in Western middle-class society. Now such characteristically Freudian phenomena are no longer seen as permanent mental functions awaiting throughout human history their discovery and revelation by Freud, but rather as new *events* of which Freud was at once contemporary and theorist. They mark, indeed, the gradual alienation of social relations and the transformation of the latter into autonomous and self-regulating mechanisms in terms of which the individual or independent personality is little by little reduced to a mere component part and, as it were, a locus of strains and taboos, a receiving

[9] *Philosophie der neuen Musik*, pp. 42-43.

apparatus for injunctions from all levels of the system itself. The former subject no longer thinks, he "is thought," and his conscious experience, which used to correspond to the concept of *reason* in middle-class philosophy, becomes little more than a matter of registering signals from zones outside itself, either those that come from within and "below," as in the drives and bodily and psychic automatisms, or from the outer circles of interlocking social institutions of all kinds. At the same time, the surviving remnant of the ego now falls victim to the illusion of its own continuing centrality: that which no longer is "in itself" continues to exist "for itself," and the subject wrongly continues to assume that there exists some correspondence between its inner monadic experience and that purely external network of circumstances (economic, historical, social) which determines and manipulates it through mechanisms beyond the horizon of individual experience.

(It is at this point, of course, that the novel, as a meaningful identification between the individual and social dimensions, begins to come apart at the seams as a form. Now that individual experience has ceased to coincide with social reality, the novel is menaced by twin contingencies. If it holds to the purely existential, to the truth of subjectivity, it risks turning into ungeneralizable psychological observation, with all the validity of mere case history. If, on the other hand, it attempts to master the objective structure of the social realm, it tends to be governed more and more by categories of abstract knowledge rather than concrete experience, and consequently to sink to the level of thesis and illustration, hypothesis and example.)

Yet atonality, however much it may testify to the loss of rational control in modern society, at the same time carries within itself the elements of a new kind of control, the requirements of a new order as yet still only latent in the historical moment. For whatever the will toward total freedom, the atonal composer still works in a world of stale tonality and must take his precautions with regard to the past. He must, for example, avoid the kind of consonance or tonal chord which would be likely to reawaken older listening habits, and to reorganize the music into noise or wrong notes. Yet this very danger is enough to awaken in atonality the first principle of a new law or order. For the taboo against accidentally tonal chords carries with it the corollary that the composer should avoid any exaggerated repetition of a single note, for fear such an insistence would ultimately tend to function as a new kind of tonal center for the ear. It is necessary only to pose the problem of avoiding such repetition in a more formal way for the entire twelve-tone system to show itself upon the horizon. For ultimately the only logical solution is that of not repeating a given note until all of the other eleven notes of the scale have first been touched on, and with this the twelve-tone "row" is born and replaces tonality. Henceforth, each work shall be composed not in a key but "in" a particular and unique row, or arrangement of all twelve notes of the scale, devised for it alone, so that in a sense the twelve-tone work is "nothing more" than an immense theme and variations with the individual row as theme, a repetition over and over again of the same series of twelve notes, but this time in either the horizontal or the vertical dimension.

For the new system has the merit of abolishing one of the most ancient and fundamental contradictions in music, that between harmony and counterpoint, between the vertical and the horizontal, between the traditions of a massive orchestral sonority, on the one hand, and those which appeal back to a rather archaic polyphony, with its fugues and canons, on the other. Hitherto, it is as though there had existed mutually exclusive vertical and horizontal types of perception, which had alternated in a kind of Gestaltlike interference with each other, obliging the listener to choose between two hearings of a given superposition of sounds, either as a momentary intersection of voices in movement or as the massive intertwining of harmonic levels in a chord structure. Now, in the seething texture of Schoenberg's mature works, this opposition is abolished, and the row, which may at first have resembled an intricate, lengthy, highly articulated theme or melody, also serves, like some elaborate and complex molecule, as the building block for the vertical dimension of the score.

Thus the twelve-tone system serves as a kind of unified field theory for music, in which the data of harmony and that of counterpoint can now be translated back and forth into each other. And with this, other inherited dilemmas are solved as well: henceforth no element is too small to require its place in the overall scheme of things, no detail too insignificant to be made to furnish its credentials and to embody a meaning. Such relatively traditional matters as instrumentation are, for example, now codified, so that in the notion of *Klangfarbenmelodie* a given succession of instrumental timbres (such as the sequence violin, trumpet, piano) takes on the functional value of a sequence of notes in a melody. Thus there is carried to completion in the musical realm that basic tendency of all modern art in general toward a kind of absolute *overdetermination* of all of its elements, toward an abolition of chance, a kind of total absorption of the last remnants of sheer contingency in the raw material, which are henceforth painfully assimilated into the structure of the work itself.

(In the form of the novel this evolution follows a rigorous and exemplary internal logic: the earliest realistic novels justify their contingent elements—descriptions, historical background, choice of a particular subject such as the life of a soap manufacturer or a doctor—on the purely empirical grounds that such phenomena already exist in the world around us, and that they therefore need no justifica-

30

tion. With Zola, however, this empirical, purely descriptive motivation is joined by a second one, which rises oddly behind it like the symptom-formation of a repressed impulse: this is the tendency to turn such facts, which seem to have no intrinsic self-justifying meaning in themselves, into symbols or grossly materialized pictures of meanings. Thus it is as if the mind, unable to bear the sheer contingency of this empirical reality, instinctively reckoned into such phenomena that unconscious, mythical, symbolic dimension which it denied them on the conscious level. Finally, with Joyce's *Ulysses*, which seemed at the time so naturalistic and conclusive a slice of life, this impulse has become a conscious intention, and the literary materials lead a double life on two separate levels, that of empirical existence and that of a total relational scheme not unlike the twelve-tone system itself, where each empirical fact is integrated into the whole, each chapter dominated by some basic symbolic complex, the motifs of the work related to each other by complicated charts and cross-references, and so forth.)

Thus, in a situation where subjective and objective have begun to split apart, Schoenberg's originality was to have driven the subjective and expressionistic to its outer limit, to the point at which the nerve-pictures and traumata of the latter slowly veer, under the pressure of their own internal logic, into the new objectivity, the more total order, of the twelve-tone system. The specificity of this solution may be better gauged against the diametrically opposed one of Stravinsky, who may be thought of as having worked out from the other, *objective* pole of the modern dilemma.

For already the privileged form in which Stravinsky works, the ballet, may be seen as a kind of applied music, which even more drastically than the "program music" that is contemporary with it reinvents a kind of distance between content and form within a medium that is otherwise nonrepresentational. Thus it is able to avoid the problems of self-justification and self-determination faced by pure music and resolved by Schoenberg in the way described above: for its musical practice is, as it were, already justified by the visual tableau itself, and after the fact by the physical movements of the dancers, which ratify it and of which it comes to seem the *accompaniment.*

And what happens to the form of these works is reproduced on the level of the content itself, particularly in the Russian ballets. Both *Petrouchka* and the *Rite of Spring* dramatize the sacrifice of individual subjectivity to an inhuman collectivity, and their deliberate primitivism (with its appeal to folk culture in *Petrouchka* or *L'Histoire du soldat,* and with its elemental, archaic, well-nigh prehistoric rhythms in the *Rite of Spring*) solicit the regression of their sophisticated listener/spectator toward a kind of sacrifice of the intellect in the sheer emotionalism of mass response. This ultrasophisticated primitivism or musical demagoguery (Adorno will go so far as to compare it as a phenomenon to Fascism) is inscribed in the technique of the works themselves, which, as opposed to the total organizational principles of Schoenberg, favors a kind of massive and discontinuous verticality. Its ritualistic beats and repetitions are broken by lapses and silences which create a syncopation with the returning shock waves of the listener's bodily reactions. Unlike Schoenberg, Stravinsky organizes the elements involved according to categories extrinsic to the musical structure, such as the isolated colors or qualities of the instruments themselves, or the psychological effects of their oppositions (loud and soft, piercing or massive).

To be sure, Stravinsky, and particularly the Stravinsky of the early ballets, is as influential and primal a musical phenomenon as Schoenberg himself; but it is instructive to compare the respective historical situations from which the innovations of each composer derived, and in particular "those 'Russian' characteristics of Stravinsky which have been so often and abusively stressed": "It has often been observed that Moussorgsky's songs are distinguished from German lieder by the absence in them of a poetic *subject* or organizational point of view, each poem being treated as the composer of operas does his arias, not as an immediately subjective expression, but rather as a kind of objectification and distantiation of whatever emotion is involved. The artist fails to coincide with the lyrical subject. The category of the subject was nowhere near so solidly established in pre-middle-class Russia as in the Western countries. Whence the alienness of a Dostoyevsky, for instance, which stems from the lack of identity of the ego with itself: none of the brothers Karamazov is a 'character' in the sense of Western literature. Now this preindividuality stands the late-capitalist Stravinsky in good stead, in his legitimation of the collapse of the individual subject."[10] His modernness is therefore the result of a kind of optical illusion, of a historical paradox in which pre- and post-individualism seem to meet, and are distinguished only by the deeper motivations at work beneath the surface. Thus where Schoenberg's expressionism was designed as a shock absorber for the unconscious material and ultimately as a means of mastering it and assimilating it to the form, Stravinsky's aim is to reproduce such effects directly as psychic events by assault on the nerve ends of his audience.

The value and direction of Stravinsky's artistic practice may be judged ultimately by the long series of neoclassical pastiches which succeed the Russian period. For here the bias toward musical objectivity may be openly observed at work in the way in which the composer renounces his own voice, abdicating that personal style which has become problematical in modern times and speaking through the fossilized subjectivity of dead composers, in a kind of witty

[10] *Philosophie der neuen Musik*, pp. 134-135.

stylistic masquerade reviving ghostly forms from a past when musical composition was still relatively free of internal contradictions. Thus Stravinsky's "way" ends in sterile imitation, in the writing of music about music (Palestrina with wrong notes, as someone has said); and indeed, in some ultimate squaring of the circle, we find him composing in the twelve-tone idiom itself, and taking his metaphysical adversary Schoenberg as his final avatar. (In literature, the theoretical justification for the use of such pastiche and parody has been made by Thomas Mann, for whom the act of speaking with irony through a dead style permits speech in a situation where it would otherwise be impossible. Joyce, once again, embodies an exemplary progress from a derivative personal style—showing period affinities with Walter Pater—through the multiple pastiches of *Ulysses*, toward something which transcends both style and pastiche altogether and which, like the twelve-tone system in the musical realm, may stand as a distant representation of some future linguistic organization of a postindividualistic character.)

It should not, however, be thought that Adorno finds Schoenberg's ultimate solution any less inherently contradictory in the long run than that of Stravinsky. How could it be otherwise, when the very inner tension and authenticity of Schoenberg's music result from the way that it at one and the same time both reflects and refuses the historical moment of which it is the memorial? This is perhaps the point at which to say something about Adorno's conception of the relationship of the work of art to its immediate historical situation, where indeed he appears to bet on all sides at once, simultaneously adopting mutually exclusive alternatives or variations on the basic model. The work of art "reflects" society and is historical to the degree that it *refuses* the social, and represents the last refuge of individual subjectivity from the historical forces that threaten to crush it: such is the position of that lecture on "Lyric and Society" which is one of Adorno's most brilliant essays. Thus the socio-economic is inscribed in the work, but as concave to convex, as negative to positive. *Ohne Angst leben*: such is for Adorno the deepest and most fundamental promise of music itself, which it holds even at the heart of its most regressive manifestations.

On the other hand, the repeated characterization of Schoenberg's system as a "total" one deliberately underscores the relationship between that work and the totalitarian world in which it comes into being. For it is no less true that this drive toward a total organization of the work which we find operative in the twelve-tone system is symptomatic of an objective tendency in the socio-economic structure of the modern world itself. Indeed, it is hardly surprising that this music, which finds its reason for being in a reaction against the debasement of hearing in general, should as in a mirror image develop all the strengths and weaknesses of its adversary, in a kind of point by point correlation. And inasmuch as that phenomenon is itself profoundly social, and is at one with the commercialization of the modern world, modern music finds itself at once deeply implicated in a social struggle without so much as straying from the internal logic of pure musical technique, and reproduces the structure of the alienated society in miniature in the intrinsic language of the musical realm.

Thus the total organizational principle of Schoenberg's system reflects a new systematization of the world itself, of which the so-called totalitarian political regimes are themselves only a symptom. For in the later stages of monopoly or postindustrial capitalism not only the multiplicity of small business units, but also distribution, and ultimately the last free-floating elements of the older commercial and cultural universe, are now assimilated into a single all-absorbing mechanism. Now, when the entire business system with its projections in government and in the military and judicial branches depends for its very existence on the automatic sale of products which no longer correspond to any kind of biological or indeed social need and which are moreover for the most part identical with each other, marketing psychology obliges it to complete its conquest of the world by reaching down into the last private zones of individual life, in order to awaken the artificial needs around which the system revolves. Thus the total organization of the economy ends up by alienating the very language and thoughts of its human population, and by dispelling the last remnant of the older autonomous subject or ego: advertising, market research, psychological testing, and a host of other sophisticated techniques of mystification now complete a thorough *planification* of the public, and encourage the illusion of a life-style while disguising the disappearance of subjectivity and private life in the old sense. Meanwhile, what remains of the subjective, with its illusions of autonomy and its impoverished satisfactions, its ever diminishing images of happiness, is no longer able to distinguish between external suggestion and internal desire, is incapable of drawing a line between the private and the institutionalized, and finds itself therefore wholly delivered over to objective manipulation.[11]

This new totalitarian organization of things, people, and colonies into a single market-system is now duplicated by the planification of the work of art itself, whether in Joyce or in Schoenberg: the absolute conscious control which modern artists seek to establish over the last remnants of free-floating contingency reflects this increasing autonomy of institutions, this increasing "conquest" of both nature and society that they feel at work in the historical moment

[11] For the most comprehensive description of this process, see Paul Baran and Paul Sweezy, *Monopoly Capital* (New York, 1966), esp. Chaps. V, X, and XI.

around them. It is no wonder, then, that Adorno's description of the relationship between art and society is ambiguous. The ambiguity had already been underlined in Thomas Mann's *Doctor Faustus*, whose theoretical sections Adorno inspired, and where the life of the twelve-tone composer Leverkühn stands in sharp allegorical parallel to the disintegration of Weimar Germany and its passage into Fascism. By which Thomas Mann meant to emphasize not the "evil" of modernism, after the fashion of a Wyndham Lewis, but rather the nature of tragedy in modern times: the possession of man by historical determinism, the intolerable power of history itself over life and over artistic creation, which is not free not to reflect what it reacts against.

In such a way, the contradictions of the age reenter the microcosm of the work of art and condemn it to ultimate failure also. Thus the system of Schoenberg, the product of an inhumanly systematized society, becomes itself a kind of straitjacket, a constraint rather than a liberating convention. The row does not replace tonality after all, but only sets itself to imitating it, and instead of evolving new forms, the new music returns to the composition of sonatas in twelve tones. But the old forms represented a triumph over the resistance of things, the result of a kind of stubborn logic in their raw material: these new ones are as distant from nature as the postindustrial universe itself, their matter as preformed and as lacking in any genuine internal logic as plastic. Nor is the identification of vertical with horizontal really achieved, but only willed: its symbol would appear to be that massive chord of all twelve tones which ends Berg's *Lulu* in a kind of blank indistinction or deathly synthesis of all the elements.

Finally, the listener's ability to hear cannot be fully regenerated, and the concrete experience of the simultaneity of the whole and its parts is no longer possible in modern times. The most successful audition of a work by Schoen-

37

berg yields, not a plenitude, but rather a kind of shadow
work, an optical illusion in which the whole somehow floats
above the concrete parts, not really at one with any of them
in any given moment; in which the parts themselves flee
hearing and extend beyond the present, are dissociated
from the physical notes through which they are expressed
and rise beyond them as a kind of blur or image superimposed: the distorted result of an attempt to imagine
wholeness in a period that has no experience of it, under
circumstances that doom the attempt to failure from the
very start.

III

WE ARE thus led little by little to reflect on the connection
between such a dialectical vision of historical change, in
which the various moments are articulated according to the
various possible relationships between subject and object,
and some hypothesis of a historical moment of plenitude or
completion against which the other historical stages are
judged and weighed. Such a moment is of course first and
foremost nothing but a *logical* possibility: the concept of
what Adorno calls *Versoehnung* or reconciliation between
the subject and objectivity, between existence and the
world, the individual consciousness and the external network of things and institutions into which it first emerges.
The naïve projection of such a logical possibility into the
realm of historical chronology can only result in metaphysical nostalgia (the golden age before the fall, the bliss-
ful state of primitive man) or in Utopianism. Yet in some
more subtle fashion all so-called "theories of history" tend
to organize themselves around the covert hypothesis of just
such a moment of plenitude: think of Jeffersonian America
or of the "unity of sensibility" of the Metaphysical poets; of
the humaneness of mediëval economic doctrine or of the

organic continuity of an *ancien régime* unsullied by regicide or by the hubris of political self-determination; not to speak of the innumerable ideological exploitations of ancient Greece.

In the cultural realm, however, where the essential working opposition between subject and object is transposed into terms of form and content, such hypotheses have perhaps greater validity, and are in any case more verifiable. For if we are in no position to judge the concreteness of life at any given moment of the past, at least we can evaluate the adequacy of form to content in its cultural monuments, and are able to measure the reconciliation of intention and medium and the degree to which all visible matter is form, and all meaning or expression concrete embodiment.

So it is that for Adorno the work of Beethoven stands as a kind of fixed point against which earlier or later moments of musical history will be judged. It is, of course, not a question of degrees of genius, but rather of the inner logic of historical development itself, and of a kind of accumulation of formal possibilities of which Beethoven is the beneficiary and which suddenly makes possible an unexpected carrying through to their conclusion of all the unfinished trends, a filling out of all the hitherto empty spaces, and an actualization of the potentialities latent in the musical raw material itself.

In musical terms, that unique reconciliation which is Beethoven's historical opportunity takes the form of a precarious equilibrium between melody and development, between a new and richer thematic expression of subjective feeling and its objective working through in the form itself, which no longer has anything of that relatively mechanical and a priori, applied execution of eighteenth-century music. For the sheer volume of the production of the great eighteenth-century composers resulted in part from the presence to hand for them of relatively simple schemes and formulae of execution. Nor had orchestration yet become so complicated and individualistic an affair: the court orchestras of feudal principalities do not yet have the variety of instruments, let alone the sheer technical virtuosity, of the later middle-class stage orchestra. For all these reasons the themes of the eighteenth-century composers cannot be said to have achieved a genuine fullness of subjective being: a melody of Mozart is not yet self-sufficient and remains functionally conceived, bearing traces of the form of which it is an indivisible component.

Nor, on the other hand, does the Beethoven melody ever reach that extreme autonomy and overripeness of those devised by the hypersubjective composers of the later nineteenth century—let Tchaikovsky stand as their archetype—for whom the contrapuntal work is reduced to a bare minimum, the working through of themes to perfunctory and monitory repetition, and in whose work the center of gravity of musical invention moves to sheer instrumental expressiveness and orchestral coloration.

Standing between these two extremes, the Beethoven melody represents a short-lived synthesis of the functional and the expressive: lengthy and articulate, it presents the appearance of autonomy while being at the same time shrewdly disposed and preformed with a view to the various developments, polyphonic or variational, which it is about to undergo. Reciprocally, the various subvoices of the development are still relatively independent and intrinsically meaningful, which cannot be said for those of late Romanticism; and they have something individual and personal about them which distinguishes them from their rather schematic and mechanical equivalents in earlier music. Thus subjectivity and the personal inform the score down to its smallest elements, but do so by working through the objective, suffusing and vivifying it, rather than by blotting it out and smothering it with the overwhelming harmonic and coloristic bias of later music. And what is true of the part holds, as we have already seen above, for the form as a whole, for the sonata as a short-lived possibility of meaningful organization on a large scale, in which the mind is momentarily able to glimpse a concrete totality, completely present at every instant of its unfolding.

Even though there is no exact literary equivalent for Beethoven and what he represents in the history of Western music, literary judgments ultimately depend on the presuppositions about form and content described above. Thus the privileged position of a Tolstoy in the history of the novel proves on closer examination to have an analogous basis. The relatively late development of middle-class literature in Russia leaves the nineteenth-century Russian novelist in a position of great freedom: everything remains to be done in the area of Russian themes, there is not the oppressive fact of earlier generations of novelists and of shelves of novels that weighs on the successors of Balzac or Dickens. Yet these Russian novelists, by their very tardiness, are contemporary with all that is most sophisticated in novelistic technique—with Maupassant and the naturalists—so that the Russian realistic novel in general and Tolstoy in particular can be born fully grown. Technique elsewhere laboriously acquired can here seem flowing and natural, resulting in that peculiar and characteristic reconciliation between the subjective intention and the novel's objective social material which we associate with the name of Tolstoy and in which both social and individual experience issue from the novelist's hand as though equally his own creations.

The dialectical structure of our negative judgments is even more apparent: think of the grimace and caricature to which we object in Balzac—is it anything more than a too hasty attempt to assimilate the objective social material—characters, furniture, institutions—to the personal enthusiasms of the author himself, imperiously deforming and distorting it for his own purposes? Think, on the other hand, of the rather metallic brittleness of Flaubert, which results from too rigid and surgical a suppression of the subjective dimensions of the work, until the hero becomes as vacuous as a recording eye, in *L'Education sentimentale*, and the work is finally, in *Salammbô*, degraded into cinematographic phantasmagoria. Think of the "mannered" quality of Henry James: those great pauses between meaningful half-sentences, the close-ups of small areas of objectivity in an attempt to infuse them with subjective intention, in the way a random word surrounded by a "pregnant" silence becomes ominous with meaning. Think of the precariousness of the synthesis of Joyce, in which matter once again seems momentarily reconciled with spirit, all the objects and detritus of the city luminous and as though informed by subjectivity—except that the seams show; there is something willful and arbitrary about the relationship of the individual chapters to each other, and the new reconciliation is paid for as dearly as that of Schoenberg in music. The novel is always an attempt to reconcile the consciousness of writer and reader with the objective world at large; so it is that the judgments we make on the great novelists fall not on them, but on the moment of history which they reflect and on which their structures pass sentence.

There can therefore be no doubt that the privileged synthesis of Beethoven's works corresponds to some peculiar freedom in the social structure of his time. Historical freedom, indeed, expanding and contracting as it does with the objective conditions themselves, never seems greater than in such transitional periods, where the life-style has not yet taken on the rigidity of a period manner, and when there is sudden release from the old without any corresponding obligation to that which will come to take its place. The dominant figure of Napoleon himself is symbolic of the basic ambiguity of this moment which follows the collapse of the feudal order in Europe and precedes the definitive setting up of the new ethical, political, and economic institutions of the middle classes which triumphed over it. He combines something of the fading values of feudality and sacred kingship with the frankly secular and propagandistic appeal of the charismatic political leaders of later middle-class society, yet at the same time can be assimilated neither to the bewigged absolute monarchs of the sixteenth and seventeenth centuries nor to the demagogues of the twentieth. Even the neoclassicism of the Napoleonic period is significant and points in two directions: for it seems to have been the last of the great Continental styles which—Gothic or Renaissance, baroque or rococo—swept across Europe in successive waves, leaving a sediment of monuments behind them; while on the other hand, it is the first form of modernism as well, in that it is secretly pastiche, art about art, and registers the contradictions of the middle-class world through its own inner contradictions in a way that will be characteristic of every artistic movement to follow.

Thus Beethoven's reconciliation between the subjective and the objective faithfully registers the enlarged horizons of the revolutionary transition period itself, when the positive and universalistic thinking of the middle class during its struggle for power has not yet given way to the *esprit de sérieux* of money, business, and *Realpolitik*; when the abstract idea of human freedom, whose optimism and heroics are eternalized in *Fidelio*, has not yet been transformed into an ideological defense of class privilege. And what is true for music holds for thought as well: philosophy, freed from the long constraint of theology, has not yet undergone the positivistic reduction to scientific empiricism, has not yet abdicated its rights to such newly invented academic disciplines as sociology or psychology, let alone begun to question its own validity in the manner of twentieth-century logical positivism. At this point in history thought is still out for the largest things, and it is to such a moment of possibility, such a moment of suspension between two worlds, that the philosophy of Hegel is the most ambitious and profoundly characteristic monument.

In the final chapter of the present work we will try to redefine the role Hegelianism is called upon to play in a Marxist framework: the problem is clearly at one with the relationship between the values of the older middle-class revolution and the revolutionary consciousness and needs of the present day. Yet it is at once evident that the very principle at work in the dialectical analyses which we have described above—that of the adequation of subject and object, and of the possibility of reconciliation of I and Not-I, of spirit and matter, or self and world—is itself the very premise of Hegel's system and may be claimed to be virtually Hegel's intellectual invention.

For Hegel made concrete the merely abstract and empty affirmations of his predecessors that the objective external world is identical with that of spirit, and set out to demonstrate the multiplicity of ways in which such an identity is realized. From the objective point of view, the *Phenomenology of Spirit* is just such a demonstration of identity, showing how the most seemingly external or material phenomena (such as the objects of our sense perception and of our scientific research) are all informed with spirit, all profoundly involved with and penetrated by ideality. But from the subjective point of view, the *Phenomenology* is the story of an ascent and a development, a description of the successive stages through which consciousness enriches and solidifies itself, and from its most individualistic and subjectively limited moments gradually arrives at the condition of Absolute Spirit, in which it learns that it ultimately includes within itself all the abundance and multiplicity of

44

the external and objective universe. Hegel is able to overcome the separation between subject and object by finding his starting point in a moment when that separation has not yet taken place: in the moment of experience itself, where the subject, still at one with its object, has not yet attained self-consciousness, has not yet learned to distinguish itself as a separate and abstractly independent entity, has not yet been able to draw back and look across a void toward the separate, equally abstract entity of things in themselves.

The dialectical method is precisely this preference for the concrete totality over the separate, abstract parts. Yet it is more complicated than any objective apprehension of a merely external kind of totality, such as takes place in the various scientific disciplines. For in these the thinking mind itself remains cool and untouched, skilled but unselfconscious, and is able to forget about itself and its own thought processes while it sinks itself wholly in the content and problems offered it. But dialectical thinking is a thought to the second power, a thought about thinking itself, in which the mind must deal with its own thought process just as much as with the material it works on, in which both the particular content involved and the style of thinking suited to it must be held together in the mind at the same time. The dialectical thinking through of a mathematical problem, for example, would involve, besides the awareness of the problem on its own terms, an implicit comparison between the way the mind felt performing the mathematical transaction and its feel during the experience of other, entirely different scientific and nonscientific operations. Dialectical thought is therefore profoundly comparative in its very structure, even in its consideration of individual, isolated types of objects; and the chapter sequence of the *Phenomenology* is merely the objective working out of the set of comparisons already inherent in it. Yet comparison involves difference, and the movement from one chapter to another, from one form of consciousness to another, is that of a series of leaps, of a constant passage from one kind of raw material to another seemingly unrelated to it.

Indeed, the most striking aspect of the *Phenomenology* for the modern reader is that it presents, to use the terminology of the novel, no unity of point of view. The transitions between the chapters are not necessarily equivalent to moments of growth and change in the life of an individual. The content of the various chapters is quite heterogeneous, some of it coming from collective or historical experience, some from individual or ethical, some relating to action, some to pure knowledge. Corresponding to these two structural irregularities, the attacks on the Hegelian system have tended to fall into two distinct groups. On the one hand, the existential objection to Hegel has always been that there is a vital difference between the knowing of a transition between two moments and the living of it: the salvation of the slave may lie in a stoicism which will result in a whole new inner life for humanity, but generations of individual slaves must die before the qualitatively new moment is achieved. Nor, on the other hand, is the *Phenomenology* ultimately any more satisfying when examined from the objective point of view, where it seems to fall apart into a series of random observations and analyses, historical notes, psychological, philosophical, scientific, artistic data which would have to be analyzed separately by the various disciplines in question before their validity could be assumed.

Yet these criticisms are based on our own historical vantage-point. They presuppose the increasing intellectual specialization of the sciences in defining their various fields and methods, as well as a greater psychological awareness of the structure and value of individual life. They represent, therefore, not so much an intrinsic, logical critique of Hegel, as an almost physical discrepancy between his moment in time and our own, and it is this paradox which is at the center of Adorno's reading of Hegel. From our inability to realize the Hegelian vision of totality it does not follow that this vision is not fuller and richer, more concrete, than anything we can presently imagine. The impossibility of the Hegelian system for us is not a proof of its intellectual limitations, its cumbersome methods and theological superstructure; on the contrary, it is a judgment on us and on the moment of history in which we live, and in which such a vision of the totality of things is no longer possible.

Just as the Beethoven sonata stood as the precarious synthesis of whole and part, so the philosophy of Hegel is one long tension between the organization of the overall dialectic, with Absolute Spirit as the end result of the process, and the individual moments, the steps of the dialectic, the concrete analyses of the various kinds of experience along the way. The two components depend on each other and cannot be considered separately: a satisfactory reading of Hegel's thought at any point resembles in structure the listening demanded by the Beethoven sonata, where the part, the note or phrase, must be apprehended both in itself and in its position with respect to the whole, as variation, modulation, reprise, and so forth. It is therefore impossible to select individual insights from the system, to separate the valid from the no longer relevant. The terminology and the intellectual equipment of the various chapters presuppose a generalizing attitude toward experience, one which demands expansion if it is to be understood at all. The key ideas of self-consciousness and recognition, of the general and the concrete, of the concept and the notion, cannot be analyzed by themselves, for they all depend on and are part of the larger ideal of Absolute Spirit, of a consciousness for which the supreme value is a development of its own powers by the assimilation of the world outside until at length it reaches the point where it recognizes in itself seeds of everything in the objective universe, where it is able somehow to recognize the latter as being of the same substance with itself.

Yet the overall organization is no longer comprehensible for us. The organizational framework, the notion of an Absolute Spirit, the possibility for the isolated subjectivity to achieve an entire self-contained world, an equivalence with the real world itself, has become inadmissible and even unthinkable in modern society, where the highly restricted worth of the individual subjectivity is only too clear, where people are at once irrevocably interrelated to each other and condemned to view the whole through the distorting windows of their own positions in it. Thus, even though one can reread Hegel, we are never able to reach the vantage point of that last chapter which would finally permit us to catch a glimpse of the work as a whole. The synthesis remains imperfect, a mere imperative to unity, a dead letter: and this imperfect focus holds true even down to the reading and rendering of the individual sentences. The very indifference to publication, the unrevised and approximate versions in which the system has come down to us and which offer the paradox of "a thought of such boundless assertions renouncing the attempt to perpetuate itself in definitive and determinate form" suggest Hegel's own awareness of this dilemma. "In the sense in which we nowadays speak of antimatter," Adorno says, "the Hegelian texts are antitexts."[12] Such a structure accounts for the unique difficulty presented by a philosopher who can only be read in fragments and only understood in the light of the whole.

What happened was that the transitional indeterminacy of the period in which Hegel lived granted him a fortunate mirage, the optical illusion of Absolute Spirit; and this

[12] T. W. Adorno, *Drei Studien zu Hegel* (Frankfurt, 1957), p. 136.

idealistic, abstract, and indeed imaginary concept was able to serve as the organizational framework for a profoundly realistic set of analyses of the world itself. For the work done depends not so much on the cast of mind of the philosopher as on the possibilities for development inherent in the organizational principle available to him. When Marx, for example, sets back on its feet this "dialectic standing on its head," as he called the idealism of Hegel, a reversal takes place in which his own material is at once more humanistic and less humane, in which he finds himself limited to the highly technical subject matter of economics. He grounds Hegel in reality but at the same time engages himself in a specialization from which it is difficult to reemerge into the wider possibilities opened up by his predecessor.

That system into which Hegel organized his thoughts and which he thought to be a property of things themselves was therefore latent in them only, and had not yet been realized in the actual historical world. A completely embodied philosophical system, a concrete intellectual reconciliation between the I and the Not-I, the subject and the world, would be possible only in a society in which the individual was already reconciled in fact with the organization of things and people around him: the concrete reconciliation would have had to precede the abstract formulation of it. So it is no wonder Hegel's system fails, just as it is no wonder that the vast artistic syntheses which are its equivalent in the twentieth century all crack under the strain of their elaborate universalizing pretense. But they already take place at a lower level of language, no longer on the level of understanding but rather on that of more elemental and immediate physical and emotional perceptions: and the real wonder is not so much that the Hegelian system fails as that it could be conceived and executed even to that degree of concreteness which it still possesses.

IV

PERHAPS the only way to keep faith with the Hegelian spirit of systematization in a fragmented universe is to be resolutely unsystematic. In this sense Adorno's thought is profoundly Hegelian, thinking its motifs through in a genuinely Hegelian spirit, facing thereby its principal formal problem: How to write chapters of a phenomenology when there is no longer any possibility of a whole? How to analyze the part as a part when the whole is not only no longer visible but even inconceivable? How to continue to use the terms subject and object as opposites which presuppose, in order to be meaningful, some possible synthesis, when there is no synthesis even imaginable, let alone present anywhere in concrete experience? What language to use to describe an alienated language, to what systems of reference to appeal when all systems of reference have been assimilated into the dominant system itself? How to see phenomena in the light of history, when the very movement and direction that gave history its meaning seem to have been swallowed up in sand?

Adorno himself, now in the guise of a theoretician of the essay as a form, has attributed its lack of development in Germany to the reluctance of German writers to surrender themselves to the almost frivolous and inconsequential freedom it presupposes, to make the painful apprenticeship of an intellectual life amidst the fragmentary and the ephemeral, to resist the ontological consolations of the *Hauptwerk* and the monumental and to stand in the very river of history itself, suffering their provisory constructions to undergo those ceaseless metamorphoses which make up the life of an idea in time.

For the fundamental formal problem of the dialectical writer is precisely that of continuity. He who has so intense a feeling for the massive continuity of history itself is some-

how paralyzed by that very awareness, as in some overload-
ing of perception too physical to be any longer commensu-
rable with language. Where all the dimensions of history
cohere in synchronic fashion, the simple linear stories of
earlier historians are no longer possible: now it is diachrony
and continuity which become problematical, mere working
hypotheses. Adorno's larger form will therefore be a construct rather than a narrative. In the work on Schoenberg,
of which we have given a brief account above, the formal
continuity is not that of Schoenberg's chronological development (although a loose feeling of chronology is maintained), but rather that of a series of abstract moments, of
the internal generation out of each other of the fundamental
elements or parts of Schoenberg's work seen as a total system. The individual work of art is therefore understood as
a balance between inner organs, as an intersection of what
we will in a later chapter call determinate categories of a
stylistic nature, separate yet profoundly interdependent on
each other, such that a modification of one (such as the
intensity of instrumental coloration) immediately involves
a shift in the proportions of the others (temporal dimensions of the work, contrapuntal development, and so forth).
Change takes place in an artist's development as a result of
such a modification in the relationships that obtain between
the fundamental categories of the work itself; the dialectical
critic, however, will plot this change on his graph as a series
of moments which generate each other out of their own internal contradictions.[13]

When we turn now to the shorter pieces, and particularly
to that series of *Notes on Literature* which is perhaps
Adorno's masterpiece, we find that as mental operations
they consist precisely in the perceptual registering and isolation, indeed in a virtual invention and naming for the first

[13] We will return to this problem, which involves the relative
validity of Hegelian and Marxist dialectics, in our concluding chapter.

time, of those categories or component parts of which the larger dialectical form had been an interlocking construction. Let the subjects of some of them—the relation of titles to works, sensitivity to punctuation, the uses of interlarded foreign words and phrases, the physical impression books make—illustrate the working method itself: they imply dialectical self-consciousness, a sudden distancing which permits the most familiar elements of the reading experience to be seen again strangely, as though for the first time, making visible the unexpected articulation of the work into determinate categories or parts. The premise remains that of the most thoroughgoing network of internal relationships, so that it is precisely the apprehension of the apparently discrete and external—the predilection in a novelist, for instance, for epigraphs to his chapters—which as a heuristic principle leads to those deeper formal categories against which the surface is organized. These essays are therefore the concrete working out of that formal category of Adorno's own production which we have described earlier under the sign of the *footnote*: an observation which may itself be thought of as a tribute to his method insofar as it amounts to a pastiche of it.

Such essays are thus the fragments of or footnotes to a totality which never comes into being; and what unites them, I am tempted to say, is less their thematic content than it is on the one hand their style, as a perpetual present in time of the process of dialectical thinking itself, and on the other their basic intellectual coordinates. For what as fragments they share in spite of the dispersal of their raw material is the common historical situation itself, that moment of history which marks and deforms in one way or another all the cultural phenomena which it produces and includes, and which serves as the framework within which we understand them. To this concrete situation itself the language makes fateful and monitory allusion: *the* administered world, *the* institutionalized society, *the* culture industry, *the* damaged subject—an image of our historical present which is Adorno's principal sociological contribution and which yet, as we have pointed out above, is never expressed directly in the form of a *thesis*. Rather, it intervenes as a series of references to a state of things with which our familiarity is already presupposed, a reality with which we are presumed to be only too well acquainted. The mode is that characteristic German sarcasm which may be said to have been Nietzsche's contribution to the language and in which a constant play of cynical, colloquial expressions holds the disgraced real world at arm's length, while abstractions and buried conceptual rhymes compare it with the impossible ideal.

At the same time, there seems to me to be a profoundly stylistic motivation behind such indirection. We have said that for Adorno—as indeed for Hegel, as for all dialectical thinkers to the degree that they are genuinely dialectical—thinking dialectically means nothing more or less than the writing of dialectical sentences. It is a kind of stylistic obedience analogous to that which governs the work of art itself, where it is the shape of the sentences themselves, above and beyond all conscious reflection, that determines the choice of the raw material. So here also the quality of the idea is judged by the type of sentence through which it comes to expression. For insofar as dialectical thinking is thought about thought, thought to the second power, concrete thought about an object, which at the same time remains aware of its own intellectual operations in the very act of thinking, such self-consciousness must be inscribed in the very sentence itself. And insofar as dialectical thinking characteristically involves a conjunction of opposites or at least conceptually disparate phenomena, it may truly be said of the dialectical sentence what the Surrealists said about the image, namely, that its strength increases proportionately as the realities linked are distant and distinct from each other.

Thus, if the work of Adorno nowhere yields that bald statement about the administered world which would seem to be its presupposition, if he nowhere takes the trouble to express in outright sociological terms that theory of the structure of the "institutionalized society" which serves as a hidden explanation and essential cross-reference for all the phenomena under analysis, this is to be explained not only by the fact that such material belongs to a study of the infrastructure rather than of ideological materials, and that it is already implicit in classical Marxist economics, but above all by the feeling that such outright statements, such outright presentations of sheer *content*, are stylistically wrong, this stylistic failure being itself a mark and a reflection of some essential failure in the thought process itself. For in a purely sociological presentation the thinking subject eclipses himself and seems to let the social phenomenon come into view objectively, as a fact, as a thing in itself. Yet for all that the observer does not cease to have a position with respect to the thing observed, and his thoughts do not cease to be conscious operations even when he ceases to be aware of them as such. Thus the overt presentation of content in its own right, whether in sociological or in philosophical writing, stands condemned as a fall back into that positivistic and empirical illusion which dialectical thinking was designed to overcome.

Yet if what Sartre would have called the "untotalizable totality" of Adorno's system, its absent center, cannot be conceptually described as a positivistic "theory of society" in its own terms, if the placelessness of so-called objective thought is ruled out by the very commitment of the system to self-consciousness, there is nonetheless another way in which such an absent totality may be evoked. It is to this ultimate squaring of the circle that Adorno came in his two last and most systematic, most technically philosophical works, *Negative Dialectics* and *Aesthetic Theory*. Indeed, as the title of the former suggests, these works are designed to offer a theory of the untheorizable, to show why dialectical thinking is at one and the same time both indispensable and impossible, to keep the idea of system itself alive while intransigently dispelling the pretensions of any of the contingent and already realized systems to validity and even to existence.

The essential argument of *Negative Dialektik* and Adorno's ultimate philosophical position, seems to me to be an articulation on the theoretical level of that methodology which we have seen at work in a concrete, practical way in the earlier aesthetic essays and critical writings. For there we found that in the long run the content of a work of art stands judged by its form, and that it is the realized form of the work which offers the surest key to the vital possibilities of that determinate social moment from which it springs. Now the same methodological discovery proves valid in the realm of philosophical thought itself; and the practice of negative dialectics involves a constant movement away from the official content of an idea—as, for example, the "real" nature of freedom or of society as things in themselves—and toward the various determinate and contradictory forms which such ideas have taken, whose conceptual limits and inadequacies stand as immediate figures or symptoms of the limits of the concrete social situation itself.

So it is, at the very outset, with the idea of the dialectic itself, which had in Hegel "as its foundation and its result the primacy of the subject, or, in the well-known language of the introductory remarks to the *Logic*, the identity of identity and nonidentity."[14] But the very mark of the modern experience of the world itself is that precisely such

[14] T. W. Adorno, *Negative Dialektik* (Frankfurt, 1966), p. 17.

55

identity is impossible, and that the primacy of the subject
is an illusion, that subject and outside world can never find
such ultimate identity or atonement under present historical
circumstances. Yet if that ultimate synthesis toward which
dialectical thought moves turns out to be unattainable it
must not be thought that either of the terms of that synthesis, either of the conceptual opposites which are its subject and object, are any more satisfactory in their own right.
The object considered in itself, the world taken as directly
accessible content, results in the illusions of simple empirical positivism, or in an academic thinking which mistakes
its own conceptual categories for solid parts and pieces of
the real world itself. In the same way, the exclusive refuge
in the subject results in what is for Adorno the subjective
idealism of Heideggerian existentialism, a kind of ahistorical historicity, a mystique of anxiety, death, and individual destiny without any genuine content. Thus a negative
dialectic has no choice but to affirm the notion and value of
an ultimate synthesis, while negating its possibility and reality in every concrete case that comes before it.

Such thought therefore aims at maintaining contact with
the concrete, painfully continuing a process of thinking
about the world itself, at the same time that it rectifies its
own inevitable falsifications at every moment, thus appearing to unravel everything it had been able to achieve.
Yet not altogether: for the genuine content acquired remains, albeit in what Hegel would have called a canceled
and transcended fashion; and negative dialectics does not
result in an empty formalism, but rather in a thoroughgoing
critique of forms, in a painstaking and well-nigh permanent
destruction of every possible hypostasis of the various
moments of thinking itself. For it is inevitable that every
theory about the world, in its very moment of formation,
tends to become an object for the mind and to be itself invested with all the prestige and permanency of a real thing

in its own right, thus effacing the very dialectical process from which it emerged: and it is this optical illusion of the substantiality of thought itself which negative dialectics is designed to dispel.

So it is, for instance, that in a classic essay on society Adorno shows not only how every possible idea we form about society is necessarily partial and imperfect, inadequate and contradictory, but also that those very *formal* contradictions are themselves the most precious indications as to how we stand with respect to the concrete reality of social life itself at the present moment of time. For society is clearly not some empirical object which we can meet and study directly in our own experience: in this sense the neo-positivistic criticism, which considers the idea of society an inadmissible abstract construct or a mere methodological hypothesis with no other kind of real existence, is justified. At the same time society—precisely in the form of such an impossible, suprapersonal abstraction—is present in the form of an ultimate constraint upon every moment of our waking lives: absent, invisible, even untenable, it is at the same time the most concrete of all the realities we have to face, and "while the notion of society may not be deduced from any individual facts, nor on the other hand be apprehended as an individual fact itself, there is nonetheless no social fact which is not determined by society as a whole."[15] Thus the contradictions of pure thought turn out to reflect the contradictions of their object as well, and that in the very moment when those initial conceptual contradictions seemed to forbid us any access to the real object to which they were supposed to correspond. Similarly, in the posthumous *Aesthetische Theorie*, the traditional foundations of aesthetic philosophy are at once discredited and given fresh justification by a constant shuttling back and forth between

[15] T. W. Adorno, "Society," *Salmagundi*, Nos. 10-11 (Fall 1969-Winter 1970), p. 145.

the historical facts of the world of artistic practice and the abstract conceptual categories through which that practice is perceived, at the same time that they reflect it.

We may therefore say that "the negative dialectic" represents an attempt to save philosophy itself, and the very idea of philosophizing, from a fetishization in time, from the optical illusion of stasis and permanency. Such antisystematic systematization, with all the deep inner contradictions it involves, reminds me of nothing quite so much as those equally contradictory monuments of modern art and literature which in their attempt to say everything end up saying only that one thing; which in their convulsive effort to present themselves, in almost medieval fashion, as the very book of the world itself, end up being but one book among others in a universe so disparate that no single thought can encompass it. Thus Barthes' observation about Proust, "whose whole work constitutes a simultaneous approach to and postponement of Literature itself," might also be applied to Adorno's philosophical position: "The writer thereby falls again into the power of time, for it is impossible to negate within the temporal continuum without at the same time elaborating a positive art which must be destroyed in its turn. Thus the greatest modern works linger as long as possible, in a kind of miraculous suspension, on the very threshold of Literature itself, in that waiting-room situation in which the density of life is given and protracted without yet being destroyed by the creation of an order of signs."[16]

It is therefore not to the discredit of *Negative Dialektik* to say that it is in the long run a massive failure; or, in different terms, that it stands as a kind of hyperconscious abstraction of that genuine totality of thought which Adorno's works taken as a whole embody. No doubt the

[16] Roland Barthes, *Le Degré zéro de l'écriture* (Paris, 1953), pp. 58-59.

emphasis on method and on the theory rather than the practice of negative dialectics risks giving an exaggerated and distorted importance to the moment of failure which is present in all modern thinking: and it is this overemphasis, more than anything else, which seems to me to account for that lack of political commitment with which radical students reproached Adorno at the end of his life. Yet his concrete studies remain incomparable models of the dialectical process, essays at once both systematic and occasional, in which pretext and consciousness meet to form the most luminous, if transitory, of figures or tropes of historical intelligibility: "like its object, knowledge remains shackled to the determinate contradiction."[17]

[17] *Philosophie der neuen Musik,* p. 33.

CHAPTER TWO

VERSIONS OF A MARXIST HERMENEUTIC

I. WALTER BENJAMIN; OR, NOSTALGIA

> Every feeling is attached to an a priori object, and the
> presentation of the latter is the phenomenology of the former.
>
> —*Ursprung des deutschen Trauerspiels*

So THE MELANCHOLY that speaks from the pages of Benjamin's essays—private depressions, professional discouragement, the dejection of the outsider, distress in the face of a political and historical nightmare—searches the past for an adequate object, for some emblem or image at which, as in religious meditation, the mind can stare itself out, in which it can find momentary, if only aesthetic, relief. It finds it: in the Germany of the Thirty Years' War, in the Paris "capital of the nineteenth century." For they are both—the Baroque and the modern—in their very essence allegorical, and they match the thought process of the theorist of allegory, which, disembodied intention searching for some external object into which to take shape, is itself already allegorical *avant la lettre*.

Indeed, it seems to me that Walter Benjamin's thought is best grasped as an allegorical one, as a set of parallel, discontinuous levels of meditation which are not without resemblance to that ultimate model of allegorical composition described by Dante when he speaks in his letter to Can Grande della Scala of the four dimensions of his poem: the literal (his hero's adventures in the afterworld), the moral (the ultimate fate of his soul), the allegorical (in which his encounters resume one aspect or another of the life of

Christ), and the anagogical (where his own drama fore-shadows the progress of the human race itself toward the Last Judgment).[1] It will not be hard to adapt this scheme to twentieth-century realities, if for literal we simply read psychological, retaining the second, moral level as such; if for the dominant archetypal pattern of the life of Christ we substitute religion in the broadest sense of the religion of art, seeing the Incarnation now as the incarnation of meaning in language; if finally, replacing theology with politics, we make of Dante's eschatology an earthly one, where the human race finds its salvation not in eternity, but in history itself.

Benjamin's work seems to me to be marked by a painful straining toward a psychic wholeness or unity of experience which the historical situation threatens to shatter at every turn. A vision of a world of ruins and fragments, an ancient chaos of whatever nature on the point of overwhelming consciousness—these are some of the images that seem to recur, either in Benjamin himself or in your own mind as you read him. The idea of wholeness or unity is of course not original with him. How many modern philosophers have described the "damaged existence" we lead in modern society, the psychological impairment caused by the division of labor and by specialization, the general alienation and dehumanization of modern life in all its aspects? Yet for the most part these analyses remain abstract; through them there speaks the resignation of the intellectual specialist to his own maimed present, the dream of wholeness, where it persists, attaching itself to someone else's future. Benjamin is unique among these thinkers in that he wants to save his

---

[1] It is at least a more familiar and less intimidating model than that proposed by Benjamin himself in a letter to Max Rychner: "I have never been able to inquire and think otherwise than, if I may so put it, in a theological sense—namely in conformity with the Talmudic prescription regarding the forty-nine levels of meaning in every passage of the Torah" (quoted in "Walter Benjamin," *Times Literary Supplement*, 22 August 1968).

own life as well: hence the peculiar fascination of his writings, incomparable not only in their dialectical intelligence, nor even in the poetic sensibility they express, but above all, perhaps, in the manner in which the autobiographical part of his mind finds symbolic satisfaction in the shape of ideas abstractly, in objective guises, expressed.

Psychologically, the drive toward unity takes the form of an obsession with the past and with memory. Genuine memory determines "whether the individual can have a picture of himself, whether he can master his own experience."[2] "Every passion borders on chaos, but the passion of the collector borders on the chaos of memory"[3] (and it was in the image of the collector that Benjamin found one of his most comfortable identities). "Memory forges the chain of tradition that passes events on from generation to generation."[4] Strange reflections, these—strange subjects of reflection for a Marxist (one thinks of Sartre's acid comment on his orthodox Marxist contemporaries: "materialism is the subjectivity of those who are ashamed of their own subjectivity"). Yet Benjamin kept faith with Proust, whom he translated, long after his own discovery of Communism; like Proust, he saw in his favorite poet Baudelaire an analogous obsession with reminiscence and involuntary memory; and in the fragmentary evocation of his own childhood called *Berliner Kindheit um 1900* he too began the task of recovering his own existence with short essayistic sketches, records of dreams, of isolated impressions and experiences, which he was however unable to carry to the greater writer's ultimate narrative unity.

He was perhaps more conscious of what prevents us from assimilating our life experience than of the form such a perfected life would take—fascinated, for example, with Freud's distinction between unconscious memory and the

---

[2] Walter Benjamin, *Schriften*, 2 vols. (Frankfurt, 1955), I, 429.
[3] *Schriften*, II, 108.   [4] *Schriften*, II, 245.

conscious act of recollection, the latter being for Freud basically a way of destroying or eradicating what the former was designed to preserve: "consciousness appears in the system of perception *in place* of the memory traces . . . consciousness and the leaving behind of a memory trace are within the same system mutually incompatible."[5] For Freud, the function of consciousness is the defense of the organism against shocks from the external environment. In this sense traumas, hysterical repetitions, dreams are ways in which the incompletely assimilated shock attempts to make its way through to consciousness and hence to ultimate appeasement. In Benjamin's hands, this idea becomes an instrument of historical description, a way of showing how in modern society, perhaps on account of the increasing number of shocks of all kinds to which the organism is now subjected, these defense mechanisms are no longer personal ones: a whole series of mechanical substitutes intervenes between consciousness and its objects, shielding us perhaps, yet at the same time depriving us of any way of assimilating what happens to us or of transforming our sensations into any genuinely personal experience. Thus, to give only one example, the newspaper acts as a shock absorber for the jolts of novelty, numbing us to events that might perhaps otherwise overwhelm us, but at the same time rendering them neutral and impersonal, transforming them into something that by definition has no common denominator with our private existences.

Experience is moreover socially conditioned in that it depends on a certain rhythm of recurrences and similarities in events which are properly cultural in origin. Thus even in Proust and Baudelaire, who lived in relatively fragmented societies, ritualistic devices, often unconscious, are primary elements in the construction of form: we recognize

[5] Quoted *Schriften*, I, 432; and see Freud, *Beyond the Pleasure Principle* (New York, 1959), pp. 49-50.

them in the "vie antérieure" and the correspondences of
Baudelaire, in the ceremonies of salon life in Proust. And
where the modern writer tries to create a perpetual present
—as in Kafka—the mystery inherent in the events seems to
result not so much from their novelty as from the feeling
that they have merely been forgotten, that they are in some
sense "familiar," in the haunting significance which Baudelaire lent that word. Yet as society increasingly decays, such
rhythms of experience are less and less available.

At this point, however, psychological description seems
to pass over insensibly into *moral* judgment, into a vision of
the reconciliation of past and present which is somehow an
ethical one. But for the Western reader the whole ethical
dimension of Benjamin's work is likely to be perplexing,
incorporating as it does a kind of ethical psychology which,
codified by Goethe, has become traditional in Germany and
deeply rooted in the German language, but for which we
have no equivalent, except in such cultural transplants as
the works of Erik Erikson. This *Lebensweisheit* is indeed
a kind of halfway house between the classical idea of a fixed
human nature, with its psychology of the humors, passions,
sins, or character types; and the modern idea of pure historicity, of the determining influence of the situation or
environment. As a compromise in the domain of the individual personality, it is not unlike the compromise of Hegel in
the realm of history itself. Where for the latter a general
meaning was immanent within the particular moment of
history, for Goethe, in some sense, the overall goal of the
personality and of its development is built into the particular emotion in question, or latent in the particular stage in
the individual's growth. For the system is based on a vision
of the full development of the personality (a writer like
Gide, deeply influenced by Goethe, gives but a pale and
narcissistic reflection of this ethic, which expressed middle-
class individualism at the moment of its historic triumph);

64

it neither aims to break the personality upon some purely external standard of discipline, as is the case with Christianity, nor to abandon it to the meaningless accidents of empirical psychology, as is the case with most modern ethics, but rather sees the individual psychological experience as something which includes within itself seeds of its own development, something in which ethical growth is inherent as a kind of interiorized Providence. So, for example, Goethe's *Orphic Words*, or the closing lines of *Wilhelm Meister*: "You make me think of Saul, the son of Kish, who went forth to seek his father's asses and found, instead, a kingdom!"

It is, however, characteristic of Benjamin that in his most complete expression of this Goethean ethic, the long essay on *Elective Affinities*, he should lay more stress on the dangers that menace the personality than on the picture of its ultimate development. For this essay, which speaks the language of Goethean life-psychology, is at the same time a critique of the reactionary forces in German society which made that psychology their own; working with the concept of myth, it is at the same time an attack on the obscurantist ideologies which made the notion of myth their rallying cry. In this, the polemic posture of Benjamin can be instructive for those of us who, undialectically, are tempted simply to reject the concept of myth altogether, on account of the ideological uses to which it is ordinarily put; for whom this concept, like related ones of magic or charisma, seems not to aim at a rational analysis of the irrational but rather at a consecration of it through language.

But for Benjamin *Elective Affinities* may be considered a mythical work, on condition we understand myth as that element from which the work seeks to free itself: as some earlier chaos of instinctual forces, inchoate, natural, pre-individualistic, as that which is destructive of genuine individuality, that which consciousness must overcome if it is to attain any real autonomy of its own, if it is to accede to any properly human level of existence. Is it farfetched to see in this opposition between mythical forces and the individual spirit a disguised expression of Benjamin's thoughts about past and present, an image of the way in which a remembering consciousness masters its past and brings to light what would otherwise be lost in the prehistory of the organism? Nor should we forget that the essay on *Elective Affinities* is itself a way of recovering the past, this time a cultural past, one given over to the dark mythical forces of a proto-Fascist tradition.

Benjamin's dialectical skill can be seen in the way this idea of myth is expressed through attention to the form of Goethe's novel, no doubt one of the most eccentric of Western literature in its combination of an eighteenth-century ceremoniousness with symbols of a strangely artificial, allegorical quality: objects which appear in the blankness of the nonvisual narrative style as though isolated against a void, as though fateful with a kind of geometrical meaning; the cautiously selected detail of landscape, too symmetrical not to have significance; analogies, such as the chemical one that gives the novel its title, too amply developed not to be emblematic. The reader is of course familiar with symbolism everywhere in the modern novel; but in general the symbolism is built into the work, like a sheet of instructions supplied inside the box along with the puzzle pieces. Here we feel the burden of guilt laid upon us as readers, in our lack of what strikes us almost as a culturally inherited mode of thinking, accessible only to those who are that culture's members; and no doubt the Goethean system does project itself in some such way, in its claim to universality.

It is the originality of Benjamin to have cut across the sterile opposition between the arbitrary interpretations of the symbol on the one hand, and the blank failure to see what it means on the other: *Elective Affinities* is to be read not as a novel by a symbolic writer, but as a novel *about* symbolism. If objects of a symbolic nature loom large in this work, it is not because they were chosen to underline the theme of adultery in some decorative manner, but rather because the real underlying subject is precisely the surrender to the power of symbols of people who have lost their autonomy as human beings. "When people sink to this level, even the life of apparently lifeless things grows strong. Gundolf quite rightly underlined the crucial role of objects in this story. Yet the intrusion of the thinglike into human life is precisely a criterion of the mythical universe."[6] We are required to read these symbolic objects to the second power: not so much directly to decipher in them a one-to-one meaning, as to sense that of which the very fact of symbolism is itself symptomatic.

And as with the objects, so also with the characters. It has for example often been remarked that the figure of Ottilie, the saintlike young woman around whom the drama turns, is somehow rendered in a different fashion from the other, more empirically drawn and psychologically realistic characters. For Benjamin, however, this is not so much a flaw or an inconsistency, as a clue: Ottilie is not reality but appearance, and it is this that the rather external and visual mode of characterization conveys. "It is clear that these Goethean characters come before us not so much as figures shaped from external models, nor wholly imaginary in their invention, but rather entranced somehow, as though under a spell. Hence a kind of obscurity about them which is foreign to purely visual images and which is comprehensible only for the reader who grasps their essence as pure appearance. For appearance is in this work not so much presented as a theme as it is rather implicit in the very nature and mode of the presentation itself."[7]

This moral dimension of Benjamin's work, like that of

[6] *Schriften*, I, 71.   [7] *Schriften*, I, 124-125.

Goethe's own, clearly represents an uneasy balance, a transitional moment between the psychological on the one hand, and the aesthetic or the historical on the other. The mind cannot long be satisfied with this purely ethical description of the events of the book as the triumph of fateful, mythical forces; it strains for historical and social explanation, and at length Benjamin himself is forced to express the conclusion "that the writer shrouds in silence: namely, that passion loses all its rights, under the laws of genuine human morality, when it seeks to make a pact with wealthy middle-class security."[8] But in Benjamin's work, this inevitable slippage of morality into history and politics, characteristic of all modern thought, is mediated by *aesthetics*, is revealed by attention to the qualities of the work of art, just as the above conclusion was articulated by the analysis of those aspects of *Elective Affinities* that might best be described as allegorical rather than symbolic.

For in one sense Benjamin's life work can be seen as a kind of vast museum, a passionate collection, of all shapes and varieties of allegorical objects; and his most substantial work centers on that enormous studio of allegorical decoration which is the Baroque.

The Origins, not so much of German tragedy (*Tragödie*), as of German *Trauerspiel*: this distinction, for which English has no equivalent, is crucial to Benjamin's interpretation. For "tragedy," which he limits to ancient Greece as a phenomenon, is a sacrificial drama in which the hero is offered up to the gods for atonement. *Trauerspiel*, on the other hand, which encompasses the Baroque generally, Elizabethans and Calderon as well as the seventeenth-century German playwrights, is something that might best be initially characterized as a pageant: a funereal pageant —so might the word be most adequately rendered.

As a form *Trauerspiel* reflects the baroque vision of his-

[8] *Schriften*, I, 121-122.

tory as chronicle, as the relentless turning of the wheel of fortune, a ceaseless succession across the stage of the world's mighty: princes, popes, empresses in their splendid costumes, courtiers, masqueraders, and poisoners—a dance of death produced with all the finery of a Renaissance triumph. For chronicle is not yet historicity in the modern sense: "No matter how deeply the baroque intention penetrates the detail of history, its microscopic analysis never ceases to search painstakingly for political calculation in a substance seen as pure intrigue. Baroque drama knows historical events only as the depraved activity of conspirators. Not a breath of genuine revolutionary conviction in any of the countless rebels who appear before the baroque sovereign, himself immobilized in the posture of a Christian martyr. Discontent—such is the classic motive for action."[9] And such historical time, mere succession without development, is in reality secretly spatial, and takes the court (and the stage) as its privileged spatial embodiment.

At first glance, it would appear that this vision of life as chronicle in *The Origins of German Tragedy*, a pre-Marxist work, is accounted for in an idealistic and Weberian manner: as Lutherans, Benjamin says, the German baroque playwrights knew a world in which belief was utterly separate from works, in which not even the Calvinistic preordained harmony intervenes to restore a little meaning to the succession of empty acts that make up human life, the world thus remaining as a body without a soul, as the shell of an object divested of any visible function. Yet it remains at the least an open question whether this intellectual and metaphysical position *causes* the psychological experience that is at the heart of baroque tragedy, or whether it is not itself merely one of the various expressions, relatively abstract, through which an acute and concrete emotion tries to manifest itself. For the key to the latter is the enigmatic central

[9] *Schriften*, I, 207.

figure of the prince himself, halfway between a tyrant justly assassinated and a martyr suffering his passion. Interpreted allegorically, he stands as the embodiment of melancholy in a stricken world, and Hamlet is his most complete expression. This interpretation of the funereal pageant as a basic expression of pathological melancholy has the advantage of accounting both for form and content at the same time.

For content, that is, in the sense of the characters' motivations: "The indecision of the prince is nothing but saturnine *acedia*. The influence of Saturn makes people 'apathetic, indecisive, slow.' The tyrant falls on account of the sluggishness of his emotions. In the same fashion, the character of the courtier is marked by faithlessness—another trait of the predominance of Saturn. The courtier's mind, as portrayed in these tragedies, is fluctuation itself: betrayal is his very element. It is to be attributed neither to hastiness of composition nor to insufficient characterization that the parasites in these plays scarcely need any time for reflection at all before betraying their lords and going over to the enemy. Rather, the lack of character evident in their actions, partly conscious Machiavellianism to be sure, reflects an inconsolable, despondent surrender to an impenetrable conjunction of baleful constellations, a conjunction that seems to have taken on a massive, almost thinglike cast. Crown, royal purple, scepter, all are in the last analysis the properties of the tragedy of fate, and they carry with them an aura of destiny to which the courtier is the first to submit, as to some portent of disaster. His faithlessness to his fellow men corresponds to the deeper, more contemplative faith he keeps with these material emblems."[10]

Once again Benjamin's sensitivity is for those moments in which human beings find themselves given over into the power of things; and the familiar content of baroque

[10] *Schriften*, I, 279-280.

tragedy (that melancholy which we recognize from *Hamlet*, those vices of melancholy—lust, treason, sadism—so predominant in the lesser Elizabethans, in Webster for instance) veers about slowly into a question of *form*, into the problem of objects, which is to say of allegory itself. For allegory is precisely the dominant mode of expression of a world in which things have been for whatever reason utterly sundered from meanings, from spirit, from genuine human existence.

And in the light of this new examination of the Baroque from the point of view of form rather than of content, little by little the brooding melancholy figure at the center of the play himself alters in focus, the hero of the funereal pageant little by little becomes transformed into the baroque playwright himself, the allegorist par excellence, in Benjamin's terminology the *Grübler*: that superstitious, overparticular reader of omens who returns in a more nervous, modern guise in the hysterical heroes of Poe and Baudelaire. "Allegories are in the realm of thoughts what ruins are in the realm of things";[11] and it is clear that Benjamin is himself foremost among these depressed and hyperconscious visionaries who people his pages. "Once the object has beneath the brooding look of Melancholy become allegorical, once life has flowed out of it, the object itself remains behind, dead, yet preserved for all eternity; it lies before the allegorist, given over to him utterly, for good or ill. In other words, the object itself is henceforth incapable of projecting any meaning on its own; it can only take on that meaning which the allegorist wishes to lend it. He instills it with his own meaning, himself descends to inhabit it: and this must be understood not psychologically but in an ontological sense. In his hands the thing in question becomes something else, speaks of something else, becomes for him the key to

[11] *Schriften*, I, 301.

some realm of hidden knowledge, as whose emblem he honors it. This is what constitutes the nature of allegory as script."[12]

Script rather than language, the letter rather than the spirit; these are the fragments into which the baroque world shatters, strangely legible signs and emblems nagging at the too curious mind, a procession moving slowly across a stage, laden with occult significance. In this sense, for the first time it seems to me that allegory is restored to us—not as a Gothic monstrosity of purely historical interest, or, as in C. S. Lewis, a sign of the medieval health of the essentially religious spirit, but rather as a pathology with which in the modern world we are only too familiar. The tendency of our own criticism has been to exalt symbol at the expense of allegory (even though the privileged objects proposed by that criticism—English Mannerism and Dante—are more properly allegorical in nature; in this as in other aspects of his sensibility Benjamin has much in common with a writer like T. S. Eliot). The preference for symbolism is perhaps more the expression of a value rather than a description of existing poetic phenomena: for the distinction between symbol and allegory is that between a complete reconciliation between object and spirit and a mere will to such reconciliation. The usefulness of Benjamin's analysis lies however in his insistence on a temporal distinction as well: the symbol is the instantaneous, the lyrical, the single moment in time; and this temporal limitation perhaps expresses the historical impossibility in the modern world for genuine reconciliation to endure in time, for it to be anything more than a lyrical, accidental present. Allegory is, on the contrary, the privileged mode of our own life in time, a clumsy deciphering of meaning from moment to moment, the painful attempt to restore a continuity to heterogeneous, disconnected instants. "Where the symbol

[12] *Schriften*, I, 308.

as it fades shows the face of Nature in the light of salvation, in allegory it is the *facies hippocratica* of history that lies like a frozen landscape before the eye of the beholder. History in everything that it has of the unseasonable, painful, abortive, expresses itself in that face—nay rather in that death's-head. And while it may be true that such an allegorical mode is utterly lacking in any 'symbolic' freedom of expression, in any classical harmony of feature, in anything human—what is expressed here portentously in the form of a riddle is not only the nature of human life in general, but also the biographical historicity of the individual in its most natural and organically corrupted form. This—the baroque, earthbound exposition of history as the story of the world's suffering—is the very essence of allegorical perception; history takes on meaning only in the stations of its agony and decay. The amount of meaning is in exact proportion to the presence of death and the power of decay, since death is that which traces the jagged line between Physis and meaning."[13]

And what marks baroque allegory holds true for the allegory of modern times, for Baudelaire as well: only in the latter it is interiorized. "Baroque allegory saw the corpse from the outside only. Baudelaire sees it from within."[14] Or again: "Commemoration [*Andenken*] is the secularized version of the adoration of holy relics. . . . Commemoration is the complement to experience. In commemoration there finds expression the increasing alienation of human beings, who take inventories of their past as of lifeless merchandise. In the nineteenth century allegory abandons the outside world, only to colonize the inner. Relics come from the corpse, commemoration from the dead occurrences of the past which are euphemistically known as experience."[15]

Yet in these late essays on modern literature a new pre-

[13] *Schriften*, I, 289-290.   [14] *Schriften*, I, 489.
[15] *Schriften*, I, 487.

occupation appears, which signals Benjamin's passage from the predominantly aesthetic to the *historical* and *political* dimension. This is the attention to the machine and to mechanical inventions, which characteristically first appears in the realm of aesthetics itself in the study of the movies ("The Reproducible Work of Art") and is only later extended to the study of history in general (as in the essay "Paris—Capital of the Nineteenth Century," in which the feeling of life in this period is conveyed by a description of the new objects and inventions characteristic of it: the commercial passageways, the use of cast iron, the Daguerreotype and the panorama, the great expositions, advertising). Yet it is important to point out that however materialistic such an approach to history may seem, nothing is farther from Marxism than the stress on invention and technique as the primary cause of historical change. Indeed, it seems to me that such theories (of the kind which regard the steam engine as the cause of the Industrial Revolution, and which have recently been rehearsed yet again, in streamlined modernistic form, in the works of Marshall McLuhan) function as a substitute for Marxist historiography in the way they offer a feeling of concreteness comparable to economic subject matter, at the same time that they dispense with any consideration of the human factors of classes and of the social organization of production.

Benjamin's fascination with the role of inventions in history seems to me most comprehensible in psychological or aesthetic terms. If we follow, for instance, his meditation on the role of the passerby and the crowd in Baudelaire, we find that after the evocation of Baudelaire's physical and stylistic characteristics, after the discussion of shock and organic defenses outlined earlier in this essay, the inner logic of Benjamin's material leads him to mechanical inventions: "Comfort isolates. And at the same time it shifts its possessor deeper into the power of physical mechanisms.

74

With the invention of matches around the middle of the century, there begins a whole series of novelties which have in common the replacement of a complicated set of operations with a single stroke of the hand. This development goes on in many different spheres at the same time: it is evident, among other instances, in the telephone, where in place of the continuous movement with which the crank of the older model had to be turned a single lifting of the receiver now suffices. Among the various gestures of sliding a mechanism home, depositing a token, or triggering an apparatus, that of 'snapping' the photograph was particularly consequential. Pressing the finger once is enough to freeze an event for unlimited time. The apparatus lends the instant a posthumous shock, so to speak. And beside tactile experiences of this kind we find optical ones as well, such as the classified ads in a newspaper, or even the traffic in a big city. To move through the latter involves a whole series of shocks and collisions. At dangerous intersections, impulses crisscross the pedestrian like charges in a battery. Baudelaire describes the man who plunges into the crowd as a reservoir of electrical energy. Thereupon he calls him, thus singling out the experience of shock, 'a *kaleidoscope* endowed with consciousness.' "[16] And Benjamin goes on to complete this catalogue with a description of the worker and his psychological subjection to the operation of the machine in the factory. Yet it seems to me that beyond the value of this passage as an analysis of the psychological effect of machinery, it has for Benjamin a secondary intention, it satisfies a psychological requirement which is perhaps in some ways even deeper and more important than the official intellectual one; and that is to serve as a concrete embodiment for the state of mind of Baudelaire. The essay, indeed, begins with a relatively disembodied psychological state: the poet faced with the new condition of language in

[16] *Schriften*, I, 447-448.

modern times, faced with the debasement of journalism, faced, as the inhabitant of a great city, with the increasing shocks and perceptual numbness of daily urban living. These phenomena are intensely familiar to Benjamin, but somehow he seems to feel them as insufficiently "rendered": he cannot possess them spiritually, he cannot express them adequately, until he finds some sharper and more concrete physical image in which to embody them. The machine, the list of inventions, is precisely such an image; and it will be clear to the reader that we consider such a passage, in appearance a historical analysis, as in reality an exercise in allegorical meditation, in the locating of some fitting emblem in which to anchor the peculiar and nervous modern state of mind which was Benjamin's subject matter.

For this reason the preoccupation with machines and inventions in Benjamin does not lead to a theory of historical causality; rather, it finds its completion elsewhere, in a theory of the modern object, in the notion of "aura." Aura for Benjamin is the equivalent in the modern world, where it still persists, of what anthropologists call the "sacred" in primitive societies; it is to the world of things what "mystery" is to the world of human events, what "charisma" is to the world of human beings. In a secularized universe it is perhaps easier to locate at the moment of its disappearance, the cause of which lies in general technical invention, the replacement of human perception with those substitutes for and mechanical extensions of perception which are machines. Thus it is easy to see how in the movies, in the "reproducible work of art," that aura which originally resulted from the physical presence of actors in the here and now of the theater is short-circuited by the new technical advance (and then replaced, in genuine Freudian symptom-formation, by the attempt to endow the stars with a new kind of personal aura of their own off the screen).

76

Yet in the world of objects, this intensity of physical presence which constitutes the aura of something can perhaps best be expressed by the image of the look, the intelligence returned: "The experience of aura is based on the transposition of a social reaction onto the relationship of the lifeless or of nature to man. The person we look at, the person who believes himself looked at, looks back at us in return. To experience the aura of a phenomenon means to endow it with the power to look back in return."[17]

And elsewhere he defines aura thus: "The single, unrepeatable experience of distance, no matter how close it may be. While resting on a summer afternoon, to follow the outline of a mountain against the horizon, or of a branch that casts its shadow on the viewer, means to breathe the aura of the mountain, of the branch."[18] Aura is thus in a sense the opposite of allegorical perception, in that in it a mysterious wholeness of objects becomes visible. And where the broken fragments of allegory represented a thing-world of destructive forces in which human autonomy was drowned, the objects of aura stand perhaps as the setting of a kind of Utopia, a Utopian present, not shorn of the past but having absorbed it, a kind of plenitude of existence in the world of things, if only for the briefest instant. Yet this Utopian component of Benjamin's thought, put to flight as it is by the mechanized present of history, is available to the thinker only in a simpler cultural past.

Thus it is his one evocation of a nonallegorical art, his essay on Nikolai Leskov, "The Teller of Tales," which is perhaps his masterpiece. As with actors confronted with the technical advance of the reproducible work of art, so also with the tale in the face of modern communications systems, and in particular the newspaper. The function of the newspapers is to absorb the shocks of novelty, and by numbing the organism to them to dull their intensity. Yet

[17] *Schriften,* I, 461.   [18] *Schriften,* I, 372-373.

the tale, always constructed around some novelty, was designed, on the contrary, to preserve its force; whereas the mechanical form "exhausts" ever-increasing quantities of new material, the older word-of-mouth communication is essentially characterized as that which recommends itself to memory. Its reproducibility is not mechanical, but natural to consciousness; indeed, that which allows the story to be remembered, to seem "memorable," is at the same time the means of its assimilation to the personal experience of the listeners.

It is instructive to compare Benjamin's analysis of the tale (and of its implied distinction from the novel) with that of Sartre, so similar in some ways, and yet so different in its ultimate emphasis. For both, the two forms are opposed not only in their social origins (the tale springing from collective life, the novel from middle-class solitude) and in their raw materials (the tale using what everyone can recognize as common experience, the novel that which is uncommon and highly individualistic), but also and primarily in their relationship to death and to eternity. Benjamin quotes Valéry: "It is almost as though the disappearance of the idea of eternity were related to the increasing distaste for any kind of work of long duration in time." Concurrent with the disappearance of the genuine story is the increasing concealment of death and dying in our society; for the authority of the story ultimately derives from the authority of death, which lends every event an absolute uniqueness. "A man who died at the age of thirty-five is at every point in his life a man who is going to die at the age of thirty-five":[19] so Benjamin describes our apprehension of characters in the tale, in antipsychological fashion, as the simplified representatives of their own destinies. But what appeals to his sensitivity to the archaic is precisely what Sartre condemns as inauthentic: namely the violence to

[19] *Schriften*, II, 248.

genuine lived human experience, which never in the freedom of its own present feels itself as fate, for which fate and destiny are always characteristic of other people's experience, seen from the outside as something closed and thing-like. For this reason Sartre opposes the tale (it is true that he is thinking of the well-made story of the late nineteenth century, which catered to a middle-class audience, rather than of the relatively anonymous folk product with which Benjamin is concerned) to the novel, whose task is precisely to render this open experience of consciousness in the present, of freedom, rather than the optical illusion of fate.

There can be no doubt that this opposition corresponds to a historical experience: the older tale, indeed the classical nineteenth-century novel as well, expressed a social life in which the individual was presented with single-shot, irreparable choices and opportunities, in which he had to play everything on a single roll of the dice, in which his life did therefore properly tend to take on the appearance of fate or destiny, of a story that can be told. Whereas in the modern world (which is to say, in Western Europe and the United States), economic prosperity is such that nothing is ever really irrevocable in this sense: hence the philosophy of freedom, hence the modernistic literature of consciousness of which Sartre is here a theorist; hence also the decay of plot, for where nothing is irrevocable (in the absence of death in Benjamin's sense) there is no story to tell either, there is only a series of experiences of equal weight whose order is indiscriminately reversible.

Benjamin is as aware as Sartre of the way in which the tale, with its appearance of destiny, does violence to our lived experience in the present; but for him it does justice to our experience of the past. Its "inauthenticity" is to be seen as a mode of commemoration, so that it does not really matter any longer whether the young man dead in his prime was aware of his own lived experience as fate. For us, henceforth remembering him, he will always be, at the various stages of his life, one about to become this destiny, and the tale thus gives us "the hope of warming our own chilly existence upon a death about which we read."[20]

The tale is not only a psychological mode of relating to the past, of commemorating it: for Benjamin it is also a mode of contact with a vanished form of social and historical existence, and it is in this correlation between the activity of storytelling and the concrete form of a certain historically determinate mode of production that Benjamin can serve as a model of Marxist literary criticism at its most revealing. The twin sources of storytelling find their archaic embodiment in "the settled cultivator on the one hand and the seafaring merchant on the other. Both forms of life have in fact produced their own characteristic type of story-teller. . . . A genuine extension of the possibilities of storytelling to its greatest historical range is, however, not possible without the most thoroughgoing fusion of the two archaic types. Such a fusion was realized during the Middle Ages in the associations and guilds of the artisans. The sedentary master and the wandering apprentice worked together in the same room; indeed, every master had himself been a wandering apprentice before settling down at home or in some foreign city. If peasants and sailors were the inventors of storytelling, the guild system proved to be the place of its highest development. In it the lore of distance, as the traveler brought it back, combined with that lore of the past that most fully reveals its riches to the stay-at-home."[21] The tale is thus the product of an artisanal culture, a handmade product like a cobbler's shoe or a pot; and like such a handmade object, "the touch of the storyteller clings to it like the trace of the potter's hand on the glazed surface."[22]

[20] *Schriften*, II, 249. [21] *Schriften*, II, 231.
[22] *Schriften*, I, 430.

In his ultimate statement of the relationship of literature to politics, Benjamin seems to have tried to bring to bear on the problems of the present this method, which had known success in dealing with the objects of the past. Yet the transposition is not without its difficulties, and Benjamin's conclusions remain problematical, particularly in his unresolved, ambiguous attitude toward modern industrial civilization, which seems to have fascinated him as much as it depressed him. The problem of propaganda in art can be solved, he maintains, by attention, not so much to the content of the work of art, as to its form: a progressive work of art is one which utilizes the most advanced artistic techniques, one in which, therefore, the artist lives his activity as a technician, and through this technical work finds a unity of purpose with the industrial worker. "The solidarity of the specialist with the proletariat . . . can never be anything but a mediated one."[23] This Communist "politization of art," which he opposed to the Fascist "aesthetization of the machine,"[24] was designed to harness to the cause of revolution that modernism to which other Marxist critics (Lukács, for instance) were hostile. And there can be no doubt that Benjamin first came to a radical politics through his experience as a specialist: through his growing awareness, within the domain of his own literary activity, of the crucial influence exerted on the work of art by changes in the public and developments in technique, in short by history itself. But although in the realm of culture the historian can no doubt show a parallelism between specific technical advances in a given art and the general development of the economy as a whole, it is difficult to see how a technically advanced and difficult work of art can have anything but a "mediated" effect politically. Benjamin was of course fortunate in the artistic example which lay before him: for he

[23] Walter Benjamin, *Versuche über Brecht* (Frankfurt, 1966), p. 115.
[24] *Schriften*, I, 395-397.

illustrates his thesis with the epic theater of Brecht, perhaps indeed the only modern artistic innovation that *has* had direct and revolutionary political impact. But even here the situation is ambiguous: an astute critic has pointed out the secret relationship between Benjamin's fondness for Brecht on the one hand and "his lifelong fascination with children's books" on the other[25] (children's books: hieroglyphs: simplified allegorical emblems and riddles). Thus, where we thought to emerge into the historical present, in reality we plunge again into the distant past of psychological obsession.

But if nostalgia as a political motivation is most frequently associated with Fascism, there is no reason why a nostalgia conscious of itself, a lucid and remorseless dissatisfaction with the present on the grounds of some remembered plenitude, cannot furnish as adequate a revolutionary stimulus as any other: the example of Benjamin is there to prove it. He himself, however, preferred to contemplate his destiny in terms of religious imagery, as in the following paragraph of the *Geschichtsphilosophische Thesen*, according to Gershom Scholem the last he ever wrote: "Surely Time was felt neither as empty nor as homogeneous by the soothsayers who inquired after what it hid in its womb. Whoever keeps this in mind is in a position to grasp just how past time is experienced in commemoration: in precisely the same way. As is well known, the Jews were forbidden to search into the future. On the contrary, the Torah and the act of prayer instruct them in commemoration of the past. So for them the future, to which the clientele of soothsayers remains in thrall, is divested of its sacred power. Yet it does not for all that become simply empty and homogeneous time in their eyes. For every second of the

[25] Rolf Tiedemann, in his "Nachwort" to Benjamin's *Versuche über Brecht*, p. 149.

future bears within it that little door through which Messiah may enter."[26]

Angelus novus: Benjamin's favorite image of the angel that exists only to sing its hymn of praise before the face of God, to give voice, and then at once to vanish back into uncreated nothingness. So at its most poignant Benjamin's experience of time: a present of language on the threshold of the future, honoring it by averted eyes in meditation on the past.

II. MARCUSE AND SCHILLER

1)

> Le seul mot de liberté est tout ce qui m'exalte encore.
>
> —André Breton, *Premier manifeste du surréalisme*

How MANY are the ideas of which we can say that we understand them conceptually, without remembering in any original sense what they mean! And even this situation —in which thinking and real experience have gone their separate ways and which leaves its mark in one way or another on everything in modern culture and modern language—standing as it does in all its banal familiarity as an illustration to its own thesis, still fails to come home to us with any of the astonishment of real comprehension unless we find within ourselves the means of constructing a moment of past history in which this was not yet so, a moment which can stand beside our own as a possibility of visionary, even visceral comparison. Let us imagine, for example, a people with no way of preserving the ideas it invents: the names of the ideas are therefore the very signs of the things themselves, endowed with all the clumsiness of primary

[26] *Über Walter Benjamin* (Frankfurt, 1968), p. 162.

spelling and all the sacred terror of origins. Yet let some internal experience, such as that of God, disappear, and not even a vacant sound remains behind; there survives to perplex future generations not so much as a stone word or indecipherable hieroglyph. In such a culture hermeneutics, the revival of the living idea beneath the layers of dead language, is a useless discipline, for there can be no twilight state between the silence of oblivion and the instantaneous transparency of human understanding, which words surround like faces with familiar expressions. Thus we measure, indeed for the first time we *understand*—in the strongest sense of the term—the quality of experience in our own culture and in our own moment of history by weighing it against this hypothetical reconstruction of a more primitive, a more natural and *original* past. The image of that past therefore serves, we may say, not so much a *historical* function (for such cultures have never existed), as rather a *hermeneutic* one.

For hermeneutics, traditionally a technique whereby religions recuperated the texts and spiritual activities of cultures resistant to them, is also a political discipline, and provides the means for maintaining contact with the very sources of revolutionary energy during a stagnant time, of preserving the concept of freedom itself, underground, during geological ages of repression. Indeed, it is the concept of freedom which, measured against those other possible ones of love or justice, happiness or work, proves to be the privileged instrument of a political hermeneutic, and which, in turn, is perhaps itself best understood as an interpretive device rather than a philosophical essence or idea. For wherever the concept of freedom is once more understood, it always comes as the awakening of dissatisfaction in the midst of all that is—at one, in that, with the birth of the negative itself: never a state that is enjoyed, or a mental structure that is contemplated, but rather an ontological impatience in which the constraining situation itself is for the first time perceived in the very moment in which it is refused. From the physical intimidation of the Fascist state to the agonizing repetitions of neurosis, the idea of freedom takes the same temporal form: a sudden perception of an intolerable present which is at the same time, but implicitly and however dimly articulated, the glimpse of another state in the name of which the first is judged. Thus the idea of freedom involves a kind of perceptual superposition; it is a way of reading the present, but it is a reading that looks more like the reconstruction of an extinct language.

This formal character of the concept of freedom is precisely what lends itself to the work of political hermeneutics. It encourages analogy: assimilating the material prisons to the psychic ones, it serves as a means of unifying all these separate levels of existence, functioning, indeed, as a kind of transformational equation whereby the data characteristic of one may be converted into the terms of other. It is not too much to say that the concept of freedom thus permits us to transcend one of the most fundamental contradictions in modern existence: that between the outside and the inside, between public and private, work and leisure, the sociological and the psychological, between my being-for-others and my being-for-myself, between the political and the poetic, objectivity and subjectivity, the collective and the solitary—between society and the monad. It is an opposition which the confrontation between Marx and Freud dramatizes emblematically; and the persistence of this attempted confrontation (Reich, the Surrealists, Sartre, left-wing Structuralism, not to speak of Marcuse himself) underlines the urgency with which modern man seeks to overcome his double life, his dispersed and fragmentary existence.

Schiller began the *Letters on the Aesthetic Education of Mankind* during the fateful winter of 1793-1794, when the absolute politization of existence which marks the Revolution even for the foreign observer was rapidly evolving toward the ultimate alternatives of the Terror or outright counterrevolution. "The gaze of philosopher as well as man of the world is fastened expectantly upon the political arena, where, it is thought, the destiny of mankind itself is at stake. Does one not betray a reprehensible indifference to the welfare of society by failing to share in the general debate?"[27]

Nonetheless, it is at such a moment in history that he will devote himself to aesthetic theory and to the reassessment of the artistic impulse itself, as it relates to the other basic activities of man. "I hope to convince you," he says, "that this subject matter is not so much alien to the needs, as rather merely to the taste, of our moment in history, and indeed that it is precisely the path through the aesthetic question that we are obliged to take in any ultimate solution of the political question, for it is through beauty that we arrive at freedom."[28] The diversion from politics is only an apparent one: in reality Schiller aims at giving a description of the artistic process such that its protopolitical character will remain visible, even for the citizens of a world fatigued by politics.

The procedure is cumbersome for modern tastes. Schiller's argument is an illustration of that hypothetical, a priori systematization so characteristic of the second half of the eighteenth century, for which the well-known remark of Rousseau, at the beginning of *Discourse on the Origins of Inequality*, may serve as an epigraph: "Let us begin by setting all the facts aside." The vices of such constructions result, no doubt, from the application of pure logical argumentation and deduction to the realm of history itself, as though the development of societies were as accessible to

[27] Schiller, *Philosophische Schriften* (Basel, 1946), p. 79.
[28] *Philosophische Schriften*, p. 80.

reason as the syllogism itself. Yet these works, which the Romantic movement relegated to the status of intellectual curiosities, were perhaps not wholly without peculiar strengths of their own. Louis Althusser comments thus upon the various seventeenth- and eighteenth-century hypotheses about the origins of society: "The various characteristics of the state of nature serve alternately to account for man's reasons for evolving out of it, and to hint at the features of the society of the future and the ideal of human relations in general. Paradoxically it is this state, bereft of any type of social relationship whatsoever, which *contains within itself and figures forth in advance the ideal of a society yet to be achieved.* The end of history is inscribed in its very origins. . . ."[29] We will return to this peculiar property of the a priori social model at the end of the present essay.

For the moment, suffice it to note that Schiller draws a signal advantage from his model: for the application of Cartesian logic—the logic of introspection, of the cogito— to the social organism already implies an identification between the inner and the outer; and Schiller's profound originality, which will leave its mark on thinkers from Hegel to Freud, was to have reversed this identification and transferred the notion of the division of labor, of economic specialization, from the social classes to the inner functioning of the mind, where it assumes the appearance of a hypostasis of one mental function over against the others, a spiritual deformation which is the exact equivalent of the economic alienation in the social world outside.

Such deformations are, however, more deduced than they are observed, and it is what ought to come last—the vision of a more fully developed human personality—which serves in fact as a kind of ideal presupposition, of ideal harmony, in the light of which the various forms of alienation may be recognized for what they are. This ideal

[29] Louis Althusser, *Montesquieu* (Paris, 1959), p. 16. Italics mine.

harmony, which is none other than the "state of nature" itself (and which one must think of more in terms of the
Greece of Winckelmann than of primitive man), is defined
by two essential characteristics: "As long as we were merely
the children of Nature, we were both happy and complete;
we became free, and lost both. Whence a double and most
unequal longing for Nature, a longing for her *bliss*, a longing for her *completeness*. Only sensual man bemoans the
loss of the first; only ethical man mourns that of the second."[30] This duality will have a significant effect on the
range and implications of Schiller's system: less a duality,
perhaps, than an overlapping, a satisfying of twin impulses
at the same time. For the superposition of these two drives
allows Schiller to satisfy both while working out the terms
of either one, allows him to translate the code of the first
into the code of the second, to deal with the phenomena of
the pleasure principle (whose terminology Freud has yet
at this point to invent) in terms of the more traditional
philosophical language of the mental functions (will, sense
perception, imagination, etc.) and of their relationship to
each other. A different Schiller will emerge depending on
which of the two basic features of the state of nature is
stressed: the emphasis on completeness yields the Schiller
of Jung's *Psychological Types*, with its ideal of the integration of consciousness, while an emphasis on the pleasure
principle results in the Freudian Schiller of *Eros and Civilization*. The paradox of the historical Schiller is precisely
that in order to arrive at a statement about happiness
(about which nothing can be said in his terminology), the
argument must be couched in the language of completeness
and of the mental functions, which permit an interplay of
opposing terms.

Neither of these forces—the *Stofftrieb* or impulse behind
the various materialistic passions and appetites, and the

[30] *Philosophische Schriften*, p. 226.

Formtrieb, or attraction to Reason, under whose influence "we are no longer individuals, but rather species-beings"[31] —is privileged: both ultimately deform, and the *philosophe* just as much as the Philistine, the abstract Jacobin personality fully as much as the personality mired in immediate self-interest and in the satisfactions of objects, fall short of a full development of their possibilities.

The conclusion is of course implicit in the starting point, and it remains only to identify some third drive in which the other two may be satisfied simultaneously, may be coordinated in the framework of a single activity in which neither is repressed at the expense of the other. Such a drive is the *Spieltrieb,* the impulse to play, which underlies artistic activity in general, and in which both the appetite for form and that for matter are satisfied together. The object of this impulse, pure appearance (*Schein*), is itself at once both form and matter, and, turning into form where you seek for matter, proving to be matter where you looked for form, stands as the sign of a kind of discipline which the human being must undergo to achieve unity, to divest himself of his historically conditioned defects and failures in development.

Freedom is at this point nothing more than the mutual neutralization of these two powerful drives (toward matter and form): like pleasure for Freud, it is the release from tension, access to and glimpse of a world in which quantity is replaced by quality, where force, weight, and mass are replaced by, or transformed into, grace. Indeed, as for Bergson, grace is for Schiller the very manifestation of freedom in the realm of the senses; beauty, to quote the ultimate formula, is the form freedom takes in the realm of sensory appearance ("Freiheit in der Erscheinung"). The qualification would be enough to remind us that Schiller's

[31] *Philosophische Schriften,* p. 124.

89

is not primarily an aesthetic, but rather still a political, system: and that the importance of beauty consists for him in the possibility the aesthetic experience affords of a practical apprenticeship for the real political and social freedom to come. In art, consciousness prepares itself for a change in the world itself and at the same time learns to make demands on the real world which hasten that change: for the experience of the imaginary offers (in an imaginary mode) that total satisfaction of the personality and of Being in the light of which the real world stands condemned, in the light of which the Utopian idea, the revolutionary blueprint, may be conceived.

No doubt such speculations, as practical political strategy, are bound to strike the modern mind as unrealistic, to say the least; making a revolution, one is tempted to say, is not like taking a course in art appreciation. Schiller, to be sure, was thinking of the middle-class revolution in Germany, and his program was a little more concrete than the above speculations suggest. For it aimed at nothing less than the creation of a new, national, middle-class culture which would be established primarily through a national theater and a national drama: the education of the German bourgeoisie to political unity and autonomy through the playhouse.

But it is more useful, and more dialectical, to turn our attention back upon ourselves and our own reactions for an instant. What if the fact of our judgment stood as a judgment on us, rather than on the Utopian speculation that we are unable to take seriously? What if our judgment were itself a measure and a symptom of our own incapacity to support such thinking, of our own repression of the principle of futurity, smothered under the realism of the reality principle and the massive weight of what is? What if it were the very psychologism, the cynical reductionism, of the reality principle itself that turned out to be not reality, but just another symptom? Thus we are scandalized when we discover the source of Rousseau's political speculations in un-disguised erotic reverie and sexual daydreaming (as in the ninth book of the *Confessions*); we find ourselves only too willing to discredit the former on the grounds that the latter was its *cause*, without understanding that such an argument cuts both ways, and that the process can be seen precisely as that return to a common source of both poetry and pol-itics, of the erotic and the political impulses, which marks a reintegration of consciousness fragmented in the modern world.

Schiller's is indeed one of the first meditations on the antinomies of cultural revolution: only after revolutionary change can the new man, the post-acquisitive human na-ture, come into being; but the Terror (and in our own time, Stalinism) stands as a warning that purges cannot complete a process for which men are not yet ready, or in other words for which objective social conditions are not yet ripe. Does it follow then that revolution can ultimately be successful only when men are psychologically receptive to its demands, which is to say, when it is no longer really necessary in the first place? The mature Schiller was of course no longer a radical; and when cultural revolution is understood as a *substitute* for social revolution, as is frequently the Western conception, it may be suspected of serving a quite different function than in a post-revolutionary society such as China today.

Yet Schiller's system provides for yet another practical outlet, of a somewhat different kind, and it is this that forms the hermeneutic section of his doctrine. For the notion of a realization of freedom in art becomes concrete only when, in *On Naïve and Sentimental Poetry*, Schiller descends into the detail of the work of art itself, there teaching us to see the very technical construction of the work as a *figure* of the struggle for psychic integration in general, to see in images, quality of language, type of plot construction the very fig-ures (in an imaginary mode) of freedom itself.

In the work of art, the older opposition between the state of nature and the state of civilization is recapitulated by the distinction between a concrete poetry, that of the "naïve" or primitive poet, and the abstract poetry of modern times, the work of "sentimental" artists—the word means a combination of "sophisticated," "intellectualistic," "artificial." Of "naïve" poetry we can in a sense only speak ex post facto. Such works exist, particularly in Greek literature, but precisely insofar as they reflect a kind of total, concrete experience, there is nothing we can really say about them, for everything we say, any terms we use, already presuppose a rift in that plenitude. Thus we can scarcely even speak of the "naïve" poet as such, for the very mark of such a poet is that he has eclipsed himself as a separate subjectivity, has abolished (or rather has never known) that distance between subject and object which is the sign of modern times, of our fall from the state of nature.

Thus, if it is difficult to characterize "naïve" poetry in any other way than as an experience of concrete plenitude, the varieties of modern or "sentimental" poetry may be computed almost deductively, as the various possible permutations of the relationship between form and matter, between subject and object, between a henceforth isolated monad and the world from which it is estranged. Clearly, there will be an essential difference in character between a literature that dwells on the situation of the abandoned subject itself and one that describes the nature of the fallen, meaningless world that surrounds it. The former may be characterized as an *elegiac* mode, whereas the latter is a *satiric* one. And insofar as modern sensibility, incapable of any genuine concrete reunification or at-one-ment with the world, still finds it in itself to dream of such a state of plenitude, attempts to project forth an impoverished vision of what such a state might be like, there is room for yet a third logical possibility, namely the *idyll*, whose irreality is inscribed in the very thinness of its poetic realization itself.

These modes of possibility are far from reducing themselves to mere questions of genre, and indeed Schiller's model is susceptible of application to any dimension of the work of art, whether it be the stylistic or the psychological, the historical or the ideological. In Hegel's *Aesthetics*, with its vision of artistic history as a set of varying relations between the poles of subject and object, as well as in Lukács' *Theory of the Novel*, with its subjective/objective classification scheme, the basic model is flattened out into a temporal progression, and becomes the foundation for a theory of history. In the American New Criticism, perhaps unconsciously, the crucial insight of a fall from "naïve" to "sentimental" is reexpressed in terms of the dissociation of poetic sensibility, which then becomes a precise analytical instrument for determining the degree and kind of poetic abstraction in a given text. In Northrop Frye's works, the classes of the genres are once more called upon to symbolize the more concrete modes of our relationship to Being. But all of these revisions of Schiller, which indicate the richness of his basic model, remain idealistic in character; and the return to Schiller himself serves to remind us of the original political intent behind the system. When that intent is lost, speculative thinking becomes futile and reaches any one of a number of well-defined dead ends: it ends up in a "theory of history," or substitutes a religious hermeneutic for the political one, or finally and most characteristically becomes involved in the sterile and circular movement of a typology, of the weighing of phenomena against a static system of classification; and such systems, whether in early Lukács, Frye, or Jung's *Psychological Types*, are always the sign of historical thinking arrested halfway, a thought which, on the road to concrete history, takes fright and attempts to convert its insights into eternal essences, into attributes between which the human spirit oscillates.

Schiller's model, we have shown, was a hermeneutic machine which permitted the critic to identify the concrete experience of the work of art with the broader problems of freedom—first on the psychological level of the integration of the personality and of the pleasure principle, and then, beyond that, on the political level itself. It was not so much a question of relating these levels to each other or of explaining one in terms of the other, as it was of providing a set of transformational equations such that the intrinsic, purely literary statements made about the work of art from the inside might be translated into the wholly distinct codes of the psychological or the political without impairment to the coherent and self-contained structure of any of these systems.

But Schiller's thinking is diagnostic rather than prophetic. A neoclassicist, for whom Utopia is essentially to be found in the past of ancient Greece, his thought is limited by the horizons of the German middle classes of his day; and even in matters of art that synthesis between the naïve and the sentimental, between the natural and the self-conscious, which his theory seems to project turns out to be little more than costume drama and a meditation on the lessons of antiquity. It would be tempting, and dialectically symmetrical, to be able to say that Schiller's vision is completed by the Romanticism that follows it chronologically, and that that vision of the new art and the new world which he was constitutionally unable to realize was there fulfilled. But from a theoretical point of view, Romanticism was only new unintentionally: it may indeed be thought of as the way a whole generation attempted to shelter itself, as an organism wards off shock, against that stupendous, total, and unprecedented transformation of the world into the henceforth barren and materialistic environment of middle-class capitalism. All the feudal postures and political daydreams, all the atmosphere of religious and medieval objects, the return as for renewal to older, more hierarchical or primitive societies are therefore to be understood first and foremost as defense mechanisms. It is nonetheless not false to say that a *certain* Romanticism comes to fulfill Schiller's system, to reinvent prophetically his vision of freedom both in the spirit and the letter, in poetry and politics alike: "at this hour," says the spokesman for such a new Romanticism, "when the authorities in France are making grotesque preparations to celebrate the centenary of Romanticism, we hereby declare that this Romanticism—for whose historical tailend we are willing to pass, but then in that case such a *prehensile tail!*—consists utterly and essentially in this year 1930 in the negation of those authorities and those celebrations; that for it, a hundred years is but as its youth; that what has wrongly been called its heroic period can in all honesty pass for nothing more than the pulings of a being only just now beginning to make its desire felt through us. . . !"[32]

It may seem incongruous to claim for Surrealism—"the future resolution of these two states, in appearance so contradictory, which are dream and reality, in a kind of absolute or sur-reality, if one may call it that"[33]—the place of that renewal of the natural or the naïve imagination, of that synthesis of the spontaneous and the conscious marked out by, yet absent from, Schiller's system; and this particularly when the Surrealist image would seem a more appropriate candidate for that logical, but impossible, fourth permutation of the Schillerian subject-object relationship: the pure productions of matter, from which the subject-pole has been effectively eliminated. Yet Schiller's thinking is dialectical to the degree to which in it phenomena are defined

[32] André Breton, *Manifestes du surréalisme* (Paris, 1969), p. 110.
[33] *Manifestes du surréalisme*, pp. 23-24.

against each other—against their situation, their surroundings, the impulses they are designed to overcome. For Schiller, we will recall, the warring impulses to be surmounted and laid to rest, the *Stofftrieb* and the *Formtrieb*, were still relatively symmetrical, so that their resolution could still take harmonious shapes. What if, in a later period of socioeconomic development, these impulses have ceased to balance each other out? What if the overwhelming predominance of one, or their mutual reorganization into something far more monstrous and oppressive, inevitably imparts its own deformity to the very movement that seeks liberation from it, as muscles might develop unequally against an unequal obstacle?

By the 1920's what Schiller called the *Formtrieb* has taken an immense lead over its rival in the gradual humanization of nature, in the organization of the market system. Little by little, in the commercial age, matter as such has ceased to exist, and has given place to commodities, which are intellectual forms, or the forms of intellectualized satisfactions: this is to say that in the commodity age, need as a purely material and physical impulse (as something "natural") has given way to a structure of artificial stimuli, artificial longings, such that it is no longer possible to separate the true from the false, the primary from the luxury-satisfaction, in them.

This is why Surrealism presents itself first and foremost as a reaction against the intellectualized, against *logic* in the widest sense of the word, subsuming not only philosophical rationality, but also the common-sense "interest" of the middle-class business world, and ultimately the reality principle itself. The Surrealist image is thus a convulsive effort to split open the commodity forms of the objective universe by striking them against each other with immense force: "Et surtout, beau comme la rencontre fortuite sur une table de dissection d'une machine à coudre et d'un parapluie!" Reverdy's definition of the image as the forcible and arbitrary interconnection of two realities as distant and unrelated as possible, which the Surrealists adopt for themselves, is remarkably faithful to Schiller's notion that freedom emerges from the neutralization of oppressive impulses; except that now the commodity impulse is turned back upon itself, its own inner contradictions transformed into the motor of its self-destruction.

But it is their theory of narration which perhaps most strikingly illustrates the way the Surrealists propose to reawaken the deadened external world around us. It is in appearance a refusal of narration altogether: for Breton hates novels, and holds the obligatory description of physical surroundings to be the basest kind of surrender to the reality principle, since in it that purely perceptual level of things to which our most superficial waking consciousness corresponds is taken for Being itself. This is to say that what is most interesting about the physical world in which we move (and the great "promenades surrealistes" of *L'Amour fou* and *Le Paysan de Paris* are there to remind us with what passion the Surrealists loved the real streets of Paris) is less a function of picturesque architecture than it is of the bizarre juxtapositions and odd chance events and objects of city living. The latter not only permit psychic identification, they serve as the pretext for a release of otherwise bound psychic energy.

For Breton, like Freud, conceives of the psyche as an endless, uninterrupted fantasy that continues beneath the surface of humdrum waking life, a kind of endless melody or "inexhaustible murmur," which at the verbal level is tapped by the technique of automatic writing. It is precisely the fact that the novel reproduces the *discontinuity* of waking life which makes it worthless from the point of view of

Surrealism, the latter aiming at nothing less than the reconstruction of the primal continuity of the unconscious itself.[34] It is an endless sentence into which we may break at any moment, in the midst of any kind of activity: "Right now, as I'm sitting at my desk, the voice of the unconscious is telling me about a man climbing out of a ditch, without of course identifying him for me. If I insist a little, it offers a fairly detailed representation: no, decidedly I don't know this man at all. But by the time I write all this down, he has already disappeared. . . ."[35]

In Freudian theory the manifest content or surface story of the dream is not merely the disguise of a repressed, unconscious desire, it is the disguise of a repressed, unconscious fantasy-satisfaction of that desire. There are thus not one but *two* stories at work in the topology of the psyche, one conscious and the other suppressed. Indeed, this notion was so important to Freud that for a long time he supposed the unconscious fantasy to have actually taken place in reality: whence the theory of the childhood seduction of neurotics. On the historical level, in fact, he maintained to the end his belief in that real and physical murder of the primal father by which, for him, civilization was founded. Yet even in the realm of the individual psyche, later on, when he had abandoned the hypothesis of childhood seduction, he never ceased to insist on its dramatic or narrative value as a *scene*; just as he never ceased to underscore the

---

[34] It is under the sign of this absolute drive toward continuity, it seems to me, that any really thoroughgoing analysis of Breton's prose style would have to be made, in which the flexing of the rhetorical apparatus—appositions, logical particles, inversions, ellipsis, dependent clauses, and elaborate qualifications—not only enjoins the twin claim on the reader's attention of both past and future as an interlocking syntactical system within the sequence of sentences; but also and above all designates some deeper logic, some buried yet irresistible continuity of thought underground, to which the devices themselves make fateful allusion, and on which they are carried relentlessly forward.

[35] *Manifestes du surréalisme*, pp. 116-117.

essentially figurative quality of unconscious or regressive thought. This is to say that for Freud there is no such thing as an instinct or drive (*Trieb*) in its pure or physical state: all drives are mediated through images or fantasies, through their object language, through what Freud calls, in an expression of which it is difficult to give an adequate rendering, the "Vorstellungsrepräsentenz" or "den Trieb repräsentierende Vorstellung," the "representational presentation."[36] It is this object-language of the unconscious which the Surrealists aim at bringing to the surface.

So it is that some chance contact with an external object may "remind" us of ourselves more profoundly than anything that takes place in the impoverished life of our conscious will. For unbeknownst to us, the objects around us lead lives of their own in our unconscious fantasies, where, vibrant with mana or taboo, with symbolic fascination or repulsion, they stand as the words or hieroglyphs of the immense rebus of desire.

And as it is with things—with "description"—so it is with people, with the "characters" of what might be the most genuine story we tell ourselves, but what is most often a dead, rationally censored articulation of the most conventional imaginary stereotypes: "the circumstantial and uselessly detailed character of each of the notations [of conventional novelists] leads me to suppose that they are amusing themselves at my expense. I am spared none of their hesitations about their character: will he be blond, what should his name be, should we see him first in summertime? So many questions resolved once and for all, by merest chance. . . ."[37] Thus the first false, one would like to say inauthentic, impulse of the novelists is to want to

[36] See Paul Ricoeur, *De l'interprétation: Essai sur Freud* (Paris, 1965), pp. 120-153, and also J. Laplanche and J. B. Pontalis, "Fantasme originaire, fantasmes des origines, origine du fantasme," *Temps modernes*, No. 215 (December 1963), pp. 1833-1868.

[37] *Manifestes du surréalisme*, p. 15.

decide, to settle once and for all the contours, the features, of their characters by fiat: as though in real life people did not stand for us as unconscious symbols, leading a second life in our fantasies of which we are only gradually, only partially, aware; as though the very interest of storytelling itself were not the slow, autonomous transformation of the characters under their own momentum, before our very eyes, the narrative process thus coming to resemble a kind of inner meditation, rather than a newspaper communiqué. This more than anything else explains the privileged position, for the Surrealists, of Lautréamont, in whose works the reader can surprise the very emergence of images, fantasies, characters from the empty idling of the waking state, where the subject of the book—in the most concrete fashion possible—is precisely its own elaboration, its stumblings, its hesitations, the sudden opening up of great stretches of automatism or psychic and narrative continuity. What Breton says of the character of Mathilda in Lewis' *The Monk*—"the most moving creation that one must credit to this *figurative* mode in literature . . . less a character than a continuous temptation"[38]—holds in even greater measure for the figments of Lautréamont, which are so clearly energy, in which the waking categories of subject and object are so essentially dissolved, or transcended, which so tangibly correspond to Freud's "Vorstellungsrepräsentenz."

Thus, to insist upon this term of Breton which corresponds both to Freudian usage and to our own hermeneutic vocabulary, it is not too much to say that for Surrealism a genuine plot, a genuine narrative, is that which can stand as the very *figure* of Desire itself: and this not only because in the Freudian sense pure physiological desire is inaccessible as such to consciousness, but also because in the socioeconomic context, genuine desire risks being dissolved and lost in the vast network of pseudosatisfactions which makes

[38] *Manifestes du surréalisme,* p. 25.

up the market system. In that sense desire is the form taken by freedom in the new commercial environment, by a freedom we do not even realize we have lost unless we think of it in terms, not only of the stilling, but also of the awakening, of Desire in general.

The liberating and exalting effect of Surrealist practice can be accounted for precisely by this notion of figuration. To put it in slightly different terms, we may observe that, contrary to what is generally supposed, automatic writing includes a reflexive moment, a dimension of self-conscious-ness: thus Breton castigates those "who are generally satis-fied to let their pens run on across the page without taking the least trouble to observe what is going on inside them at such a moment—this self-consciousness being, however, both easier to seize and more interesting to contemplate than that of ordinary conscious writing."[39] It is this reflexive dimension of apparently unreflexive, purely automatic texts which more than anything else explains the uncertain posi-tion of historical Surrealism from a purely literary point of view: in themselves, these texts are local and contingent, and their effect no doubt depends on the accidents of our own fantasies and our own fascinations. It is only when they are perceived as *examples* of Surrealism that they once again begin to take on the stronger colors of their origin. This is to say, if you like, that the *idea* of Surrealism is a more liberating experience than the actual texts. Breton himself could hardly have had in mind anything else when he excluded the so-called "right-wing deviationists," those Surrealists too given over to the ultimate values of art itself and of the production of an art object. But we can go fur-ther than that: for the quasiphysical enlargement of our be-ing produced by this idea—and analogous in that, as in its causes, to the more expansive pages of Whitman or Hart Crane—is the exact correlative of the aeration of the text

[39] *Manifestes du surréalisme*, p. 116.

by the larger figural meaning or generalization which stands behind it. Thus in Whitman's catalogues, the individual finite items are released against the background of the general, indeed the universal, for which they stand. Thus in Surrealism there is at work a hermeneutic process in which Desire is identified behind all the individual and limited desires of an individual associative system, in which Freedom is felt, instinct, behind the more limited and contingent freedoms of image and language. We are accustomed, in our time, to make a fetish of the concrete, by which we normally understand the particular: yet the effects in question here demonstrate, on the contrary, that the particular can be an enslavement under certain conditions, and that under those conditions it is precisely the movement of abstraction that can come as liberation. Thus, whoever speaks of Surrealism as a meditation on the figures of Desire is also at the same moment describing a technique for the release of the subjectivity from the single limited desire, the desire which is "only that," which is therefore at the same time the renunciation of other desires; and for the satisfaction, through such release, of all desire, of Desire as a force.

This new satisfaction, which Schiller, looking back to the state of nature, called bliss, is most adequately conveyed, in its Surrealist version, through the word *mystery*. Indeed, the status of the two terms in the two systems is analogous, and there is in Surrealism also something of the overlapping, superimposed duality which we found in Schiller's description of the state of nature, and for much the same reasons. For about the feeling of mystery there is nothing to be said: it is in itself merely a sign that that long-hoped-for enlargement of our beings, release from the repressive weight of the reality principle, has taken place, that life is suddenly once more transformed in quality, has somehow recaptured its original reasons for being. If we wish to say

more about this relatively ineffable value, we must somehow shift to a more precise, or at the least more articulable
terminology, and it is at this point that the Surrealists have
recourse to the words for the privileged experiences in
which the sense of mystery is most frequently released:
love, the dream, laughter, automatic writing, childhood.
They describe, however, the external conditions, the essential situations, of the pleasure principle, rather than the
quality of that principle itself.

Is this to say that Surrealism, as a theory and a practice,
retains for us the burning actuality which it had in its own
day? The answer is contained in the question: for the
theory remains actual while the practice has ceased to be
so. The reasons for this lie not only in that inner contradiction between the text and the idea described above; they
are also profoundly rooted in historical conditions themselves, and may perhaps best be grasped by a return to the
kind and nature of the imagery that we associate with Surrealism—not, indeed, the images so much as the objects
themselves, the mysterious pieces of junk, inexplicable artifacts which seem to bear some hidden message, the letter-
ing that leaps out from a shop window in passing as
a miraculous coincidence or a thinly disguised omen, the
grade-B melodramas in cheap movie theaters, the store
windows of inner passageways, now long since torn down,
flora and fauna of the city, whose emblematic value is
underlined by their presence as photographs, bound into
the text of the books themselves, as though it were necessary for them to come before the reader with an extra-
verbal density, a tangible reality-quotient which alone lends
them the opacity of the dream object and permits them to
resist the verbal thinness and impoverishment of the dream
protocol.

These objects—the places of objective chance, or of
preternatural revelation—are immediately identifiable to

us as the products of a not yet fully industrialized and systematized economy. This is to say that the human origins of the products of this period—their relationship to the work from which they issued—have not yet been fully concealed; in their production they still show traces of an artisanal organization of labor while their distribution is still predominantly assured by a network of small shopkeepers. Advertising, in the dimensions so familiar to us, is scarcely developed at all; indeed, the very ads themselves, whether *affiche*, the sandwich man of *Ulysses*, or that crude painting on a vacant wall which was Gertrude Stein's first introduction to the secret prestige of oil paints, can still be apprehended as objects of fascination in their own right. Thus what prepares these products to receive the investment of psychic energy characteristic of their use by Surrealism is precisely the half-sketched, uneffaced mark of human labor, of the human gesture, on them; they are still frozen gesture, not yet completely separated from subjectivity, and remain therefore potentially as mysterious and as expressive as the human body itself.

By the same token, they remain linked forever to a determinate stage in our socio-economic development. This we can see more clearly who look back upon that stage, already completed and now historical, with a nostalgia which is that of the suburb for the traditional city on its way to becoming extinct. Breton does not seem to have been aware of the degree to which the very possibility of the Surrealist image is historically conditioned, although he was well aware of the historical character of its raw material: "The marvelous," he tells us, "is not identical at all moments in history; it obscurely participates in a kind of general revelation the detail of which alone is handed down to us: romantic *ruins*, the modern *mannequin*, or any other symbol apt at stirring human sensibility for a time. . . ."[40] The

[40] *Manifestes du surréalisme*, p. 26.

104

mannequin: veritable emblem of the sensibility of a whole age, supreme totem of the Surrealist transformation of life —in which the human body itself comes before us as a product, where the nagging awareness of another presence, as in the terror of the blue gaze that meets us from the doll's eyes, the secret premonition of a lifeless voice somehow about to address us, all figure emblematically the central discovery by Surrealism of the properties of the objects that surrounded it. We need only juxtapose the mannequin, as a symbol, with the photographic objects of pop art, the Campbell's Soup can, the pictures of Marilyn Monroe, or with the visual curiosities of op art; we need only exchange, for that environment of small workshops and store counters, for the *marché aux puces* and the stalls in the streets, the gasoline stations along American superhighways, the glossy photographs in the magazines, or the cellophane paradise of an American drugstore, in order to realize that the objects of Surrealism are gone without a trace. Henceforth, in what we may call postindustrial capitalism, the products with which we are furnished are utterly without depth: their plastic content is totally incapable of serving as a conductor of psychic energy, if we may express ourselves that way. All libidinal investment in such objects is precluded from the outset, and we may well ask ourselves, if it is true that our object universe is henceforth unable to yield any "symbol apt at stirring human sensibility," whether we are not here in the presence of a cultural transformation of signal proportions, a historical break of an unexpectedly absolute kind.

It is enough to invoke—not so much as a fully developed concept, but rather as an essential mystery and as the sign of a problem to be explored in its own right—that older vocabulary of nature which was still that of Schiller, for us to realize the extent of the transformation already accomplished. For is it not precisely the ultimate and total humanization of the world that is here in question, the final liquidation of the last surviving pockets of an older, "natural" economy, as in agriculture, the definitive subordination of all forms of production to the market system itself, with its computerized centralization, its obligatory standardization? Does this not mark the ultimate establishment of the reign of the purely human upon the earth, of the antiphysis? In this light, the Romanticism of the Surrealists becomes clearer, for their nature was precisely the city itself, to which they attached themselves with all that profound longing which the Romantics satisfied through the presence of landscape; and this they were able to do, ironically enough, only because the French economy of the period was itself retrograde and archaic, and came before them as the vestiges of the natural. Henceforth, however, it is the very memory of nature itself which seems to face obliteration.

2)

> L'aînée, celle qui ne parle pas! l'aînée, ayant le
>   même âge! Mnémosyne qui ne parle jamais!
> Elle écoute, elle considère.
> Elle ressent (étant le sens intérieur de l'esprit),
> Pure, simple, inviolable! elle se souvient.
> Elle est le poids spirituel. Elle est le rapport
>   exprimé par un chiffre très beau. Elle est
>   posée d'une manière qui est ineffable
> Sur le pouls même de l'Etre.
>
> —Paul Claudel, *Cinq grandes odes*

It is in this context that the originality of Herbert Marcuse's reflection and writings may be most clearly seized: for his work, which takes the form of a commentary on Hegel and Marx, on Freud and Schiller, aims precisely at rethinking these earlier systems, and their consequences, in the light of the utterly new socio-economic environment of postindustrial capitalism which began to emerge at the end of World War II. The new environment is one in which the possibility of eliminating poverty and hunger definitively for the first time in history goes hand in hand with the technical possibility of unparalleled control and total organization in the realm of social life. It is neither a completely technological nor a completely political development: for the purely scientific Utopias of food from the sea and world government ring hollow, while at the same time the older class analyses no longer seem applicable to a situation in which there are no longer any visible "agents" of the historical process, in which the working classes become assimilated in their values and politics to the bourgeoisie, while the "power elite" often seems, in comparison to the older types of ruling classes, as much a pawn as a master of the enormous forces at its disposition.

Abundance and total control: such is the paradoxical context in which Marcuse prepares to rethink Freud and Marx, to reevaluate the classical opposition between individual happiness and social organization with which they were both concerned. Indeed, his cultural reflections may be taken as a kind of ironic reversal of those of Freud in *Civilization and Its Discontents*, which posited an irreversible and unavoidable interdependency between progress in the evolution of society and unhappiness in the repressed psyche of individual man, between individual self-denial and the diversion of psychic energy for collective purposes. For Marcuse, on the other side of the great watershed of postindustrial capitalism, things no longer look quite the same, and it turns out that it is precisely increased sexual freedom, greater material abundance and consumption, freer access to culture, better housing, more widely available educational benefits and increased social, not to speak of automotive mobility, which are the accompaniment to increasing manipulation and the most sophisticated forms of thought-control, increasing abasement of

107

spiritual and intellectual life, a degradation and dehumanization of existence. Thus it is that the happier we are, the more surely we are given over, without even being aware of it, into the power of the socio-economic system itself.

It is this feature of Marcuse's thinking which has lent renewed actuality to the ancient Platonic debate about the nature of the good: for his analysis raises precisely the problem of happiness, and forces us to ask whether people can know what is good for them, whether the social good can be judged in terms of a subjective feeling of contentment, in a world in which brainwashing and manipulation exist as everyday mechanisms. At the same time, his books have been the target of the classic objection to the trustworthiness of the philosopher king or the philosophical elite who are expected to make the ultimate judgments on the good of society in the absence of a reliable voice from the people themselves.

It seems to me, however, that the problem is most usefully posed the other way round, and that the thrust and persuasiveness, the basic unity, of Marcuse's work can best be felt if we reverse these conceptual priorities and take as his basic theme not happiness, but rather the nature of the *negative* itself. Indeed, what his discussion of Freud's instinctual dynamics has in common with his sociological doctrine, as it emerges from Marx, as well as with his tactical positions expressed in *Repressive Tolerance* and *An Essay on Liberation,* is the notion that the consumer's society, the society of abundance, has lost the experience of the negative in all its forms, that it is the negative alone which is ultimately fructifying from a cultural as well as an individual point of view, that a genuinely human existence can only be achieved through the process of negation.

Thus seen, Marcuse's relationship to Adorno and the Frankfurt School becomes that of the practical to the theoretical. For where Adorno drafted the *theory* of negative

108

or critical thinking (or of a "negative dialectic"), where in his essays on literature or philosophy or music he traced the effects of a weakening of the negative upon the superstructure, Marcuse's works may be thought of as explorations of the psychological and socio-economic infrastructure of the same massive historical transformation.

For we find essentially the same circumstances at work on all the levels of modern life, whether on the political or the psychological, that of action or that of contemplation. The basic development in the light of which all of Freud must be rethought is the collapse of the family, the disappearance of the authoritarian father, that is, of oppression at the level of the cellular family unit. With this liberalization, the Oedipus complex and the superego themselves are greatly weakened, so that the apparently liberated individual is at the same time denied that path toward genuine psychic individuality once offered him by the revolt against the father. The ego of modern man "has shrunk to such a degree that the multiform antagonistic processes between id, ego and superego cannot unfold themselves in their classic form. . . . Their original dynamic becomes static: the interactions between ego, superego, and id congeal into automatic reactions. Corporealization of the superego is accompanied by corporealization of the ego, manifest in the frozen traits and gestures, produced at the appropriate occasions and hours. Consciousness, increasingly less burdened by autonomy, tends to be reduced to the tasks of regulating the coordination of the individual with the whole."[41] In much the same way, on the social level, the overt burden of societal repression and enforced sublimation is withdrawn: the older restraints, characteristic of a period of "primitive accumulation of psychic capital," have given way to "repressive desublimation," in which the so-

[41] Herbert Marcuse, *Eros and Civilization* (New York, 1955), pp. 90, 93-94.

ciety of sexual abundance encourages overt but specialized sexual activity as a way of reducing conscious unhappiness within the system, of foreclosing conscious dissatisfaction with the system, while at the same time compensating for the necessarily increased impoverishment of the environment from an emotional or libidinal point of view, a phenomenon we have described above.

On the political level, the withdrawal of the right to revolt against the father is reproduced as a disappearance of any effective possibility of negating the system in general. The weakening of the class struggle, the assimilation of the working classes into the bourgeoisie, is the objective condition for this universal neutralization; and with the extension of the media, the very content and gestures of revolt are exhausted, in the sense in which television performers speak of the "exhaustion" of their raw material through overexposure. In this sense, tolerance in our society can be said to be genuinely repressive, in that it offers a means of defusing the most dangerous and subversive ideas: not censorship, but the transformation into a fad, is the most effective way of destroying a potentially threatening movement or revolutionary personality.

Attenuation of the Oedipus complex, disappearance of the class struggle, assimilation of revolt to an entertainment-type value—these are the forms which the disappearance of the negative takes in the abundant society of postindustrial capitalism. Under these conditions, the task of the philosopher is the revival of the very idea of negation which has all but been extinguished under the universal subservience to what is; which, along with the concepts of nature and of freedom, has been repressed and driven underground by the reality principle. This task Marcuse formulates as the revival of the Utopian impulse. For where in the older society (as in Marx's classic analysis) Utopian thought represented a diversion of revolutionary energy into idle wish-fulfillments and imaginary satisfactions, in our own time the very nature of the Utopian concept has undergone a dialectical reversal. Now it is practical thinking which everywhere represents a capitulation to the system itself, and stands as a testimony to the power of that system to transform even its adversaries into its own mirror image. The Utopian idea, on the contrary, keeps alive the possibility of a world qualitatively distinct from this one and takes the form of a stubborn negation of all that is.

We may therefore say that for Marcuse it is the Utopian concept—"the attempt to draft a theoretical construct of culture beyond the performance principle"[42]—which henceforth, absorbing and replacing the function of art for Schiller and for the Surrealists, embodies the newest version of a hermeneutics of freedom. For Utopian thinking may be said to unite both the philosophical and the artistic impulses, at the same time that it transcends both: it is philosophy become concrete, it is art which takes as its object not products and works but life itself. The impulse of fantasy, in which alone the pleasure principle remains pure and unrepressed, now negates the existing real world, the "realistic" world, and prepares for that world a future. For Adorno had also shown, after his fashion, that the production of works of art is in our time undermined by powerful internal contradictions, and that the resulting art objects are immediately absorbed back into the immensity of what is. Now Marcuse sees in the new sensibility and the new sexual politics an application of the artistic impulse to the creation of a new life-style itself, to a concrete acting out of the Utopian impulse.

But the political limits of the new sensibility are inherent in the very notion of a hermeneutic: its political implications can only be clear when it is itself understood as a dress rehearsal of Utopia, as a foreshadowing of ultimate con-

[42] *Eros and Civilization*, p. 144.

crete social liberation. The immediate contingent freedoms of the new life-style must therefore function as *figures* of Freedom in general; and without this characteristic movement in them from the particular to the general which we have described above, from individual experience to that universal liberation for which the experience stands, they remain a matter of individual narcosis, of individual salvation only in the midst of the collective shipwreck. Now indeed we are in a better position to resolve the traditional problem of happiness evoked above; for it is only when individual happiness, subjective contentment, is not positive (in the sense of ultimate satiation by the consumer's society), but rather *negative*, as a symbolic refusal of everything which that society has to offer, that happiness can recover its right to be thought of as a measure and an enlargement of human possibilities.

Marcuse's work is not, however, exhausted by this description, for at the same time that it develops the vital urgency of Utopian thinking, it also lays the groundwork for the very possibility of such thinking in the first place. At the same time that it develops a new hermeneutic, it establishes the conditions of existence of hermeneutic activity in general. This theoretical foundation takes the form of a profound and almost Platonic valorization of memory, anamnesis, in human existence. Indeed, it is not too much to say that Mnemosyne occupies something of the same emblematic and mythopoetic position in Marcuse's thinking that the deities of Eros and Thanatos hold in Freud's late metapsychology.

The functional value of memory may be judged by the fact that it is for Freud the very source of conscious thought itself, the latter being "merely a detour from the memory of gratification . . . to the identical cathexis of the same memory, which is to be reached once more by the path of motor experiences."[43] On account of the diagnostic character of so much of Freud's writings, we are tempted to think of memory chiefly in terms of pain, in terms of trauma, whereas in reality memory's primary function is in the service of the pleasure principle. "The memory of gratification," Marcuse tells us, "is at the origin of all thinking, and the impulse to recapture past gratification is the hidden driving power behind the process of thought."[44]

Now the origin of Utopian thinking becomes clear, for it is memory which serves as a fundamental mediator between the inside and the outside, between the psychological and the political, whose separation we described at the beginning of this essay. It is because we have known, at the beginning of life, a plenitude of psychic gratification, because we have known a time before all repression, a time in which, as in Schiller's nature, the elaborate specializations of later, more sophisticated consciousness had not yet taken place, a time that precedes the very separation of the subject from its object, that memory, even the obscured and unconscious memory of that prehistoric paradise in the individual psyche, can fulfill its profound therapeutic, epistemological, and even political role: its "truth value lies in the specific function of memory to preserve promises and potentialities which are betrayed and even outlawed by the mature, civilized individual, but which had once been fulfilled in his dim past and which are never entirely forgotten."[45] The primary energy of revolutionary activity derives from this memory of a prehistoric happiness which the individual can regain only through its externalization, through its reestablishment for society as a whole. The loss or repression of the very sense of such concepts as freedom and desire takes, therefore, the form of a kind of amnesia

---

[43] Quoted, *Eros and Civilization*, p. 29.
[44] *Eros and Civilization*, p. 29.   [45] *Eros and Civilization*, p. 18.

or forgetful numbness, which the hermeneutic activity, the stimulation of memory as the negation of the here and now, as the projection of Utopia, has as its function to dispel, restoring to us the original clarity and force of our own most vital drives and wishes.

The theory of memory, indeed, furnishes an unexpected theoretical justification for such a priori social models as those of Schiller, for we may say that such apparently indefensible reasoning is as it were the conceptual disguise which memory takes, and it is as though the eighteenth-century philosophers were able to reinvent the psychological truth of individual existence only by imagining themselves to be in the act of deducing, through reason, the characteristics of the historical state of nature and of original human society in general. Thus, what looked most abstract turns out to be concrete on a wholly different and unexpected level, and Schiller's famous words about the objects of nature win a new and profound resonance: "They *are* what we *were*; they are what we must once more *become*. We were Nature just as they are, and our culture must lead us back to Nature along the path of Reason and Freedom. They are therefore the representation of our lost childhood, that which will eternally remain dearest to us; for that reason, they fill us with a certain sadness. At the same time, they symbolize for us our highest possible completion in the realm of the Ideal, and for that reason they awaken in us the noblest exaltation."[46] But what Schiller took to be the hypothetical origins of humanity itself turns out to have been but reason's way of misinterpreting the prehistory of the individual psyche.

Marcuse's position with respect to Freud is in many ways markedly similar to that of Schiller in the face of Kantian critical philosophy. The latter had set itself the task of exploring the conceptual preconditions of what already exists,

[46] *Philosophische Schriften*, p. 210.

of formulating the necessary conditions of possibility of the experiences of sense perception and of beauty, of free will. Schiller, as we have seen, continues to deduce conditions of possibility: but these are now the preconditions not of an existing but of a hypothetical state. Schiller wishes to determine, in other words, how man's psyche would have had to have been constructed for a genuinely free and harmonious personality to become one day a real possibility; but in the very terms of this argument, there remains the logical alternative that such a being does not and can never exist.

In much the same way, where Freud's instinctual theory is designed to explain the structure of real and existent mental phenomena, of hysteria and the neuroses and psychoses, Marcuse's use of that theory has a more speculative and hypothetical cast: for it aims at describing the conditions of possibility of a society from which aggression will have been eliminated and in which libidinally satisfying work will be conceivable. Thus, for example, the ingenious hypothesis of a "maternal super-id"[47] is designed to show how in a Utopian future the apparently contradictory claims of the pleasure principle and of some form of social morality might be harmonized and justified by the topology of the instincts themselves.

To be sure, there is always the possibility that such a society is precisely impossible: and this final alternative, which the a priori model leaves open for us, is itself the source of Marcuse's realism, of his insistent reminder that salvation is by no means historically inevitable, that we do not even find ourselves in a prerevolutionary, let alone a revolutionary, situation, and that the total system may yet ultimately succeed in effacing the very memory of the negative, and with it of freedom, from the face of the earth.

---

[47] *Eros and Civilization*, p. 209. This is perhaps the psychic equivalent, for Marcuse, of Marx's and Engels' valorization of the stage of matriarchal communism in social development.

115

Yet whatever the outcome, it pleases me for another moment still to contemplate the stubborn rebirth of the idea of freedom, in three such profoundly different shapes, at three such profoundly different moments in history: its re-invention by the historian-playwright, dreaming the heroic gestures of political eloquence in his tiny feudal city-state open to the fields, stimulated by the news of revolutionary victories there where in a few years the shock of Napoleonic armies will cause the earth to tremble; by the poet, stalking his magical fun-park for the neon omens of objective chance, behind the hallucinatory rebus of the street scene never ceasing to hear the pop gun volleys of the vicious, never-ending military pacification of colonial empire; by the philosopher, in the exile of that immense housing devel-opment which is the state of California, remembering, re-awakening, reinventing—from the rows of products in the supermarkets, from the roar of the freeways and the omi-nous shape of the helmets of traffic policemen, from the incessant overhead traffic of the fleets of military transport planes, and as it were from beyond them, in the future—the almost extinct form of the Utopian idea.

III. ERNST BLOCH AND THE FUTURE

So our campaign slogan must be: reform of consciousness, not through dogma, but through the analysis of that mystical consciousness which has not yet become clear to itself. It will then turn out that the world has long dreamt of that of which it had only to have a clear idea to possess it really. It will turn out that it is not a question of any conceptual rupture between past and future, but rather of the *completion* of the thoughts of the past.
—Marx, Letter to Ruge (1843)

ALLEGORY and Communism make strange bedfellows. If, as I believe, the work of Ernst Bloch is best grasped as an attempt to do for Marxism what the four levels of meaning did for medieval Christianity, to furnish a hermeneutic technique of great flexibility and depth, there remains, floating over the whole enterprise, the suggestion of some more basic affinity between Marxism and religion that remains to be worked out, the suspicion that Bloch is not so much a Marxist philosopher, even a Marxist philosopher of religion, as he is rather (in the terms of his description of Thomas Münzer) a "theologian of the revolution."

For the notion that Marxism is itself a kind of religion is one of the principal arguments of the anti-Communist arsenal; the idea, no doubt, is that it is shamefaced religion, a religion which does not wish to know its own name. Yet it has always seemed to me a peculiar reproach, one which cuts both ways: an assimilation of Marxism to religion in particular would seem to reduce the religions to the status of purely secular ideologies. The revealing analogy, in other words, is at this point not so much that of Marxism with religion, as that of religions with Marxism. And in a more general way it has always seemed to me that the nonbeliever strengthens his adversary's case by his tendency (a properly superstitious one, we might point out) to attribute some unique and specialized, intrinsically *other* type of psychological or spiritual experience to the believer; and this, even though it is made plain in theological literature from the very outset that faith is to be described essentially as the longing to have faith, that the nature of belief lies not so much in some apprehension of the presence of God as rather of his silence, his absence—in short, that there is basically no real difference between a believer and a nonbeliever in the first place.

What Marxism shares with Christianity is primarily a historical situation: for it now projects that claim to universality and that attempt to establish a universal culture which characterized Christianity in the declining years of the Roman Empire and at the height of the Middle Ages.

117

It is therefore not at all surprising that its intellectual instruments should bear a structural similarity to those techniques (among them figural analysis) with which Christianity assimilated populations of differing and wholly unrelated cultural backgrounds. Medieval hermeneutics, indeed, served two essential functions: a doctrinal one, designed to satisfy the intellectual and philosophical needs of the believers themselves, and a missionary one, for the purpose of absorbing the cultural or religious attitudes of those still outside the church (as in the assimilation of pagan festivals to Christian).[48] From this common historical mission of Marxism and Christianity all more superficial resemblances derive: thus, for instance, if the works of Marx and Engels have become what are derisively called sacred writings, sources of abusive quotation and misinterpretation, this stems not so much from some unconscious parody of the Bible as from the essential structure of a universal culture itself, and the central position within it of that text or letter around which it is organized, and which serves as a common language or code, constituting, not a common set of solutions or dogma, of universally imposed content, but rather a common set of problems, a shared form through which the most culturally heterogeneous situations may be understood.

In a more limited way, the problem of a Marxist hermeneutic arises whenever we are called upon to determine the place of what we may call right-wing literature, whether it be the traditional conservative literature of the past, of a Flaubert or a Dostoyevsky, or in our own time a Fascist literature of great quality, as is the case with Wyndham Lewis or Drieu, or with Céline. If it is as Marxism has always claimed, namely that there can be no such thing as a right-wing philosophy, that a Fascist system is a con-

---

[48] See Michel Van Esbroeck, *Herméneutique, structuralisme et exégèse* (Paris, 1968), pp. 113ff.

tradiction in terms, not thought but the optical illusion of thought only; if indeed this accounts for the fact that Fascist revolutions have always been obliged to borrow their trappings from the left and to disguise themselves as national "socialisms"; then the official opinions and positions of such reactionary authors may be considered surface phenomena, rationalization and disguises for some more basic source of energy of which, on the analogy of the Freudian model of the unconscious, they are unaware. A Marxist hermeneutic would then have the task of restoring to that energy the political direction which rightfully belongs to it, of making it once more available to us. "The fact of the genuine originality and specificity [of a thought like Marxism] does not mean that such thinking, which needs no external borrowings, cannot at the same time enter upon a *heritage*."[49] Bloch's philosophy offers one of the forms which such a reconversion process, such an expropriation of apparently alien or antagonistic cultural monuments, might take, although, as I hope to show elsewhere, it is not the only possible one.

There are a number of coordinates by which such a hermeneutical operation might be located. We must, for example, distinguish between what Paul Ricoeur has called negative and positive hermeneutics, between the hermeneutics of suspicion and the hermeneutics of a restoration of some original, forgotten meaning,[50] between hermeneutic as demystification, as the destruction of illusions, and a hermeneutic which offers renewed access to some essential source of life. For Ricoeur, of course, the latter cannot be imagined as anything other than the *sacred*, so that the only form of positive hermeneutic of which he is able to conceive remains an essentially religious one. Negative hermeneutic, on the other hand, is at one with modern philosophy itself,

---

[49] Ernst Bloch, *Das Prinzip Hoffnung* (Frankfurt, 1959), p. 1380.
[50] See Ricoeur, *De l'interprétation*, pp. 33-44.

with those critiques of ideology and illusory consciousness which we find in Nietzsche and in Marx, in Freud ("for Freud," Bloch tells us, "the dream's manifest content is essentially carnival time, wearing masks; the interpretation of the dream is the Ash Wednesday that follows").[51] With these twin, irreconcilable characteristics, that of demystification and that of an essential restoration of access, the requirements for any genuinely successful and concrete hermeneutic are given, and the ingenuity with which Bloch manages to satisfy both on a secular basis may be judged.

But there are other coordinates according to which we may evaluate the various hermeneutic attempts as well. Medieval exegesis, for instance, may with its four levels of meaning be thought of as essentially a vertical, or, if you prefer, an idealistic, operation, a way of introducing increasing conceptual richness into an object which itself remains relatively static. Bloch's hermeneutic, on the contrary, finds its richness in the very variety of its objects themselves, while its initial conceptual content remains relatively simple, relatively unchanging: thus little by little wherever we look everything in the world becomes a version of some primal figure, a manifestation of that primordial movement toward the future and toward ultimate identity with a transfigured world which is Utopia, and whose vital presence, behind whatever distortions, beneath whatever layers of repression, may always be detected, no matter how faintly, by the instruments and apparatus of hope itself.

Hence the truly encyclopedic character of Bloch's major work, *Das Prinzip Hoffnung*, which is less an ascending ladder of forms like Hegel's *Phenomenology of Spirit* than it is a vast and disorderly exploration of the manifestations of hope on all levels of reality: from the ontological itself, in the central and crucial analysis of human time, fanning out

[51] *Das Prinzip Hoffnung*, p. 91.

to touch upon existential psychology (the meaning of such phenomena as anxiety and disappointment); ethics (the study of hope institutionalized in traditional ideals and values); logic (the conceptual categories of the possible); political science, both of a conventional type, in the studies of the various theories of the state and of social organization, and of a Marxist character, in the analysis of revolutionary strategy; the social planning inherent in the conception of Utopias of all kinds; *Technik*, not only in the sense of the scientific achievements of the world of the future, but also in terms of the way in which it alters our relationship to the objects around us; sociology, in the form of the analysis of the wish-fulfillments of advertising and popular culture; ideological and literary criticism, finally, in its all-embracing account of the archetypes of Utopia in art, myth, and religion. Thus *Hope the Principle* is necessarily unsystematic in its very conception: either too long or too short, its essential scheme may be rehearsed in a few pages or expanded indefinitely to match the infinite realities of the world itself.

Such an exploration, however, does not begin without some initial attention to its own conditions of possibility, without some initial contemplation of the very process by which these figures of Hope, of the imperceptible tending of all things toward Utopia, of the future which stirs at its convulsive but microscopic work within the smallest cells of the vast universe itself, make themselves known to us as *Spuren* in the world both without and within: traces, spoor, marks, and signs, "signatures of all things I am here to read." The centrality of this concept in Bloch may be measured against Benjamin's brittle world of script and allegorical fragment, in which the incomprehensible sign alone survives as the mark of a forgotten disaster; or against Derrida's theory of the "trace," where only the pure temporal movement of signification itself, as it deposits itself in object

121

or in letter, is retained, without any ultimate sense of the direction or meaning of that movement.

For the trace in Bloch is both an external object and an immediate experience: its authenticity is certified, before any conscious intellectual interpretation, by the sheer fact of the astonishment with which we pause before these glowing emblems in which some urgent yet utterly personal secret seems to be concealed. Philosophy here rejoins its origins as a concrete working out of the astonishment we feel before the world itself: yet how many philosophers, remarks Bloch, "have kept faith with the directions implied by such beginnings? Almost none of them held the pose of questioning wonderment for any longer than the arrival of the first answer."[52] Astonishment is therefore for Bloch (to use a different philosophical terminology) one of the most concrete possible modes of our being-in-the-world, the correlative, on the subjective side, of an objective disposition of the world itself: "Just as the darkness of the lived instant represents one pole of conscious anticipation and of the anticipatory disposition of the world as well, so also material astonishment [Realstaunen], with that outright adequation which is its content, constitutes the other one; and each tugs powerfully at the other, the symbolic intentions of the Supreme and the Omega imply the darkness of the Alpha or of closest proximity. [Astonishment] is the very source or origin of the world itself, ever at work and ever hidden away within the darkness of the lived instant, a source which becomes aware of itself for the first time in the signatures of its own estuaries as it resolves itself into them."[53]

Thus real philosophizing begins at home, well beneath the official abstractions of the metaphysical tradition, in lived experience itself and in its smallest details, in the body and its sensations, at the very sources of the word as

[52] Ernst Bloch, Spuren (Frankfurt, 1960), p. 286.
[53] Das Prinzip Hoffnung, pp. 353-354.

it comes into being. This accounts for the presence, from one end of Bloch's work to the other, of those tiny expressionistic sketches, often as enigmatic as a Zen Buddhist koan, which regularly alternate with the more formal philosophical disquisitions, as though repeatedly to return us to some more primordial renewal of thought in astonishment itself.

And no doubt there is always a place in Bloch's scheme of things for the smallest realities as well as the greatest and most apocalyptic, for the humble in a Germanic sense: if not Biedermeier, then at least the simplicity of what he calls "peasant Tao," as exemplified in Hebel and Jeremias Gotthelf (who occupy a place in his constellation of values perhaps analogous to that of Leskov for Benjamin)—the finite happiness of the lighted window in the fields, of the return from the furrows, of rest after labor as a symbol and a figure, in its own way also, of Utopian fulfillment.

But this aspect of Bloch's sensibility must be sharply distinguished from that mystique of the peasant landscape which we find in a Heidegger, as must Bloch's experience of astonishment from the more ritualistic mysteries of the Heideggerian *Seinsfrage*. Bloch refuses the "metaphysical question" as Heidegger formulates it ("Why is it that there is something, rather than nothing at all?"), inasmuch as for him being is precisely incomplete, in process, not yet altogether there: what astounds is therefore not so much being itself, but rather the latency of being-to-come at work, the signs and foreshadowings of future being. It is for this reason that we may think of Bloch's epiphanies, in contrast to those of Heidegger (and I'm thinking, for instance, of the Van Gogh painting of peasant shoes upon a chair evoked in *The Origin of the Work of Art*), as dramatic rather than lyrical, involving not a contemplative perception of the being of the world's network as it issues from some central object at rest, but rather a convulsive stirring within ob-

123

jects, a stirring which unfolds itself in time. Hence the content of *Spuren* as a lingering over strange anecdotes and peculiar experiences, as a recounting of paradoxical destinies, of ironic legends, of objects with unexpected powers: that which "gives pause," that which expresses itself most properly in storytelling rather than description. For insofar as astonishment constitutes an implicit or explicit perception of the future concealed within that which exists, it already carries within itself a story line, the trajectory of the not-yet-finished, the struggle of the incomplete to free itself from the as-yet-formlessness of the present: "In short, it's also good to think in fables. For there is much that fails to be exhausted by the taking place, or even by a good telling of it. Things have an odd way of keeping on going, there's a problem here somewhere, it's pointing this way or beginning to strike. Such stories are not only re-counted [erzählen], you also count up [zählen] what is making itself heard through them, or you perk up your ears: Who goes there? An unexpected Mark! emerges from perfectly ordinary circumstances; or else a Mark! that was already there turns up traces and examples of its presence in all kinds of insignificant incidents. They draw our attention to a More or Less that ought to make us reflect while we're telling stories, or tell stories while we reflect; one that isn't quite right, because it's out of tune with us and with everything else. So much can be grasped only through such stories, and not in the grand and full-blown manner, or at least not in the same way. How some of these things attracted attention we will now try to tell and to mark: lovingly, marking in the telling of them, and in the marking attending to that which has been told. They are little traits from life and other things which were somehow not forgotten; nowadays there's a lot worth throwing away. But that older impulse was there too, to listen to stories, good and inconsequential alike, stories of different sorts and from different times, noteworthy stories, which, if they come to their end, have to end by touching us. It's a reading of traces everywhere, in all directions, in bits and pieces variously divided. For in the long run, everything that meets us, everything we notice particularly, is one and the same."[54]

1)

Next year in Jerusalem!
—Old Jewish Prayer

Any description of Bloch's ontology must, it seems to me, distinguish sharply between the *philosophical* system—for which there is a right and a wrong way of presenting human reality, for which the judgments of truth and falsehood still exist as valid conceptual categories—and its *hermeneutic* use, in which the "false" is but a disguise of the "true," in which that which is wrong on a purely conceptual level may itself ultimately be delivered of that secret truth which dwells within it as a figure and which lends it even that vitality which it possesses.

From the philosophical point of view, it is first of all a question of time and of the proper account to give of it. For what strikes the random observer of the history of philosophy is the lack of attention given the future as such, as though there were something essentially frivolous in a consideration of that which does not yet exist, when so much exists already. In that the philosophers resemble M. Terentius Varro, "most learned of all the Romans," who "is supposed to have forgotten the future tense in the first version of his Latin grammar."[55]

Yet it is not enough merely to make a place for temporality: even Bergson, who first in modern times revealed the essential spatiality of logical concepts and insisted on the

[54] *Spuren,* pp. 15-16.   [55] *Das Prinzip Hoffnung,* p. 4.

uniqueness and specificity of lived time and *durée* as opposed to them, failed to evolve an adequate formulation of the reality of time. For insofar as he defined the latter as process or change, it is always in another sense the same at any moment; Bergson never managed to think his way through to the fundamental conceptual category which presides over the experience of the future and which is precisely the *novum*, the utterly and unexpectedly new, the new which astonishes by its absolute and intrinsic unpredictability. Whereas for Bergson, "the new is perceived and celebrated only under the form of meaningless changes in fashion styling . . . merely as the abstract opposite of repetition, indeed very often as the mere reverse of mechanical uniformity."[56]

On a somewhat deeper level, however, in the realm of existential emotions or affects, it is clear that we already have at our disposal two different ways of visualizing the future and that well before any conceptual formulation our emotions themselves have evolved two quite different and distinct ways of living time. This is the sense in which Bloch distinguishes between "filled affects or emotions" and "expectation-affects": the former (greed, envy, adoration, for example) are to be sure fully as temporal as the latter, in that they also ask something of the future, they also are at their very heart a type of wishing or desiring. Yet the so-called filled emotions project their wish into a psychic space which is properly unreal; they project what Bloch calls an "inauthentic future." For they ask for fulfillment in a world at all points identical to that of the present, save for the possession of the particular object desired and presently lacking. Such affects are primitive or infantile to the degree that they amount to magical incantations, a conjuring up of the object in question just exactly as we long for it, at the same time that we hold the rest of the world, and our own desire,

[56] *Das Prinzip Hoffnung*, p. 231.

126

magically in suspension, arresting all change and the very passage of real time itself. As though everything in the world were not interrelated and interdependent in the most astonishing and imperceptible fashion! As though the very changes in the world required to bring about our ultimate possession of the longed-for object did not run the risk of transforming the very object itself to the point where it no longer strikes us as very desirable, or of transforming ourselves to the point where we no longer desire it! Such emotions or feelings therefore not only imply a kind of provincialism of the present, into which we are plunged so utterly that we lose the very possibility of imagining a future which might be radically and constitutionally *other*; their analysis also implies a kind of ethics, a keeping faith with the open character of the future, a life in time which holds to the prospect of the absolutely unexpected as the only expectation: certainty, not of the abstract, but of the concrete new in its unimaginable plenitude.

It is in this sense that by contrast the so-called "expectation-affects," whether of a positive or negative type, whether hope and belief or anxiety and fear, aim less at some specific object as the fetish of their desire, than at the very configuration of the world in general or (what amounts to the same thing) at the future disposition or constitution of the self. From the point of view of temporality, the experience of hope consists in a coming to consciousness of that relationship to the as yet inexistent implicit in all these emotions, and may therefore stand as their structural archetype and at the same time as their most concrete affective manifestation.

At this point there intervenes in Bloch's system a mechanism of self-justification which is in one way or another a necessary and constituent element in all modern philosophy: namely, a kind of hypothesis about conceptual censorship, an explanation of the type of intellectual resistance which has prevented the philosophical system in question—inasmuch as it presents itself as the truth—from having been thought of until that particular moment in intellectual history. Such a mechanism—Bergson's spatiality, Sartre's bad faith, Heidegger's forgetfulness of the ontological question, Freud's censorship, Marx's class consciousness—takes the form in Bloch of what he calls the *Sperre* or "block," the resistance of static logic to the very content of the novum, to any genuine opening onto the future itself; and this anxiety before the future, this flight from the new, finds a conceptual rationalization in the myth of absolute presence, in the notion that there exists something like a plenitude of being and that for this reason something like a full and self-contained present instant of time is ontologically possible.

Paradoxically, however, this hypostasis of the present ends up in the long run by glorifying the past; and the most stubborn philosophical version of the myth of an absolute presence turns out—we have already seen a revolutionary version of it in Marcuse—to be the Platonic doctrine of anamnesis, of memory as a return to lost sources of plenitude before birth. For Bloch, indeed, the doctrine of hope has not one, but two basic philosophical adversaries: nihilism and anamnesis; or to put it another way, the experience of hope has not one, but two opposites: anxiety and memory. The structure of nihilism, however, as we shall see shortly, is simply the reverse or negative of that of the doctrine of hope; whereas the doctrine of memory is so to speak its obverse side, its absolute inversion, in which everything which in reality belongs to the future is attributed to the past, in which time is stood on its head conceptually.

Hence the dialogue with Freud: for Freud's topology is the most striking model of time oriented around the past, a picture of an apparent movement toward the future whose vital incentives lie buried in early childhood; for such a model comprehension consists in a working back to origins. The Freudian unconscious is therefore a no-longer-consciousness, an unconsciousness of a world and a self which have officially, in the eyes of the reality principle, ceased to be: and this formulation is in itself enough to suggest the lines along which Bloch corrects it. For in this sense there is room, alongside this no-longer-consciousness, for a new and very different type of unconscious, a blankness or horizon of consciousness this time formed not by the past but by the future: what Bloch calls a not-yet-consciousness, an ontological pull of the future, of a tidal influence exerted upon us by that which lies out of sight below the horizon, an unconscious of what is yet to come.

That this new unconscious is something other than a flatus vocis or purely logical construction, that it generates a psychic energy at least equivalent to that of the Freudian unconscious, may be judged by the existence of a type of psychic possession specific to it, which corresponds to the compulsions of Freudian neurosis and psychosis, but which this time is a white life-giving possession, a possession oriented toward and determined out of the future. It is that same power which Goethe believed himself "to have discovered in nature, both animate and inanimate, both souled and soulless, something which manifested itself only in contradictions and could therefore not be formulated in concepts, let alone in words. It was not divine, for it seemed irrational; not human, for it had no understanding; not diabolical, for it was beneficent; not angelic, for it often betrayed *Schadenfreude*. It was like chance in its inconsequentiality; like Providence in the interrelationships it revealed. Everything that has limits for us seemed to it penetrable; it seemed willfully to recombine the most necessary elements of our existence, eclipsing time and extending space. Only in the impossible did it seem at home, and to

129

thrust the possible from itself in scorn. This being, which seemed to interpose itself between all the others, to sunder or unite them, I called the *Demonic*. . . ."[57] The Demonic names such possession by vocation, by destiny, by some powerful latency in existence itself; and such Faustian vocations are just as surely forms of possession, mark their owners just as surely as driven beings, as the darker regressive compulsions of mental illness: but here they are driven forward by their demons into the not-yet-existent, rather than back into the endless repetition of childhood fixations. The Demonic is indeed that which presides over all creation, all production, insofar as the latter represents the most concrete form of possession by a work which does not yet exist anywhere.

To this philosophical correction of the tradition of anamnesis and of the model of past-oriented time, there corresponds a whole artistic commentary as well: for just as there are true and false models of human time, so there are true and false forms as well, authentic and inauthentic, forms based on the mystique of the past and forms that reveal the essential movement of human reality toward the future. Hence, for instance, Bloch's distinction between the fairy tale and the heroic saga, a distinction based not only on the peasant or aristocratic character of their raw materials or of their respective publics, but above all on the quintessential relationship of the fairy tale to that wish which is its privileged content, to those most naïve and emblematic visions of the heart's desire which are the table groaning beneath ample bread and Würstchen, the warm fire, the children back home happy at last. Whereas the heroic saga unfolds under a baleful spell; the power of destiny hangs as a sentence of doom over all the heroic gestures of its characters, most properly furnishing the symbol of domination by a past which is their only future.

[57] Goethe, *Dichtung und Wahrheit* (Zurich, 1950), pp. 839-840.

130

But the most striking example of such a construction of formal opposites is to be found in the great essay-diptych which is one of Bloch's masterpieces: "Philosophical View of the Detective Story—Philosophical View of the Novel of the Artist." For the detective story is the very archetype of Oedipal construction in the manner in which everything in it, events and sentences alike, draws its ultimate value and even its meaning from an event in the past, an event necessarily external to the work's structure. In this the detective story shows a profound affinity with those past-oriented religious cosmologies for which the world itself begins with crime or violence: "What is true about all these various versions of the Oedipal metaphysic, above and beyond their mythological content, is that they reflect, if not, certainly, any initial dreamed-up *crime*, then at least the very *darkness* or *incognito* of origins themselves. Every fundamental type of research is related to the Oedipus form in the way in which its incognito is treated not so much as an unknown of a logical type but rather as something monstrous, something unclear even to the bearer himself. No Oedipus has ever yet replied to, let alone resolved, that most basic ontological incognito of all, that riddle alone worthy of the Sphinx, namely why something is, why the world is, in the first place."[58] Yet for Bloch this is a riddle which is answered, not at the beginning, but at the very fulfillment of time itself: for the meaning of Being itself comes into being, if at all, only at the moment when the world passes over into Utopia, and when that final Utopian destination returns upon the past to confer a sense of direction upon it.

To this regressive form, the novel of the artist stands in unexpected juxtaposition: for the artist-novel always revolves around an absent center also, but this center is no longer some secret about an event in the past, but rather the empty place of that imaginary work of art which alone con-

[58] Ernst Bloch, *Verfremdungen*, 2 vols. (Frankfurt, 1963), I, 58.

fers upon the novel's hero his right to be called an artist, a work of art whose absence stands as a kind of aesthetic imperative to the novelist himself, but one which he is necessarily and structurally unable to fulfill. For it is notorious that descriptions of imaginary art works, of non-existent paintings or novels or pieces of music (with the striking exception, perhaps, of those in Thomas Mann's *Doctor Faustus*), fail to ring true, and that this failure is not accidental but inevitable: a work of art not being an object (which could be represented or used artistically) but a system of relationships. For Bloch, however, this emptiness of the work within a work, this blank canvas at the center, is the very locus of the not-yet-existent itself; and it is precisely this essentially fragmentary and aesthetically unsatisfying structure of the novel of the artist which gives it its ontological value as a form and figure of the movement of the future incomplete before us.

In all of this, Bloch's system is still operating from a *critical* rather than from a *prophetic* standpoint, if I may put it that way. We are, in other words, still in the realm of philosophical judgment and not yet in that of hermeneutic interpretation. When we pass over into the latter, matters of truth and falsehood give way to techniques of conversion, to modes of recovering that which is authentic and instinct even within the most regressive forms, to a decipherment of the figures of hope beneath the immediate surface realities of despair or destiny.

Thus it is that the dialogue with Freud, the attack on anamnesis, gives way to an interrogation of Heidegger and of existence philosophy, with its dominant experience of anxiety, with its stress not on the past but on the present. In this context, the conversion mechanism used by Bloch consists in a changing of valences, a translation from negative to positive, which suggests the deeper underlying principle that every negative in some fashion implies a positive which is ontologically prior to it; indeed, that every negative may therefore serve as a means of access to that positive which it conceals.

Thus, if one cannot refute an experience like anxiety, one can at least transform it into that positive anticipation which is its correlative: and this even on the physiological level itself, where the limited bodily concomitants of both emotions (rapid heartbeat, sweating, lowered skin temperature, facial pallor) are identical. Indeed, a kind of prodigious enlargement of the existential horizon, a kind of lifting of the soul by its own bootstraps, suffices to transform the most acute anxiety into a breathless eagerness, an expectation of the future in which joy and terror are indistinguishable.

As with physiological sensations, so with nihilism itself as a world view, with those visions of boredom or of the absurd, those images of the death cell which most surely describe the modern feeling of being in the world. For despair, whether personal or historical, remains an emotion oriented to the future, one which "intends" the future in as total a fashion as hope: only it projects nothingness as its ultimate, rather than the all, the in-vain rather than the supreme. We are here very far from that self-righteous ethical dismissal which modern art and so-called nihilism receive at the hands of a Lukács, for instance: for Bloch, on the contrary, horror and the black emotions are infinitely precious insofar as they also constitute forms of that elemental ontological astonishment which is our most concrete mode of awareness of the future latent in ourselves and in things. Nor may Bloch's use of these emotions be assimilated to any facile optimism of a historical or personal kind: it is not a question, here, of replacing anxiety with hope, of revealing new horizons to the sufferer, or of making a convert in the last stages of desperation. Bloch wishes, on the contrary, to locate the positive *within* the negative itself; to hold the negative fast as the very authentication of the positive as it reveals itself through it; and it is most instructive, I think, to compare this teaching with that negative path to God which is one of the classic forms of religious mysticism, but which, according to Bloch's reversal of priorities, may now be seen as a kind of distorted foreshadowing of a secular truth. To seek the absolute through guilt, sin, and despair, through the absence of God himself, thus comes to serve as a kind of idealistic figure of this technique of reading anxiety as one of the most powerful forms of our longing for Utopia.

But, clearly, to long is not necessarily to find; and it is equally clear that a philosophy of this kind, which cannot reckon with the immortality of the soul, remains a dead letter unless it comes to terms in one way or another with death itself. This holds for the political-historical as well as for the personal and ontological level of reality: for the most urgent question of socialist construction remains that of individual sacrifice, and of the renunciations made by present generations for the benefit of generations in a future they will not themselves see.

Revolutions, of course, have their martyrs just like the older religions, and it is instructive to compare the church martyrs with the portrait Bloch offers us of *Thomas Münzer as Theologian of the Revolution.* For it is in a sense the very belief of the tortured Christian saints which disqualifies their existential agonies for us: their part in paradise—imaginary as it is—transforms the events themselves into the decorations of golden legend. It is reserved for those who die for good—the Indians and forgotten indigenous tribes, the witches, the peasants slaughtered after uprisings not even recorded in the history books, the torture and lynching of potential troublemakers from the very beginnings of time—to give the most anguishing glimpse of a death in absolute despair. Here obliteration from the minds of men stands as a figure of the oblivion of death itself: and the execution of Münzer signals not the end of the peasant war alone, but also—no doubt for the man himself, and for the people who believed in him—the very collapse of history itself as a meaningful process, as hope. It is with this absolute that any dialectic of history must ultimately come to terms: and the meditation on these bloody pictures, with their medieval apparatus of torment—tongs, rack, scourge, and stake—is not, as in religious contemplation, designed to console, but rather precisely to provoke that ultimate anxiety beyond which alone a revolutionary vocation is ratified.

Thus when Bloch (quite rightly) evokes the fearlessness in the face of death of the revolutionary, who, having passed to the level of collective solidarity, no longer really has an individual life to lose in the older sense, he nonetheless here remains within the realm of empirical psychology, or of political ethics, if one may put it that way, and has not yet come to terms with the deeper, ontological roots of the death anxiety and of death itself. The appeals to the technological aspects of Utopia, moreover—the progress of medicine in prolonging life, the prospect of a relatively painless type of extinction—are even less satisfactory in this respect. Yet we will not be able to understand Bloch's ultimate response without a long detour through the present itself, and through the instant: for from a temporal point of view what characterizes death is precisely its structure as that instant in which no future (and no hope) is any longer possible.

The present of time is characterized for Bloch above all by the absence of any real presence, any real plenitude of being: it is a hollowness, an insufficiency, a kind of darkness, and we think of words of Mallarmé which in the language of art ring with the same chiliastic overtones: "Il n'est pas de Présent, non—un présent n'existe pas. . . . Faute que se déclare la Foule, faute—de tout. Mal informé celui qui se crierait son propre contemporain. . . ."[59] The present is indeed for Bloch a kind of blind spot, its grotesque symbol that naïve drawing inserted by Ernst Mach into an analysis of self-perception and showing, through its own eyes, a body stretched out at rest upon a couch, from crudely foreshortened legs in the distance to the beard flowing down the chest from out of the rim or frame of perception, where the head is supposed to be and through which the observer is himself gazing.[60]

For the darkness of the present, the structure of its temporality, is at one with the whole question of identity itself, with the degree to which we are ultimately able to rejoin or to possess our selves: "So it is with regard to the non-self-possession of that intensive temporal element which has not yet, unfolding in time, revealed its own content as process. It is not the farthest away but rather *the closest which is still the darkest of all,* and this precisely because it is the closest and the most immanent; *in this proximity lies the very knot of the riddle of existence* [he uses the Heideggerian term *Da-sein* or Being-there]. The life of the now, the most truly intensive kind, has not yet come before itself, has not yet been brought to itself as something seen and revealed; it is least of all a *Da-sein,* a revelation of being. The now of existence, which drives everything else forward and toward which everything else is driven, is that which has been experienced the least. . . . Hence the strange fact that nobody has ever yet really *been there,* nobody has ever yet really lived. For life also means being present, it doesn't only mean beforehand or afterwards, anticipation or aftertaste. It means seizing the day, in the simplest as well as in the most thoroughgoing sense, it means holding concretely to the Now. But insofar as precisely that closest, most gen-

---

[59] Mallarmé, *Oeuvres* (Paris, 1945), p. 372.
[60] *Verfremdungen,* I, 14.

uine, continuing being-present to the world is really nothing of the sort, no human being has ever really lived, at least not in this sense. . . ."[61]

This is why, for all the emphasis on hoping and wishing, such experiences in the concrete world of our own imperfect here-and-now are always themselves figures of a wishing that has not yet fully revealed itself: by the same token, those instants which satisfy the most intense wishes are always, according to ancient psychological insight, in their very essence disappointing. Thus the title of Bloch's Tübingen inaugural lecture, in this context an astonishing one: "Can Hope Ever Be Thwarted?" receives an even more astonishing answer: hope is *always* thwarted, the future is always something *other* than what we sought to find there, something ontologically excessive and necessarily unexpected. Thus the negative is reabsorbed back into the positive, not as facile consolation, but as a kind of *via crucis* of hope itself, an enlargement of our anticipations to include and find satisfaction in their own negations as well.

The essential allegory of this process is for Bloch the legend of the Egyptian Helen in which Menelaus lands at the island of Pharos on his homeward voyage from Troy, only to find there a second Helen identical in all respects to the first, whom he carries with him on the ship. The Egyptian Helen claims to be the real one, spirited away by the gods and concealed here pure and undefiled during the ten years of the Trojan War while a simulacrum took her place in Paris' arms. Menelaus refuses to believe. "I trust the sufferings endured in battle more than I trust you!" he shouts in Euripides' version, but with that the shipboard Helen disappears in fiery smoke, and Menelaus must be content with the satisfaction of his wish, a satisfaction identical at all points to that desired for so long and so passionately, yet somehow hollow to the core, although *real*. "In each fulfill-

[61] *Das Prinzip Hoffnung*, p. 341.

ment, insofar as it is fully realizable in the first place, there remains a very specific type of hope whose *mode of being* is not that of present reality, or *at least not of present reality as it now is*, and which persists, complete with its own content. . . ."[62] It is this essential dissatisfaction at the very core of hope which drives time forward and which transforms each contingent wish into a figure of the Utopian wish itself, each contingent present into a figure of that ultimate presence of Utopia. "Yet rest comes on the day when the Egyptian Helen is endowed with all the prestige of the Trojan one."[63]

It is instructive to compare this doctrine not only with that of Heidegger, but also, as George Lichtheim has shrewdly suggested, with that of Sartre, or at least with that of the Sartre of *Being and Nothingness*, to whom Bloch shows some surprising resemblances, in spite of enormous stylistic and cultural disparities, along with some even more revealing differences. For Sartre also insists on this empty nature of the present which pro-jects us forward into the future, but for him the emptiness is one of *lacking* rather than of *wishing*; and he shows how temporality is to be seen as the passion of consciousness to overcome this essential ontological lack and to attain that ultimate identity which would be found in the union of consciousness or lack with that being which it lacks, or in other words with the external world. (Indeed, Sartre even sketches out a doctrine of the figures which this pro-jection of human reality deposits in the elements of the external world—Bloch calls them "reality ciphers"—and which a Bachelardian analysis of matter is called on to explore.)

But from a Sartrean point of view, the union of consciousness and being is a contradiction in terms, remains forever unrealizable. It is clear, therefore, that for Sartre the system

[62] *Das Prinzip Hoffnung*, p. 213.
[63] *Das Prinzip Hoffnung*, p. 213.

of Bloch is one which remains a prisoner of the optical illusion that *Being and Nothingness* attempted to exorcize.
Bloch's doctrine of Utopia thus finds itself reduced to a kind
of philosophy of as-if, a kind of lie which helps live.

The argument is not unanswerable from Bloch's point of
view, but a reply involves a shifting of its basic terms. For
it would seem clear that from the standpoint of *Hope the
Principle* existentialism itself is a kind of optical illusion,
one generated by an absolute valorization of the present as
such. This was already the case in Pascal, for whom the real
and desolate truth of existence is revealed only through a
thoroughgoing reduction of existence to the present instant:
reality becoming visible to us only on condition that we
divest ourselves of the mirages or ontological diversions
(*divertissements*) of both future and past, only on condition that we come to terms with the emptiness of life in the
present. So also in Sartre, for whom it must be said, in spite
of his emphasis on our pro-jection forward in time, that the
future remains imaginary in the most morbid sense: nothing, indeed, draws down the whole corrosive force of
Sartrean irony more surely than the mere wish to change
in the future, or, what amounts to the same thing, the wish
to have changed in the past: idle daydreams, or remorse.
Such wishes in reality have their function in the present
alone: one wants to change (think of the horror of Electra,
when her bloody daydreams are—as though through some
terrible misunderstanding—actually realized) only in order
to feel oneself superior to an intolerable present, only to
dissociate oneself mentally from a present reality one does
not care to see. Thus Sartre reduces the wish to its structure
as an illusion in the present, where Bloch reads its very
abstractness, its very ontological insufficiency, as a symbol
and a cause of the concrete future to come. Yet if one takes
Sartre's system not as a timeless description of the necessary
structure of all consciousness, but rather as a particularly

acute reflection of the feeling of existence in the historical here and now, in the empty present of modern industrial capitalism, then history is once again reintroduced into the philosophical debate, and it is no longer quite so certain that it is Bloch's system that in the long run is the more "Utopian" in the pejorative sense of the word.

There remains the problem of the nature of that ultimate Utopian identity which for Sartre is impossible and which for Bloch stands as the very sign of the realization of Utopia itself. It is at this point that *Faust* takes on its relevance for Bloch, whose entire work, indeed, may in one sense be seen as an immense commentary on Goethe's poem (in this light the peculiar and untraditional characteristics of his dialectic may be accounted for by the hypothesis that his is a Marxism which springs not from Hegel but from Goethe himself, not from the *Phenomenology* but from *Faust*). For it will be remembered that the work of Goethe is organized around the key episode of the wager with the devil, the terms of which involve refusal of, or consent to, the Instant. The customary image of Faust as an embodiment of restless dissatisfaction, and of the almost quantitative desire for ever greater amounts of experience, is an oversimplification which fails to come to terms with the resolution of the wager in *Faust II*. For there Faust's initial boast—that he will never find an instant so pleasurable that it would make him long to suspend time—is corrected; and with the reclamation of land from the sea and the prospect of a new and transformed *collective* existence ("Solch ein Gewimmel möcht ich sehn / Auf freiem Grund mit freiem Volke stehn!"), a present approaches to which precisely the fatal words of longing may be addressed. With this genuinely concrete and indeed profoundly political vision, the Instant for the first time throws off its ontological incognito: "The hic et nunc is that which everywhere takes on the form and being of a question [Bloch here deliberately reverses the Heideggerian slogan of a *Seinsfrage*], that which completes all the inadequate or only half-adequate images of world-being as process. But only in the flash of its proper identification or revelation of itself would for the first time that emerge, which had otherwise throughout the universe been announced and foreshadowed in the form of the marvelous: namely figures of identity. . . . The marvelous is a lightning bolt from subject and from object alike, in the light of which there no longer exists anything alienated, and in which subject and object have simultaneously ceased to be separated from each other. The subject, along with its truest characteristic, namely the Desiderium or longed-for object, has ceased to exist; the object has ceased to exist, along with its most ungenuine property: alienation. This realization is triumph, and the goddess of triumph stands, like ancient Nike, upon a single point: as that concentration of being created and ingathered to the genuinely human. . . ."[64] The fact of Faust's salvation underlines a profound qualitative difference between this ultimate, genuinely concrete Instant, and those lesser present moments with which Mephistopheles sought to fascinate Faust and to win his soul.

It is in this notion of an ascending ladder of forms of the instant that *Faust* most closely resembles Hegel's *Phenomenology*, a similarity which not Bloch alone, but Adorno and Lukács also have pointed out. If in the long run it is the Goethean vision which wins out in Bloch, this is on account of the essential idealism of that Absolute Spirit which is the final moment of fulfillment for Hegel and whose principal characteristic is the total elimination from the subject of any remnants of the external object itself, of any last shreds of objectivity as such. Hegel's system, as we have seen in the

[64] *Das Prinzip Hoffnung*, pp. 1549-1550.

critiques of Adorno and Marcuse, ultimately aims not at reconciliation with the world but at its total absorption, at the complete digestion of the world in all its contingency and otherness, its transformation into the self and into pure subjectivity. But for Bloch, for whom, in both a phenomenological and an emotional sense, consciousness pines away without an object, this ultimate suppression of the object-pole is constitutionally distasteful; and the lived source of Bloch's materialism may be found in this conviction of the boredom of consciousness left to its own devices, of the necessity of an object which justifies, not labor in the sense of the work of the fallen world, but rather activity of a higher, nonalienated, Goethean nature, in a Utopian external world now reconciled with the self, but not for all that swallowed up inside it.

The Faustian instant is, of course, but one possible symbol of the ultimate among many others: indeed, the structural force of Goethe's poem lies in the manner in which this essentially floating character of the symbol is reduplicated within the work itself. For Faust never really does live the moment in question; rather he imagines it as we imagine the poem itself, and the conditional in which his fatal words are couched stands as a mark of the essentially analogical character of the fable as a whole. The Utopian moment is indeed in one sense quite impossible for us to imagine, except as the unimaginable; thus a kind of allegorical structure is built into the very forward movement of the Utopian impulse itself, which always points to something other, which can never reveal itself directly but must always speak in figures, which always calls out structurally for completion and exegesis. We will examine some of the individual figures shortly, but for the moment it is enough to indicate the derivation of both art and religion, with their symbolic and allegorical expressions, from this deeper allegorical structure of being itself.

There exist, however, existential experiences which may be understood as foreshadowings of what the plenitude of such an ultimate Utopian instant might be like: this is the sense of the mystical union of the religions; in an even more concrete way, it is the most genuine function of music as a limited and yet pure feeling of that unity of outside and inside which Utopia will establish in all the dimensions of existence. For in music the tone itself is that most rarefied objective existent conceivable, one which enters in at our ear and mingles with our being intimately, without for all that ever losing its essential separation from us as a distinct object in its own right. Moreover, the sonata itself is proof of a kind of dialectic inherent in the musical experience, whereby this ontological relationship to the tone finds its fulfillment in that unfolding in time, in that temporal process and movement toward a future plenitude, which we know as musical form. Thus music is profoundly Utopian, both in its form and in its content.[65]

Now it may be clearer how the Utopian instant, or indeed the Utopian eternity, if it cannot abolish death, may at least rob it of its sting: for where normally at the moment of dying the individual is brutally wrenched from that future in which alone he might have found completion, now the transfigured time of Utopia offers a perpetual present in which there is a specific, yet total ontological satisfaction of every instant. Death, in such a world, has nothing left to take; it cannot damage a life already fully realized.

Yet there are stages in this conquest of death; for initially, even in our own world, there is a sense in which death and the present instant (as a darkness or hollowness) are re-

[65] See in particular "Philosophie der Musik," in Ernst Bloch, *Geist der Utopie* (Frankfurt, 1964), pp. 49-208.

lated: "The unobjectified existence, the sheer fact of existing which has not yet become a *Da-sein* or real presence to the world, is undoubtedly among the very future sources of *becoming* itself and of the attempt to externalize that existence in a mediated *Da-sein*; but to the degree that it is the source of this entering of existence into process, it is also the source of the *passing away* of things. And this to the precise degree that the instant has been unable adequately to externalize itself, to the degree that the sheer fact of existing has not yet been realized. But because the *central instant* of our existence has not yet entered upon the process of its objectification and consequently of its realization, *for that very reason it cannot fall prey to decay.* . . . Precisely because the very core of existence has not yet betaken itself into sheer process and change, it cannot be touched by the transitoriness inherent in that change; in the face of death it is surrounded by the protective circle of the not-yet-living. Yet if that inner core of being should enter upon process, then even that self-objectification, and ultimately that self-intensification and consequently self-realization, would no longer be one of process: with such an emergent instant the devouring reign of Chronos would be at an end. . . . The core of existence, therefore, having at length been brought into being and therein consequently fulfilled, would through that very *fulfillment* for the first time have become *extraterritorial* to death; for death would, along with that process-oriented insufficiency to which it belongs, have become inconsequential, indeed would itself have died off."[66] So it is that the citizens of Utopia, while still mortal, will know eternal life; and this deathless promise, these intense, only dimly perceptible intimations of the triumph over death are among the ultimate symbols of hope, distorted in their otherworldly religious forms, and now restored to us with all the exalting force of secular revolution.

[66] *Das Prinzip Hoffnung*, pp. 1387, 1390-1391.

2)

L'Art est une anticipation du travail tel qu'il doit être pratiqué dans un régime de très haute production.

—Georges Sorel, *Réflexions sur la violence*

Thus for Bloch the world is an immense storehouse of figures, and the task of philosopher or critic becomes a hermeneutic one to the degree that he is called upon to pierce this "incognito of every lived instant,"[67] and to decipher the dimly vibrating meaning beneath the fables and the works, the experiences and the objects, which surrounding us seem to solicit our attention in some peculiarly personal fashion.

The privileged objects of such hermeneutic analysis are of course myth and art; and they are distinguished from each other not as popular versus sophisticated culture, but rather as content versus form. For in the myth and the fairy tale the act of wishing, which is the most authentic dramatization of the Utopian impulse, constitutes the very story line of the fable itself. And the elaboration of fairy tale or myth is essentially a process of transformation or disguise, of distortion or displacement of that basic content, operations which no doubt correspond to the various modes of concealment from censorship which Freud exhaustively described in the *Interpretation of Dreams*. Only for Bloch, as we have seen, it is not a prehistoric wish, but rather a Utopian longing which is concealed behind the symbols of the gods, or in the displacement of the golden age either into a supernatural beyond or into a paradise at the beginning of time.

But when the literary work attempts to use this Utopian material directly, as content, in secular fashion, as in the various literary Utopias themselves, there results an impoverishment which is due to the reduction of the multiple levels of the Utopian idea to the single, relatively abstract

[67] *Das Prinzip Hoffnung*, p. 1548.

field of social planning. There is, of course, a sense in which all plot may be seen as a movement toward Utopia, in its working through to some ultimate resolution of the basic tensions: this is the position of Lukács in *Theory of the Novel* (1918), which is indeed contemporaneous with Bloch's *Spirit of Utopia* and which may serve to remind us that the preoccupations to which Bloch remained faithful were those of a whole intellectual generation. Yet this use of the notion of Utopia is already a figurative, or in the present context I would prefer to say a *formal* one, inasmuch as it has less to do with the wishing of the hero alone than with the development of all the various elements of the work through the time of form.

Bloch has never systematically worked out the modes of formal analysis his thought implies; yet it is clear that in his system a theory of figures would benefit from a kind of double coding not unlike that described with respect to Schiller in the previous chapter. For Bloch has essentially two different languages or terminological systems at his disposition to describe the formal nature of Utopian fulfillment: the movement of the world in time toward the future's ultimate moment, and the more spatial notion of that adequation of object to subject which must characterize that moment's content. These two aspects of Utopian fulfillment may be described as the "tendency" and the "latency," respectively, of things in the present: dynamic possibilities of historical development on the one hand, and the more perceptual or aesthetic potentialities of the same objects on the other. They thus correspond to dramatic and lyrical modes of the presentation of not-yet-being.

At the same time, from a figural point of view, this opposition corresponds to Bloch's characteristic distinction between the allegorical, as an opening onto otherness or difference, and the symbolic, as a folding back of all things into the unity of the same. Allegory no doubt itself aspires to the ultimate unity of the symbol, and to that degree these two movements are the same, the symbol "governing something like a *determination of the end,* which is to be distinguished from allegory as an identity-relationship to otherness, expressed through otherness: [the latter being] therefore essentially a *determination of the way.* Art is in its representation of the way just as completely allegorical as it *remains indebted to the symbol* for the end which determines that way (and which remains for all its unity and totality a human one)."[68] Yet inasmuch as the reality of the symbol is not yet given in the world itself, inasmuch as the world has not yet attained that unity of being designated by the symbol, there remains something as premature and willful about it as there is fragmentary and insufficient about allegory. The two, indeed, correspond at this level to the difference between religion and art: "Art is a pluralism which in its mode of presentation, and in spite of possessing an intrinsic meaning of its own, follows the indirect and multivocal movement of the allegorical; while centralistic religion, in spite of its use of transparent poetic modes, aims at taking a single direction, and at accomplishing a convergence of symbols."[69]

In the context of a lyrical, rather than a dramatic, mode of representing reality, however, both types of representation may be seen as forms of *completion:* "To be sure, the doctrine of the last things is far from being as accessible to modern man as it was in those blessed times when the gods were near; yet for that very reason the artists among men once more take up the sluggish and long-unused arrows of expression to let them fly in henceforth esoteric directions; and since the sacred can come no closer to earth than within the work of art itself, the darkly colored luminous

[68] *Das Prinzip Hoffnung,* p. 951.
[69] Ernst Bloch, *Tübinger Einleitung in die Philosophie,* 2 vols. (Frankfurt, 1963-1964), II, 46-47.

transparency of expressionistic art, with its Utopian content- and object-orientation, is to be honored as the courtyard before the dwelling of a parousia to come. . . . The images of art, like little islands before us, are as paintings on glass which have only just begun to glow, stimulating our attention, and which people indicate, explicate, and then again abandon. And this is indeed the criterion of a purely *aesthetic* illumination, viewed from the point of view of its ultimate categories: *how may the things of this world be completed without their ceasing, apocalyptically, to exist. . . ."*[70] Thus, what the sonata form completes in time, the dome, for instance, completes in space, as the very figure of that cupola of earth which was "for Columbus an 'indicio del paraýso terrenal,' when he transferred the latter from Ceylon, where the Arabic geographers set it, to the delta of the Orinoco (still, to be sure, closely neighboring Ceylon in his mind), indeed beyond that still, to that unattained realm in which one cannot set foot, where the earth become Eden passes over into the dome of the azure sky."[71]

In painting, in lyrical expression generally, we catch a glimpse of the transformation and transfiguration of objects in the world to come: "Just as Franz Marc said that pictures represent our own reemergence into a different place, so here, in placelessness, where interior and perspective interpenetrate and suffuse each other with a sense of the beyond, *a whole existence emerges into elsewhere*: here there no longer exists anything but the wish-landscape of this everywhere, this at-home-ness in the universe."[72] It is precisely this sense of mystery or the marvelous, whether conveyed by Surrealism, by Flemish still life, or by the glorious encasement of a Renaissance Madonna, which is negated by modern civilization, whose "most unquestionably original

[70] *Geist der Utopie*, p. 151.
[71] *Das Prinzip Hoffnung*, p. 908.
[72] *Das Prinzip Hoffnung*, pp. 980-981.

148

achievement" Bloch sees in the "modern bathroom and water closet, just as surely as furniture, in the Rococo, and cathedrals, in Gothic art, furnished the architectonic dominants around which the rest of the style of the periods in question organized itself. Now washability dominates, somehow water flows down all the walls, and the magic of modern sanitary installations imperceptibly intervenes as an a priori of completed machine production even in the most precious achievements of the industrial technique of our time."[73]

This is not to say that functionalism is necessarily unaesthetic: for it is precisely the humbler artifacts, the crudely carved peasant pipes and drinking cups, which embody the most authentic way in which man attempts to rejoin himself through the things around him, attempts to rejoin his ultimate identity through a passionate shaping of the tools and artifacts among which he lives and works and through which he externalizes himself. The making of artifacts is thus the basic archetype, the most fundamental gesture, at the heart of lyric expression.[74]

When we turn now to temporal forms, and in particular to the unfolding of the fable in time, it is evident that the very time of the work may itself stand as a figure of Utopian development: "Every great work of art, above and beyond its manifest content, is carried out according to a *latency of the page to come*, or in other words, in the light of the content of a future which has not yet come into being, and indeed of some ultimate resolution as yet unknown."[75] A phenomenology of the temporal forms of the novel is implicit in this idea, but one which would transcend mere typology and deal rather with the Utopian significance of the various concrete experiences of time which the various narrative modes embody.

[73] *Geist der Utopie*, p. 21.
[74] See *Geist der Utopie*, pp. 17-19.
[75] *Das Prinzip Hoffnung*, p. 110.

It is this significance which gives art its truth content, which makes of artistic practice a preconceptual philosophical exploration of the world in its own right: "Artistic appearance [Schein] . . . has the sense of a being driven further on, a sense disguised in images but only communicable through them, *where the stylization and the construction of the fable themselves represent an ontological anticipation [Vorschein] of the real which both transcends that limited and temporally developing object of the work and intends it at the same time,* an ontological anticipation precisely representable in an aesthetically immanent way. Here is illuminated what dull or habituated sense still scarcely sees, both in individual events, as well as in social or natural ones. . . ."[76]

In this context the various techniques or categories of the work of art take on their ultimate meaning only when their analysis is pursued as far as the ontological level itself, where they become transparent as modes of Utopian realization: "*Art is at one and the same time a laboratory and a carnival of possibilities brought to fulfillment.*"[77]

All of which, no doubt, remains abstract and itself unfulfilled, a set of empty critical imperatives, without some concrete technical demonstration of the way in which such a method would function. And this is all the more the case owing to Bloch's characteristic choice of primarily popular or at least traditional artistic examples. I am not aware, for instance, that he has ever spoken of Proust, whom Benjamin translated, whose "temps retrouvé" Marcuse sees as the very archetype of instinctual anamnesis, whose great work indeed would seem to offer the very prototype of the novel of the artist; yet it seems to me that the creation of Proust suggests itself as privileged material for a Utopian hermeneutic, both as an illustration and as a test case.

[76] *Das Prinzip Hoffnung*, p. 247.
[77] *Das Prinzip Hoffnung*, p. 249.

For it is hard not to think frequently of Proust when we read Bloch's accounts of the fortunes of hope, when we observe his sensitivity not only to experiences of fulfillment, but also to those of disappointment and to the ironies of satisfaction. The storyline in Proust is precisely one of wishes; and indeed the force of the work lies in its experience of wishing in its most powerful and infantile form: as a longing for an object, a rendezvous, a dinner invitation, a trip to the theater, so total that for the moment it blots out the rest of the world, so absolute it has all the peremptory force of the desires of a child. And it is precisely such wishes which yield the purest archetype of the Utopian impulse.

With the structure of such a wish, the time of Proustian narration is given as well. As in Bloch, the future always turns out in Proust to be that which is more, or other, than what was expected, even if what was expected had in the last analysis been dissatisfaction itself. Think of that long-desired letter from Gilberte which the narrator composes over and over again in his mind until he stops in terror: "I understood that were I to receive a letter from Gilberte, it could in no case be that particular one, since I had just myself composed it. And from that moment on I forced myself to avoid thinking the words I would have loved to have her write me, for fear of excluding precisely those words—the dearest and most longed for—from the field of possible realizations by pronouncing them myself."[78] Thus for Proust also, whatever the content of the future, it must necessarily come with the force of the utterly new, the utterly unexpected, and the narrator is therefore driven into an agonizing and self-contradictory, profoundly superstitious process of conjuring the wish: consciously imagining less in order to receive more, formulating the wish in one way only so as

---

[78] Proust, *A la recherche du temps perdu*, 3 vols. (Paris, 1954), I, 409.

to have it realize itself in that stronger form secretly longed for.

Proustian plot is therefore constituted by a series of episodes each of which negates the immediately preceding one, while at the same time raising it to a higher plane; and emotionally, this negation of the negation has an immense impact. We have only to think of the opening sequence, in which the kiss is unexpectedly denied by the mother who is ordinarily so permissive, and then just as unexpectedly permitted by the father who is ordinarily so severe. Proust thus reduplicates the characteristic plot rhythms of his master Balzac, whose novels also turn around a wishing or desiring; but what was there an appetency for the external goods and objects of nascent capitalism is here interiorized, and translated by Proust onto a psychological level.

This is what we may call the inner plot in Proust, whose content is the private life of the narrator. When we turn now to the outer plot, to the other characters and their unexpected destinies, it becomes clear that this expectation-affect, so to speak, so profoundly emblematic of our relationship to the future, has been shifted from emotion to contemplation, has been transferred from protagonist to reader. For in these multitudinous reversals of fate and reputation, Proust's fascination with the unexpected matches that of Bloch in *Spuren*; and the various anecdotes of which the Proustian work is composed might have served as material for the latter: the imbecilic Dr. Cottard, who turns out to be at the same time a diagnostician of genius; the great painter Elstir, who turns out to have been the vulgar and clumsy habitué of Madame Verdurin's earliest salon; the transformation of Madame Verdurin herself into the Princesse de Guermantes, and Odette into the Duchesse; the very incognito of the Swann and Guermantes ways themselves, which prove to have been one and the same all along. It is in the analysis of such material, and of

152

the interest in such material, that we can perhaps best confront a reductive with an expansive hermeneutic: for from
a psychological point of view, it is not hard to see how such
twists of fate are Proust's way of revenging himself on
external appearances, on his own reputation for snobbery
and frivolity, of affirming, with a prodigiously inventive
mauvaise foi, that he also is other than he seems. Such motivation, the crudest form of wish-fulfillment, is not contra-
dicted but rather transcended by the hermeneutic system
of *Hope the Principle*. It is, we may say, itself one of the
"ruses of hope"—the content of the oldest fairy tales and
myths, in which prince or princess wait, bewitched, beneath
the ugly forms of toad or hag. And one would have to perform a dialectical reversal to the second power, one would
have to interrogate the motivation of reductive psychology
itself, and the *Schadenfreude* with which the appearance
is stripped from the cynical reality, to understand our misunderstanding of the positive motive power behind even
mauvaise foi itself, the powerful yearning for a perfected
self which behind all superficial egotism is part and parcel
of a drive toward a world itself transfigured.

When we turn now to the actual social content of Proust,
the hidden significance of such passions as snobbery and
social climbing is at once revealed: so many the mystified
figures of that longing for perfection, of an as yet unconscious Utopian impulse. At the same time, such social raw
material, with its eternal receptions and drawing rooms and
its pronounced class limitations, and the deliberate intention of Proust to paint a nobility in decay and on the point
of vanishing into nothingness—all of these things come to
seem not so much reactionary as anticipatory. For it is precisely the leisure of this class, given over completely to
interpersonal relationships, to conversation, art, and social
planning (if one may so characterize the energy that goes
into the building of a salon), fashion, love, which reflects in

153

the most distorted way the possibilities of a world in which alienated labor will have ceased to exist, in which man's struggle with the external world and with his own mystified and external pictures of society will have given way to man's confrontation with himself. The Proustian leisure class is a caricature of that classless society: how could it be otherwise? Yet since it is (at least in Proust's society) the only leisure culture which exists, it alone can serve as a source of concrete images of what such a Utopia might be like. Behind Proust stands of course his other great model, Saint-Simon; and the court of Louis XIV exerts an analogous fascination in the picture it gives of the very center of the world itself, complete in itself, freed from need, yet swarming with the most intense interpersonal relationships: a kind of harem of genuinely human existence within the brutalities of baroque absolutism. In this sense it is perhaps not too much to say that *gossip*—that meeting place of conversation and art, that profoundly fertile vice of both Saint-Simon and Proust (and indeed of Balzac as well, in a very different social milieu)—may itself stand as a kind of distorted figure of that passion for the human in its smallest details which will be ours in the transfigured society and the transfigured world.

It is a misconception to believe that Proust's novel is circular, or that the end, with its withdrawal from life and its intimations of the cork-lined room, really marks a return to the beginning. In this context the work may rather be seen as an immense phenomenology of the forms of the repressed artistic impulse itself, a kind of ladder of attempts at expression (in which gossip returns to its secondary place and the passions of snobbery and position are put in perspective), stretching from the first enthusiastic "Zut, zut!" of the youthful narrator on a beautiful day, from the loving care with which Odette works out details of her costume which no one else will see, from the diagnostic flair of the otherwise mediocre Dr. Cottard, all the way to the paintings of Elstir and the narrator's artistic vocation itself. Thus, there is yet a second structure of progressions toward the future within the novel, this one a series of forms all striving blindly toward the lucidity of artistic practice itself; and this valorization of art is itself an anticipatory phenomenon. "Art," said Sorel, "is an anticipation of the way all work will feel in the society of the future":[79] or, to put it another way, all activity in the society of the future will be as profoundly satisfying and as without constraint as is the practice of art in our own.

Yet for Proust art finds its immediate justification in the ontology of time, in a darkness of the present instant very similar to that described by Bloch. In Proust also the present only gives us the raw material of genuine experience, and not experience itself. For whatever reason—the over-intellectualization of modern life, a too intense and willful hyperconsciousness about ourselves—real life seems able to take place only when we are least expecting it, only when, so to speak, we happen to be looking in another direction. Thus, in our world and our society, experience is given as necessarily fragmentary; it is never lived with that full and genuine self-consciousness which Bloch attributes to that ultimate adequation of subject with object; and the task of art and language is to recover this wholeness of experience, or rather to make it possible for the first time. Thus in no sense can Proustian art be said to be memory-oriented, to be obsessed with the past and its restoration: rather, that past is itself structurally deficient, ontologically inadequate, and it is only at the moment of expression through language that it can really be lived *as though for the first time*. Thus Proustian composition, and the reading of Proust, is itself a figure of the experience of eternity, of the experience of Utopian adequation; and for the first time

[79] Georges Sorel, *Réfléxions sur la violence* (Paris, 1950), p. 53.

also that empty space within the novel of the artist, that empty canvas which is his putative work of art, is filled (in this Proustian superposition of the experiences in the fallen world, and their expression, from beyond the end of the novel, from beyond the end of that world, by the narrator) by the concrete time of verbal expression.

Thus the vital Utopian reality of Proust's work contradicts the limits of its official philosophy, of that Platonic anamnesis which proves to be a return to the past only in appearance; as though the Utopian impulse itself were able to do its work only in disguise, were obliged to realize its projections of the future under the cloak of a mystique of nostalgia.

Art as a "displaced prophetic vocation":[80] this phrase perhaps best illuminates the relationship between art and religion in Bloch's system, the authentic value of the so-called religion of art, and at the same time the deeper sources of Bloch's own language as well, which, particularly in the earlier works, is of a deliberately prophetic cast, overtly inspired by the Biblical prophets, and which through its very rhetorical molding, and unmolding mimes and conjures up that apocalyptic moment when, in Münzer's words, "the Lord will lay mightily around him with an iron rod among the clay pots."

For what distinguishes the force of religion from the less binding, more contemplative play of art proper is the conjunction of absolute belief and collective participation which are united in the concept of the millenarian or the chiliastic. Through the second of these twin concepts, religion is distinguished from philosophy, where there can theoretically be such a thing as solitary truth: in Münzer's theology, the very truth-coefficient of a theological doctrine is measured by collective need, by the belief and recognition of the multitudes themselves. Hence a theological idea,

[80] *Geist der Utopie*, p. 150.

in contrast to a philosophical one, already implies in its very structure a church or group of believers around it, and exists therefore on a protopolitical, rather than a purely theoretical, level.

Yet the "seriousness" of religion, the absolute quality of its belief, also marks its profound affiliation to praxis and to politics in the larger sense. I am tempted to compare this aspect of Bloch's description with Sartre's discussion of the physiological concomitants of emotion which constitute, he said, something like the "sérieux" of the subjective feelings themselves: without genuine physical blushing, trembling, sweating, rapid heartbeat, the emotions are reduced to so many figments of pure mind, so many velleities floating across consciousness. So also with this absolute conviction of the religions, which marks our access to the most genuine Utopian longings of mankind, "treasures which neither moths nor rust can corrupt, nor either the Lysol of a modern 'philosophical outlook.' "[81]

The value of religion for revolutionary activity lies therefore in its structure as a hypostasis of absolute conviction, as a passionate inner *subjective* coming to consciousness of those deepest Utopian wishes without which Marxism remains an objective theory and is deprived of its most vital resonances and of its most essential psychic sustenance as well: " 'Know,' says an ancient manuscript of the Zohar in this sense, 'that there exists for all worlds a double form of vision. One shows their exterior, and the general laws of the worlds according to their outer form. The other shows their inner essence, namely the very essence of the human soul itself. And there exists, accordingly, two ways of acting, that of works and that of prayer; for works are in order to fulfill the worlds in the respect of their external appearance, prayers to make the one world hold within the others and to lift them up.' In such a functional relationship between

[81] *Verfremdungen*, I, 158.

liberation and spirit, between Marxism and religion, united in a single will toward the ultimate kingdom, their eventual confluence draws together a multitude of neighboring streams: the soul, Messiah, Apocalypse, which is the form taken by the act of an awakening to totality, give the last impulse both theoretical and practical, constitute the a priori of all politics and culture."[82] Thus Bloch's thought in its ultimate twin source, as a kind of explosive reopening of the "vases communicants" of religion and politics.

3)

> This science [hermeneutics] has had a peculiar destiny. It wins esteem only during some great historical movement for which such comprehension of historical existence in its singularity has become an urgent theoretical problem, only to vanish thereafter once more into darkness.
>
> —Wilhelm Dilthey, Notes to "Die Entstehung der Hermeneutik"

Bloch's work, it would seem, is more honored than influential in either of the two Germanys in which he has lived and worked; of all the philosophers and critics discussed in this book he is certainly the least well known abroad. Partly, no doubt, this is due to the total and all-embracing character of his system, which like the universal culture of which it is an expression implicitly demands the absorption into itself of all the lesser philosophical languages and perspectives to which we have become accustomed. All the more difficult is this when we have to do with a doctrine of figures for which there can be no ultimate terminology, no bedrock of language which the mind can feel as a kind of absolute. In this, too, it demands an adherence perhaps more religious than philosophical in nature.

Mainly, however, the neglect of Bloch is due to the fact that his system, a doctrine of hope and ontological antici-

[82] *Geist der Utopie*, pp. 345-346.

pation, is itself an anticipation, and stands as a solution to problems of a universal culture and a universal hermeneutic which have not yet come into being. It thus lies before us, enigmatic and enormous, like an aerolite fallen from space, covered with mysterious hieroglyphs that radiate a peculiar inner warmth and power, spells and the keys to spells, themselves patiently waiting for their own ultimate moment of decipherment.

Meanwhile his work, like that of Marcuse and Benjamin, may serve as an object lesson in some of the ways available to a Marxist hermeneutic to restore a genuine political dimension to the disparate texts preserved in the book of our culture: not by some facile symbolic or allegorical interpretation, but by reading the very content and the formal impulse of the texts themselves as figures—whether of psychic wholeness, of freedom, or of the drive toward Utopian transfiguration—of the irrepressible revolutionary wish.

CHAPTER THREE

THE CASE FOR
GEORG LUKÁCS

For WESTERN READERS the idea of Georg Lukács has often seemed more interesting than the reality. It is as though, in some world of Platonic forms and methodological archetypes, a place were waiting for the Marxist literary critic which (after Plekhanov) only Lukács has seriously tried to fill. Yet in the long run even his more sympathetic Western critics turn away from him in varying degrees of disillusionment: they came prepared to contemplate the abstract idea, but in practice they find themselves asked to sacrifice too much. They pay lip service to Lukács as a figure, but the texts themselves were not what they had had in mind at all.[1]

Such discomfort is hardly surprising, for it marks the approach of Western relativism to its own conceptual limits: we conceive of our culture, indeed, as a vast imaginary museum in which all life forms and all intellectual positions are equally welcome side by side, providing they are accessible to contemplation alone. Thus, alongside the Christian

[1] Susan Sontag: "I, too, am inclined to give Lukács all the benefit of the doubt, if only in protest against the sterilities of the Cold War which have made it impossible to discuss Marxism seriously for the last decade or more. But we may be generous toward the 'late' Lukács only at the price of not taking him altogether seriously, of subtly patronizing him by treating his moral fervor aesthetically, as style rather than as idea . . ." (*Against Interpretation* [New York, 1966], p. 87). Adorno: "Lukács' person is above suspicion. But the conceptual framework to which he sacrifices the intellect is so narrow as to smother everything that needs to draw free breath to live: the *sacrifizio del' intelletto* does not leave the latter unscathed . . ." (*Noten zu Literatur*, 3 vols. [Frankfurt, 1958-1965], II, 154). George Steiner: "German is Lukács' principal language, but his use of it has grown brittle and forbidding. His style is that of exile; it has lost the habits of living speech" (*Language and Silence* [London, 1969], p. 295).

mystics and the nineteenth-century anarchists, the Surrealists and the Renaissance humanists, there would be room for a Marxism that was but one philosophical system among others. Nor can it be some requirement of absolute belief that prevents Marxism from being assimilated in this fashion, for the religions themselves, transformed into images, easily coexist in the eclectic tradition with which we are familiar. No, the peculiarity of the structure of historical materialism lies in its denial of the autonomy of thought itself, in its insistence, itself a thought, on the way in which pure thought functions as a disguised mode of social behavior, in its uncomfortable reminder of the material and historical reality of spirit. Thus as a cultural object, Marxism returns against cultural activity in general to devalue it and to lay bare the class privileges and the leisure which it presupposes for its enjoyment. It thus ruins itself as a spiritual commodity and short-circuits the process of culture consumption in which, in the Western context, it had become engaged. It is therefore the very structure of historical materialism—the doctrine of the unity of thinking and action, or of the social determination of thought—which is irreducible to pure reason or to contemplation; and this, which the Western middle-class philosophical tradition can only understand as a *flaw* in the system, refuses us in the very moment in which we imagine ourselves to be refusing it.

No wonder, then, that Lukács' life work fails to be understood from the inside, as a set of solutions and problems developing out of one another according to their own inner logic and momentum; no wonder his works are taken to be external signs of arbitrary positions, symptoms meaningless in themselves and comprehensible only in terms of shifts in the party line. His intellectual development is replaced by a myth of the career of Lukács which all his Western commentators repeat in one form or another without reflection.

After a neo-Kantian period, we are told, after studies with Simmel and Lask and contact with Max Weber, the Hegelian Lukács of the *Theory of the Novel* (1914-1915) begins to emerge. And just as the Kantian had become a Hegelian, so during the war the Hegelian becomes a Marxist, joins the Hungarian Communist Party, participates in the revolutionary government of Béla Kun. The third Lukács, a Bolshevik with strong activist leanings and unrepentant Hegelian tendencies, writes a seminal work, *History and Class Consciousness* (1923), which the party condemns. In the wake of his autocritique, the most familiar and mature Lukács takes form: the Stalinist Lukács of the 1930's and 1940's, the theoretician of literary realism, easily assimilable to the official socialist realism of the same period, and expressed in such works as *Balzac and French Realism* (1945), *Goethe and His Time* (1947), *Russian Realism in World Literature* (1949), and *The Historical Novel* (1955), as well as numerous studies of nineteenth- and twentieth-century German literature and thought, published in East Berlin after the war. With the thaw, a more moderate Lukács restates his general position on modernism in *On Critical Realism* (1958), and after the Hungarian uprising goes into retirement, preparing the two-volume *Aesthetics* (1963) in which, along with the projected *Ethics* and *Ontology*, he returns, but from a Marxist point of view, to the neo-Kantian theoretical projects of his youth.

It will be noted that the elaboration of this biographical myth depends on the division of a life into discontinuous "periods," an operation which presents a two-fold advantage. On the one hand, the passage from one period to another falls outside the myth proper. Thus the transitions from one position to another turn out either to exceed (as in the notion of a semireligious *conversion* to Communism) or to fall short of (as in the spectacle of servile obedience to the party line) what even the most sympathetic historical consciousness may be expected to relive and to understand from the inside. On the other, the various periods may now be played off against each other without our having to commit ourselves to any of them. So the young Marx was used against the older one; and early Lukács (whether that of the *Theory of the Novel* or of *History and Class Consciousness*) serves to discredit the later theoretician of realism; indeed, the final Lukács, with his return to the beginning, is bound to suggest the failure and the vanity of the whole enterprise.

Yet what if the earlier works proved to be fully comprehensible only in the light of the later ones? What if, far from being a series of self-betrayals, Lukács' successive positions proved to be a progressive exploration and enlargement of a single complex of problems? In the following pages, we will show that Lukács' work may be seen as a continuous and lifelong meditation on narrative, on its basic structures, its relationship to the reality it expresses, and its epistemological value when compared with other, more abstract and philosophical modes of understanding.

I

THE CHIEF conceptual opposition within which all of Lukács' examination of literature has taken place is the familiar Hegelian one of the concrete and the abstract. Hegel's originality, of course, lay in the transformation of this purely logical distinction into an ontological one; in the demonstration of how lived experiences and life forms themselves could be in its light evaluated against each other; in the evolution of a comparative, or indeed dialectical, mode of thinking such that every perception of a given experience or work is at the same time an awareness of what that experience or work is not. It is clear that the feeling of concreteness, of filled density of being, or that of abstractness and impoverishment of experience, are essentially derived from just such implicit comparisons between one experience and another, one work and another, one moment of history and another.

What is perhaps less evident is the degree to which this Hegelian opposition overlaps the more familiar contemporary notion of *alienation*: for the abstract and the alienated, no doubt, name the same object. Only it is easy to see why Western thinkers have on the whole preferred the concept of alienation: the latter permits the diagnosis of an evidently fallen and degraded reality without demanding of the mind any reciprocal attempt to imagine a state in which man no longer is alienated. It is thus a negative and critical concept, from which the Utopian moment has been quietly eliminated; whereas the term abstract forces us, through its very structure as an antithesis, to preserve and develop the idea of concreteness in order to complete our thought.

The most characteristic Marxist use of this opposition is of course that according to which society itself is seen as the ultimate source of the concreteness or the abstractness of individual existence. In literary terms, this means that society is conceived of at any given historical moment as that preexistent and indeed preformed raw material which ultimately determines the abstractness or the concreteness of the works of art created within it. "Men make their history themselves," said Engels in a famous passage, "only they do so in a given environment which conditions it, and on the basis of actual relations already existing, among which the economic relations, however much they may be influenced by the other, the political and ideological relations, are still ultimately the decisive ones, forming the keynote which runs through them and alone leads to understanding."[2] It

[2] Letter to Starkenburg, 25 January 1894 (Marx and Engels, *Basic Writings on Politics and Philosophy*, ed. L. Feuer [New York, 1959], p. 411).

would be a truism to say that the airplane and the department store, the bearer of the *Légion d'honneur* and the problems of women's emancipation cannot be elements of works of art from societies in which these things do not exist: what is more important is the influence of a given social raw material, not only on the content, but on the very form of the works themselves.

In the art works of a preindustrialized, agricultural or tribal society, the artist's raw material is on a human scale, it has an immediate meaning, requiring no preliminary explanation or justification on the part of the writer. The story needs no background in time because the culture knows no history: each generation repeats the same experiences, reinvents the same basic human situations as though for the first time. The social institutions are not felt as external traditions, as forbidding and incomprehensible edifices; authority is vested in the king or priest, is immanent to them. As human actors they express it fully in a three-dimensional way. The physical objects of such a world are equally immediate: they are clearly human products, the results of preordained ritual and of an immediately visible hierarchy of village occupations. Even the supernatural, the magical or religious, ideology of such a way of life returns to man in the anthropomorphic shape of gods and personalized forces; no doubt it is a projection, but the very mechanism of projection is still naïvely undisguised in the storytelling structure of the myths themselves. The works of art characteristic of such societies may be called concrete in that their elements are all meaningful from the outset. The writer uses them, but he does not need to demonstrate their meaning beforehand: in the language of Hegel, this raw material needs no *mediation*.[3]

---

[3] "What man requires for his external life, house and home, tent, chair, bed, sword and spear, the ship with which he crosses the ocean, the chariot which carries him into battle, boiling and roasting,

When we turn from such a work to the literature of the industrial era, everything changes. The elements of the work begin to flee their human center: a kind of dissolution of the human sets in, a kind of centrifugal dispersal in which paths lead out at every point into the contingent, into brute fact and matter, into the not-human. Even those most basic components of the story, the characters themselves, become problematical: now they have *personalities*, and the choice of personality traits, the portrayal of the hero as dreamy and idealistic rather than choleric and cynical, demands organic justification within the work itself. Thus the hero's temperament will be explained in terms of his father and his family situation; or will perhaps be given as emblematic of a certain relationship to the existing society and its predominant values; will be shown as bearing metaphysical value as a defiance of the universe, or in the end simply remains unjustified, whereupon the work tends to sink to the level of accident, to become a kind of case history.

---

slaughtering, eating and drinking,—nothing of all this must have become merely a dead means to an end for him; he must still feel alive in all these with his whole sense and self in order that what is in itself merely external be given a humanly inspired individual character by such close connection with the human individual" (Hegel, *Aesthetik*, 2 vols. [Frankfurt, 1955], II, 414, quoted in Lukács, *Studies in European Realism* [New York, 1964], p. 155). See also the section on the "world of prose," quoted below, pp. 352-354. Indeed, the sections of Hegel's *Aesthetics* which we as modern readers find most interesting are perhaps not so much those which describe epic structure as such, but rather precisely those which either directly or by implication show what it is in the modern world that rules out such wholeness in advance. We read Hegel negatively rather than positively, and Lukács' *Theory of the Novel* is in this sense but the logical continuation of the Hegelian aesthetic after the death of Absolute Spirit. Thus in the present instance Hegel adds: "Our present-day machinery and factories, together with the products they turn out and in general our means of satisfying our external needs would in this respect—exactly like modern state organization—be out of tune with the background of life which the original epic requires."

The same loss of immediate comprehensibility takes place on other levels as well: in the time of the work, in the institutions that form its background, in the objects among which the characters move. For the unquestioned, ritualistic time of village life no longer exists; there is henceforth a separation between public and private, between work and leisure, and the story must find its elbowroom in a world in which men's lives are divided between routine drudgery and sleep. So the novelist arranges his plot to take place on weekends (Camus' *Stranger*), during vacations (Thomas Mann's *Magic Mountain*), during great crises in which the routine breaks down (war literature). If the hero's profession leaves him enough free time for his private life (Joyce's *Ulysses*), then somehow the very choice of the profession must be justified in its turn (advertising as work with language). Where there is inherited wealth and leisure, either it is based on a kind of unexamined social presupposition (as in the case of the landed gentry who furnish the actors for nineteenth-century English and Russian novels); or else it remains a mere family accident, and the problem is not solved, but only thrust into the past, into earlier generations (and here the very emblem of the process might well be that unmentioned chamber pot which Henry James privately admitted to have been at the origin of the Newsome fortune in *The Ambassadors*).

So also with the very framework of the story itself: the institutions of the modern world, within which the characters live out their dramas, end up as something merely *given*, as the result of the accidental origin of the work in a particular national situation, at a particular moment of historical development. The village, the city-state, is a whole world in itself: but the superhighway, the modern university, the American army, or the great industrial city —all these things constitute unrealized, and ultimately unrealizable, foreign bodies within the work of art. And what is true of overall social organization is all the more visible in the individual commodities of a given society, in the various objects and products among which the characters move: the chairs and motorcycles, the food, houses, and revolvers which are no longer felt as the results of immediate human activity, which inhabit the work like so much dead furniture, tear through the human surface of the work like so much alien inorganic matter.

It will be observed that modern literature has developed special techniques, elaborate methods of symbolism, in the express hope of giving meaning to such stubbornly resistant things, of assimilating them to the humanized substance of the work of art. And symbolism as such is a central phenomenon of modern literature: we will discuss it later at more length. For the moment it is enough to say that whatever the merits of symbolic and symbolizing modes of thought as a solution to this dilemma, their presence in the work always stands as an indication that the immediate meaning of objects has disappeared: the process would not arise in the first place if objects had not already become problematical in their very nature.

A far more telling objection might be made to the reality of this contingency in modern life: it is contingency, it might be said, in appearance only. In fact, all such apparently inhuman institutions and things are intensely human in their origin. Never has the world been so completely humanized as in industrial times; never has so much of the individual's environment been the result, not of blind natural forces, but of human history itself. Thus, if the modern work of art were only able to enlarge its point of view far enough, if it were able to make enough connections between such widely disparate phenomena and facts, the illusion of inhumanity would disappear: once again the content of the work would be completely comprehensible in human terms, even though on a far vaster scale than before. Yet it is precisely this enlargement which is irreconcilable with the very form and structure of literature. The framework of the work of art is individual lived experience, and it is in terms of these limits that the outside world remains stubbornly alienated. When we pass from individual experience to that collective dimension, that sociological or historical focus in which human institutions slowly become transparent for us once again, we have entered the realm of disembodied abstract thought and have left the work of art behind us. And this life on two irreconcilable levels corresponds to a basic fault in the very structure of the modern world: what we can understand as abstract minds we are incapable of living directly in our individual lives and experiences. Our world, our works of art, are henceforth *abstract*.

We may therefore conclude this preliminary discussion by emphasizing the two basic characteristics of concreteness in art. First of all, its situations are such as to permit us to feel everything in them in purely human terms, in terms of individual human experience and individual human acts. Second, such work permits life and experience to be felt as a totality: all its events, all its partial facts and elements are immediately grasped as part of a total process, even though this essentially social process may still be understood in metaphysical terms. For the most important aspect of this feeling of totality for us is not at the moment the ideological explanation given it but rather its immediate presence or absence in that particular social life from which the writer draws his raw material. As we have already shown, if this feeling of immediate wholeness and interrelationship is not there in real life to begin with, the artist has no means at his disposal to restore it; at best he can only simulate it.

In the *Theory of the Novel*, Lukács' first full-scale attempt to apply these categories to literature, they take the form of an opposition between essence (*Wesen*) and life, or in

169

other words, between meaningfulness on the one hand and the events and raw materials of daily existence on the other. The development of forms in ancient Greece provides him with a kind of scale model or dialectical myth of the various possibilities, the various relationships, inherent in this basic opposition. (And we should add that for the moment the historical accuracy of this picture of ancient Greece is of no consequence for us: we may take it merely as a convenient conceptual framework for the presentation of Lukács' discussion of the modern novel.)

The first of the three basic stages which Lukács finds in Greek literature is that of the epic, which is concrete in the sense developed above: in it meaning or essence is still immanent to life, and genuine narration, epic narration, is possible only when daily life is still felt to be meaningful and immediately comprehensible down to its smallest details. After this Utopia, in which essence and life are one, the two terms begin to fall apart, and the place of epic is taken by tragedy. For in tragedy meaning and daily existence have become opposed to each other: they coincide only at the moment of the tragic crisis itself, when the hero holds them together for an instant in his own agony, maintaining his absolute demands on life, his ultimate passion for meaning, even on the point of destruction by that meaningless outside world which denies him. Tragedy therefore no longer offers a continuity, but is organized around and dependent on those heightened instants of crisis alone, fitful and unstable in their very structure. When they also disappear, when meaning and life part company irreparably, then the third stage of Greek art is at hand, that of Platonic philosophy. Here, in a world in which the raw materials of daily life have become utterly worthless, essence or meaning takes refuge in the purely intellectual realm of the Ideas, and has, except insofar as it expresses itself in the Platonic myths and fables, become itself unrealizable.

Already, in spite of their common methodology, the differences between the Lukács of *Theory of the Novel* and Hegel himself, particularly in the *Aesthetik*, become apparent. Despite the great value Hegel places on the Greeks, he sees the history of Western art, and history in general, as an ascension of forms, from the symbolic forms of Oriental art, in which the spirit is still caught and imprisoned in matter, in the monstrous forms of the Assyrian and Egyptian deities, through the classical forms of Greece, in which spirit finds its adequate expression in the purely human figure, to the Romantic art of the modern world, in which matter little by little falls away and pure spirit comes to expression in language. No doubt Hegel had already felt the novel to be a modern replacement of epic, in Lukács' sense. But for him, as is well known, the fulfillment of art lies not in any art form but in its self-transcendence, in the transformation of art into philosophy: what human beings at first naïvely projected in religion, what they then made visible to themselves in artistic creation, they ultimately bring to self-consciousness only in philosophy itself.

But for Lukács, as we will see again and again in varying contexts, pure thought never has absolute value as a privileged means of access to reality. On the contrary, it is narration which is for him the absolute, and even the preliminary sketch of the stages of Greek art has as its premise the primacy of narration. Only the epic can be considered a purely narrative form: tragedy is drama—that is to say, it presents instants only, can no longer have recourse to the techniques of narrative continuity; and in philosophy, of course, the dominance of pure thought, far from being a virtue, is judged and evaluated precisely by its elimination of narration as a formal possibility.

It is against this preliminary background that the basic idea of the *Theory of the Novel* emerges: the novel as a form is the attempt in modern times to recapture something

171

of the quality of epic narration as a reconciliation between matter and spirit, between life and essence. It is a substitute for epic, under life conditions which henceforth make the epic impossible: "it is the epic of a world abandoned by God."[4]

As such, the novel is no longer a closed and established form with built-in conventions, like tragedy or epic; rather, it is problematical in its very structure, a hybrid form which must be reinvented at every moment of its development. Each novel is a process in which the very possibility of narration must begin in a void, without any acquired momentum: its privileged subject matter will therefore be the search, in a world in which neither goals nor paths are established beforehand. It is a process in which we witness the very invention of those problems whose solution is its story. Where the epic hero represented a collectivity, formed part of a meaningful, organic world, the hero of the novel is always a solitary subjectivity: he is problematical; that is to say, he must always stand in opposition to his setting, to nature or society, inasmuch as it is precisely his relationship to them, his integration into them, which is the issue at hand.[5] Any reconciliation between the hero and his environment which was given from the beginning of the book and not painfully won in the course of it would stand as a kind of illicit presupposition, a kind of cheating with

---

[4] Georg Lukács, *Theorie des Romans* (Neuwied, 1962), p. 87. In this sense Lukács' book may be seen as an application of the categories of Max Weber's social analyses to the various plot structures, which take their place in a characteristic Weberian dialectic between human activity and that essential meaning which may no longer be immanent to it, but rather transcendent and otherworldly, or indeed, as in the bureaucratic and secularized (*entzauberte*) world, wholly missing: as with Weber also, these analyses find their ultimate fulfillment in a typology.

[5] Lucien Goldmann's theory of the problematical hero, which emphasizes this aspect of the novel's content at the expense of other, more formal elements, seems to me far more limited than the idea of Lukács which inspired it.

the form, in which the whole novel as process would be invalidated. The prototype of the novel's hero is therefore the madman or the criminal; the work is his biography, the story of his setting forth to "prove his soul" in the emptiness of the world. But of course he can never really do so, for if genuine reconciliation were possible, then the novel as such would cease to exist, would once more give place to epic wholeness.

Thus the novel, as an attempt to give meaning to the outside world and to human experience, is always the result of subjective will, subjective willfulness. It is not the world from which such unity springs, as in the epic, but rather the mind of the novelist which attempts to impose it, by fiat. For this reason, the activity of the novelist always takes place under the sign of what the German Romantics called Irony; for Romantic irony is characterized by a structure in which the work takes its own subjective origin into account, in which the creator completes his creation by pointing to himself: *larvatus prodeo*. Thus it can be said that for Lukács the most basic image of human freedom is not the hero of the novel, for he can never succeed in his quest for ultimate meaning, but rather the novelist himself, who in telling the story of failure succeeds—whose very creation stands as that momentary reconciliation of matter and spirit toward which his hero strives in vain. The creative activity of the novelist is the "negative mysticism of godless epochs."[6]

The novel therefore has ethical significance. The ultimate ethical goal of human life is Utopia, that is, a world in which meaning and life are once more indivisible, in which man and the world are at one. But such language is abstract, and Utopia is not an idea but a vision. It is therefore not abstract thought, but concrete narration itself that is the proving ground for all Utopian activity, and the great

[6] *Theorie des Romans,* p. 90.

novelists offer a concrete demonstration of the problems of Utopia in the very formal organization of their styles and intrigues themselves, whereas the Utopian philosophers only offer a pallid and abstract dream, an insubstantial wish-fulfillment.

Given the opposition between matter and spirit on which Lukács' theory rests, it is clear that novels will tend to fall into two general groups, depending on which term is accented. Yet in another sense the simplicity of this typology is deceptive, for the starting point of the novel must always be subjective, must always be human experience: the objective term, the outside world, scarcely bothers to dream of its reconciliation with man. So the world-oriented novel (which Lukács calls the novel of *abstract idealism*) proves to be based on a kind of optical illusion. Its hero is characterized by a blind and unshakable conviction in the world's meaning, by an unjustified and obsessive faith in the success of his quest in the here and now, in the very possibility of reconciliation. For such an obsessed hero (whose prototype is of course Don Quixote), the apparent resistance of the real world can be easily accounted for by magic and the hostile operations of evil sorcerers: thus he never really comes into contact with outside reality, but only with that Utopian vision of it which was his starting point. The paradoxical effect of such an attitude upon the form is that the novel of abstract idealism will result in a series of objective events and adventures, will offer a seemingly objective surface, even though this surface objectivity is nothing but the result of madness and subjective obsession.

The precondition for the creation of *Don Quixote* was a social world in which secular rationality was still imperfectly disengaged from the superstitious and ritualistic world view of the Middle Ages, in which, therefore, Don Quixote's madness was not capricious, but corresponded to a reality in the outside world itself. This reality is of course interiorized in the novel in the form of the romances and dreams of chivalry, so that the novel as a whole becomes not the unquestioned and degraded storytelling of these popular adventure stories, but a reflection on the very possibility of storytelling itself, a coming to self-consciousness of narration. Yet as the modern world grows increasingly secularized, the tension which gave *Don Quixote* its vitality begins to dissolve: the heroes of abstract idealism no longer find their justification in their moment of history, but tend increasingly to become arbitrary, mere grotesques, whose *idée fixe* is capricious; and in a novelist like Dickens we find a static, lifeless opposition between amusing eccentrics on the one hand, and a sentimentalized middle-class universe on the other (sentimentalized precisely because the novelist has taken it at face value, has smuggled into his work a preconception as to the nature of that external reality which it was the business of the novel to explore without any preconceptions).

Only in Balzac perhaps is some ultimate version of the novel of abstract idealism possible; and even here, in the henceforth secularized world, it is based on a formal tour de force. On the one hand, we find the familiar obsessed hero, the man of an *idée fixe*, inventor, poet, businessman, aristocrat. Yet the second term of the opposition, that outside reality without which no tension is possible, is now nothing more than the sum total of all the other obsessed characters of *La Comédie humaine*, or in other words, of society itself. Thus once more a genuine totality comes into being in which the other works of the series provide a density of external reality, a massive resisting outside world, for use in the individual conflict within any given story. Yet obviously this tension is bought at great cost: *La Comédie humaine* is what Sartre would call a detotalized totality; it is never completely present in any individual work, only the fragments of the whole are fully realized

175

before us. With Balzac the novel of abstract idealism is exhausted as a form; the reality of the modern world no longer offers adequate materials for its construction.

So slowly the second general type of narration, the novel of *romantic disillusionment*, comes into being to replace the first. Here the emphasis is squarely on the soul itself, on the subjective experiences of the hero, whose task is to interpret the world from within his own consciousness. Where the first form threatened to disintegrate into a series of empty adventures, into hollow picaresque or entertainment literature, this second type of novel is immediately menaced by solipsism. Its hero is passive-receptive, contemplative, and his story is forever on the point of dissolution into the purely lyrical and fragmentary, into a series of subjective moments and moods in which genuine narration is lost.

Yet at this point Lukács makes one of his most remarkable observations (and it has often been pointed out that in this he anticipates the whole direction of the modern novel at a time—1914—when it was only just coming into being). For whereas the external world of the earlier novel form was primarily spatial, whereas the hero's experience of such a world took the form of a series of adventures and wandering through geographical space, now, in the novel of romantic disillusionment, the dominant mode of being of external reality will be time itself. It is this shift in metaphysical emphasis which will save the most illustrious examples of the new form, such as Flaubert's *Education sentimentale*, from mere static poetry, which will once more justify and permit a kind of genuine narration in them. Now once again the passive-contemplative hero can act, his life can be told as a story: yet these acts are now acts in time, are hope and memory. Now once again the novel can express a kind of unity of meaning and life, but it is a unity thrust into the past, a unity remembered only. For in the present the world always defeats the hero, frustrates his

176

longing for reconciliation: yet when he remembers his failure, paradoxically he is at one with it. The process of memory has therefore drawn the resistant outside world into subjectivity, there, in the past, reinstating a kind of unity with it. In this the remembering hero is a little like the novelist himself: for both, time is profoundly ambiguous in nature, a force both life-giving and life-destroying. In the hero's life it is the source of all pain, all loss, the very element in which he comes to know the vanity of human existence. Yet time is also the very fabric of life itself, for reader as well as for hero the very substance of experience; it is therefore at once duration and flow, and founds the density of the narrative at the same moment at which the latter tells of the tragic passage and ephemerality of all things.

After these two basic types of narration, Lukács presents us with attempts at synthesis, in Goethe's *Wilhelm Meister* and in the novels of Tolstoy. And as we might expect, these syntheses are themselves polarized into subjective and objective orientations respectively. In *Wilhelm Meister* a hero of a relatively passive-receptive, romantic type ends by discovering a meaningful external universe, a social environment which no longer resists the individual, but offers fulfillment to his subjective talents and potentialities: one which is not characterized by dehumanized, alienated institutions, but rather reflects purpose in its hierarchy of tasks, and is therefore once more on a human scale. Yet this reconciliation is based on a tour de force: for the form of the book as a whole is dependent on the existence of the masonic elite who appear at its conclusion. All the apparently accidental adventures and encounters of Wilhelm Meister turn out to be deliberate tests and object lessons planned for him by this all-knowing priestly caste into which he is then ultimately received. Thus the apparent solidity of Goethe's novel is the result of a forcing, a deformation, of external reality along the lines of wish-fulfillment: Utopia is not won concretely line by line, but established by fiat at the end of the book, which reaches back and transforms the beginning.

Tolstoy, on the other hand, profits from the existence in his historical situation of an element absent from the experience of the Western European novelist: the presence of nature itself, which grounds the portrayal of the external world, the second term of the novelist's opposition, with renewed solidity. Whereas in the West the drama of the individual and his passions was opposed to the empty conventionality of his society, in Tolstoy both of these phenomena are seen as ultimately deformed and vitiated, both enter into opposition with nature itself, with glimpses of some primal reunified genuine natural existence. Yet once again this tension is a precarious one: for it depends not on any realized and fully achieved narration of the natural term, the natural life, but on mere lyric glimpses of what such a life might be. In this sense Tolstoy falls short of a reinvention of the epic, creating fragments that strive toward epic unity only.

For it is clear to Lukács, at the end of his work, that the transformation of novel into epic has as its precondition not the novelist's will but the transformation of his society and his world. The renewed epic cannot come into being until the world itself has been transfigured, regenerated; and his final comment, that the novels of Dostoyevsky offer a glimpse into such an ultimate, totally humanized Utopia, must be taken more in the way of prediction than of formal analysis.

The great richness and suggestiveness of the *Theory of the Novel* result more from the problems its speculative framework permits it to raise than from the solutions it offers. In the first place, there is in it a contradiction between form and content which ultimately casts doubt on its conclusions. For on the formal level, as an analysis of the

work of the novelist himself, of his perpetual effort to reconcile spirit and matter, the *Theory of the Novel* is irre-
proachable; yet insofar as the book also involves a theory
of the hero, a theory of the novel's content, we may be sur-
prised to detect a whole set of hidden presuppositions, a
whole preconceived psychology which is in conflict with the
neutral or purely formal Hegelian conceptual framework
of the rest of the book. Here indeed we find Lukács describing the hero's quest as an attempt to "prove his soul"
(Browning), to overcome the primal homesickness of being
by "returning home" in a metaphysical sense (Novalis:
"Immer nach Hause!"), by reintegrating that "transcendental site" which was the original dwelling of the soul. The
objection is not to this doctrine as such, which has its own
fascination for the modern mind and suggests ideas of Heidegger and Kierkegaard, but to its incompatibility with
Lukács' formal description of the novel as a process in
which no guidelines are given in advance, in which, therefore, even this characterization of man's metaphysical quest
in the world is not permissible, and stands as a preconceived
value imposed on the initial formlessness of existence.

We may state this contradiction in another way by recalling the degree to which all of Lukács' analyses of the novel
depend on what is a kind of literary nostalgia, on the notion
of a golden age or lost Utopia of narration in Greek epic.
No doubt, as we indicated above, such a conception of literary history may simply be taken as an organizational fiction, as a mythological framework, for the concrete analyses
of the book; yet in the long run, the historical inadmissibil-
ity of the framework returns to vitiate the individual
analyses. By the same token, any change in the framework
will entail a far-reaching reevaluation of the empirical history of the novel itself. Obviously the ultimate realization
of a reconciled universe will now be projected into the
future, and with such a shift in perspective we are already

179

well within a Marxist theory of history. But more than this, we would expect the removal of the idea of a golden age to result in a new interpretation of modern literature as well, and to allow for the possibility of at least partial moments of reconciliation in modern times, of at least isolated examples of genuinely concrete works of art, in a way which the overall historical scheme of the *Theory of the Novel* seemed to preclude.

Yet even in the Hegelian framework of the book itself there are weaknesses which Lukács' later work will attempt to rectify: the aim of the work is the creation of a typology, of a characteristically Hegelian working out of pure formal possibilities in the chronological unfolding of history itself. The evident weakness of such a typological viewpoint can be seen in such passages as the one in which Lukács, having established the novel of romantic disillusionment as a general category, as a genus, admits that it has perhaps only one genuine representative or member, namely Flaubert's *Education sentimentale*. And just as Marx, standing the Hegelian dialectic on its feet, dissolved the Hegelian series of ideal forms into the empirical reality of history itself, so from this logical defect of the *Theory of the Novel* it is but a step to the abandonment of novelistic *types* as such, to the apprehension of Flaubert's work itself as a unique concrete empirical historical phenomenon, as a unique moment of the history of the novel, an ungeneralizable combination of circumstances. At this point, then, we would expect further development along the lines of the *Theory of the Novel* to result in the replacement of the all-encompassing typological theory by a series of concrete historical monographs, by a dissolution into concrete literary history itself.

Finally, it should be noted that even within the framework of the *Theory* itself there are signs of an important shift in perspective. In the first two typological chapters (those which defined the novels of abstract idealism and of romantic disillusionment), the content of the novel was characterized as an opposition between man and the outside world. Even when the resistance to the hero comes in the shape of other characters, Lukács basically thinks of this resistance in terms of a struggle between man and his environment, between man and the universe, between man and things: the human elements of the conflict are always assimilated to the more general category of the world itself, the Not-I, the being of nature. Such a way of looking at the drama of human life cannot but be metaphysical, for the basic model is always the relationship of man to some absolute outside himself.

Yet when we turn to the chapters on Goethe and Tolstoy, we find that, perhaps without any conscious awareness on Lukács' part, this metaphysical second term, the world, has imperceptibly glided into a new one, namely society. But at this point everything changes, and the very quality of the opposition is different: the new tension is not a metaphysical but a historical one, and man's relationship to his social environment is no longer the static and contemplative one of his metaphysical situation in the universe. For society is an evolving and changing organism, and for the first time it is given to the hero of the novel as Lukács sees him not only to contemplate his distance from external reality in a fixed manner, but to *change* it. Now external reality is not alien to him, but of the same substance as himself, for it is history, and the result of the activities of men. At this point, therefore, there intervenes Vico's great insight, so significant for Marxism and indeed for historiography in general, that we understand what we have made, so that it is history rather than nature which constitutes the privileged object of human knowledge.[7] Thus in the very working out of the

---

[7] "The world of civil society has certainly been made by men . . . its principles are therefore to be found within the modifications of our own human mind. Whoever reflects on this cannot but marvel that the philosophers should have bent all their energies to the study

problems of the *Theory of the Novel* itself there are decisive signs of that shift from a metaphysical to a historical view of the world that will be ratified by Lukács' conversion to Marxism. Indeed, I would be tempted to reverse the causal relationship as it is generally conceived, and to claim that if Lukács became a Communist, it was precisely because the problems of narration raised in the *Theory of the Novel* required a Marxist framework to be thought through to their logical conclusion.

II

LUKÁCS' NEXT WORK, *History and Class Consciousness* (1923), would, however, seem to have little to do with these purely literary problems. Its title is misleading enough, for the new book is not so much political as it is epistemological, and aims at laying the foundation in a technical manner for a new Marxist theory of knowledge. By "class consciousness," therefore, Lukács means not so much an empirical and psychological phenomenon, or those collective manifestations explored by sociology, but rather the a priori limits or advantages conferred by affiliation with the bourgeoisie or the proletariat upon the mind's capacity to apprehend external reality. Thus this immensely influential work of Lukács distinguishes itself from the outset from the more familiar Western critique of *ideology* as it is practiced by such writers as Lucien Goldmann and Sartre. For the concept of ideology already implies mystification, and conveys the notion of a kind of floating and psychological

---

of the world of nature, which, since God made it, He alone knows; and that they should have neglected the study of the world of nations, or civil world, which, since men had made it, men could come to know" (Giambattista Vico, *The New Science*, trans. T. G. Bergin and M. H. Fisch [Ithaca, N.Y., 1968], p. 96). See also Erich Auerbach, "Vico and Aesthetic Historicism," in *Scenes from the Drama of European Literature* (New York, 1959).

world view, a kind of subjective picture of things already by definition unrelated to the external world itself. The consequence is that even a proletarian world view is relativized, and felt to be ideological, while the ultimate standard of truth becomes the positivistic one of some "end of ideology" which would leave us in the presence of the facts themselves, without any subjective distortions.

It is, however, because Lukács takes so-called bourgeois philosophy seriously that he can evolve an adequate theory of proletarian knowledge. For him, we may say, what is false is not so much the *content* of classical middle-class philosophy as its *form*; and in this, Lukács applies to the realm of philosophy the method that Marx himself had already practiced in his critique of middle-class economics. For Marx's criticism of his predecessors (Smith, Say, Ricardo) was aimed not so much at the details of their work—theory of ground rent, market circulation, accumulation of capital, etc.—most of which he takes over into his own system, but rather at the overall model, or lack of it, in which these details find their interpretation, in which they are to be put in perspective as parts or functions of some larger totality. Marx is able to show not only that the middle-class economists were unable to evolve a unified field theory into which these various empirically observed phenomena might be integrated, but indeed that they instinctively avoided doing so. It was as though they sensed the dangerous social and political consequences of the kind of total and systematic model of economic reality which will later be embodied in *Das Kapital*; in order to avoid those consequences they are obliged to pursue their research on a fragmentary and empirical level only.

Marxism is frequently misunderstood as a theory of material or economic interest, even though at the level of individual psychology the notion of self-interest originates much earlier, at the time of Hobbes and La Rochefoucauld. Yet it would be less erroneous to claim that Marxism is a theory of *collective* or *class* self-interest. For while it is not at all surprising or paradoxical to find a man willing to sacrifice his immediate personal interests for some greater ideal or cause, the very passionate adherence to such a cause, its binding force, is almost certain to derive from its collective basis, from its structure as a defense mechanism of the group or class with which the individual feels himself at one. The member of a given class therefore defends not so much his own individual existence and privileges, as the very preconditions of those privileges in general: and in the realm of thought also he is willing to venture only to the point at which those preconditions begin to be called into question. We may therefore in a more abstract way say that the influence of class consciousness on thought is felt not so much in the perception of the individual details of reality as in the overall form or Gestalt according to which those details are organized and interpreted.

As with Marx's critique of middle-class economic theories, so also for the Lukács of *History and Class Consciousness* the limits of middle-class philosophy are signaled by its incapacity or unwillingness to come to terms with the category of *totality* itself. That this is no mere external standard of judgment but rather a dilemma with which the classical philosophers were themselves concerned may be seen in the orientation of pre-Marxist German philosophy around the problem of the universality of the individual subject or knower—a universality which is posited in abstract form only in the concept of the transcendental ego of Kant or in Hegel's Absolute Spirit. Lukács' originality is to have returned this abstract philosophical problem to its concrete situation in social reality itself, and to have posed the question of the relationship between universality on the epistemological level and the class affiliation of the individual thinker himself.

For Kant's critical philosophy had already assigned its ultimate limits to the universality to which middle-class rationalism had aspired. (For Kant, of course, these limits are not those of middle-class thought alone, but of the human mind in general: but this ahistorical manner of posing the problem only marks his profound identification with the type of thought he is studying.) According to Kant, the mind can understand everything about external reality except the incomprehensible and contingent fact of its existence in the first place: it can deal exhaustively with its own perceptions of reality without ever being able to come to terms with noumena, or things-in-themselves. For Lukács, however, this dilemma of classical philosophy, to which Kant's system is a monument, derives from an even more fundamental, prephilosophical attitude toward the world which is ultimately socio-economic in character: namely, from the tendency of the middle classes to understand our relationship to external objects (and consequently our *knowledge* of those objects) in static and contemplative fashion. It is as though our primary relationship to the things of the outside world were not one of making or use, but rather that of a motionless gaze, in a moment of time, suspended, across a gap which it subsequently becomes impossible for thought to bridge. The dilemma of the thing-in-itself becomes, then, a kind of optical illusion or false problem, a kind of distorted reflection of this initially immobile situation which is the privileged moment of middle-class knowledge.

Yet this static relationship to the objects of knowledge is itself but a reflection of the life experience of the middle classes in the economic and social realm. Their relationship to the objects that they produce, to the commodities, the factories, the very structure of capitalism itself is a contemplative one, in that they are not aware of capitalism as a historical phenomenon, as being itself the result of historical forces, as having within itself also the possibility of change or of radical transformation. They can understand everything about their social environment (its elements, its functioning, its implicit laws) except the sheer historical existence of that environment itself: their rationalism can assimilate everything but the ultimate questions of purpose and origin. In this sense, capitalism is itself the first thing-in-itself, and the primal contradiction upon which all later, more specialized and abstract dilemmas are founded.

When we turn now to the class consciousness of the worker, to those new possibilities of thought inherent in the structure of a proletarian epistemology, it is clearly not enough simply to claim that the philosophical problems are different, that the old problems and dilemmas no longer obtain. What Lukács must show is that proletarian thought has precisely the capacity for resolving antinomies which middle-class thinking by its very nature was unable to deal with. He must show how something in the structure of proletarian thought itself permits access to the totality or reality, to that totalizing knowledge which was the stumbling block of classical bourgeois philosophy, with the resultant replacement of the static model of knowledge from which the classical middle-class dilemmas sprang. Something must be found in the very existential situation of the proletarian himself which corresponds, as a concrete reality, to that union of subject and object, of knower and known, which Hegel posited as a solution to the Kantian problem of the thing-in-itself in the domain of pure thought. This privileged nature of the worker's situation lies, paradoxically, in its narrow, inhuman limits: the worker is unable to know the outside world in a static, contemplative manner in one sense because he cannot know it all, because his situation does not give the leisure to intuit it in the middle-class sense; because, even before he posits elements of the outside world as *objects* of his thought, he feels *himself* to be an object, and this initial alienation within himself takes precedence over everything else. Yet precisely in this terrible alienation lies the strength of the worker's position: his first movement is not toward knowledge of the work but toward knowledge of himself as an object, toward self-consciousness. Yet this self-consciousness, because it is initially knowledge of an object (himself, his own labor as a commodity, his life force which he is under the obligation to sell), permits him more genuine knowledge of the commodity nature of the outside world than is granted to middle-class "objectivity." For "his consciousness is the self-consciousness of merchandise itself, or in other words, it is the self-consciousness, or the revelation to consciousness of capitalist society based on commodity production and exchange."[8]

Implicit in this new type of self-consciousness are all the elements of a successful solution to those epistemological dilemmas in which middle-class thought found itself involved. It is commodities that structure our original relationship to objects of the world, that shape the categories through which we see all other objects. Yet such objects are ambiguous; they vary in appearance accordingly as their objective nature or their subjective origin is emphasized. Thus for the bourgeois, a commodity is a solid material thing whose cause is relatively unimportant, relatively secondary: his relationship to such an object is one of pure consumption. The worker, on the other hand, knows the finished product as little more than a moment in the process of production itself: his attitude toward the outside world will thereby be significantly altered.

For he will see the objects around him in terms of change,

---

[8] Georg Lukács, *Histoire et conscience de classe* (Paris, 1960), p. 210.

rather than in the timeless "natural" present of the middle-class universe (with its corresponding emphasis on man as a universal). Moreover, inasmuch as he knows the inter-relationship of tools and equipment to each other, he will come to see the outside world not as a collection of separate, unrelated things, but as a totality in which everything depends on everything else. Thus, in both of these ways, he will come to apprehend reality as process, and the *reification* into which the outside world had frozen for the middle classes will be dissolved. The privileged relationship to reality, the privileged mode of knowledge of the world will no longer be a static, contemplative one, will no longer be one of pure reason or abstract thought, but will be the union of thought and action that the Marxists call *praxis*, will be one of activity conscious of itself. At this point the Kantian problem of the thing-in-itself, of the predicate of being, is doubly resolved: first of all, being is found to be an abstraction, and the consideration of it as a separate phenomenon is bound to lead to antinomies, inasmuch as the basic reality of the world is one of becoming and process. And second, as was already foreshadowed in Hegel's system, the outside world, as the result of human labor, considered now not as nature but as history, is of the same substance as the subjectivity of the worker himself: the subjectivity of men can now be seen as the product of the same social forces that create commodities and ultimately the entire reality of the world in which men live.

Henceforth, following the usage of Lenin in *Materialism and Empiriocriticism*, Lukács will characterize the process of knowledge itself as one of a reflection (*Widerspiegelung*) of reality. But the various polemics to which the so-called reflection theory of knowledge has given rise may be avoided by seeing in this figure of speech not so much a theory in its own right as the sign of a theory to be elaborated: "the discovery of a reflection . . . always indicates the existence of an articulated link between at least two systems of relationships; the notion of *reflection* at this point functions as an indication ('signal') of this articulated link. But when it is a question of thinking this link as such . . . then the concept of *process* alone proves to be genuinely operative, that is to say productive of the knowledge of such a link."[9] The figure of the reflection of reality in thought is therefore simply a kind of conceptual shorthand designed to mark the presence of that type of mental operation we have elsewhere described as a *historical trope*, namely the setting in contact with each other of two distinct and incommensurate realities, one in the superstructure and the other in the base, the one cultural and the other socioeconomic.

We may now draw some conclusions as to the implications of *History and Class Consciousness* for the literary problems with which Lukács had previously been concerned. It would indeed seem that it is epistemology, and abstract philosophy in general, which tends under its own internal momentum to reduce the phenomenon of reflection to a static type of mental image more or less adequate to the realities outside. What Lukács describes as proletarian truth is, on the contrary, a sense of forces at work within the present, a dissolving of the reified surface of the present into a coexistence of various and conflicting historical tendencies, a translation of immobile objects into acts and potential acts and into the consequences of acts. Indeed, we are tempted to claim that for the Lukács of *History and Class Consciousness* the ultimate resolution of the Kantian dilemma is to be found not in the nineteenth-century philosophical systems themselves, not even in that of Hegel, but rather in the nineteenth-century *novel*: for the process he

[9] J. L. Houdebine, "Sur une lecture de Lénine," in *Tel Quel: Théorie d'ensemble* (Paris, 1968), pp. 295-296.

describes bears less resemblance to the ideals of scientific knowledge than it does to the elaboration of plot.

Thus, with its humiliation of middle-class philosophy, *History and Class Consciousness* lays the groundwork for that differentiation of the aesthetic experience which Lukács will later exhaustively work out in the *Aesthetik*,[10] where indeed narration is valorized in that it presupposes neither the transcendence of the object (as in science) nor that of the subject (as in ethics), but rather a neutralization of the two, their mutual reconciliation, which thus anticipates the life experience of a Utopian world in its very structure.

Yet inasmuch as the construction of Utopia henceforth no longer falls to literature, but rather to praxis and political action itself, the whole organizational framework of the *Theory of the Novel* must now be reconsidered. Now indeed that nostalgic vision of some golden age in which an epic wholeness was still possible gives place to a view of history which sees men as already implicitly reconciled to the world around them, in the sense in which that world is itself necessarily the result of human labor and human action. Yet the failure to see through the reified surface of the outside world is itself historically conditioned: for before the nineteenth century, when the bases of modern capitalism were laid in the form of thoroughgoing industrialization of the environment and worldwide organization of the market system, the prerequisites for a genuinely historical understanding of life were not yet complete. It was not until the nineteenth century, therefore, that what had previously been understood (and expressed) in terms of a conflict between man and destiny or nature can be narrated in the purely human and social categories of what Lukács will henceforth call *realism*.

[10] But already sketched out in the early "Subject-Object Relationship in Art," *Logos*, VII (1917-1918), 1-39.

III

AFTER *History and Class Consciousness*, therefore, there can be no question of a return to the kind of Hegelian and typological deduction of possible novelistic structures which had been undertaken in the *Theory of the Novel*. Now, on the contrary, Lukács sets himself the task of exploring the conditions of possibility of precisely those works which have been able to "reflect" social reality in its most concrete historicity, in short, of accounting theoretically for the existence of what he will call the great realists, of Goethe and Scott, Balzac, Keller, Tolstoy. That he will later shift, more questionably, from description to prescription and attack modern writers in the name of some a priori model of realism does not invalidate this starting point, where the word merely designates the empirical existence of a concrete body of works to be explored.

No doubt the most obvious and immediate method of characterizing what is distinctive in realism lies in an analysis of the content of the realistic works, and in particular of the human motif in them, of the characters themselves. For Lukács realistic characters are distinguished from those in other types of literature by their *typicality*: they stand, in other words, for something larger and more meaningful than themselves, than their own isolated individual destinies. They are concrete individualities and yet at the same time maintain a relationship with some more general or collective human substance. The notion of *typicality*, which for Western literary theory has become old-fashioned if not downright suspect, was already present in what must be the first full-scale specimen of Marxist literary criticism, namely the long exchange of letters between Marx, Engels, and Lassalle about the latter's play, *Franz von Sickingen*. It was therefore explicitly related to the problem of the historical drama or of the historical work of art in general; and

Lukács' own version of this idea is worked out at great length in his book *The Historical Novel.*

For if its relevance to other forms of literature may be questioned, there can be at least no doubt that the historical work, aiming explicitly at a picture of a whole period of history, bears thus in itself a standard by which it may then be judged, so that the question as to whether the characters and situation of a historical work are adequate to reflect the basic historical situation itself has validity in terms of the form itself. The problem is one of the role of the accidental and of the necessary in the work of art: Does the free shaping power of the historical playwright or novelist extend to certain kinds of liberties with the subject matter which he has (through his initial free choice) assigned himself? For Lassalle, the tragedy of Sickingen (which he meant to be exemplary of the general tragic situation of the German revolution in 1848) lay in a moral and intellectual flaw: the leader of the first revolt against the great princes during the upheavals of the German Reformation fell because of his ingrained diplomatic and political mentality, because as a statesman he allowed himself to be unduly fascinated with the intricacies of *Realpolitik* and intrigue among the princes and lost sight of the vital revolutionary energies generated by the revolutionary goal itself. Lassalle's defense of his play seems at first glance unanswerable: *this* was the tragedy he wanted to write, he tells Marx and Engels, although at the same time there were many others he could have chosen. Had he told the story of Thomas Münzer, he admits, the whole basis of the tragic situation would no doubt have been quite different.

But for Marx and Engels the play is faulty because the intellectual flaw which Lassalle stresses is not the real cause of Sickingen's downfall. This cause was not a moral but a social one: Sickingen could never have had the support of the revolutionary peasants because his basic social aim was

192

utterly different from theirs, focused not on a liberation of the land but on reestablishment of the petty nobility, which itself suffered from the domination of the great princes and of the church. Thus for Marx and Engels the tragic situation of Sickingen was an objective one, and had nothing to do with any agonizing moral choices inside his mind, any grandiloquent moral postures he might strike on stage. As the play stands, the character of Sickingen does not typify the real historical dilemma, the situation of the play does not give a genuine model of the forces at work during the period; and Marx and Engels show how all the formal weaknesses of the play (its endless speechifying, its reminiscences of Schiller rather than Shakespeare) flow from this more fundamental weakness, this inadequacy of the work to its raw material. The interest for us of such an analysis, as well as those of Lukács in *The Historical Novel*, which follow much the same line of reasoning, lies in the idea that the form of the work is dependent on some deeper logic of the raw material itself; the word *typical* merely serves as a name for the articulation into individual characters of this basic reality which is the substance or content of the work of art.

Of course this category has been mishandled in the vulgar Marxist practice of reducing characters to mere allegories of social forces, of turning "typical" characters into mere symbols of class, such as the petit bourgeois, the counterrevolutionary, the landed nobleman, the Utopian socialist intellectual, and so forth. Sartre has pointed out that such categories are themselves idealistic, in that they presuppose immutable forms, eternal Platonic ideas, of the various social classes: what they leave out is precisely history itself, and the notion of the unique historical situation, to which Lukács himself has always been faithful in his criticism.

We cannot here discuss the more immediate and interest-

193

ing features of Lukács' discussion of types in the historical novel, in particular his distinction between world-historical figures (that is to say, the great names of history, the Richelieus or Cromwells or Napoleons) and the average, relatively anonymous, invented figures that Scott, for example, places at the center of his novels. It is enough to point out that here, as everywhere, Lukács' method is a formal one; in this case it turns on a distinction between the forms of the drama and of the novel, and on the relative functional differences between characters in each. The great historical figures, the real leading actors of history, will be central in drama (Macbeth, Wallenstein, Galileo) because the dramatic collision is a far more concentrated and heightened one; whereas the novel, which aims at a total picture of the historical background, can only tolerate such figures in secondary, episodic appearances, for it is only in such a distant, secondary way that they appear in our everyday lives, in our own lived experience.

But the essential characteristics of the typical are to be found elsewhere: in particular, it should be noted that for Lukács the typical is never a matter of photographic accuracy. In that perennial confrontation of Balzac with Zola, to which we will return, he points out that the Balzacian character, as melodramatic as it is with its romantic exaggeration and unrealistic grotesqueness, is far more expressive of underlying social forces, is far more profoundly typical, than are the highly schematic, stereotyped characters of Zola (the rich peasant, the miner, the factory owner, the shopkeeper, and so forth), even though the latter would seem at first glance to be far more adequate to the basic aims of realism itself. It is as if, in the works of Zola, the idea, the preconceived theory, intervened between the work of art and the reality to be presented: Zola already *knows* what the basic structure of society is, and this is his weakness. For him the basic raw material, the professions,

194

the socially determined character types are already established in advance: this is to say that he has succumbed to the temptation of abstract thought, to the mirage of some static, objective knowledge of society. Implicitly he has admitted the superiority of positivism and science over mere imagination. But from Lukács' point of view, for which narration is the basic category and abstract knowledge a second best only, this means that the novel in Zola's hands has ceased to become the privileged instrument of the analysis of reality and has been degraded to a mere illustration of a thesis.

Whereas Balzac does not really know what he will find beforehand. The Avant-Propos to *La Comédie humaine* shows that his aim is to construct a typology, a vast zoology of human society, but that the vast energies of the work are released by the idea of a method, rather than by the discovery ahead of time of a kind of table of the basic elements. Moreover, Balzac's feeling for historicity and for historical change is so intense that he would be incapable of imagining a fixed archetype of the social types, of the petit bourgeois for example: the petit bourgeois in his work is always characteristic of a given period, of a given decade, he is in constant evolution, in his style of clothing, in his furniture, in his language and mentality, from the days of Napoleon to the last years of Louis-Philippe. Thus a Balzac character is not typical of a certain kind of fixed social element, such as class, but rather of the historical moment itself; and with this, the purely schematic and allegorical overtones of the notion of typicality disappear completely. The typical is not at this point a one-to-one correlation between individual characters in the work (Nucingen, Hulot) and fixed, stable components of the external world itself (finance aristocracy, Napoleonic nobility), but rather an analogy between the entire plot, as a conflict of forces, and the total moment of history itself considered as process.

At this point, it would perhaps be well to observe that this entire discussion of the content of works of art is in reality a formal one. If we began by seeming to discuss content, this was because of the nature of the historical novel or play itself, in which a built-in distinction between form and content is maintained in its very structure. For where the ordinary novel gives the illusion of absolutely disengaged reading, of a self-sufficient work which needs no object or model in the outside world, the historical novel is characterized by the manner in which it always holds such a model, such a basic external reality, before our eyes in the very act of reading it. It does not matter whether we have no intellectual interest whatsover in the historical exactitude of Scott's pictures of the Middle Ages, of Flaubert's Carthage, we cannot help but intuit this external reality, we cannot help but *intend* a real object (in the Husserlian sense), no matter how emptily and vaguely; the very structure of our reading of the historical novel involves comparison, involves a kind of judgment of being.

Thus, when we leave this specialized form and turn to the realistic novel in general, we may restate the above discussion in purely formal terms: but in these terms, the human elements of the work, the characters, become raw materials just like any others, just like the material settings of the book, for example, and the notion of the *typical*, no longer quite appropriate for this more general formal point of view, gives way to another kind of terminology. Here, the principal characteristic of literary realism is seen to be its antisymbolic quality; realism itself comes to be distinguished by its movement, its storytelling and dramatization of its content; comes, following the title of one of Lukács' finest essays, to be characterized by narration rather than description.

It is perhaps easiest to begin with the negative part of the definition, with that hostile diagnosis of symbolism which will be a constant throughout Lukács' career: for him, symbolism is not just one literary technique among others, but represents a qualitatively different mode of apprehending the world from the realistic one. Symbolism, we may say, is always a second best, always a kind of admission of defeat on the part of the novelist; for by having recourse to it the writer implies that some original, objective meaning in objects is henceforth inaccessible to him, that he must invent a new and fictive one to conceal this basic absence, this basic silence of things. The symbolic mode is of course not so much the result of the writer's personal aesthetic as of the historical situation itself: in their origin, all objects have a human meaning. Even nature itself is humanized, by the manner in which man makes his home within it, in which he converts it to his own use (thus the rocky and barren landscape of Greece is turned inside out like a glove, domesticated, by an economy that adapts to it with seafaring and commerce, artisanal production). This original meaningfulness of objects becomes visible only when their link with human labor and production is unconcealed. But in modern industrial civilization this link is hard to find: objects appear to lead an independent life of their own, and it is precisely this illusion which is the source of the symbolic. In Zola, the mine comes to be felt as a beast, nightmarishly inhabiting the landscape, devouring human flesh. In Joyce, the newspaper office comes to seem the cave of the winds: whatever realistic, historical meaning it also possesses has come to seem too drab and prosaic for the work of art. Henceforth the furniture in *The Spoils of Poynton*, the brooding cities of Dickens and Dostoyevsky, the morally expressive landscapes of a Gide or a D. H. Lawrence, exist in the work of art as self-sufficient elements, carrying their meaning built into them. Even the neutral objects of a Robbe-Grillet are the result of this symbolizing process: for they also reply, but by silence, and the eye continues to search them for some obsessive pattern, some immediate visual comprehensibility, which remains forever in doubt. Thus symbolism results not from the properties of the things themselves but from the will of the creator, who imposes a meaning on them by fiat: it represents the vain attempt of subjectivity to evolve a human world completely out of itself. In this, it is much like the earlier middle-class ethic of the moral imperative, the ideal or the *Sollen*, which Lukács criticizes in *Theory of the Novel*. In symbolic works of art, we strive for some meaningful relationship to the outside world, to objective reality, only to return empty-handed, having lived our life among shadows, having touched nothing but ourselves in the world around us.

This is perhaps the moment to comment on the rejection of modern art and of modernism in general which is implicit in this idea of Lukács. In Kafka's *Castle*, after one of the characters has shown K. that all of his actions can be interpreted in a quite different and far more unfavorable light, the hero replies: "It's not that what you say is false: it's just that it's hostile." Such might be the motto for Lukács' observations on modern art. It is both diagnosis and judgment: yet the whole dimension of judgment rests on an ambiguity, for it presupposes that the modernist writer has some personal choice in the matter, and that his fate is not sealed for him by the logic of his moment in history. The same ambiguity is visible in Marxist revolutionary theory as well, where the revolution cannot come into being until all the objective conditions are ripe for it, but where at the same time Lenin can apparently force this condition by sheer willpower, can create a proletarian revolution before the preceding middle-class revolution has had time to run its course.

If, therefore, we set aside that part of Lukács' work which constitutes a set of recommendations to the artist (and which is complicated by the fact that Lukács aims here at two publics at once—at the writers of socialist realism just as much as at the "critical realists" of the West), we find that his analysis of modernism is based on a fundamental fact of modern art: namely, the observation of a qualitative leap in recent times, of an absolute difference between that literature which is ours, and which began around the time of Baudelaire and Flaubert, and the classical literature which preceded it. No doubt, depending on the width of our historical lens, this absolute break could be located earlier, perhaps around the beginning of the nineteenth century, with the French Revolution and German Romanticism. In this connection it is significant that the attitude of Lukács reproduces almost exactly that of Goethe and Hegel toward Romanticism itself. Classicism is the healthy, said Goethe, Romanticism the sick. And Hegel criticized the subjectivism of the Romantics in much the same terms that Lukács reserves for the modernists. The judgment is the inevitable one that a philosophy of the concrete must pass on the abstract, and it should be added that it is very often precisely from a relatively old-fashioned, anticontemporary, even reactionary viewpoint (see Yvor Winters and, indeed, Edmund Burke himself) that the most penetrating analyses of the actual are made. The advantage of Lukács over sympathetic theoreticians of the modern lies in the differentiating and profoundly comparative thought mode which is his. He is not inside the modern phenomenon, completely given over to its fundamental values, able to see it only through its own eyes: he can define it and mark off its limits as a historical moment from that which it is not; yet such comparisons will always, in their very structure, seem to imply a judgment on the side of the older term.

At this point it should be noted that Lukács' criticism of modernism was already implicit in the *Theory of the Novel* itself. We showed how the four typological chapters of the

199

latter tended to fall into two groups, the first (on the two basic types) apprehending man's relationship to the world in a metaphysical way, the second (on Goethe and Tolstoy) seeing it in social or historical terms. It was no accident that the first two chapters were so rich in suggestions and intimations of modernism: for modern or symbolic art is characterized precisely by its ahistorical, metaphysical way of viewing human life in the world. The distinction between realism and symbolic modernism was therefore already present in the shift toward a novel which apprehended reality, and the human environment, in terms of human history. Thus, by a kind of detour, we find that the basic methodology of the earlier work, the separation between soul and world, meaning and life, retains its vitality in the later writings: it has merely gone underground, and, having shed its familiar Hegelian terminology, will continue to inform the distinction between symbolism and realism, between a merely willed synthesis between meaning and life and one which is somehow present in a concrete way in the historical situation itself.

Yet for Lukács the symbolic mode of presentation is itself merely a symptom of some deeper underlying mode of apprehension which he will call description, that is, a purely static contemplative way of looking at life and experience which is the equivalent in literature to the attitude of bourgeois objectivity in philosophical thought. For the realistic mode of presentation, the possibility of narration itself, is present only in those moments of history in which human life can be apprehended in terms of concrete, individual confrontations and dramas, in which some basic general truth of life can be told through the vehicle of the individual story, the individual plot. Yet such moments have become relatively rare in modern times: and there are others in which nothing real ever seems to happen, in which life is felt as waiting without end, perpetual frustration of the ideal (Flaubert); in which the only reality of human existence seems to be blind routine and the drudgery of daily work, forever the same day after day (Zola); in which, finally, the very possibility of events seems to have disappeared, and the writer seems relatively reconciled to a framework in which the truth of the single day can stand as the microcosm of life itself (Joyce). In these historical situations, even when the literary work itself seems violent and agitated, such explosions will turn out on closer inspection to be mere imitations of events, pseudoevents, imposed from above by the novelist, who despairs of evolving any genuine events from the colorless stream of experience itself. Indeed, melodrama (as in Zóla) is one of the principal devices by which modern literature has sought to conceal its contradictions: the violent clash between larger-than-life collective units (the mob in *Germinal*, the barbarians in *Salammbô*) or between absolute good and evil conceals the absence of any genuine human interrelationship on the individual level, in individual lived experience. And where modernism resolutely assumes its situation, it abandons plot entirely, renounces narration in the older sense, and seeks to make a strength of its basic weakness.

Thus description, as a dominant mode of representation, is the sign that some vital relationship to action and to the possibility of action has broken down. Lukács compares the horse race in Zola's *Nana* with the similar episode in *Anna Karenina*. The first is a brilliant set piece observed from the outside, having little to do with the fates of the characters. In the second, the characters are passionately involved: lengthy external descriptions are unnecessary because we feel the intensity of the event, not through visual contemplation, but through the hopes and expectations of the characters themselves. Thus description begins when external things are felt to be alienated from human activity, come to be viewed as static things-in-themselves; but it is fulfilled

201

when even the human beings who inhabit these lifeless settings become themselves dehumanized, become lifeless
tokens, mere objects in motion to be rendered from the
outside.

Lukács tends to account for the realistic, genuinely narrative moments in literature in two ways: through the personal situation and attitudes of the writers themselves, and
through their objective historical situation. The analysis of
the subjective precondition of realism forms a parallel to
the analysis of the preconditions of knowledge of the totality in *History and Class Consciousness,* although on the
literary plane the explanation may seem relatively simplistic: the great realists, Lukács tells us, are those who somehow fully participated in the life of their times, who were
not mere observers, but actors also, "engaged" in a far less
limited and political sense than in Sartre's familiar usage.
Yet in his examples of such engagement, Lukács follows his
materialism through to a further and even paradoxical conclusion: if it is the material substructure, the social situation that takes precedence over mere opinion, ideology, the
subjective picture someone has of himself, then we may
logically be forced to conclude that under certain circumstances a conservative, a royalist, a believing Catholic can
better seize the genuine forces at work in society than a
writer whose sympathies are relatively socialistic. This is
the ultimate force of Lukács' comparison between Balzac
and Zola. It may seem willful and perverse to claim that the
champion of Dreyfus was detached from the basic issues of
his time; yet even so unpolitical a writer as Henry James
shrewdly observed not only that Zola's political engagement
followed the end of his creative career in literature, serving
as a substitute for the latter, but also that it seemed to reflect some nagging sense of unfulfillment in the writer's private life as well, some feeling that he had never really come
to grips with genuine experience. And there can be no ques-

tion that Zola's methods of work (a kind of rationalistic division of labor, choice of theme before characters, careful background documentation and notes, a visit to the locale, and so forth) are those of the observing outsider rather than the imaginative participant./Whereas Balzac, for all his intellectual and moral criticism of the age of the middle classes, the secular corruption of the July Monarchy, lived out its basic ambitions and drives in his very bones, in his life passions, dreaming of the riches of the Sardinian silver mines, of a quick fortune made in the theater, feverishly collecting spurious treasures, furnishing one house after another, longing for the ultimate stability of the landed proprietor, finding the causal forces of his moment in history already full-blown within himself, without having to observe them in others, from the outside. No doubt it is vain to recommend such a life as a model for the realistic writer, as Lukács sometimes seems to do: but it should be pointed out that newer kinds of psychological analyses, such as Sartre's of Flaubert, are merely refinements, using psychoanalytic techniques, on this basic model. Thus the formal practice of Flaubert is seen as reflecting his detachment from the possibilities of lived action in his situation as a second son to whom the practical fulfillments of middle-class life seemed denied.

But this subjective disposition of the realistic writer is only the reverse of the objective possibilities of the historical situation in which he lives, and which his work reflects. It was Balzac's historical luck to have witnessed, not the later, fully evolved and finished capitalism of the time of Flaubert and Zola, but the very beginnings of capitalism in France; to have been contemporary with a social transformation which permitted him to see objects not as completed material substances but as they issued from human work; to have been able to apprehend social change as a network of individual stories. We can dramatize this by saying that in Balzac, factories do not yet exist as such: we watch not the end products but the efforts of the great capitalists and inventors to construct them. Social and economic reality is still relatively transparent, the result of human activity still visible to the naked eye. But the only factory in the works of Flaubert is that pottery works which is but a passing stage in Arnoux's checkered career, and through which Frédéric passes with infinite boredom, attentive only to Madame Arnoux's eyes and hands as she patiently explains the mechanics of production ("'Ce sont les patouillards,' she said. He found the word grotesque, somehow wholly unsuitable in her mouth."). Like Frédéric, Flaubert is condemned by his historical situation to a life of monotonous tourism amid industrial monuments that mean nothing to him. And as has already been shown, when Zola, impatient with this massive lifelessness, tries to breathe vitality into it, he can do so only by recourse to myth and melodramatic violence.

Thus realism is dependent on the possibility of access to the forces of change in a given moment of history. At the time of Balzac such forces are those of beginning capitalism, but the nature of the forces is not itself so important: for in another situation, Tolstoy's literary vitality comes from the existence in Russian society of the rising class of the peasantry, with which he identifies himself in a Utopian and religious manner, but whose very presence gives him a strength inaccessible to his Western contemporaries. (Here also, it should be noted that the analysis of the *Theory of the Novel* is maintained: except that for the relatively metaphysical formulation of a primal nature in Tolstoy's environment, Lukács here substitutes the social reality behind the ideal of nature and the natural life, namely the peasantry itself.)

Thus that ideal of the concrete which was inscribed in the *Theory of the Novel* as a will to reestablish epic narration remains intact in the later theory of realism, where it is shown, in the spirit of *History and Class Consciousness*, and indeed, like revolutionary praxis itself, to depend on those privileged historical moments in which access to society as a totality may once again somehow be reinvented. At the same time, the valorization of narrative implied here emphasizes a preoccupation which is increasingly central to the most divergent schools of modern thought. So in the best of the recent studies of the philosophy of history from an analytical point of view, an American philosopher has shown that even so-called scientific historiography may be said to have an essentially narrative structure;[11] while linguists like A. J. Greimas have reinforced such interests in their domain by analyzing all kinds of verbal materials, even abstract philosophical argumentation, in terms of a storytelling model which is itself but the central mechanism of the sentence as such.[12] Lukács' work, however, provides a theoretical framework for such essentially empirical observations through its insistence on the relationship between narrative and totality: it thus confirms the opinion of no less an expert than Martin Heidegger himself, who saw in Marxism not merely a political or economic theory but above all an ontology and an original mode of recovering our relationship to being itself.[13] But of such an opening onto being, now conceived as a social and historical substance, it is narration which is both the formal sign and the concrete expression.

[11] "It seems to me that there is just as much justification for the claim that we can reconstruct a 'scientific explanation' as a narrative, as there is for the reverse claim, and that an account in narrative form will not lose any of the explanatory force of the original" (Arthur C. Danto, *Analytical Philosophy of History* [Cambridge, Eng., 1965], p. 237).

[12] A. J. Greimas, *Sémantique structurale* (Paris, 1966), pp. 173-191.

[13] Heidegger, *Brief über den Humanismus* (Frankfurt, 1947), p. 27. Lukács' own projected *Ontologie* is described in his *Gespräche* with Holz, Kofler, and Abendroth (Hamburg, 1967).

CHAPTER FOUR

SARTRE AND HISTORY

> It has always seemed to me that a working hypothesis as
> fruitful as historical materialism never needed for a founda-
> tion the absurdity which is metaphysical materialism.
>
> —*Transcendance of the Ego* (1936)
>
> Some day I will undertake to describe that strange reality
> which is History, and which is neither completely objective
> nor completely subjective, in which the dialectic is resisted,
> pervaded and corroded by a kind of anti-dialectic, itself how-
> ever still dialectical in character.
>
> —*What is Literature?* (1947)[1]

THE CUSTOMARY description of the *Critique of Dialectical
Reason* as an attempt to reconcile existentialism and Marxism has always seemed to me to betray a fundamental
naïveté about the relationship of thought in general, and
political thought in particular, to our being as a whole, to
that total human reality of which it is an expression. Intellectual systems are not here opinions which can be tinkered
with, adjusted, manipulated until we somehow manage to
fit them together properly; and such an operation is all the
more ironic when it takes as its object two philosophical
approaches which explicitly deny the priority of thought
over being (existentialism with the principle that existence
precedes essence, Marxism with the teaching of the determination of consciousness by social reality). It seems to me,
indeed, that the situation is quite the reverse of what is
implied above: the very project of such a "reconciliation"
is the sign that it already *has* been effected in lived reality,
that somehow a lived synthesis of the two systems exists

---

[1] These are, according to Pietro Chiodi (*Sartre e il marxismo*
[Milan, 1965], pp. 21-22, note 9), the earliest hints in Sartre's works
of what will later become the *Critique de la raison dialectique* (Paris,
1960).

already, preceding, motivating, and founding the purely intellectual working out of the synthesis in the domain of thought. This is, indeed, what Sartre's account of his own intellectual development confirms. For Marxism was not something to which Sartre came *after* existentialism, but rather an interest concurrent with it, which has coexisted with the other philosophy throughout Sartre's career. It is worth stressing, for the American reader, the profound difference between the American and the European context in this respect: for in Europe Marxism is an omnipresent, living mode of thought, one with which every intellectual is bound to come into contact in one way or another, and to which he is obliged to react. Thus Sartre studied *Das Kapital* in 1925, two years *before* the publication of *Sein und Zeit*; his close friends Paul Nizan and Raymond Politzer were later to become leading theoreticians of the French Communist Party. Most significant, however, in his own words, "was the *reality* of Marxism, the heavy presence on my horizon of the masses of workers, an enormous, somber body which *lived* Marxism, which *practiced* it, and which at distance exercised an irresistible attraction on petit bourgeois intellectuals."[2] We will return to this "attraction at distance" later on, for it is one of the fundamental lessons that the *Critique* has to teach us.

Thus one of the most striking characteristics of Marxism as a philosophy is underscored in Sartre's experience, which is not an atypical one: that Marxism as such, for whatever reason, does not seem to exclude the adherence to some other kind of philosophy; that one can be both a Marxist and an existentialist, phenomenologist, Hegelian, realist, empiricist, or whatever. No doubt this paradox is partly the result of the ambiguity of the verb to be—as though it

[2] J. P. Sartre, *Search for a Method*, trans. Hazel Barnes (New York, 1963), p. 18.

meant something to say that someone "is" a Marxist or an existentialist or whatever. The more basic explanation is, however, that Marxism takes as its object something utterly distinct from the object of the more academic philosophical systems; that there can be no contradiction (even where the exact relationship of the two remains to be worked out) because two wholly different types of reality, which each mode of thought properly governs, miss each other in mid-air, as it were, fail to intersect at any point. "We were convinced," says Sartre of his generation, "*at one and the same time* that historical materialism furnished the only valid interpretation of history, and that existentialism remained the only concrete approach to reality."[3] Marxism is a way of understanding the objective dimension of history from the outside; existentialism a way of understanding subjective, individual experience. The "search for a method" therefore does not take the form of a reconciliation of contraries, but rather of a kind of unified field theory in which two wholly different ontological phenomena can share a common set of equations and be expressed in a single linguistic or terminological system.

This is what Sartre himself means when he describes the relationship of an "ideology" (existentialism) to a "philosophy" (Marxism): implying thereby that a genuine contradiction could only take place between two entities of the same type, between two different "philosophies." His model is, however, perhaps more useful than his terminology, which owing to the customary uses of these words seems to me to give rise to a number of false problems.

It is clear, however, that if the above description is correct, it will not logically be possible to describe the *Critique* as a radical break with the position of *Being and Nothingness*. The fact is that in genuinely Sartrean fashion the new book has *changed* the old; *Being and Nothingness* can no

[3] *Search for a Method*, p. 21.

longer be read in the same way after its appearance. The idea of logical inconsistencies between the two positions is a static one: it is more satisfactory to think that the *Critique* comes to complete *Being and Nothingness* in certain basic areas where it remained abstract or insufficiently developed; and that this act of completion, lifting all the problems onto a higher dialectical plane, ends by utterly transforming the very appearance of the earlier system.

The *Critique* is a difficult work and one which does not yet seem to have had all the attention and influence it deserves. For one thing, it aims at a multiple public (orthodox Marxists, orthodox existentialists, even American sociologists); for another, its style reflects the tortuous straining of the ideas it expresses toward totality ("each sentence," Sartre himself has said, "is as long as it is, as full of parentheses, of expressions between quotation marks, of 'qua's and 'inasmuch as's, only because each sentence represents the unity of a dialectical movement").[4] But the importance of the work may best be measured, perhaps, not in the realm of thought but in the realm of historical action itself: for the May Events of 1968, coming some eight years after the publication of the *Critique*, fully bear out its conclusions and testify to its significance as an expression of some of the deepest tendencies of its historical period.

I

The *Critique* and the brief *Search for a Method* that precedes it attack the same problem from opposite directions: the former as a theory about the collectives in and through which our individual lives are pursued, the latter as a method of interpreting those individual existences from within, working back from the individual life to the objec-

---

[4] Interview, *Revue d'esthétique*, XIX Nos. 3-4 (Winter, 1966), 329.

tivity of history. This pamphlet therefore completes the task Sartre had set for himself at the end of *Being and Nothingness*, that of laying the groundwork for a theory of existential psychoanalysis.

At the same time, it forces upon our attention something about Sartre's work which had not been so evident up until now: the crucial importance that the problem of *biography* has always had for him, the formative role which a self-conscious awareness of biographical models has played in all the forms his work has taken. For it is no accident that his first hero Roquentin should have been a biographer, with the peculiar anxiety caused by his own capricious power to arrange and rearrange the past: "Did Rollebon take part in the assassination of Paul the First or didn't he? That's the question for today: I've got that far and I can't go on without making up my mind."[5] For the past is essentially that about which one must "make up one's mind": it is sheer fact, inertia, it must be formed from the outside, by a *decision*. And in the earlier plays, particularly in *No Exit* and *Dirty Hands*, this basic indeterminacy of the past, this dizzying possibility of rearrangement of models, takes the form of a nagging uncertainty about *motivation*:

> GARCIN: Estelle, am I a coward?
> ESTELLE: But I don't know, honey, I'm not in your shoes.
> You have to make up your mind for yourself.
> GARCIN: I can't make up my mind.[6]

But the "solution" which is given in these plays is just as surely a repudiation of history-writing and of its claims to knowledge as is Roquentin's disgusted abandonment of his project ("It's my fault: I said the one thing I never should have said: I said that the past didn't exist. And with that, without a sound, M. de Rollebon returned to nothing-

---

[5] J. P. Sartre, *La Nausée* (Paris, 1962), p. 28.
[6] J. P. Sartre, *Théâtre* (Paris, 1947), pp. 171-172.

ness").[7] In the plays, the only way Garcin or Hugo can "really" decide why they did what they did is to go on acting in such a way that the rest of their lives, their future acts, confirm or refute the motivation decided on. Yet the implication of this revision of past by present[8] is that it is not the mere hypothesis of the historian which fixes the meaning of the past event in definitive form, but rather simply yet *another* concrete event in time. The biographer's model is an abstraction from three-dimensional existence: Sartre now modifies the segment of past events not by imposing a new form on it but by adding new events which alter its relative proportions. In other terms, his is an implied critique of the idea of motivation as self-contradictory.

In an earlier work, I showed how Sartre's novels resulted from the intersection of two different kinds of forces: the one a phenomenological sense of the expressiveness of objects, of the way in which objects reflect states of consciousness, the other a melodramatic impulse which shaped those relatively atemporal moments into a storyline.[9] It is now clear, however, that in order to account fully for the concrete determination of these works, yet a third line of force must be postulated: and this is precisely the biographical impulse itself. For it becomes apparent that character formation in the *Roads to Freedom* (particularly when we juxtapose them with the biographically oriented preparatory sketches of *The Wall*), turns out to be an attempt to resolve, by the doing, through novelistic practice, those problems of motivation and biography that the earlier plays had set for abstract thought. There the powerlessness of the abstract mind to analyze genuine three-dimensional action

[7] *La Nausée*, p. 138.

[8] See in particular "Mon Passé," *L'Etre et le néant* (Paris, 1948), pp. 577-585; and also Danto, *Analytical Philosophy of History, op.cit.,* Chap. VIII.

[9] Jameson, *Sartre: The Origins of a Style* (New Haven, 1961), pp. 189-192.

was demonstrated; here Sartre shows that even if the actual production of the act by a determinate personality remains inaccessible to analytical thought (and that act of production is what is called *freedom* in his terminology), nonetheless it is possible to *recreate* such action imaginatively. It is this which lends character formation in Sartre's novels its peculiar distinguishing qualities. For his characters are all virtually constructed around formulas: the clinical ones of *The Wall*, Boris with his obsession with aging and older people, Daniel with his pathological introspection, even Mathieu himself with his philosophical disengagement and "placelessness." Yet for all that they are not lifeless figures, since they do not submit to and undergo their formula or character like a destiny, but rather reinvent it at every instant: the theory of the "original choice" is the intellectual justification for this unity of character that we constantly renew and enrich in our freedom at every moment. Such characters are deceptively realistic, and what we watch in them is, I believe, just as much their process of elaboration as it is the final, objective form of the characters themselves. They are like the result of a *bet*, in which Sartre dares us to witness the recreation of the most morbid states from the inside, thus demonstrating, by his very act of creation, that they themselves are indeed the result of free choice and self-invention. The problems of biography analyzed elsewhere, and theoretically illustrated through such models as the existential psychoanalyses of Baudelaire, Genêt, and Flaubert, are here resolved by a kind of biographical-narrative praxis.

In this sense the play form is always more critical. In the novel, everything—environment, character, thoughts, acts, feelings—must be created out of nothingness. But in the play form, a certain number of things are given from the outset: the existence of the characters themselves, which does not have to be initially proven because they stand before us in the physical presence of the actors; the existence of the situation also, which precedes the rising of the curtain or maintains itself offstage as a place of genuine action, as opposed to the dramatic dialogue *about* action which the stage itself offers. Thus in the play, the character is in some sense a spectator of his own past, of his own acts, *along with* the audience: we bend over that past, those acts, together with him in an effort to understand or to articulate them.

So it is that in later Sartre, particularly in *Lucifer and the Lord* and *The Condemned of Altona*, the play takes the form of a psychoanalysis acted out before our eyes. The essential problem of Goetz, of Frantz, is to interpret their own past, to find out just exactly what their original choice was in the first place; and the analytical instrument for such interpretation is simply Husserl's intentionality. For if it is useless to try to determine the meaning of an act by introspection, in these later plays we proceed in reverse, on the assumption that whatever was done, whatever objective results the act in question had, must have been in some sense willed or desired by the actor himself. Thus, if Goetz's kindness, if his game of sainthood and his Utopian doctrine ultimately result in cataclysm and universal civil war, then one must conclude that somehow, obscurely, Goetz wanted it that way. His gift of the lands is a way of destroying the landed nobility around him, who refused to accept him as one of them; his generosity to his own peasants a way of revenging himself for their instinctive suspicion of him.

It is in *The Condemned of Altona* that this pyschoanalytic structure is enlarged and developed to the point where it displays all the problems around which *Search for a Method* will be organized. For here the choice between possible alternative motivations stands revealed as a coexistence between two different explanatory systems, two wholly different behavioral models. The atrocities committed by Frantz during the war can be understood either way: psychologically, as the son of a powerful father who has robbed him of any chance to become himself, they are his attempt to assert himself through absolutely irremediable action, through acts that cannot simply be hushed up by the father's wealth and influence. But on the socio-economic plane, Frantz can be seen as the crown prince of an industrial empire, who arrives at the age of reason only to confront a managerial structure that no longer needs a chief. His violence therefore both expresses the imperialistic tendencies inherent in the economic empire itself and aims at the latter's destruction as well.

If, therefore, there is any question of a "reconciliation" during this period of Sartre's thought, it rather takes the form of a reconciliation between Marxism and *Freudianism*, which are revealed in *The Condemned* to be at one, two codes or languages into which behavior may be alternately translated. The play is also instructive as to the relationship to these other two of the existential moment itself, which turns out to be a function of the impossibility of the situation itself, and of the closed and final character of history and the impotence of individuals. For in this paralysis only the cogito remains, that sheer helpless affirmation of his own existence which indeed survives Frantz' physical death and rings out as a voice from a tape recorder on an empty stage, repeating the one possibility, the one certainty, in the universal negation of human freedom: "O tribunal de la nuit, toi qui fus, qui seras, qui es, j'ai été! j'ai été!"

CHARACTERISTICALLY, the resolution between the Marxist and the Freudian models implied in *The Condemned of Altona* took the form of a simple equation, of the assertion of the verb to be,[10] of the identification of the two dimen-

---

[10] *Sartre: The Origins of a Style*, pp. 141-142.

sions by fiat. In *Search for a Method*, however, Sartre takes the problem up at a logically prior moment of its development: for the relationship between two different systems, or models, or series of phenomena, cannot serve as a point of departure until both systems genuinely exist in their own right. Thus the vulgar Marxist analysis of Valéry as a petit bourgeois (which continues by furnishing an analysis of petit bourgeois psychology and concludes by showing how Valéry may be seen as a manifestation of that kind of mentality) is unacceptable because it is really an idealism in disguise. The concrete work of Valéry has been, in such an analysis, linked to and translated into an abstract idea: namely the concept of the petite bourgeoisie, a concept as Platonic and timeless as anything in German *Geistesgeschichte*, with which, indeed, this mode of thought is contemporary. To link Valéry to the *real* petite bourgeoisie, to a determinate form of it at a given historical period, would in fact raise more problems than it would solve, since we could not first know that social class without having dealt meaningfully with a host of individual concrete existences such as that of Valéry himself, which was the problem to be solved in the first place.

The "method" of Sartre will therefore here take the form of a rectification of this idealistic pseudo-Marxism, and it seems to me that this rectification basically takes three forms: first, in objecting to the simple intellectual equation between an existence and an abstract idea, it tries to substitute for that intellectual link a genuinely lived one. That is, for Sartre, the problem of *mediation* is also the problem of character formation, of social influence, of genuine lived experience of class and society. Second, it attempts to plunge this problem back into history by showing that there is nothing timeless about it, and that in social and individual life we are constantly faced with overlap and time lag, with the coexistence of hosts of different time schemes at the same moment. And finally, it replaces the relationship between idea and human existence (which in pseudo-Marxism had been a purely logical one: the idea is the universal, the man the particular of it), with a dynamic one, namely that of existence as project, and of class relationship and affiliation as the free invention of a role projected toward the future, rather than determined by the past.

To return to the first point, for Sartre Marxists have had no use for Freud because they have consistently neglected the importance of childhood in the formation of the adult personality (with all its ideological and class affiliations). This is, however, precisely the domain of Freudianism, whose object is childhood itself and family experience. (In neglecting this area of study, Marxists have ignored the hint of Marx himself, who in a sentence written at the age of seventeen declared: "Our social relations have to some extent already commenced before we are in a position to determine them."[11])

Clearly, it must be through the mediation of the family itself that the child learns his social affiliations and class values; but even here the problem is more complex than it would at first seem. For we do not simply reduplicate the values of the father within ourselves (in the form of the censor), since in reality we do not know what those values are in themselves; the child constantly overestimates the father, who looms as a kind of gigantic and menacing shadow. Moreover, this kind of analysis generally neglects the mother, and fails to take note of the way in which the family is in reality a construction based on two separate social and characterological environments, maternal as well as paternal, which are rarely identical. It is between these two complete alternatives of character that the child enjoys a measure of freedom: for the formation of his own per-

[11] Quoted in H. P. Adams, *Karl Marx in His Early Writings* (New York, 1965), p. 14.

sonality results precisely from a choice between the alternate traits (or, what amounts to the same thing, between their opposites, their determinate negations, in the sense that the child can rebel against any one and convert it into its opposite). Thus the part of necessity inherent in this Sartrean model (which was prefigured in Simone de Beauvoir's account of her own childhood, where she showed how her own character, including her literary and philosophical ambitions, resulted from a conflict between a devout and prudish mother and a dilettantish, artistically inclined father) may be understood in analogy to the model of genetic inheritance, where the new organism has available to it two complete sets of genes and chromosomes from which to evolve its own particular pattern; characteristically, this necessity is not determinism, but is rather an inherent and external limit on the system itself within which the free choices are being made. The child cannot know that any particular human component, trait, or experience is lacking in his closed world, in his family situation, precisely because he is inside it and because it is all he does know.

Sartre's recent chapters on Flaubert offer us the most complex description of this process, in which the religion of art of the later Flaubert proves to have been a synthesis between the religious devotion of a mother of aristocratic origins and the analytical skepticism of a middle-class father only a generation away from the soil. In his case, this opposition is complicated by the presence of an older brother, who preempts the possibility of any absolute filial identification with the father by becoming a doctor himself, so that the second son is driven toward a more personal resolution which is at the same time a kind of social paralysis. Hence the contradictory character traits with which we are familiar in Flaubert: analytical skepticism derived from his father and beyond him from the eighteenth-century Enlightenment; hatred of his own class insofar as it is both hatred of his father and hatred of himself as a kind of classless monster; mysticism of art which derives from the mother's devotion; femininity (particularly as revealed in the creation of Madame Bovary herself—"Madame Bovary, c'est moi!") as social passivity and inability to act; grossness and boorishness ("le Garçon") as interiorization of what he imagined to be his own class (i.e., himself) seen from the outside, etc.: these contradictions are moments of a total movement which is the very process of inventing a solution to the problems of class conflict faced by Flaubert as a child in the family situation, under the guise of problems of a psychological order. (We will come upon this ultimate translation of psychology into class reality again in the *Critique*, where, however, it will be shown from the other direction: how what are essentially class conflicts ultimately come to be translated into the psychological dimension of individual existence.)

Already in this description we have been able to sense the presence of the second Sartrean principle, namely, the recognition that this invention is a temporal process, or, in different terminology, the reincorporation of the essentially timeless or synchronic model of pseudo-Marxism back into genuine diachrony itself. Clearly, the child is vitally absorbed in last year's social conflicts; his choice of self in the present takes place on the basis of the realities of the previous generation, namely those of his parents. Indeed, in some cases the institutional lag is even more striking, and of this there is no better illustration than the experience of Sartre himself as a child (described in *Words*), who, having lost his father, and with a young and weak mother whom he essentially regarded as a sister rather than an authority figure, grew up in the world of a grandfather whose characteristic values and traits and ideology were formed in the

1840's. Hence, if one likes, the relatively distinctive nature of Sartre's own literary production, in which he was able to skip a whole generation of false problems and react in a wholly different fashion from contemporaries still struggling against the realities of 1890 and 1900.

On the cultural level, this phenomenon takes the form of what Sartre calls perimated signs: that is, the inertia of the very language and ideas we use, which have in them, to anticipate the terminology of the *Critique*, a kind of counter-finality of their own, and which alienate our own thoughts and works to the degree that our original intention is deflected by this resistance and this previous history of the material itself.

Underlying all this, it seems to me, is an insistence on the existential fact of the absolute break between the generations of individual lives in history. In this sense also, pseudo-Marxism is really idealistic in character, because it insists on seeing history as a kind of continuity, whereas the only continuity in history (made up of ever renewed waves of finite, individual lives) is that within the historian's mind as he thinks his way down the centuries. (It follows from this that the only genuine continuity in history must come not so much from the generations that die as from the material objects and industrial plant that survive them—but this is once more to anticipate the subject matter of the *Critique* itself.)

Finally, implicit in both of the principles treated above is the requirement that the new biographical model permit understanding of action not as the *result* of some larger entity (such as class being) which "manifests itself" through the act in question, but rather as free invention directed toward the future, as being essentially a *project*. The illustration Sartre gives of this principle of analysis is that of the meaning of the war policy of the Gironde during the

French Revolution, in a critique of Daniel Guérin's treatment of the same subject in *La Lutte des classes sous la première république.*

For Guérin, the Gironde represent mercantile interests in Bordeaux, and their declaration of war on Austria and Prussia is a first move in a new economic struggle with England for commercial superiority. For Sartre, such an analysis too quickly dissolves the autonomy of the purely political "series" (i.e., parliamentary phenomena, speeches, policy, tactics, personality of the orators, struggle for preeminence within the Gironde itself, and so forth): those phenomena are of course not really separate from the economic, as they would have been thought to be in the older kind of purely political chronicle. Yet they do have a kind of semiautonomy of their own, a kind of intrinsic coherence, which Guérin disregards in his attempt to *reduce* the political to immediate economic motivation and to dismiss it as a kind of epiphenomenon of history. (Here Sartre is still basically following the thinking of Engels in a famous letter which we will discuss in our concluding chapter.)[12]

But there is yet another side to this objection: for Guérin's analysis illustrates the tendency of schematic Marxism to replace the subjective with the objective, to reinterpret intention in terms of objective results (hence the classic Stalinist notion of the "objective traitor" as someone who with the best will in the world commits what turns out to be treasonable or socially harmful activities). The Gironde could not have known *at that point* that England would enter the war (which later on, of course, did become economic in character), and to attribute this motive to them at the earlier date is to prevent us from discovering what exactly was their reasoning and the ultimate value of those particular concrete actions. Oddly enough, we have al-

[12] Engels to Conrad Schmidt, 27 October 1890 (Basic Writings, ed. Feuer, pp. 400-407).

ready seen in our analysis of *Lucifer and the Lord* that Sartre is not at all reluctant to use this argument from objective results in the interpretation of individual, relatively psychological behavior such as that of Goetz: you are what you do, you must have really wanted what ultimately happened. Thus the Sartre who in the realm of individual experience used the doctrine of intentionality *against* psychology and subjectivism and the doctrine of the subjective intent, here appears to return to the more old-fashioned school of historical writing which took the thoughts and words of the actors of history at face value. We will see shortly that this is not quite the case; but this apparent exoneration of the Gironde (based on a view of the limits of their own existential situation) will not really be put in its proper perspective until we reach the end of the *Critique* itself.

AT THIS POINT, it is useful to distinguish as sharply as we can between the interpretive method Sartre offers us and that practiced by orthodox Marxism. It would seem, indeed, that by reinserting between the act and its functional economic meaning a whole set of mediations and of semiautonomous series, his method tends to restore the older historiography of intention and rational analysis. It amounts to a distinction between the conscious and the unconscious: for the faithfulness to lived experience which Sartre proposes amounts to a priority of the conscious thoughts and experiences of Brissot, Vergniaud, Guadet over that "unconscious" economic motivation which is the object of Marxist historiography.

All this can be said in a much simpler way by observing that for Sartre orthodox Marxism practices a *reduction* of history and of experience. This, although true, tends to prejudice the argument somewhat. For it may be maintained that in a sense all understanding, all abstract thought

is reductive: indeed, the very process of *abstraction* itself
is in its very essence a reduction, through which we substitute for the four-dimensional density of reality itself simplified models, schematic abstract ideas, and thereby of necessity do violence to reality and to experience. On the other
hand, it is difficult to see how we could understand or deal
with reality in any other way than by such reduction.

Insofar as existentialism is in its very origins a reaction
against this process of abstraction, we must also observe
that it depends on it as a prior moment: no return to things,
no return to lived experience, unless we have first abandoned them in the process of abstraction.

It will be objected that the basic thrust of the existential
critique of such reduction is directed against the notion of
causality, but I do not really think this is so. In effect, causality is the empty form of the reduction itself: or if you
prefer, it is the pretext for that mental operation which for
the psychological, anecdotal, parliamentary reality of the
Girondins substitutes the simplified economic and commercial model. That this is so can be judged from the fact that
Sartre's polemic is addressed indifferently to either Marxism
or structuralism; for structuralism is just as much a reductive mode of thought as the orthodox Marxism in question
here. Only for the Marxist terminology of economic motivation or determination, structuralism substitutes the notion
of the *sign*, in which the initial surface phenomenon is a
signifier (*signifiant*) that stands for or represents some deeper underlying signified (*signifié*), and where the process
of understanding is precisely the translation or reduction
of the one into the other. (Indeed, this basic similarity of
the reductive process in both Marxism and structuralism
explains how the latter can have assimilated the former as
one version of itself.)

To return to Guérin's book, it seems to me that its reader
cannot but be impressed by the sense which such reductive

thinking makes of history, and the way in which a mass of data and detail falls into place when the socio-economic model is taken as the guide to interpretation. Indeed, it is precisely this feeling of events falling into place which is what we mean by *understanding* history; it is precisely this feeling of the most disparate facts ordering themselves around a model that is meant by the claim that history has a *meaning*. I would therefore propose that this reductive model of thought be considered a "historical trope" in the sense in which we have earlier used this term, as a type of rhetorical figure or form in time, thus avoiding epistemological polemics and underlining the temporal process itself by which the mind confronts and deals with reality.

It now remains to determine the structure of that quite different historical or rhetorical figure which Sartre opposes to the reductive one. I have already described elsewhere[13] the process by which, throughout Sartre's works, abstraction is evoked only to be resolved back into what is essentially a novelistic vision, and this is, I believe, essentially the process at work here. The aim is not only to "understand" the Gironde (in the reductive sense described above); but once understanding has been attained, to use it as a way back into what is essentially a concrete reexperiencing of the Girondins' actual situation itself, a reenactment of their thoughts and acts, in something of the form they might take for a historical novelist. This is, indeed, the sense of what Sartre (following Marc Bloch) calls the "progressive-regressive method": after having analytically worked back from the present to what must have been the meaning and value of past acts at their moment of performance, synthetically to recreate them in thought in such a way that justice is done their original richness and complexity. This was also the method of Marx, who in speaking of the understanding of religious beliefs (and thus of ideological phe-

[13] *Sartre: The Origins of a Style*, pp. 147-156.

nomena in general) declares that "it is, in fact, much easier to find by analysis the secular kernel of the religious mysteries than, conversely, to derive their exalted forms from the prevailing real conditions. The latter is the unique materialistic and therefore scientific method."[14] Thus Sartre's theory recapitulates the very course of his creation itself: and the visionary act is asked to fulfill, complete, and somehow to verify the abstract process of analysis which had preceded it.

We may underline the differences between the two historical or rhetorical forms of abstraction and vision by describing the relationship which each one implies between the various series of phenomena, or the various levels of data (the psychological, the oratorical, the political, the economic, the geographical, and so forth), of which a given historical event is composed.[15] It is convenient to describe the reductionist model in terms of *signs*, in which the various series stand to each other as signifier to signified, and where the basic specification of semiology is maintained: namely, that the relationship between signifier and signified be an *arbitrary* one (which amounts, as we have already seen, to something like a hypothesis of an unconscious). The basic problem or task faced by such a model is therefore the choice of some ultimate explanatory series which can stand as the signified to the other more superficial signifiers: in Marxism, of course, this ultimate series is the socio-economic one, or the form of the mode of production; for the structuralists it is language itself.

By contrast, the relationship between the various series in Sartre's mode of interpretation must be described as

[14] Quoted in Karl Korsch, *Karl Marx* (New York, 1963), p. 176.

[15] See, for a classic analysis of the relationship between such series or "factors" and for an account of the concept of "mediations" in general, Antonio Labriola, *Essays on the Materialistic Conception of History* (New York, 1966), Chap. VI. Labriola's book is still one of the best overall introductions to Marxism.

symbolic; which is to say that their relationship is precisely *not* arbitrary, but that in some fashion each series reflects and contains within itself all the others. Thus, Baudelaire's peculiar gait in walking ultimately (and if properly analyzed) contains the secret of his psychology, his socio-economic ideology, and his poetic sensibility itself. Thus Genêt's style recapitulates his whole life experience, and a purely tactile reaction such as that toward stickiness (*viscosité*) is inherently symbolic of an original choice of being itself. Earlier, of course, Sartre maintained the position that the basic series, the ultimate signified, was the relationship to being. It is now clear, however, that even granting the priority of the economic in his present thought, this particular model does not demand the priority of any particular series over any other, for they are all implicit in each other, taken separately.[16]

The real theoretical problems inherent in this model lie elsewhere. The attractiveness of the notion of a *sign*, or of the hypothesis of an unconscious, stemmed precisely from the way in which it allowed something else, something disproportionate and incommensurable, to be substituted for the immediate data of consciousness itself. Now, however, Sartre's model implies that in some fashion the actors of history are conscious of what they are doing and why they are doing it; and this simply does not seem to do justice to our feeling of the impersonality of history, of the alienations of all kinds involved in its process, of the relative insignificance of the individual actor.

Sartre had already faced such a dilemma earlier, when, attacking the Freudian model of the unconscious (another

[16] Implied in this is a whole new type of logic as well, in which the static model of the relationship of universal to particular would be replaced by one in which each particular symbolically realizes in itself and in its own mode the totality of the universal in question. For indications of such a theory in the *Critique* see pp. 180-182, on language; and for a typical concrete example, p. 644, on the relationship of group to class.

such reductive model, which can easily be reinterpreted in semiological terms), he found himself obliged to substitute in its place something else which would do justice to our lived experience of dimensions of the mind beyond rationalistic consciousness—which would preserve, in other words, the truth of Freud's discoveries, while eliminating the unacceptable hypothesis of an unconscious. His solution to this dilemma took the form of the theory of bad faith (*mauvaise foi*), in which he showed how one can be aware of the intention of one's acts on an unthematic, unselfconscious level, while at the same time failing to *know* that intention thematically or "consciously," in the ordinary sense of the word. *Mauvaise foi* is an enterprise of self-mystification designed to persuade ourselves that the unpleasant facts in question do not exist, all the while that we are still dimly aware of being in the process of so persuading ourselves. It is a structure of self-deception which becomes ever more intricate as we attempt to maintain it in being, and may aptly be symbolized by the desperate and contradictory attempt to keep ourselves from thinking about something (which we have to think about in order to know what we want to avoid). Thus the notion of *mauvaise foi* provides a means whereby a given act may be seen as both containing and not containing an awareness of its own basic intention or conscious purpose.

It is to this notion (without naming it) that Sartre has recourse in *Search for a Method*, when he wishes to substitute a symbolic for a reductive model of interpretation. In the intervening period, however, it has been enriched by the whole meditation on the imaginary and on irrealization[17] and has ultimately come to take a form which is not inconsistent with certain observations of Marx himself:

[17] See my "Three Methods in the Literary Criticism of Jean-Paul Sartre," in *Modern French Criticism*, ed. John K. Simon (Chicago, forthcoming).

Of course, someone will tell us that the proclaimed goal of the followers of Brissot is a mask, that these bourgeois revolutionaries considered themselves and presented themselves as illustrious Romans, that it is the objective result that really defines what they did. But we must be careful: the original thought of Marx, as we find it in *The Eighteenth Brumaire of Louis Bonaparte* attempts a difficult synthesis of intention and of result; the contemporary use of that thought is superficial and dishonest. If we push the Marxist metaphor to its limit, in fact, we arrive at a new idea of human action. Imagine an actor who is playing Hamlet and who is caught up in his role. He crosses his mother's room to kill Polonius hidden behind the arras. But that is not *what he is actually doing*. He is crossing a stage before an audience and passing from "court side" to "garden side" in order to earn his living, to win fame, and this real activity defines his position in society. But one cannot deny that these *real* results are present in some way in his imaginary act. One cannot deny that the movement of the imaginary prince expresses in a certain indirect and refracted manner the actor's real movement, nor that the very way in which he *takes himself* for Hamlet is his own way of *knowing himself* as an actor. To return to our Romans of 1789, their way of *calling* themselves Cato is their way of *making* themselves bourgeois, members of a class which discovers History and which already wants to stop it, which claims to be universal and which establishes the proud individualism of its members upon a competitive economy—in short, the heirs of a classical culture. Everything is there. It is one and the same thing to declare oneself Roman and to want to *stop* the Revolution. Or rather, the better one can pose as Brutus or Cato, the better one will be able to stop the Revolution. This thought, obscure even to itself, sets up mystical ends which enclose the confused awareness of its objective ends. Thus we may speak simultaneously of a subjective drama (the simple play of appearances which hides nothing, which contains no "unconscious" element) and of an *objective, intentional* organization of real means with a view to achieving real ends—without any organization of all this by a consciousness or a premeditated will. Very simply, the truth of the imaginary *praxis* is in the real *praxis*, and the real, to the extent that it takes itself as merely imaginary, includes implicit references to the imaginary *praxis* as to its interpretation. The bourgeois of 1789 does not pretend to be Cato in order to stop the Revolution by denying History and by substituting virtue for politics; neither does he tell himself that he resembles Brutus in order to give himself a mythical comprehension of an action which he carries out but which escapes him. He does both at the same time. And it is precisely this synthesis which allows us to discover an imaginary action in each one as a doublet and at the same time the matrix of real, objective action.

But if *that* is what is meant, then the followers of Brissot, at the very core of their ignorance, must be the responsible authors of the economic war. This external, stratified responsibility must have been internalized as a certain obscure awareness of their political drama. . . .[18]

This crucial passage may stand as the essential theory of Sartre's later biographical practice, and indeed, of his vision of history itself, insofar as we see it from the inside out, through the actions of individuals. It should be noted that, far from being a revisionistic weakening of historical interpretation, in fact this analysis only serves to intensify the personal responsibility of the Girondins for their own actions. Moreover, the emphasis on their own complex inten-

[18] *Search for a Method*, pp. 45-47.

tions and imaginary self-justifications has the further effect of reemphasizing, rather than explaining away, the alienation and distortion undergone by those individual intentions as they enter the field of history itself. If there remains anything problematical about this ultimate version of the Sartrean model, it has to do with the nature of the judgments passed on the Gironde: to describe them as a certain type of bourgeois revolutionary is to categorize them from the outside, to evaluate them in a larger context with which they themselves could not have been familiar. Even to the degree that they knew themselves in some such fashion, in the obscure kind of self-awareness Sartre is describing here, such self-knowledge could only have resulted from some previous judgment on them from the outside, by enemies who saw them in a certain light, who stamped them with a certain label and a certain accusation, which they themselves then attempted to recuperate and to interiorize, to justify. At this point, therefore, we begin to pass outside the traditional area of existential analysis, the world of lived experience or the monad, in the direction of judgments made from the outside, and seemingly unjustifiable in existential terms. It will be the ultimate purpose of the *Critique* itself to found such judgments, and in doing so, to replace the relativism inherent in an intrinsic analysis of any given historical moment (such as the Gironde) in and for itself with a more absolute sense of the ultimate meaning of history itself.

II

THE INITIAL difficulties in reading the *Critique* come from the fact that its opening chapters deal not so much with genuine social experience as with the abstract structures underlying such experience. As the title suggests, the work is an attempt to lay a philosophical foundation for research that has already been done, analyses that have already been made. In this sense, Sartre's book takes for granted the validity of Marxist analyses of history, just as Kant took for granted the validity of the physical sciences of his time. It therefore asks the question: What preconditions are necessary, what must the structure of human existence be, in order for history thus to prove dialectical in its movement?

It seems useful to discuss this groundwork under three general groupings: praxis or totalization, negation, and reciprocity; or in other terms, dialectical action as such, and then the two poles into which it seems to resolve itself, our relationship to objects on the one hand, and that with other people on the other.

1. The word dialectical already governs several different kinds of objects: it may refer to history or to individual action, or it may refer to the kind of thinking which can apprehend either of those types of events. The advantage for Sartre of the word "totalization" is that it can apply indifferently to any of these three types of dialectical phenomena.

The term clearly corresponds to what in *Being and Nothingness* was called the project; for the latter also passes through a collection of objects, unifying them as it does so, on its way toward a determinate end. My project thus *totalizes* my environment, in that it causes it to order itself around me, and to reveal its own inertia, its own "coefficient of adversity," by resisting my future end: thus the desert, as I try to survive it, is revealed as an inhuman landscape; thus the open freeway redoubles my own speed, and the ski slope lends itself to my downward flight. The project then leaves behind it these aggregates of matter in the form of *totalities,* or husks of dead projects, traces of human action which has long since vanished. In this sense, our cities are sedimentations of such totalities, like a sitting room whose owner has died.

It is because individual human action, or the project, or my totalization, is dialectical in its very structure, and involves my own negation of the things around me, with the synthesis of them which that negation performs, as well as the transformation of my own act itself by its success, and the production of a new order of projects out of the very structure of the old ones—it is because of this structure that history, as a locus of millions of human acts, and understanding, as that which is born of my experience of action and only later becomes specialized as a purely intellectual process, can both be dialectical also.

But the word totalization, thus applied, begins to have consequences which transcend the suggestions of the word project: for now it begins to imply a kind of hierarchy among the projects themselves, some clearly more "total" and more "totalizing" than others. In history, then, such totalizations will increasingly involve greater numbers of people, and be more profoundly implicated in the most minute details of the socio-economic structures of their lives. In this sense the Revolution of 1789 was obviously something far vaster and more all-embracing than, say, a *jacquerie* or a civil war in a medieval Italian city-state.

From the intellectual point of view also, it is apparent that the system of Hegel includes more within itself and understands more than an analytical or empirical type of thinking which can only deal with one isolated and specialized phenomenon at a time.

Finally, the concept of totalization enables Sartre to do away with the relativism inherent in the notion of the project (and indeed strongly implied in the very system of *Being and Nothingness*, where—since all life is a failure to be—all projects in the long run are of equal value). It is only on this condition that history as a whole can have a meaning, or a single direction, in the sense that projects are acquiring increasingly vaster fields of influence in all senses.

We may anticipate the thesis of the projected second volume of the *Critique* hinted at here and there in the present volume, by saying that the "meaning" of history is just such a totalization. It is a becoming rather than a being; and in genuine dialectical fashion, we may assume that in prehistoric times, when men lived in unrelated groups and tribes, history, in effect, had no single meaning. Only now, when the world is becoming one, and when events in any given area are involved in and affect the very being of people in wholly distinct countries and societies, can we begin to have even a vague realization of what human life would be like if it were a single project, had a single meaning, constituted a single "totalization in course."

2. The content of a project or a totalization, however, depends essentially on the world in which that project comes into being, and on which it attempts to operate. It is instructive to compare the new version to that of *Being and Nothingness*, where the very origin of action (as nothingness in a domain of pure being, i.e., of objects) was found in the structure of the human being as *lack*, as ontological privation, attempting to satisfy itself, to fulfill itself, and thereby to arrive at some definitive state of being.

The new term for this process is *need*, which is little more than a translation of the ontological terminology into a relatively more socio-economic kind. Both are, of course, Hegelian in origin: not only is the notion of human action, work, experience as a negation of existing being characteristic of Hegel; but for him the very history of self-consciousness begins precisely with desire (*Begierde*), which functions, however, in much the same way as Sartre's idea of need.

This initial terminological shift brings others with it: just as lack, as an abstract way of characterizing human existence, takes place in a world abstractly characterized as *contingent*, whose essential structure, with respect to man, is *facticity* (that is to say, incommensurability with human thought and human existence, or, in the terminology of a more literary existentialism, absurdity or meaninglessness); so in these new concrete terms, in which man's emptiness takes the form of *need*, the resistance of the world to man is now defined in terms of *scarcity*. For scarcity is precisely the unanalyzable starting point, the contingent datum, of the world in which we exist. Unintelligible in itself, simply a fact to which we cannot assign any metaphysical significance whatsoever, it nonetheless is the framework in which we must act, and conditions and alienates our acts and projects even in their very conception.

The concept of scarcity permits Sartre to articulate human need as a lack which is at one and the same time a relationship to the objects of the outside world and a determinate type of distance from other people as well. Just as the fact of scarcity forces each individual to search desperately for the objects of his need, laboriously to create them out of unfavorable materials and under difficult conditions, so also each object which I can consume is one implicitly wrested from my neighbor; and in a more general way, my very existence, in a world of scarcity, is a threat to my neighbor's existence, as is his for me. Thus Manichaeanism and violence have their source in the very contingent structure of the world of matter itself, and it is with the accents of an older rhetoric, the homo homini lupus, that Sartre evokes this absolute otherness imposed on human life by scarcity: "the century would have been a good one, had not man's cruel, immemorial enemy lain in wait for him, that carnivorous species that has sworn his destruction, that hairless, malignant beast, man himself!"[19]

It is worthwhile underlining another consequence of this notion, which will be crucial for the development of the

---

[19] This passage comes of course from the ending of *The Condemned of Altona*, but there are many analogous pages in the *Critique*, e.g., p. 208.

whole argument of the *Critique* as well as for its ultimate evaluation. For the concept of scarcity is the first manifestation, and also, in a sense, the source, of a basic duality in Sartre's thinking and in his terminology: the twin possibility of expressing any given phenomenon either in terms of human action or in terms of objects. Scarcity provokes a human reaction which can be expressed in terms either of work on the outside world or of struggle with other human beings, for it is essentially both at once. Thus we have at our disposal two languages or codes in which to formulate events or experiences: what look like static physical objects can be translated into the human relationships of which they are the disguise, or what look like direct, face-to-face human relationships can be seen to constitute mere reflections of inert objects and material systems of things. The results of this duality will be obvious later; here it is enough to say that as a perception of reality, and even as a philosophical notion, it is not a new but rather a very old component in Sartre's work, and derives, indeed, not so much from anything in Marx, as from Heidegger. For the latter distinguished in *Sein und Zeit* between two essential modes of the perception of objects: as *vorhanden*, simply there, inert and disconnected, and as *zuhanden*, or as action latent, tools and instruments lying ready to hand in case of need.[20] And for Heidegger, as later on for Sartre, it is this second dimension which is ontologically prior: we apprehend things first and foremost as tools and only thereafter as the static objects of contemplative or scientific knowledge. Hence things may stand as shorthand for human actions, and such a point of view forms the very basis for the Sartrean evocation of the outside world as a network of frozen imperatives or a "hodological" space, as objects filled

[20] Martin Heidegger, *Sein und Zeit* (Tübingen, 1957), pp. 66-88; and see also "Der Ursprung des Kunstwerkes," in Heidegger's *Holzwege* (Frankfort, 1950).

with implicit life and feelings swarming about us as so many objective modes through which being is revealed.[21]

The idea of scarcity has struck many critics, however, as being more Malthusian and Darwinian than Marxist; just as the Manichaeanism of otherness and the struggle for existence has reminded readers of Hobbes rather than of the *Communist Manifesto*. Such categorization is of course not real philosophical argument; but it is at least worth pointing out the complexities of Sartre's position on this first moment of social life, or work on matter, which he sees as involving not one but *two* separate negations. Work is of course in itself a negation of matter; yet it is a determinate negation, a negation of a particular sector of materiality with the aim of transforming it into a determinate object of need, into some specific product. Thus Sartre insists on the priority of some earlier and more fundamental global negation of the world of being itself: for without some initial global negation, the "world" as such in the phenomenological sense could not come into being over against man, and there would be no total field to serve as a background against which local and determinate zones could be perceived. Thus, need is what causes the entire inert sphere of external being to organize itself into a unified field[22] which is "world" or nature itself; and it is only on this basis that the more specific and determinate negations which are the various forms of toil and work can take place. Work is therefore a negation of a negation; and in the sense in which this expresses a rather value-charged rhythm in traditional Marxist thought, we may observe that it has the result of putting the accent on work and activity, rather than consumption and satisfaction.

[21] *Sartre: The Origins of a Style*, pp. 73-88, 125ff.
[22] From *Being and Nothingness* on one finds an increasing affinity between certain of Sartre's thought patterns and those of Gestalt psychology; I myself, however, am inclined to see the latter as a kind of disguised dialectical thinking in its turn.

It has other consequences as well, however, and they are far from being as abstract as the whole problem would at first seem to suggest. First of all, the idea of an initial, global negation of the world permits Sartre to preserve the idea of total responsibility which had been presented in *Being and Nothingness*. There, it was because I could never experience facticity face to face, because there was no such thing as a direct experience of pure contingency which had not already passed through a human consciousness or a human project, that every perception of the world represented an assumption of facticity on my part (or in other words, a negation of the initial contingency of being). It was in this sense that, in the context of *Being and Nothingness*, everyone was in some way responsible for their own moment of time and for the whole world around them: the war that faces me is "my" war, if only in the sense that I have to interiorize it somehow and react to it, that I am not free *not* to make it my own by some kind of reaction. This global responsibility, which more than anything else was responsible for Sartre's characterization as Jansenistic by some of his critics, was, however, a relatively ahistorical concept; in the new context of scarcity, need, work, and history, it takes a quite different form. For here the initial negation by which man causes the world and nature to come into being over against him is in a sense the enabling act that lends matter its human power, and invests what otherwise would have been sheer inertia and externality with that malignant and destructive power which matter uses against men and which Sartre will call counter-finality, or the practico-inert. Thus man is still "responsible" for what destroys him, but in the new, collective, historical context, this responsibility falls apart into two different moments: one in which man, by his action and his work, confers on matter a kind of surplus-value or stored human energy; and the second, in which that energy awakens and returns against him in a form he cannot comprehend and which he takes to be matter or nature acting on its own.

The second consequence of this scheme of the two negations is that through them man not only works on the outside world, but on himself as well. He makes himself an object in order to work on objects, he makes himself inertia in order to overcome inertia, just as one converts one's hands and arms into tools in order to use tools. Thus initially man's ultimate possibility of being alienated or dehumanized is given in this first basic structure of his relationship to matter.

Perhaps this is the moment to discuss the whole question of whether Sartre is here reinventing *idealism*, as several critics have maintained, and whether, beyond that, his notion of alienation is consistent with that of Marx. It does seem that you would not use language of this kind, which describes man *making himself* inert, *making himself* matter, in order to work on matter, unless you somehow initially thought of him (perhaps in spite of yourself) as something else, and thought of his entry into the world of matter as a kind of primal fall. And there can be no question but that for Sartre matter is somehow the source of evil: we have seen this already, insofar as the structure of matter is scarcity. But this is true in another sense also, where matter is read as the equivalent of exteriority and consequently of multiplicity and number as well. Thus, for Sartre, the peculiar alienation of human action by sheer numbers of other human actions which we will examine shortly is basically simply the result of the interiorization of exteriority, which is to say the contingent fact that there are many human beings, rather than just one.[23]

From another point of view, this Manichaean and indeed

[23] "Number may be considered the absolute abstraction of man, or as his absolute materiality taken in the abstract" (*Critique*, p. 366). *Le Sursis* (*The Reprieve*) is of course a dramatization of this concept.

in some ways pre-Socratic evaluation of matter is merely the result of the insistence, already basic in *Being and Nothingness*, on what we might call an arrested dialectic: on the absolute irreducibility of the contingent, of facticity, of what here is called matter. Indeed, Sartre's most perceptive philosophical critic, Pietro Chiodi, has diagnosed the ultimate failure of the *Critique* as a result of the idea of the project, which, contrary to Heidegger's practice, has always been conceived by Sartre in Cartesian fashion as a linking of subject and object poles. From this untenable distinction comes the overestimation of matter (as a hypostasis of the object pole) as well as the confusion between alienation and objectification which, for Chiodi, ultimately stamps Sartre's thought as un-Marxist.

It is worthwhile quoting Chiodi's argument in a little detail, for it has the merit of clarifying this problem very sharply: "Thus three related but irreconcilable positions may be defined: 1/ the Hegelian one, for which alienation can be suppressed, but for which, inasmuch as relationship and alienation coincide, it is necessary to suppress relationship as such in order to suppress alienation; 2/ the Marxist one, which shares with the Hegelian the requirement that alienation must be suppressed (and this is the profound reason for the revolutionary continuity between Hegelianism and Marxism), but which denies the coincidence between relationship and alienation, so that its requirement of the suppression of alienation is accompanied by a recognition of the ineliminability of relationship as such; 3/ the protoexistential position, which shares with Marxism the thesis of the ineliminability of relationship, but which, since it preserves the Hegelian identification of alienation and relationship, ends up implying the ineliminability of alienation itself."[24]

[24] *Sartre e il Marxismo*, p. 13. For Chiodi, whose point of view may be characterized as a kind of Heideggerian Marxism, Sartre's

In other words, Hegel uses the terms objectification and alienation interchangeably, and for him this process is the very motor of history itself; but insofar as his system ultimately glorifies the purely intellectual activity of the philosopher, it implies a negative judgment of any involvement of man with the material objects around him, and ultimately foresees the suppression of all such involvement in pure thought and purely intellectual activity itself.[25] For Sartre, of course, such suppression is as inconceivable as it is for Marx. But what seems suspect in his point of view is his continuing insistence, carried over from *Being and Nothingness*, on the manner in which *all* action, *all* projects, involve a loss of self and an alienation of consciousness in objects and in the realization of work; on the manner in which consciousness objectifies itself and deposits itself in its work in the form of being, and in which its work returns to it unrecognizable and profoundly *other*. But if this is so —and it seems to me, particularly judging from the kinds of examples that Sartre uses, that he has in mind a relatively literary model, the way a writer objectifies and alienates himself in language—then there is really no way to distinguish clearly between what we might call normal, human objectification, and what Marx sees as alienation caused by the socio-economic system. This objection, however, does not take into account the basic duality we have described above; for we must always remember that for Sartre any relationship to an object can be retranslated back into terms of human relationships. At that point, it becomes clear how we are to distinguish objectification from alienation: the first is a relationship to objects which in human terms translates into a generosity or a freedom with respect to other

---

basic error is to have confused the otherness or *alterité* of my relationship to other people with objectification itself.

[25] See Herbert Marcuse, *Reason and Revolution* (Boston, 1960), p. 163.

men, while the second translates into work for another man, and into a relationship of oppression by him.

To return to the question of negativity, we may finally observe that its origin has implications for the reading of history as well, and for the problem of the beginnings of class society and of the division of labor. The interest of Marx and Engels for Morgan and for studies of the institution of primitive communism was an ambiguous one: sometimes the fact of primitive communism was used simply to show that private property, as a legal category and a social institution, was not somehow eternal and thus natural.[26] At other times, however, particularly in Engels' hands, the fascination with primitive communal institutions results in a version of history which is unacceptable because it is, in disguise, simply the myth of the garden of Eden and the fall of man. Such a myth is untenable, if for no other reason than that if has at its disposal no means of accounting for the origins of history: it cannot show how out of such a positive, a negative could be made to evolve. Sartre's initial negations, and the stress he lays on scarcity, have the advantage of restoring to primitive societies (no matter what their property system) that dimension of misery and toil, early death, ignorance, and earth-scraping desperation which we know to have been theirs, and of restoring to history its inhuman, nightmarish quality from which myths as such only serve to distract us.

3. Something of the same problem of logical and ontological priorities and initial structures reappears when we turn to the question of our basic relationship to other people as it is described in the *Critique*. Sartre begins by insisting on the priority of some fundamental reciprocity between men which precedes any later and historical form of antagonism and conflict; at the same time, particularly in the light of *Being and Nothingness*, it would seem that the structure of

[26] See Korsch, *Karl Marx*, pp. 68ff.

that "fundamental" reciprocity is rather difficult to determine.

The intention behind the concept is somewhat clearer: for by the idea of initial reciprocity, Sartre wishes to undermine the purely economistic doctrine of the manner in which particular, historically determinate modes of human relationships are the result of the modes of economic production at that particular period. Human relationships would thus seem to be mere instinctual or biological reactions and adjustments to different types of material surroundings; and Sartre rightly points out that this is to take reification at face value, and to think, not that human relations are thing*like*, but that they actually are inert objects subject to quasiphysical and external influences in the first place. At that point, genuine history turns into something like a mechanical evolution of economic institutions from which man, either as an individual or as a collective being, is excluded. But for Sartre there cannot be alienation unless there was first something to alienate, some prior form of human relationship to serve as the object of distortion.

I suspect, however, that what is really meant by reciprocity here is no more than that traumatic and absolutely inescapable fact of recognition of another consciousness or freedom which was described in *Being and Nothingness*: I cannot, in other words, pass a man by as though he were a stone. His existence immediately puts him in relationship to me, and the project to treat him like an object can only come after that initial recognition.

Indeed, judging from the very schematic indications of the *Critique*, it would seem that human relations here undergo much the same development as they did in *Being and Nothingness*, where they entered on a vicious circle of various types of subject-object domination. For here both subjects are centers of totalization, and it would seem inevitable that one would end up being totalized by the other, or forming part of the other's perceptual field, being unified just as surely as the other objects in the path of the project.

The *Critique*, however, draws conclusions from this situation which were implicit, but never really spelled out, in the earlier work. For the implication of the above situation was that two monads, two freedoms, always conflict, in the sense that each has to *face* the other, that they cannot share a common world since each one sees it from the other end, since each is an object in the other's perceptual field. The new conclusion Sartre draws from this situation is one of the most original notions in the *Critique*: namely that the couple, or the dyadic relationship, is not the most fundamental form of interpersonal life, in spite of its clear priority for common sense. Since the couple cannot really be a unity, unification must be operated by a third party, by an outside observer or witness; and the crucial role thus played by the "third" confirms the priority of the triadic relationship over the dyad, which is a later phenomenon logically and ontologically.

This notion is bound to strike the reader as paradoxical at the outset; and although it will eventually become clear just why Sartre needs this particular idea for the later development of his argument, that is not in itself an adequate defense either. Ultimately, a phenomenological analysis must appeal to lived experience, and we cannot really understand the justification for the idea of the "third" until we form some picture of the phenomenon it tries to *name*.

For one thing, it tries to correct the common-sense view of direct, face-to-face dyadic human relationships by showing that this view is secretly abstract. We never are all alone with each other; every confrontation always takes place against the background of what is a little hastily called society, or at least against the background of swarms of other human relationships. In this light, the notion of the couple, and the resistance to the idea of the "third," is a way of making room around ourselves, trying to persuade ourselves that our world is filled with empty spaces, and that there is such a thing as genuine solitude or genuine privacy.

For we must never forget that in the Sartrean system the role of other people can provisorily be filled by objects; and frequently it is precisely objects as such which function as an absent or latent third to the apparently solitary dyad. Thus, the honeymooners are alone with their motel, which is to say, with the rest of middle-class American society.

But there is a more subtle and fundamental way in which the third is necessarily implied in all dyadic contacts, and this is, so to speak, as a medium of exchange. For exchange as such is comprehensible only as a system devised by a third party: for the judgment of identity, the act of setting two different things in equivalence with each other, can only come from the outside. Thus, I exchange a sum of money for an amount of fish: but since these two objects are utterly incommensurate, and since each partner to the exchange sees only his own property (unless he puts himself in the position of a third), the parties to the exchange must of necessity have recourse to some external system of equivalence which fills the function of the third. But inasmuch as all direct contact presupposes a common world of some kind, all such contact must necessarily be mediated by a principle of identity which puts the two freedoms, the two totalizations, in equivalence with each other. Normally, of course, language is itself this third party. (It is in this sense that Sartre's triadic model is an implicit challenge to structuralism, whose binary oppositions fail to take into account precisely the movement of the exchange itself as a third element, as a mediation.)

It seems to me that this notion of the primacy of the triad is rich with all kinds of suggestions and possibilities (some of which I will sketch in later). For one thing, it provides an ontological foundation for the idea that human life is, in its very structure, collective rather than individualistic. For another, it would seem to offer the promise of a whole new system of psychology worked out on the basis of the triad.[27] Finally, it is dynamic, where the concept of the dyad is static and circular (as was apparent in the vicious circle of concrete relations with other people described in *Being and Nothingness*). By showing that interpersonal experience can never precede group experience, it immediately forces the argument of the *Critique* to transcend the individualistic level at which the analyses of *Being and Nothingness* had been undertaken, and to move at once to the ways in which the solitary individual tries to overcome his ontological and socio-economic weakness by the invention of collective acts and collective units.

III

To THE basic duality of those reciprocal interrelationships we have just described, mediated as they are either by third parties or by things, corresponds a basic duality in the forms of collective existence: human beings can be united either by matter or by other human beings. Yet it would seem that for Sartre the first, relatively unselfconscious and passive kind of grouping is the predominant one, and also generally prior, both in the logical and in the historical sense.

For the most part, in other words, in our fragmented and atomistic society, we are united to each other by what Sartre calls the "practico-inert": matter which has been invested with human energy and which henceforth takes the place of and functions like human action. The machine is of course the most basic symbol of this type of structure, but

[27] For just such a theory, worked out independently of the *Critique*, see René Girard, *Mensonge romantique et vérité romanesque* (Paris, 1961), translated as *Desire, Deceit and the Novel* (Baltimore, 1965).

it is really only a physical symbol of it, and in concrete daily life the practico-inert most frequently takes the form of social institutions. Yet the idea of an institution is a kind of intellectual shorthand, in the long run contradictory insofar as it implies that such objects have some genuine supra-individual being, insofar as it tends to mistake the reification of human relationships for actual inert objects of a quasiphysical variety. The practico-inert is a physical object (subway, policeman's uniform, checkbook, sidewalk, calendar) which functions *like* an institution, which replaces direct human relationships with something more ordered and more indirect.

A heightened and intensified language goes into the evocation of these strange, parasitic, vampiristic objects, which draw their being from man and drain him of his own in return: "In order to maintain the status of a lodging, a house has to be *inhabited*, in other words kept up, heated, swept out, whitewashed, etc.; otherwise it goes to pot; this object-vampire incessantly absorbs human action, lives on man's blood and finally lives in symbiosis with him. All of its physical characteristics, temperature included, come from human action, and for its inhabitants there is no difference between that passive activity that we might call the process of inhabiting and the pure *reconstitutive praxis* which shelters the house against the Universe, or in other words serves as a mediation between exterior and interior. It is in this sense that one can speak of *the* Mediterranean as a real symbiosis between man and things, which tends to petrify man in order to *animate* matter. . . ."[28]

This counter-finality inherent in the practico-inert is Sartre's way of solving the problem raised in the previous section in connection with Engels' notion of history, namely the production of a negative fact out of a positive one (i.e.,

[28] *Critique*, p. 238. (Henceforth, for convenience, page references to the *Critique* will be cited in the text).

the creation of a mining proletariat with its misery out of the pure positivity of a geographical area rich in coal, or out of the scientific invention of extractive processes). For in this profoundly dialectical reversal, every act by which man seems to progress further and further toward a control of nature or matter only results in increasing his dependency and putting him ever more deeply into the latter's power.

It is important to distinguish between this process, which is one of alienation, and simple failure: in the latter, human action is annihilated, whereas in the former it continues to exist and operate as a freedom, but has secretly been stolen or volatilized from without, has become a kind of "dead freedom," an exercise of "dead possibilities." It is no accident that this description initially (in *Being and Nothingness*) applied to alienation through the look of other people; for it is precisely to interpersonal conflict that Sartre will appeal for an example to clarify the way in which worked matter alienates man. It is, he says, analogous to the struggle between two armies, where one is led into a tortuous ambush in which each military tactic is foreseen and reckoned into a higher plan by the other: in this example my freedom remains intact, but has been reversed and used against me (pp. 292-293). So it is that matter is like an other, who welcomes my free exercise of my own praxis the more surely to draw me into its own power and to subjugate me.

This alienation takes yet another form, owing to the identification already commented on between matter and sheer multiplicity or number, where the source of deflection is less some external object than it is simply the uncontrollable result of a host of collective actions and wills working together. Sartre's examples of this process are the deforestation of China and the inflation which took place in Renaissance Europe as a result of the influx of Spanish gold from the New World. In both cases, a host of individually positive actions (each peasant removes trees from his own land in order to make it cultivable; each conquistador enriches himself personally, encouraged in that by the state itself) add up to a negative sum: with the trees gone, the Chinese landscape enters its classic rhythm of devastating floods; and Spanish currency depreciates at a pace terrifying to contemporaries. The basic experience of this kind of alienation for Sartre himself seems to have been the outbreak of World War II, in which a million freedoms seemed to cancel each other out in total helplessness.[29] This type of alienation by the fact of collectivity itself was already described by Engels in one of his letters of the early 1890's in which he said: "history is made in such a way that the final result always arises from conflicts between many individual wills, of which each in turn has been made what it is by a host of particular conditions of life. Thus there are innumerable intersecting forces, an infinite series of parallelograms of forces which give rise to one resultant—the historical event. This may again be viewed as the product of a power which works as a whole *unconsciously* and without volition. For what each individual wills is obstructed by everyone else, and what emerges is something that no one willed."[30] The dialectical twist given to this model is, however, the idea that even if everyone wills the *same* thing, quantity turns over into quality and indeed into negation.

The mode of human interaction which corresponds to the domination of the practico-inert is that of *seriality*, another one of the new ideas developed in the *Critique*.[31] In seriality (that is, when individuals are arranged together in a

---

[29] See *Situations*, 7 vols. (Paris, 1947-   ), II, 252ff., and the novels of the *Roads to Freedom* series, particularly *The Reprieve*.

[30] Engels to Joseph Bloch, 21-22 September, 1890 (*Basic Writings*, ed. Feuer, p. 399).

[31] I have examined aspects of Joyce and Robbe-Grillet in the light of this concept in a study entitled "Seriality in Modern Literature," *Bucknell Review*, XVIII, No. 1 (Spring 1970), 63-80.

"series" instead of being united in a "group"), my basic relationship to other people is something that might be described as statistical anonymity, with all that those words imply of isolation and at the same time profound uniformity with everyone else. Thus, when performing most of the acts characteristic of industrial civilization—waiting for a bus, reading a newspaper, pausing at a traffic light—I seem alone, but am in reality simply doing exactly what everyone else does in the same situation; and this is not an external, but an internal identity. For I make myself an other or the Other, and deliberately pattern my behavior on what I imagine the other's to be. The ontological irony of this mode of being is, of course, that all the while I am modeling myself and my behavior on the being of other people outside me, all the rest of them are doing exactly the same thing; in fact, there is no Other, only an infinite regression, an infinite flight in all directions. "Each is the same as the Others to the degree that he is Other from himself," Sartre says (p. 311), and in this sense seriality is a vast optical illusion, a kind of collective hallucination projected out of individual solitude onto an imaginary being thought of as "public opinion" or simply "they." But public opinion does not exist, and it is rather the belief in it and the effects of such belief which "unite" individuals in the series.

Seriality is thus a basic social mechanism; as such, it is the ontological foundation of statistics as a science, when statistics *is* a science. It is the structure of such phenomena as panics or inflation, and can never be anything other than collective impotence and helplessness, owing to the way in which each isolated individual feels being to be elsewhere, to be outside of him, and serial action to be something to which he passively submits. Indeed, it is important to stress the way in which, in a serial situation, the actions of individuals only serve to intensify their serial helplessness, and, inasmuch as such action is *other* in its very origin, return against them as an alien force. Think of the man who at the onset of an inflationary spiral begins to hoard his gold: what he is afraid of, in other words, is that thousands of other people in identical situations will in exactly the same way refuse to surrender gold for paper, causing the paper to become worthless. He is thus an other to himself to the very degree that he causes that which he fears in the future, that he himself does what he apprehends from other people.

Given the impotence of individuals in the serial situation, the motivation behind the formation of genuine groups is easily understood as a way of regaining autonomy, of reacting against dispersal through a new type of unity and solidarity. The group thus always comes into being on the ruins of seriality, and history can be seen alternatively as either a perpetual oscillation between moments of genuine group existence and long periods of serial dispersal, or, at any given moment, as a complicated coexistence of groups at various stages of their development and masses of serial individuals surrounding them.

It is instructive to compare this basic opposition of series to group with its early form in *Being and Nothingness*, where the same phenomenon was described as the distinction between the "we-subject" and the "we-object." There, of course, the crucial role in the formation of a collective type of being was played by the look of the third party, the outside observer (which was, of course, the source of the notion of the "third" described in the earlier section). It is only when I feel myself become an object along with someone else under the look of such a "third" that I experience my being as a "we-object"; for then, in our mutual interdependency, in our shame and rage, our beings are somehow mingled in the eyes of the onlooker, for whom we are both somehow "the same": two representatives of a class or a species, two anonymous types of something, two workers or intellectuals or Americans or whatever. Then my being is outside me, inextricably involved with that of my partner and his with mine, in that we share a common situation, face a common enemy, and submit to a mutual alienation or reification.

The "we-subject," however, is not a genuine ontological experience as described in the earlier work; it is subjective only, and corresponds to nothing beyond the bounds of my own consciousness of it. It is no doubt a real feeling: in the theater, among other witnesses at an accident, anywhere I am a spectator along with other people, I feel myself part of something, just as I do at political rallies, perhaps, or in a parade. But this feeling has no consequences for the other people around me; and the proof of this is that I can feel the same exaltation in total solitude, or when nobody else does. The reader will call to mind the mystical experience of the Self-taught-man in the prison camp as it is described in *Nausea*, a kind of religious feeling of participation in humanity itself which may serve as the outside limit for this kind of illusion of fraternity or communion.

The earlier description thus corresponds fairly closely to experience of seriality, but its terms do not yet seem altogether adequate. In particular, the relationship of the two structures (the one ontological, the other subjective) to consciousness or awareness was never really clear. And given the thrust of Sartre's philosophy, which aimed at suppressing the false dualism between objectivity and subjectivity, it would seem that the recourse to the subjective as a term of judgment is more a sign of theoretical uncertainty than of anything else, an uncertainty which the *Critique* will dispel. The source of such judgment is of course the idea of inauthenticity as first developed in Heidegger, the notion of the "anybody" (the German "man" or French "on"), mass-man, the anonymous and faceless crowds in the streets and factories of the industrial world. But with

Heidegger, and with the other anxious critics of modern civilization in the twenties, this concept was essentially an antidemocratic one: Sartre reverses it, turning it against the middle classes themselves.

What is particularly striking about the comparison between Sartre's two versions of this idea is that even the Sartre of the earlier work immediately links the experience of the we-subject to that of manufactured objects. There is, we might say, no personal way of opening a can, of punching a time card, of turning on a faucet: each of these objects has built into it an impersonal directive, a set of instructions as to the way in which "anybody" must use them, so that in doing so, we lose our own personal individuality and become mere delegates of that "undifferentiated transcendance" which is the we-subject. Thus, as in the later work, objects reflect back to me my own anonymity, my participation in a we-subject; and indeed, all the themes of the later work are implicit in the earlier illustration. For the worker is also alone with things, with his tools and machines and raw materials: yet insofar as they stand as commands to him to produce a given object *for* someone else, he feels them as an alien presence, as the look of the third, before which he himself becomes a kind of object along with his fellow workers. Yet the consumer who ultimately uses these manufactured objects feels himself "at one" in a profoundly depersonalized, anonymous sense with all those others who also buy and use the merchandise in question. Thus even in *Being and Nothingness* the commodity is the disguised bearer of interpersonal relationship, interpersonal struggle. Yet in the scheme of *Being and Nothingness* the we-relationships tended to be too rapidly assimilated to the vicious circle of the individual ones, and to be seen in cyclical and ultimately ahistorical fashion. This was the result of the initial terminology of subject and object, the alternation between which limited the possibilities with fairly

251

mathematical strictness. There remains a trace of this cyclical, random oscillation in the *Critique*, but the notion of increasing totalization puts it in a new light and gives it for the first time a genuinely historical direction.

In the new version of the formation of a group given in the *Critique*, the "third" plays a role analogous to that which it had in the creation of the we-object (and clearly, it was to prepare for this function that Sartre introduced the idea earlier, in connection with reciprocity itself). Only in the *Critique*, what seemed before relatively simple and straightforward has undergone an amplification of imposing proportions, a complication which may seem to make this concept as cumbersome as that of the rotation of Ptolemaic epicycles. For the basic problem we face when we come to the question of group dynamics is that of the possible autonomy of the group as a unit: if the experience of the we-object, of group participation and ontological solidarity with others, remains bound to the look of the third party or the outsider, then it is hard to see how the group could ever become an independent force in its own right, for it would always depend for its being on something outside itself.

And there is no doubt that in the beginning, the group always comes into being *against* some third party, against an external menace of some kind. It is fear of possible repressive action by the royal troops arriving at the Tuileries (a move similar to that which had resulted in a massacre only three months earlier) that galvanizes the Faubourg Saint-Antoine out of its serial dispersal and unifies it into a group which will eventually seize the key stronghold of the Bastille (pp. 391-393). Thus already in this first example, the external stimulus initially furnished by the third (the enemy, the troops of the Prince de Lambesc) is replaced by a new center or common object in the Bastille itself, around which the group organizes and disposes itself.

Yet this new organization in itself is not enough either,

for seriality was also defined as a disposition of people around some central (practico-inert) object. The group needs to interiorize its unity in some more basic way, and this is done by the interiorization of the formerly external third party. Now each member of the group becomes a third to all the rest, and this is to be understood not statically but dynamically. It is not a form fixed once and for all, but a process of rotating or revolving thirds, in which everyone in turn serves as the unifier of the other members. Now the group no longer has to depend on the look of the outsider or the enemy: a structure has been evolved such that the group carries its own source of being within itself, and moreover this structure is a profoundly democratic one, for in it there are no leaders, only agitators (in other words, thirds who attempt to verbalize the implicit feelings and aims of the group), and at this stage in the group's development everyone is equally a member, or third.

Despite the complication of this model, I think that anyone with an existential experience of groups will judge that as a phenomenological account it is not a bad description of what groups actually feel like. It is certainly the case that in real group action, we are ourselves both observer and participant at the same time, in unequal proportions. We both feel the group as something larger than ourselves, which we are able to observe in the others from without (and here we are ourselves functioning as a third to them); and at the same time, particularly when we ourselves are involved in action, we feel ourselves so observed as making up the group in question. As for the crucial distinction between leaders and mere agitators, it ought to be evident in the way in which, at this stage, the suggested actions or watchwords *must* somehow correspond to and articulate the profound intentions of the group itself; for it is not the prestige of the leaders which brings about the adoption of this or that proposed course of action. Rather, the leaders enjoy respect precisely to the degree to which they are able to anticipate and give voice to the unformulated thinking of the group itself.

Yet, particularly as the life of the group extends in time, the interiorization of the third is an insufficient guarantee of group autonomy, for the danger which it came into being to combat may disappear, or at least momentarily abate. The Bastille falls, the enemy beats a prudent retreat. Now, although the various members of the group may be intellectually aware that the danger is far from over and that the king's troops may return any minute in greater force, the enemy presence is no longer there to maintain the necessary sense of urgency, and the members of the group are tempted to drift back into the private life of serial dispersal. So at this point, reinforcing the system of revolving thirds, the group interiorizes the danger itself in the form of the *oath*. Its classic form and paradigm is of course the tennis court oath, its purpose to maintain by sheer internal determination that cohesion which had previously been little more than a response to external stimuli. The original oath, which pledged the members of the National-Assembly-to-be "never to separate and to reassemble wherever circumstances should require until such time as the Constitution shall be established and placed on solid foundations," has the additional interest of pointing beyond this "hot" moment of the group-in-fusion toward a gradual cooling and institutionalization. What is not present in this wording, but is implied in the very nature of an oath, as a necessary corollary, is the Terror: for it must include its own principle of enforcement, and implicitly each member pledges his own death should he in the future break the unity of the group and turn traitor to it. He therefore, in a sense, consents in advance to the Terror.

This component of the oath would seem at first glance to justify Merleau-Ponty's accusation of ultra-Bolshevism (leveled at Sartre not on the basis of the *Critique*, which he only heard in lecture form, but of *Les Communistes et la paix*); for with it, as in the purge trials of the 1930's, the children of the Revolution implicitly ask to be devoured by it, and justify their own elimination in advance. Yet as a phenomenological description, Sartre's theory is only designed to account for the empirical fact of the very real sense of life-and-death urgency which a group-in-fusion confers on itself. He explicitly underlines, moreover, the ultimate failure of the Terror as such: "Of the two possible negations of the group—individual *praxis* and seriality—the first, as we have seen, constitutes the moment of the realization of the common enterprise; it is ontological negation and practical realization; the other is definitive and it was against it that the group was originally formed. However, it is the first of these negations which is suspect for the machinery of the Terror" (p. 578). Thus, in its very structure, the Terror fails of its aim. Born of an attempt to prevent the return of seriality and dispersal, it engages instead in the liquidation of individual freedoms. In place of a recreation of the original group-in-fusion, in place of a return to that earliest moment of group euphoria and group cohesion, the Terror results only in that progressive desolation of the Convention so vividly described by Michelet, with its empty benches, its sense of the absence of the famous voices, the picture—charged with psychological suggestion as well—of Robespierre and his followers now left alone with themselves.

But the Terror is only part of the oath itself, which plays something of the role of a social contract in Sartre's thinking.[32] Even the differences with Rousseau are somehow profoundly akin to the spirit of the latter. Rousseau, of course, thought in terms of a larger community, a state or city-state, whereas the Sartrean concept of the group aims at a much

---

[32] See Georges Lapassade, "Sartre et Rousseau," in *Etudes philosophiques* XVII, No. 4 (Winter 1962), 511-517.

smaller guerrilla-type unit, and even tends, as we shall see shortly, to preclude the idea of a social class as an actor in history, let alone such an abstract unit as a state or a society or a nation. Yet implicit in Rousseau's concept was a reduction of the viable society to relatively manageable proportions, as in the city-state; and Sartre's further reduction to little groups, to relatively existential, lived proportions is really an operation undertaken in the same spirit, but at a later moment in the development of the middle-class society, when henceforth there is no longer any national or social unit, only a jumble of various groups and ruins of groups, serial collectivities, and groups of all kinds coming into being simultaneously.

It is at this point that Sartre, attempting to integrate into his scheme the whole dimension of historical time (in existential terms, the succession of the *generations* in time), enters on what are for him relatively new kinds of speculation. Thus, birth itself becomes the implicit swearing of a series of oaths, of a series of group affiliations. The baptism of newborn children (rather than of consenting adults) may serve as the symbol of this process which allows the newborn to join the larger group unities at once, to preserve the continuity of social institutions, to avoid the suspension of a "state of nature": "baptism is a way of creating freedom for the common individual [Sartre's term for the member by oath of an already constituted group] at the same time that he receives his function in the group and his reciprocal relationship to the other members" (p. 491n). This defense of an implicit social continuity, of an implicit ongoing life of institutions, may strike us as a flagrant contradiction of the very spirit of Sartre's existentialism itself; indeed, I believe that the idea of a social contract has been used to serve conservative as well as radical ends, and Sartre's own language at this point shows some hesitation ("I used to think this reasoning reflected some kind of timid conformism or fear . . .". It is, nonetheless, an essential link in his argument, as we shall see shortly, for the continuity of the oath, implicit or explicit, is the means by which a kind of inheritance of guilt is constituted from generation to generation, by which individual responsibility in the present is intensified with the burden of all the class responsibility of the past.

With the notion of the oath, the description of the structure of the initial group-in-fusion is complete. The distinction between group and seriality should now be evident: where in seriality no one was a center and the center was always and for everyone *elsewhere*, here in the group, everyone is the center, the center is everywhere, present wherever any members of the group are present. It is in this sense that the formation of the group is for its members a recuperation of their lost being, of their serial and individual dispersal in the world. On a mythical level, the formation of the group and the taking of the oath are, in Sartre's words, "the beginning of humanity" (p. 453). Now, for the first time, men are somehow self-caused, have become the foundation of their own being, have through mutual solidarity overcome both the abstract isolation of individual existence and the alienation of serial man in objects and otherness.

IT is perhaps worthwhile, at this moment in which the mystique of the group is strongest, to pause for an evaluation of the spirit in which group action is here treated by Sartre, and beyond that, of the notion of revolution itself which is implicit in his descriptions and in his frequent recourse to the French Revolution as a paradigm of group behavior. In this, of course, he himself is representative of a larger current in contemporary French intellectual life which may be described as that of revolutionary nostalgia, governed by a value-charged myth of revolution itself. I use the word myth not in the negative sense of that which calls for demystification, but rather in the positive meaning it has come to have for American literary criticism as a kind of ordering of experience; for it seems to me that this notion of revolution can be best understood not so much in direct political and theoretical terms, but precisely in terms of time and of narration, in what are ultimately literary categories.

What if, in other words, revolution were to be understood not so much in terms of content as in terms of *form*? What if the power of the revolutionary idea came fully as much from the new temporal reorganization of experience that it permits, as from any practical consequences which might flow from it as effects from a cause?

This is nowhere so clear as in the realm of historiography itself. The basic difference between academic and Marxist histories lies, it seems to me, in the types of rhythm each establishes between permanence and revolution, between social custom and social change, between the continuous and the sudden break in the thread. For the academic historian, as for the conservative in general, the truth of social life is somehow a deep underlying permanence, a slow and organic continuity whose first image and rhythm is derived from the landowner's fields themselves. Synchronic pictures of history are possible only at that price, for how else would a historian be justified in writing a description of England in the 1740's, let us say? Yet the experience of living in a numbered and historical decade is something that no one feels at the time: it is an optical illusion of the historian, a mirage of being projected after the fact. Thus Sartre's characters and Sartre himself are shocked, at the end of the 1930's, to realize that all this time they had been "a" generation, living through a period which would go down in the history books as the period "between the two wars": they themselves had merely thought they were living.

Faced with an absolute break in continuity, the conservative historian tries to reabsorb it into that continuity itself: thus Taine shows us that in its essential structures (centralization, rationalism), the Revolution was not something new, but only fulfilled the work of the eighteenth century, of the *ancien régime* itself. Thus the Revolution becomes but one manifestation of the eighteenth century among others.

For Marxist historiography, on the other hand, it is permanence and continuity which are the illusion, and change and struggle the reality. These two modes of understanding the past, indeed, reflect a kind of Gestalt alternation, in which everything changes depending on whether you see history as a continuum only occasionally broken by upheavals, or as a constant working out of hidden contradictions, a perpetual but concealed violence which comes to the surface from time to time as a reminder of the nature of the underlying reality. (The very concept of continuity is of course an *idealistic* one, criticized from their own respective points of view by both existentialism and Marxism.)

Thus the scandal of the revolutionary event for academic historiography lies in the radically new type of event which it offers to historical narration. In ordinary continuous life, the life of custom and tradition, nothing really changes or happens, there is basically nothing to tell in the narrative sense: there are only "institutions" on the one hand, and the random stories of individual life on the other, which therefore lose even what existential density they possess and become mere *examples* of the former (the life of a peasant in the Middle Ages, the daily routine of a seventeenth-century burgher's wife, and so forth).

The peculiarity of the revolutionary moment is that in it, for the first time, history takes the form of narratable events, reveals itself as a continuity with a beginning, middle, and end, marks a shift to a new and qualitatively different temporal organization. We have seen in an earlier chapter how for Lukács the novel was a means of salvaging and organizing the aimless, drifting (*existential*) time of the individual and giving it a kind of ritual meaning, albeit in imaginary fashion and in an imaginary mode. The revolutionary moment now does so in reality, through the new relationship which comes into being between the individual and the collective, and the transformation of individual time which comes as a consequence. In other words, whereas under ordinary peacetime conditions there is still a difference between real life and mere existence, or between genuine existence and mere dead stretches of time or duration, this distinction is suppressed by the revolutionary continuum itself, in which everything—all gestures and thoughts, routines, decisions, private life as well as public life—is henceforth drawn into relationship with the revolutionary process, reorganized around it and reevaluated automatically by its juxtaposition with the central revolutionary fact itself.

This total process, which Malraux (in *L'Espoir*) called apocalypse, is for the first time one in which the total collectivity is involved, whether it wants to be or not. Wartime would seem to be an analogous state of total mobilization, but it is, of course, initiated from the outside: the revolutionary moment, on the other hand, which insofar as it is violence is basically a civil war, contains its own cause and maintains itself in its own being.

Such a description, on the other hand, would seem to stress unduly the process of change at the expense of the actual nature of the socio-economic change itself; for it would seem that where the revolutionary moment becomes an end in itself, as apocalypse or group euphoria, as a transfiguration of existence rather than as an instrument to transform a system of production or legal relationships, then there would be no way of distinguishing the value of one group experience from another, and the old quarrel between Communism and anarchism would seem once more to raise its head. For it is actual again, and not only in France, in the theoretical differences between student movements and the older institutional Left; and one can rephrase the criticism in temporal terms as Pietro Chiodi does when he objects to the instantaneity inherent in Sartre's concept of the group, its basic timelessness, or the way it can experience time and change, *durée*, merely as a gradual deterioration from that initial moment of intensity in the formation of the group.

We may say all this yet another way by pointing out that what is so fascinating about the French Revolution of 1789, what makes it so useful as a paradigm and seems patently to justify Sartre's use of it in his book, is precisely its *bourgeois* character; for this particular revolution took the form of a conquest of *political* power by the middle classes, and played itself out in parliamentary form. Hence the importance in it of "characters" in the novelistic sense, of individualities: for it was both by their oratorical language and by the emblematic value of their personalities (Danton's appetites, Robespierre's stiffness) that they were able to be functional in that "ruse of history" whereby France was transformed from a hierarchical feudal-absolutist state to a centralized middle-class one. Thus the Great Revolution, like the novel form, like the sonata or the great systems of idealistic philosophy, is implicitly governed by the category of middle-class individuality (or, if you prefer, of *humanism*), and thus allows itself to be told in the form of a story —witness Michelet, whose great history yields in nothing to the novelists with whom he is contemporary (Balzac, Dickens, Flaubert).

There are, indeed, other literary categories which are instructively applied to the notion of revolution as well:

that of the point of view, for instance. Such a category, with its implication that we must be in situation even with respect to the past, is already inherent in that logical distinction between subject and predicate in the historical process, of which Marx made so much and which he originally derived from Feuerbach (i.e., the proletariat is the actual subject or bearer of the historical process). There is a basic sense in which this means that even in the study of the past, *insofar as it is told as a story*, we are obliged by the very form itself to take sides. Thus Aragon's Géricault, listening in the dark to a complicated argument between revolutionary conspirators, finds himself obliged to adopt a point of view in order to comprehend: "Here, in order to follow the *plot* [and the ambiguous term *histoire* designates either *story* or *history* itself], Theodore had to make up his mind one way or the other, his sympathy had to go out to this set of actors as against those others. And the odd thing was that this King's Musketeer, this Don Quixote of the world of yesterday—a world which today was in headlong flight—as he listened to these clashing arguments, seemed to be taking Napoleon's side as though his anxiety were that these nobodies, these wretches, this priest, these middle-class citizens, these day laborers, might not understand the new role the Emperor was going to assume. He was afraid the play might not have the ending he wished, like those members of the audience in the gallery who are carried away to the point of shouting to the hero on the stage that the traitor is standing behind him. . . ."[33] In this, Géricault as witness only reproduces the movement of the reader of the historical novel itself, who looks in as spectator and is forced, by the mechanism of point of view, into complicity with the acts he witnesses.

This relationship between history and situation or point

[33] Louis Aragon, *Holy Week*, trans. Haakon Chevalier (New York, 1961), pp. 298-299.

of view is indeed the focus of that thoroughgoing attack on the validity of historical thinking undertaken, on the occasion of Sartre's *Critique*, by Lévi-Strauss, who emphasizes precisely the dependency of historical analysis on taking sides. Yet inasmuch as these sides or alternative points of view are conceived of in terms of that modern spectrum of positions from extreme Right to extreme Left which the French Revolution exhaustively articulated for the first time, our possibilities of point of view and identification become uncontrollable as an event recedes further and further into the past. Understanding the Fronde, for instance, becomes a frenzied effort to determine whose is the legitimate "right to revolt," who represents privilege and who the attack on privilege. "It suffices therefore that history be increasingly removed from us in time, or that we be removed from it in thought, for it to cease to be interiorizable, and to lose its intelligibility, which was only an illusion that was attached to a provisory interiority."[34] As scandalous as such an argument may seem from the point of view of academic or "objective" historiography, it seems to me that in the present framework we may well admit its validity, without for all that conceding the invalidity of historical thinking as a whole. For it amounts to saying that we ourselves are in situation only with respect to middle-class history, and that history as such has acquired a unified or "totalized" meaning only since the advent of capitalism itself; that the earlier past and its artistic monuments are available to us only analogically, and at the price of some essential translation or adaptation of them to our own socio-economic situation. It is in any case certain that the problem of a point of view in the past is among the crucial ones that Sartre will have to solve in the *Critique* if history is not to dissolve into a series of unrelated group movements and discontinuous events. The error of Lévi-Strauss is, however,

[34] Claude Lévi-Strauss, *La Pensée sauvage* (Paris, 1962), p. 338.

not so much the notion that the distant precapitalist past is inaccessible to historical thought as such, but rather the idea that we can in any genuine way "be removed" from our historical present in postindustrial monopoly capitalism, that we are in any sense free *not* to understand events in that historical mode which is contemporaneous with it. The argument may be put in perspective by juxtaposing it with Lukács' position in *History and Class Consciousness*, where he shows that the proletariat and the party of the proletariat are both practically and theoretically the bearers of history in the sense of the basic "point of view."

But it was Michelet who first sensed the scope of this problem and worked out the consequences in his historiographic practice. Like Balzac, Michelet anticipated the transformations necessary in the category of the point of view when it was raised from the story of individual life to that of the collectivity: "every history of the Revolution up to now," he says in his conclusion, "has been essentially monarchistic. (This one in favor of Louis XVI, this one in favor of Robespierre.) The present history is the first republican one, the first to break the idols and the gods. From first page to last, it has had but one hero: the people."[35] Michelet marks, therefore, the passage from individualism (with its implicit "cult of the personality") to a new type of collective narration which, whatever the differences in historical content (*people*—1853, rather than *proletariat*—1923), is formally identical with that proposed by Lukács. The result is that the portraits of individual characters, through whom we witness the events, undergo a relativization which is thoroughly modern in its literary character. We still take sides, but as in the Sartrean system of revolving thirds, we are no longer bound in sympathy to a single actor. We take up our heroes and let them drop ruthlessly;

[35] Jules Michelet, *Histoire de la révolution française*, 2 vols. (Paris, 1952), I, 991.

and from this point of view, our reading is itself an abnega-
tion of that individual personality to which we are instinctively so attached, already virtually a training in the new
forms of collective existence. But let Michelet describe his
own practice, for he is well aware of what he is doing: "We
have rarely made any total and indistinct judgment, rarely
given a *portrait* as such; all, or almost all, are unjust, resulting from an averaging out of a character at a given moment,
where good and evil cancel each other out and make each
other false. . . . How many men in one man! How unjust it
would be to stereotype a definitive image of this variable
creature! Rembrandt made, I believe, thirty self-portraits,
all similar, all different. I have followed this method; both
art and justice equally urged me to it. If you take the trouble to follow each of the great actors through these two
volumes, you will see that each consists of a whole gallery
of sketches, each retouched at its particular date according
to the moral and physical modifications which the individual had undergone. The Queen and Mirabeau come before
us again and again, five or six times; at each appearance
time has marked them in passing. Marat seems the same,
but under shifting traits, all true, although different. The
timid and comfortless Robespierre, hardly glimpsed in
1789, is drawn in profile before us in November 1790, in an
evening session, at the rostrum of the Jacobins; we give a
full-face portrait of him (in May 1791) in the National As-
sembly, magistral, dogmatic, already full of menace. We
have thus carefully and punctiliously dated men and questions, and the moments of each man. Again and again, we
have had brought home to us an idea which struck us
greatly and which dominates the present work: *history is
time*."[36]

Point of view is, of course, not the only literary category
of significance for the study of the revolutionary moment

[36] *Histoire de la révolution française*, I, 290-291.

and of its possible historiography. The very temporal structure itself is displayed in the crucial importance of the choice, inevitably an artificial one, of the frame, of the beginning and the ending, of the points between which the narrative is to run. The history of the French Revolution is customarily thought to begin with the Estates General (or the elections to it) and to end with the death of Robespierre —and in this, Michelet himself follows the customary pattern. Yet the effect of such a choice of termini is significant: for the coincidence of the fall of Robespierre with the end of the Revolution as such implies that the Terror was at one with the Revolution itself. It is an implication written into the form, and even a writer hostile to Robespierre and the Jacobins, as Michelet is, will find himself, by his own time scheme, forced into profound sympathy with Robespierre at the moment of his downfall. That this is something more than a literary question may be judged by a comparison with a history which chooses a wholly different temporal framework, such as that of Daniel Guérin mentioned above. *La Lutte des classes sous la première république*—the omission of the word revolution from the title is already a program in itself—begins with the ministry of the Gironde and ends not with the fall of Robespierre but with the execution of Babeuf. Essentially, Guérin has rewritten the classical schema of the Great Revolution along the lines of Marx's *Eighteenth Brumaire,* as a kind of holding operation by the victorious middle classes. The functional purpose of Robespierre in this new reading of the Revolution was to eradicate whatever elements—whether counterrevolutionary or genuinely popular—remained to endanger the control of the middle classes; and when this was done, he himself was dispensable and could give way to that enjoyment of the fruits of the enterprise which was the Directory. Thus, his death is not the end to the basic process but only one of its moments, and the Revolution itself does not really come to a halt until the failure of Babeuf's conspiracy eliminates the last progressive forces from the scene. This analysis has the merit of reminding us that the word revolution is in itself a very ambiguous one: on the one hand, all revolutions are akin in the new *kind* of temporal organization they offer, in the sudden outbursts of collective energy, in their relentless development "toward the Left." But what this generic similarity often causes us to forget is that a middle-class revolution is not really a revolution at all in the modern sense; so that one cannot take sides *for* the revolutionaries of the Convention without contradiction, without confusing our whole reading of the past. That the Jacobins of 1793 were heroic, while those of 1848 were petty, should not blind us to the fact that *both* were middle class, and aimed essentially at the conquest of power by the middle classes.

This is, I think, the gravest formal objection to Sartre's use (and he is not alone in this) of the French Revolution as a paradigm. It suffices to think of a modern socialist revolution to realize that there the whole temporal structure of the process is quite different. The actual "revolution" itself is only an instant—the seizure of power by the Bolsheviks, the entry of Fidel into Havana—for it is no longer in terms of *political* control but of total economic transformation that the essential problems are posed: such a process is a story whose beginning and ending is more difficult to determine, for it expresses itself not so much in terms of personalities at a revolutionary podium as in production statistics and collective enterprises. No doubt, the protagonists of the French Revolution also spoke of the need to "continue the Revolution" or to "end the Revolution," but what they meant thereby was merely the definitive choice of a particular political form of government and the elaboration of a constitution. Whereas the continuation of the revolution in a socialist country has to do with a social and technological transformation which has no foreseeable end, and to which correspond rather such ideas as that of the "permanent revolution" in both Trotsky's and Jefferson's sense. It remains to be seen, however, what narrative or historiographic form can be devised to express the reality of this new mode of revolutionary time; and in that sense, Sartre's basic model of groups, although I do not think it seriously affects the outcome of his argument, risks misleading the reader into an overestimation of the moment of group formation, and into a mystique of apocalypse.

ONCE THE group has been formed, the question of its subsequent development cannot be worked out until some basic description of its being has been given. It is here that the continuity between the Sartre of *Being and Nothingness* and the Sartre of the *Critique* is most striking, and I insist on the point both because it is crucial and because most studies of the *Critique* seem to gloss over it. Just as the being of the individual is in reality a lack of being, an inability to be, to reach some ultimate and definitive stability and ontological plenitude, so also the group is characterized not as a substance or a hyperorganism, but as a set of individuals trying in vain to become a substance, straining toward some ultimate hyperorganic status which they can never attain. The group is not an organic community or collectivity, but a common project: and the formal sense of that common project is to *become* just such an organic community. But even in the case of the we-object, the collective "being" which I shared with my fellows was that of my materiality, my objective quality, and not that of my subjectivity: a world soul, an interfusing of minds and subjectivities is clearly an impossible and contradictory notion. Thus, the group experience, like that of the individual consciousness in *Being and Nothingness*, is an ontological failure,[37] in that

[37] *Being and Nothingness* does not admit the possibility of a global we-object because at that point there would remain no outside third to effect the process of objectification through the look.

it sacrifices itself in vain to become something which does not and cannot exist. But we cannot make an evaluation of this idea of a "failure" until we first see what concrete form it takes.

Already the oath and the Terror were implicit attempts on the part of the group itself to preserve itself in being from within, and to stave off an eventual collapse back into seriality. But as this danger increases, the group undergoes an even more decisive transformation and adaptation. It prolongs its life as a group primarily by developing an organization, and it is clear that the demarcation of separate responsibilities, the assignment of tasks of different orders, the division of labor, are ultimately inconsistent with the total democracy and equality of the revolving thirds. Where before anyone could fill any role, now little by little, in the differentiation of roles, the immediate reciprocity of the thirds to each other is replaced by a reciprocity mediated by the group structure.

The term is significant, for it is at this point that Sartre raises in his system the whole problem of structure, particularly as it is formulated by Lévi-Strauss for linguistically patterned, supraindividual structures such as those of kinship in primitive tribes. Such structures, which the followers of Lévi-Strauss take as the *object* of their research, are here by Sartre subjected to a phenomenological analysis which reveals them to be a kind of optical illusion: they are, indeed, the optical illusion of the outsider, seeing the group not as praxis or action in course but as a type of being or constituted object. They are the hypostasis, along synchronic lines, of what is in reality a diachronic process.

On the other hand, these complex systems, which can be mapped out before us in charts, these kinship laws susceptible of being reduced to mathematical language, are clearly not imaginary and correspond to some particular mode of being of the social phenomenon in question. It is precisely because the group has made itself inert, has given itself an inner, resistant, material structure, that this aspect of it is henceforth accessible to statistical and mathematical analysis. Structure is not a timeless characteristic of all groups, but rather a phenomenon characteristic of a single moment of a group's historical development. It is, in this sense, the reverse of the practico-inert: where there man had to make himself inert in order to work on the objects around him, where he lost himself as freedom in order to fulfill the requirements of the object, here the group gives itself objective being from the inside, in order to be able to work on itself. Thus structure enables the group to become not only self-causing, but self-repairing, in its persistence of being, that is, in its renewed adaptation to changing situations; but at the same time, of course, it marks the ultimate, implicit limits of that development and that adjustment.

Now, with structure or organization, the group becomes itself a grouping of subgroups, and in psychological terms the problem of maintaining group unity may be stated as the difficulty of making every member of the specialized subgroups feel his place in the whole and realize the way in which his own perhaps limited technical responsibilities are on the contrary indispensable to the group effort and remain, as in the group-in-fusion, an omnipresent center. Now slowly membership in the group comes to be felt not so much from the inside as from without; and I learn my group affiliation through the surrounding seriality, which identifies me as a group member, and thus as a symbol for the group as a whole. At this point, the relationship of thirds to each other becomes a more distant and indirect one: it is clear to them that the group is no longer transparent, no longer pure praxis, no longer immediately assimilable to their own actions. It has come to acquire its own opacity, its own inertia, and its members feel themselves at once both a part of it and external to it. This new distance, which Sartre calls quasisovereignty, is of course nothing more than a resolution of the third back into its original components—actor versus witness. But the term is chosen to underline the fact that a total return to seriality has not taken place: the sovereign still remains in some way a member of the group (p. 589), although his relationship to the group itself is quite different in character from the relationship of pure manipulation and oppression which he establishes with the outlying seriality. Yet it is part of the natural history of the group that as the rotation of the thirds slows down, as institution and organization begin to come into being, at length a single third finds himself in the dominant position in the now petrified group structure: in him, in his unity as a human organism, the group still tries to see an image of its own organic unity (p. 595).

At this point, of course, the implicit frame of reference has been shifted from the French Revolution to the control of Stalin over the Soviet apparatus; and with this development the life, the vital evolution of the group has for all practical purposes ceased. This is not yet a dissolution back into seriality, which might indeed be the next stage in the group's history, if it can still be said to have one: for it is important to remember that along with the oath and the Terror, along with structure and organization, the taking of a sovereign is something the group does to itself in order to remain in existence, in order precisely to ward off the increasingly insistent forces of seriality at work all around it.

What confuses the issue perhaps is our tendency to think in terms of society as a whole as the ultimate unit of study; and it is important to remember that for Sartre the group does not, and can never, correspond to society as a whole, or to the nation as such (pp. 608-610). Thus, the concept of a society or a nation is an artificial one, which tends to mask the reality of social life as a complicated interrelationship of groups and series, in which groups use and manipulate

271

through extero-conditioning the various series dependent on them (pp. 614, 621). Sartre's theory is not for all that a return to microsociology, or to a form of nominalism of the various types of groups: for the dialectical result of this refusal of the national categories is precisely to throw the problems of group-formation open on a worldwide basis, as is appropriate in a situation where both the market system and the movement of liberation opposed to it have ceased to be national and have become international phenomena.

As with the life of the organism, so in the life of the group there is a temporal irreversibility: once having grown rigid in its structures, having given itself a sovereign, the group cannot swim back up the river of time to its heroic moment of formation. However, as with other apparently pessimistic aspects of Sartre's thinking which we will examine shortly, it is important to draw the right practical consequences from this situation before judging the theory out of hand. Clearly, it has something to tell us about reform from above, and about all attempts to revivify group praxis and to restore more genuine revolutionary feeling from the hierarchy on down. The bureaucracy, Sartre seems to warn us, cannot transform itself back into a guerrilla unit: the ossified group cannot be renewed, it can only be *replaced*, by a new thrust of group-formation.

The relevancy of these analyses becomes evident when we think, for instance, of the Chinese cultural revolution. Whatever may have seemed confusing in that period of social upheaval now takes on the clarity of a textbook demonstration: a deliberate attempt, not to revive the party apparatus, but to provoke a new and fresh wave of group-formation and revolutionary cohesiveness to take the place of the older, ossified groups; an attempt to put the notion of the permanent revolution into practice.

Another corroboration of Sartre's theory, a little closer

to home, is to be found in the French May Events of 1968, in which the official Communist Party apparatus was by-passed, both inside and outside the party, by a new type of revolutionary group-formation. Yet it is necessary to under-score the fact that the existing group institutions are not wholly without function; for they are, as we have seen, the material inertia, the structural, quasimathematical rem-nants of what was formerly genuine group action, and as such they function a little like reminders. Thus, for instance, it seems clear that it was the party apparatus in France which by its very existence kept the idea of revolution alive —through its cellular organization, through manifestations, through the various types of revolutionary education and training, through the dissemination of Marxist culture and the commemoration of the past history of the labor move-ment. The fact that the new revolutionary moment was obliged to express itself structurally in the formation of new groups does not mean that it could have succeeded in doing so without this institutionalized reminder, this mnemonic device, as it were, holding the place in the pages of history.

In a more general way, it is clear that objections to the "pessimism" of the *Critique* only recapitulate in different language those leveled against *Being and Nothingness* some twenty years earlier: for both essentially aim at undermin-ing the central doctrine of the lack of being of individual consciousness, or of groups. Thus, the implication of Sar-tre's new work would seem to be that in some sense the revolution must always fail, since the inevitable perspective of groups is bureaucracy or Stalinist dictatorship, ultimate loss of spontaneity to rigid forms. Sartre's political system would therefore seem to be a defeatist one.

What this criticism fails to note is that it is precisely the antiorganic bias of Sartre's group theory which renders it unserviceable for right-wing group mystiques, whether of the people, the nation, the army, or whatever. For the effects of mass hypnotism and mystification would not seem possible without the firm illusion of some organic communion to which the individual surrenders himself.

As for the notion of an inevitable petrification of groups, I believe that what is objected to here is not the forecast as such, but in reality time itself. For to say that consciousness or human life is a lack of being, an emptiness striving toward stasis and plenitude, toward being itself, is only in effect to give a definition of time. Thus, Sartre's description of the failure (*échec*) of group action, like that of the failure of the individual human relationships, is to be understood in ontological rather than empirical terms. When Sartre says in *Being and Nothingness* that the project to love is an ontological failure, this means neither that there is "really" no such thing as love, as a lived experience, nor that love cannot last, but merely that love as such never succeeds in fulfilling the ontological function it sets for itself, namely to bring about some ultimate plenitude, or in other words, to achieve the very end of time itself. On the level of groups, therefore, the doctrine of ontological failure lays emphasis on the passage of time, on constant change, both in group and in situation, and on the succession of the generations. As in *Being and Nothingness* it has what is essentially an ethical function: it aims at dispelling the illusions of an ethic of being, and at reconciling us to our life in time. On the collective level, we can still find traces of those illusions everywhere when we think about the future in political or economic terms: where Marx saw Utopia as the beginning of genuine history itself, and contemptuously described our own "history" as "prehistory," most of us tend instinctively to think of it as the point at which history stops. These are the remnants of idealism, of the thought modes of the illusion of being, which the existential component of the *Critique* attempts in its severity to dispel.

274

IV

BEFORE discussing the conclusion of the *Critique*, it therefore seems useful to pause and to review Sartre's earlier ethical positions, in order to see to what degree the *Critique* completes that earlier development, and in what sense it can be said that the later work corresponds to the *Ethics* promised on the last page of *Being and Nothingness* and never forthcoming.

In reality, there never was a problem about the ethical position of *Being and Nothingness* where the isolated individual was concerned. The question was not one of the nature of authenticity as an individual life style or mode of living, but rather of its implications for the collectivity, and the relations it implies or fails to imply with other people.

As we have already indicated, the ethical thrust of *Being and Nothingness* aimed at dispelling the substantialist illusion, the illusion of possible being, in all its forms. Insofar as it is an instrument of demystification, therefore, this ethic will take as many forms as the initial mystification itself. Thus we find a relatively conventional version of it toward the end of the work, where the inevitable failure to be provides a standard by which the various original choices, the various life-styles, can be judged and ranked in a hierarchical system of evaluation. The lowest, and most base, of the original choices will be those which confuse being and matter, which take matter as a substitute for being, and long to find an ultimate stability in the possession or enjoyment of material objects. It is therefore logical that above these passions should be ranked those which involve increasing spiritualization of their object, which conceive of being in less tangible and material terms: this would be, for example, the situation of the writer who attempts to objectify himself and to realize his being in a work of art, which,

as language, and as appeal to the other, no longer has anything material about it. Yet here still the illusion of being is
present, for what drives the project forward is the obscure,
instinctual, unarticulated feeling that it is still in some sense
possible to "realize oneself," that is to say, to objectify oneself in the form of an object for consciousness, so that one
can be at once both object and subject, which is to say, the
in-itself-for-itself, or God. There would therefore seem to
be room for yet another kind of life passion, one which did
not aim at self-objectification or at some ultimate form of
stasis, but which took its own freedom for an end and which
therefore, in any of the various possible forms it might take,
can be described by the general term of *play* in Schiller's
sense (and the term is clearly chosen for its offensiveness
to the *esprit de sérieux*, as Sartre terms the mode of consciousness caught up in the illusion of being). With the
state of play as an absolute, then, we reach a point where
we glimpse the possibility of some free, nonreified authenticity, no longer bound to the myths and illusions of being.[38]

Yet the ethic of play is at the same time positive and
abstract: what is concrete is that which prevents its realization. Genuine, concrete authenticity must therefore be defined in terms of that against which it has to struggle, rather
than as a type of ideal. Indeed, for both Heidegger and
Sartre, authenticity is seen as a later form than that inauthenticity which has priority over it and which constitutes the primary mode of being of human life. Genuine
authenticity is therefore not a state (to think so would be
to fall back into precisely that illusion of being which is at
issue), but rather something precariously wrested from inauthenticity, reclaimed and reconquered from it, and in

[38] It is paradoxical that Marcuse, in his convincing analysis of
Being and Nothingness as the historical expression of an alienated
society (*Kultur und Gesellschaft*, 2 vols. [Frankfurt, 1965], II, 49-84,
and see below pp. 347-348), fails to underline the significance of
this ethic of play, so close to his own.

perpetual danger of collapsing back into the older form
(for Heidegger anonymity, for Sartre *mauvaise foi*). For
this reason we would do well, I think, to consider the idea
of authenticity a *critical* one: for it cannot be defined in itself but only against some preexisting situation and state of
inauthenticity which it is designed to correct or remove.

We are thus led to explore the idea of authenticity
through its opposite. Thus, insofar as *mauvaise foi* is designed to give me a feeling of self-justification, and to help
me avoid that realization of my total freedom and solitude
which is anxiety (*angoisse*), the experience of authenticity
will always take place in anxiety, and will always involve a
sense of the unjustifiability of my own existence—a purification of consciousness which strips it of all its defenses and
rationalizations and leaves it without a past from which to
draw self-respect, without a future in which to put blind
faith.

Even so, this remains a relatively psychological or formal
description of authenticity (its apprehension as an *experience*). The peculiar force of Sartre's dramatization of the
problem comes from his instinctive feeling for the form
which the illusion of being takes for the middle class:
namely, *regret* and *remorse*, or perhaps even more than
regret, the *fear* of regret and remorse. This cuts both ways:
for remorse dissociates me from my own past, from my own
past actions; whereas the fear of remorse prevents me from
taking any binding step in the future that I might be sorry
about. This complex of fears has a positive version in the
notion of availability (*disponibilité*), where in the attempt
to keep myself free for anything that might come along, I
hoard my present like a miser, fearing to squander it, in
case I should need it in the future. Images of this stubborn
clinging to the self, this terror at the thought of abandoning
that inner middle-class privacy and elbowroom which is
known as the *personality*, are familiar to every reader of

Sartre's works: Clytemnestra, and after her Electra, disowning their crimes (in *The Flies*); Mathieu (in *The Age of Reason*) hesitating to do anything that might deprive him of his future freedom. But a scene in *Peer Gynt* offers perhaps an even more striking dramatization of this situation. Peer, in the kingdom of the trolls, and about to acquire eternal luxury through his marriage to the daughter of the troll king, must first fulfill one condition: that he allow his face to be mutilated, so that he will be as ugly as the trolls themselves and have no desire to return to the land of human beings in the future. Peer is horrified at the thought of being thus marked for good, irreparably; but the genuine Sartrean heroes are those who, like Orestes, long for the irreparable, the act by which they will become once and for all marked men.

The Flies, of course, ends at this point and is in any case a kind of parable. Indeed, I think that this is the moment at which one might invoke the notion of realism developed by Lukács, and maintain that the truth of such an ethical concept must be measured by the degree to which it can be realized in the concrete work of art, through the raw materials furnished by contemporary reality. Thus it is the series of the *Roads to Freedom* which must ultimately serve as the key to what is really meant by authenticity.[39]

Mathieu is able to be released from his self because he is already at distance from it: he is aware of examining his personality, his freedom, from the outside, and from there it is but a step to the abandonment of everything but his own present in time, to the realization that at every moment he is at one with his freedom. What is not so clear, however, is the enabling role of the historical situation in this proc-

[39] Any analysis of the work must henceforth draw on Simone de Beauvoir, *La Force des choses* (Paris, 1963), pp. 212-214, where the projected ending of the unfinished fourth volume is told for the first time.

ess: for even at this point it would seem that it is because of the war and the mobilization, it is because he has already become a serial number and a statistic, that it is so easy for Mathieu to free himself of his individualism and of the past that went with it.

The process involved, a kind of purification and disintoxication which we witness elsewhere in Sartre's works, in *The Flies*, in *Lucifer and the Lord*, in *Words* itself, can be described in psychological terms as the destruction of the ego, or in religious terms as the "cruel and long-drawn-out enterprise of atheism."[40] It requires the remorseless extirpation of every form of belief in transcendance, whether open or disguised: of history (Brunet and Frantz), external values (Mathieu), posterity (Sartre), the audience (Kean), as well as God (Goetz). Later on, in the unfinished fourth volume, when Mathieu joins the Resistance, when he is tortured and dies, it is clear that his authenticity consists in this absolute fidelity to the present and to the immediate situation of the present, this total disregard for the future and for his own death imminent in it, which has come to be known by the term *engagement* or commitment, and which is thus an ethical category long before it is a political one.

Yet once again the historical ambiguity presents itself, and we may emphasize it most clearly by returning to the work of art itself and to the aesthetic of the *extreme situation* on which it is constructed. For it is all one to say that without the war Mathieu could not have become authentic, and to say that without an extreme situation (that is, one involving death) one cannot *dramatize* the notion of authenticity. It is here, perhaps, that Sartre is closest to Heidegger, whose notion of the being-unto-death, whose mystique of the death anxiety, he does not share. If authenticity is dependent on crisis, in other words, then ultimately it is dependent on history itself and on contingent historical cir-

[40] *Les Mots* (Paris, 1964), p. 210.

cumstances; and with this, ethics already abolishes itself and makes way for the overtly political perspective of the *Critique*.

There is, however, still another aspect of this problem which accounts for the historical direction that Sartre's later thought has taken, and that is the private quality which authenticity still seems to have in this series of novels. To put this dilemma in its sharpest form, we may ask what there is to distinguish Mathieu's salvation, as it is presented here, with its consent to time and death, from an ethic of heroic Fascism, with its own cult of death and action, intensity of experience, with its analogous distaste for middle-class individuality. At this point, it is obviously not Sartre's own political sympathies which are in question, but rather the adequacy of his ethical formula as such: Is there anything built into that formula which necessarily implies a particular mode of being with others and a sympathy with oppressed rather than oppressing groups?

The only solution Sartre seems to have devised during this period[41] is the classic Kantian one, that I cannot realize my own freedom unless I realize that of others as well, that I cannot take my own freedom as an end unless I so take that of others as well. This position is disappointing, not because it is false, but because it is ahistorical, based upon a judgment from the outside and from above, rather than on the inner conditions of the concrete situation itself.

The new thrust forward in Sartre's ethics follows on the elaboration of his idea of the *imaginary*[42] and is contemporaneous with what has been called his political conversion

[41] See, for provisory expressions of this solution, Simone de Beauvoir, *Pour une morale de l'ambiguité* (Paris, 1947); Francis Jeanson, *Le Problème morale et la pensée de Sartre* (Paris, 1947); and Sartre's own (later repudiated) *L'Existentialisme est un humanisme* (Paris, 1946).
[42] See Section II of my "Three Methods," in *Modern French Criticism, op.cit.*

(that is, the writing of *Les Communistes et la paix*). It represents a radical reversal and interiorization of the Kantian position described above: now, in place of the abstract recommendation that the attitude toward others should be the same as that held toward the self, it is shown that in a psychological sense it is the attitude toward the self that conditions our attitudes toward other people. Thus the bad faith of Goetz (in *Lucifer and the Lord*), his frenzied attempt to justify his own existence either through evil in the absolute (he will be a greater criminal, a greater monster, than anyone else) or through good in the absolute (he will be holier, more saintly, more humble, than anyone else) is shown to be at one with the defense of *privilege*, both on the psychological and the socio-economic levels. His final conversion to humanity, his ultimate "death to self" thus involves an abandonment of the special pleading of the ego. The new psychological anonymity and impersonality that he wins thereby allows him not only to love for the first time, but also for the first time to accept his own position as "a complete man, made up of everybody else and worth any of them, but no better than any of them either" (to recall the closing language of *Words* as it describes Sartre's own development). This new concept of an inner, psychological identification between self-justification and special privileges, between *mauvaise foi* and privilege in general, is the intellectual instrument whereby Sartre converts his earlier ethical system into a politics or a theory of history. There cannot, therefore, be a Fascist authenticity: for the Fascist point of view always involves the defense of some form of privilege, and is the sign that some dank corner of the soul still clings to its own unjustifiable feelings of status and of innate superiority.

The final step in the argument is a relatively empirical one: What is to insure the continuity between the psychological disposition and the actual political choice? One may presumably renounce privilege and still be uncertain as to the exact composition of those privilege-defending groups to which one is then bound to be hostile. In aesthetic terms, we may once again recall that *Lucifer and the Lord* is simplified historical pageant, and that a model which articulates peasants, nobles, and burghers in conflict is far from having the statistical complexity of the politics of the modern world (for one thing, it offers a precapitalist situation). It is at this point that the *Critique* takes its place in the working out of the solution to the problem.

V

> . . . je vouai à la bourgeoisie une haine qui ne finira qu'avec moi.
> —"Merleau-Ponty vivant"

THE FINAL section of the *Critique* is devoted to a lengthy historical and phenomenological analysis of the life-styles and mentalities of both worker (and colonial subject) and bourgeois as they were formed in the course of the nineteenth and early twentieth century.[43] It is here, therefore, that we reemerge from the abstract structures of isolated individual and group action studied in the first five hundred pages of the book back out into the "level of the concrete, the place of history itself" (p. 632). This reemergence is both a fact of our reading and a significant conclusion to the argument: for it annuls whatever objections might have been made to the previous chapters on the basis of their abstractness, and confirms the presence of the earlier structures within that dense existential reality which we recognize as history itself. Indeed, this conclusion of the book, which many readers are perhaps too fatigued to reach or at least to consider with the intellectual alertness they may

---

[43] These pages complete the analysis of French "Malthusianism" begun in *Les Communistes et la paix*.

have been willing to devote to the earlier chapters, is as indispensable to an understanding of Sartre's position as its ending to a novel that one ought (in an ideal world) to read at a single sitting. For it is at this point, with a prodigious whirring of dialectical machinery in which quantity turns around into quality, that the earlier, self-contradictory impressions of revisionism and Stalinism are wholly canceled out and replaced by the first genuinely political writing in the *Critique*, which, with its passion, intransigence, and attachment to the lived fact, matches the Sartre already familiar to us from *Les Communistes et la paix* and the political articles in *Les Temps modernes*.

For the ideal groups we have been considering up to now are as abstract as the isolated individuals with which we began ("there are revolutionary idylls about the group which are the collective counterpart of the Robinsonade" [p. 643]). When, however, we attain the concrete reality of social class as such, we find that it is a complex of both serial and group structures: on the one hand, class is serial, both to the degree that it can never completely be transformed into a group, and in the sense that it originates as a serial structure: "it is qualified and determined by exigencies of the practico-inert: the first, negative relationship of the worker to the machine (nonpossession), the mystification of the free contract and work becoming a force hostile to the *worker himself*, beginning with the salary system and the capitalist process—all these things are realized in the context of serial dispersion and antagonistic reciprocity on the work market" (p. 644). Class affiliation, in other words, is defined as a particular relationship to a particular, determinate mode of economic production; and in this sense, what Sartre describes as seriality is what Marx calls conditioning (we will examine the possible differences between these two models shortly). From a different point of view, however, the "whole class is pres-

ent in the organized group which springs into being within
it and its collective seriality is, as a limitation, the inorganic
being of its practical community" (p. 644): so that the
group can, at least symbolically, realize the union of the entire class in its action.

Thus the status of a class is already given in the structure
of the practico-inert (factory system, machinery, salaries,
mode of distribution, rate of industrial development) at any
given moment. But this inert, impotent seriality is, as we
have seen already, first galvanized into group-formation by
the presence of external danger, by the threat of a common
enemy, who is, of course, in this context none other than the
middle class itself, the property owner. That danger is real,
for the middle classes fear the mass of workers and react
preventively to what is felt to be a working-class threat: not
only economically, in the lowering of salaries to assure
profits, in the closing down of factories during periods of
overproduction and in the fostering of useful forms of un-
employment, but overtly and politically as well. The first example of this political preventive warfare is still the classic
one: the deliberate repression and massacre of the workers
in June 1848 after the success of the middle-class revolution
had been assured and the working-class agitation for guar-
anteed employment had become an impediment to the
development of business.

This initial crime, this founding violence as we might call
it, has grave consequences for the formation of the middle-
class character as well; and it is at this point that the dimension of genuine history, the succession of the generations,
the dialectical change and development from one moment
to another, begins to come into view. For like the worker,
the factory owner emerges into a world whose external conditions are already given, into a situation fixed in advance
(even though the response to that situation is invented
freely), and the acts and life styles of the previous genera-

tion are precisely a part of the basic situation faced by their successors. Thus, an essential part of the inheritance of the middle class, from generation to generation, is the fact of their own past violence, which is to say, the violence done by their fathers and grandfathers, and it is this that in a previous section we have called blood guilt. This is not a theological idea but a dialectical one: the generation of 1848 decimates the workers, the workers remember and pass the memory on to their sons, the new generation of factory owners must now face a sullen, resentful, and mistrustful working class which has made up its mind about them *in advance*. Thus the act, once committed, passes into the structure of the world itself, leaves its traces as repressive legislation on the one hand and as profound suspicion on the other, and returns to confront the second and third generations as an *objective* situation to which they are not free *not* to react.

No matter how cultivated these later generations have become, inasmuch as they owe their new polish and sophistication both to the act of past violence and its fruits on the one hand, and to the increasing sophistication of the repressive apparatus on the other, we may say that they have interiorized the earlier violence in the form of an implicit oath of allegiance to their class and have thus taken on themselves responsibility for the actions of their predecessors. This responsibility is not to be understood as a marginal fact about the new middle classes, but as a total thing, as the basic choice, the key fear, around which everything else in their personal life-styles is organized.

It is at this point that we find some of Sartre's most characteristic analyses, such as the following passage on middle-class "distinction" (a *distinguished* man, great *distinction* of table manners, etc.): "The distinguished man is the result of *selection* (on the part of his superiors): he is the superior individual recruited by class cooption (or maintained in his class by permanent recognition). But he isn't *born* (even if he is in fact a bourgeois and the son of a bourgeois). For nature and blood confer their privileges on the aristocracy. But in the 'democratic' world of capitalism, it is nature that represents universality, with the result that *at first glance* the worker is a man just like the bourgeois. Distinction is an antinature: the bourgeois is *distinguished* in that he has suppressed needs in himself. And in fact he does suppress them, both by satisfying them on the one hand, and by hiding them on the other (occasionally displaying a certain asceticism): he maintains dictatorship over the body in the name of an absence of need; or in other words a dictatorship of culture over nature. His clothing is *constraint* (corsets, stiff collars and false fronts, top hats, etc.); he draws attention to his own *sobriety* (girls eat ahead of time when they are invited to dinner, in order to fast publicly), his spouse does not conceal her *frigidity*. This violence permanently exercised against the body (it is real or a pretense depending on cases, the important thing about it is that it be public) seeks to crush and negate it insofar as it [the body] is universality, insofar, in other words, through the biological laws that control its development and above all by the needs that characterize it, as it is the presence within the oppressor of the oppressed in person" (p. 717).

Insofar as the *Critique* began with a definition of man as *need*, this passage forms a kind of thematic climax. It is also the ultimate and definitive form taken by the method of existential psychoanalysis as it developed from *Being and Nothingness* to the study of Flaubert. That method aimed at showing how everything in a life, no matter how seemingly specialized and unrelated (gestures, tastes, opinions, skills), was the symbolic manifestation of a single basic choice of being, and was part of a single totality. Now Sartre shows us that the primary situation to which this choice is a reaction is class struggle itself. Thus, *everything* in the character of the bourgeois, his original choice even as it seems to express itself in his "private life," is but a disguised acting out of his participation in the historical struggle in which he is involved with the working class. There is in this sense nothing unpolitical any longer, no relief from history—and this not only synchronically but diachronically as well. There is no relief from the past as class struggle either, and it is precisely against the background of that struggle itself that the very need for relief, for mystification, for the illusion of the private and the personal, the nonpolitical and nonhistorical, can be understood as a project: it is, indeed, the equivalent of those blinks and moments of oblivion that were so sorely missed in *No Exit*.

It now becomes clear, I think, in what way the *Critique* aims at resolving the two basic historical problems it posed for itself: the responsibility of the individual for collective events over which he clearly has no control, and the manner in which the material and contingent accidents of history are to acquire a kind of meaning (without which, history itself becomes accidental and contingent).

The first problem is related to the classic opposition of freedom and necessity; and since ideas are best located and defined with respect to their opposites, it is worth recalling that the opposite of freedom, in *Being and Nothingness*, was neither necessity nor constraint, but rather *determinism*. Freedom is therefore positively defined neither as supreme power nor as the absence of obstacles, but rather as responsibility; the paradoxical element of Sartre's notion of freedom is of course precisely the manner in which we are responsible for everything that happens to us (even through necessity or constraint), in that we are *not* free *not* to react to the fate in question. The diachronic or historical dimension in which this notion is placed in the *Critique* transforms it into the more familiar one of total political responsibility or complicity. The fact that I do not make the basic decisions in no way releases me from responsibility for them: abstention is consent in the sense of being part of the solution or being part of the problem. And it is because of the continuity of the class struggle across the various generations that everyone can be seen to be reacting to a single situation, to a single such "problem."

We have already dealt with the way in which men, by the mere fact of their needs and their work, humanize the inert, material world around them and invest it with a human meaning as well as with the destructive possibilities of counter-finality. Now, as we begin to see how this relatively technological history looks when it is translated into terms of class antagonism, it is perhaps the right time to confront this ultimate picture of the Sartrean system with the view presented by orthodox Marxism. I will reserve the whole problem of the relationship between idealism and material-ism for a concluding chapter: here we will compare the positions of both models with respect to the determinant role of the economic in history.

For there can be no doubt that they offer us pictures of history which, if they are not inconsistent, are at least quite different from each other. The classical Marxist picture shows history as a relatively autonomous development and unfolding of economic institutions themselves, a develop-ment which is of course not linear or organic, but rather bound up with the working out of internal contradictions and the creation, out of the system itself, of the ever fresh problems which it will have to face and to which it will be called on to adapt: the emergence of capitalism from the sporadic commerce of the Middle Ages, the landless serfs driven into the cities by enclosure and adding their life-force and labor power to the primitive accumulation of capital realized by merchants and entrepreneurs through whose individual passions, through whose greed and thrift history works as by a ruse, making of them the instruments of its own self-development.

Whereas in the *Critique*, although it does not of course call into question the above linear description as an account of the facts, the picture of lived history that emerges strikes us as being far more markedly cyclical—a kind of alternation between moments of group-formation and moments of group decay, an almost Viconian recurrence of the fixed stages of seriality, group-in-fusion, institutionalization, and the ultimate fall back into seriality itself.

In fact, however, we may understand the difference in emphasis inherent in these models by seeing the Marxist one as relatively more diachronic, in the way in which it evaluates each moment with respect to its position on the curve of developing capitalism over a long period; while the Sartrean analysis is more synchronic in the manner in which it permits any given moment to be resolved back into the lived reality of the class struggle.

It is perhaps in this context that the vexing problem of the reflection theory of ideology is best posed: for the very notion of a reflection presupposes a preliminary separation between the two phenomena that reflect each other. When these phenomena are diachronic in nature and extend over a long period of time, reflection is fairly imperceptibly translated into simple parallelism. Thus, the development of the character of the bourgeois (from its early Protestant origins to the various modern national varieties) forms a kind of general parallel to the development of the economy, and this parallelism allows room for whatever incidental time lags or premature developments, whatever asymmetries and irregularities between the systems prove empirically to have been present. "The further the particular sphere which we are investigating is removed from the economic sphere and approaches that of pure abstract ideology, the more shall we find it exhibiting accidents in

289

its development, the more will its curve run zigzag. But if you plot the average axis of the curve you will find that this axis will run more and more nearly parallel to the axis of economic development the longer the period considered and the wider the field dealt with."[44]

Now whenever Sartre deals with the relationship of character or ideology to a given moment of historical development, his analyses are not inconsistent with the above model. Thus in describing the evolution of working-class organizations he shows how the type of machine used (in the particular case studied, the "universal machine," like the lathe) and the economic organization to which it corresponds preselect a proletariat divided into skilled and unskilled labor; so that the anarcho-syndicalism characteristic of this period is in reality the ideology of a skilled proletariat and is as such an idea latent in the machine itself, the "thought of the machine," which changes when it changes in the last years of the nineteenth century (pp. 292-297).

Paradoxically, however, it is the diachronic Marxist model that proves to be synchronic in the analysis of any given moment, while it is the relatively more synchronic Sartrean model that articulates such moments into diachronic steps. Thus, where for classical Marxism such ideology-formation is a determination of a conditioning by, a reflection of, the mode of production (in other words, where the superstructure and the infrastructure are somehow simply corresponding units of the same phenomenon), for Sartre the former must be seen as a reaction to the situation which the latter constitutes. The economic base is therefore inert matter which is transformed by human action, and which, in the act of transformation, leaves its traces within the new act as a kind of inert structure or skeleton; in other terms, it may be seen as the past (*passé*)

[44] Engels to Heinz Starkenburg, 25 January 1894 (*Basic Writings*, ed. Feuer, p. 412).

transcended (*dépassé*) by the act of the historical agent. The Sartrean model is therefore closer to the original Hegelian one of a datum which is both negated and sublated (*aufgehoben*) or preserved: and this rearticulation of the reflection model into two consecutive moments, into situation and freely invented response, gives a more realistic content to the idea of alienation itself, as something which circumstances force us to *do to ourselves*, and that without clearly knowing it. This is the spirit of a henceforth classic passage of the *Critique*: "In the early period of semiautomatic machines, interviews have shown that the girls involved in this specialized work drifted into specifically sexual daydreams while working, recalled their room, their bed, the night, the most private details about the couple in its solitude. But in reality it was the machine that dreamed through them about erotic experience: for the type of attention required in that particular kind of work allowed neither for complete distraction (thinking of something else entirely) nor complete concentration (thinking interferes with physical operation); the machine thus requires and creates in the human being an inverted semiautomatism in order to complete itself: an explosive mixture of unconscious vigilance; the mind is absorbed without being used, involved in a kind of *lateral* control, while the body functions 'mechanically' under a kind of *surveillance*. Conscious life overflows the task assigned it: it has to live these minutes of artificial distraction one by one; it has to live them at a lower level of concentration, refusing any attention to detail as well as any genuine systematic thought, in order not to interfere with the lateral control mechanism, in order not to slow down the operation; thus an abandonment to passivity is an appropriate response: in analogous situations, men have nowhere near the same tendency to sexual daydreaming; but they're the 'first sex,' the active sex: if they thought about *possession*, their work would suffer, and

291

inversely their work, absorbing their total activity, leaves no room for sexuality: the working girl, however, dreams of *sexual surrender* because the machine requires of her that she live her conscious life passively in order to maintain a flexible, preventive state of alertness without ever allowing it to become active thought. . . . The truth is that through the attempt to *escape* her situation the working girl has found an indirect way to make herself what she is: the vague feeling of desire which she maintains—and which is limited by the incessant operation of the machine and of her own body—is a means of preventing thought from reforming, a means of holding consciousness back, absorbing it in the body, while keeping it available. Is she aware of this? Yes and no: undoubtedly she seeks to fill the empty boredom caused by the specialized machine; but *at the same time* she tries to maintain her mind within the limits permitted by the operation, by the objective task: accomplice in spite of herself of the managers who have set the norms and the production quotas in advance. Thus the profoundest interiority becomes a means for realizing oneself as total exteriority" (pp. 290-291).

The Sartrean model also offers a different mode of relationship to the past than does the classical Marxist picture, which sees history as a relatively objective series of events. For Sartre, as we have already shown, each generation reinteriorizes the past, assumes responsibility for it and in doing so, in a sense, recreates it as well. Thus the Sartrean model, synchronic as it is, is able to contain the whole past within itself (that past of violence interiorized by both bourgeoisie and proletariat, and still at work virulent in the present), where the Marxist model is that of a relatively external succession.

Every model has its limits and produces a type of distortion characteristic of it; and it would seem clear that the classical or orthodox Marxism we have been describing here (and developed not so much by Marx himself as by Engels and later writers), with its emphasis on the primacy of the economic, has the disadvantage of drawing attention to the separation and relatively autonomous development of each class, rather than to their constant interaction in the form of the class struggle. It is not only, and not even, a question of determinism: for if one considers each of these theories as a model, the notion that the economic factor is determinant seems less important than the picture of the autonomous, somehow self-developing evolution of each class which the parallelism with the economic evolution suggests. The insistence on the primacy of economic over purely human agencies is a distortion not because it deprives the individual human actor, or even the individual class, of its freedom and efficacity, but rather because it abstracts from and destroys the basic concrete form which human action takes in history, namely the struggle *between* classes, and it is this which most discussions of the role of human action in history leave out: *that on which* men act, or in other words *other* men and *other* classes. Sartre underlines this sharply in his discussion of Engels' economism: "If the two classes are each in themselves the inert—or even the practico-inert—product of economic development, if they have both equally been forged by the transformations in the mode of production, the exploiting class supporting its own statute in passivity, like a constitutional law, and the powerlessness of the wealthy reflecting that of the wretched, then struggle disappears: both serialities are purely inert, the contradictions in the system reveal themselves through them, that is to say, through each in a state of otherness to itself. That kind of opposition between capitalists and wage-workers does not deserve the name of *struggle* any more than does that of the shutter to the wall it strikes against" (p. 669).

And it is certain that, in opposition to Engels, Sartre

293

aims at replacing the "primacy" of the economic with that of praxis and the class struggle. He wishes, he tells us at several points, "to substitute history for economistic and sociological interpretations, or in more general terms, for all determinisms" (p. 687); "sociology and economism must both be dissolved back into *history itself*" (pp. 673-674). One is tempted to recall those ancient controversies in which an earlier Sartre was accused of trying to invent a third way between the East (in present terms, economism) and the West (now American sociology and French structuralism). In reality, however, this operation is more appropriately compared with that undertaken by Marx himself when he dissolved philosophy into economics. For it strikes me that the "end of philosophy" proclaimed by Marx has often been misunderstood, either as the notion that philosophy is in its very nature idealistic and must be replaced by materialism or as the idea that philosophy, as one specialized discipline and mode of research, was to be replaced by another such specialized discipline, in the form of economics or social science in a more general sense. On the contrary, it seems to me that in aiming to dissolve philosophy, Marx intended to strike at the very category of the specialized discipline as such and to restore the unity of knowledge. In renouncing philosophy, he aimed at replacing the abstract in its various forms by the concrete, by history itself—and at this stage in nineteenth-century thought the discovery of economics was *the same* as the discovery of concrete history. In Sartre's time, where economics has become itself an abstraction and a mode of specialization, a return to the concrete in history is bound to involve a partial dissolution of the economic as well as the other abstract disciplines; and ironically enough, it was Engels himself, the father of economism, who in his old age became increasingly apprehensive about the crude isolation of the economic factor practiced by some of his followers. (It is important to add, however, that Sartre presupposes the existence of the economic and of economic research as that which is to be dissolved: in other words, his method, as we have shown before, is a secondary rather than a primary one, an "ideology" in the special sense Sartre has given this word.)

In reality, the two tendencies we have been describing are themselves but signs and symptoms of a profound ambivalance in Marxism, in the thought of Marx himself, or, more precisely still, in the historical reality which Marx studied and analyzed. The concept of "fetishism" is an attempt to fix this ambivalent reality, where things behave like people and people like things, in tangible form before our eyes, and it is described thus in a famous page of *Das Kapital*: "A commodity is a mysterious thing, simply because in it the social character of men's labor appears to them as an objective character stamped upon the product of that labor; because the relation of the producers to the sum total of their own labor is presented to them as a social relation, existing not between themselves, but between the products of their labor. This is why the products of labor become commodities, social things whose qualities are at the same time perceptible and imperceptible by the senses. In the same way, the light from an object is perceived by us not as the subjective excitation of our optic nerve, but as the objective form of something outside the eye itself. But, in the act of seeing, there is at all events an actual passage of light from one thing to another, from the external object to the eye. There is a physical relation among physical things. But it is different with commodities. There, the existence of the things *qua* commodities, and the value relation between the products of labor which stamps them as commodities, have absolutely no connection with their physical properties and with the material relations arising therefrom. There it is a definite social relation between men that assumes, in their eyes, the fantastic form of a relation between things. In order, therefore, to find an analogy, we must have recourse to the mist-enveloped regions of the religious world. In that world the productions of the human brain appear as independent beings endowed with life, and entering into relation both with one another and the human race. So it is in the world of commodities with the products of men's hands. This I call the Fetishism which attaches itself to the products of labor, so soon as they are produced as commodities, and which is therefore inseparable from the production of commodities."[45]

The result of this basic insight into the structure of the modern world is that the latter stands resolved into an appearance and an underlying reality. The appearance is that of commodities and of the "objective" network of relationships which they entertain with each other and which ultimately include within themselves the whole legal and property system itself, as well as the economic modes of distribution and production: yet paradoxically, this illusion of objectivity forms the very existential fabric of our lives, which are characterized by *belief* in this reified appearance (fetishism is a form of belief) and which are wholly absorbed with the acquisition and consumption of commodities in general. The reality of social life, on the other hand, lies in the labor process itself, in the transparency of human work and action which is ultimately responsible both for the commodities produced and for the very social mode in which commodities form the principal category of production. But in our own society, this truth of social life is concealed, and can be made visible only mediately through critical analysis; and it seems clear that only in a more rationally organized society would objects and production-relations once more become transparent, the illusion of

[45] Karl Marx, *Capital*, trans. S. Moore and E. Aveling (New York, 1906), p. 83.

reification dissolved back into the reality of human action: "the social relations of the individual producers, with regard both to their labor and to its products, [would be] in this case perfectly simple and intelligible, and that with regard not only to production but also to distribution."[46]

This is to say that Marxism, owing to the peculiar reality of its object of study, has at its disposal two alternate languages (or codes, to use the structuralist term) in which any given phenomenon can be described. Thus history can be written either subjectively, as the history of class struggle, or objectively, as the development of the economic modes of production and their evolution from their own internal contradictions: these two formulae are the same, and any statement in one can without loss of meaning be translated into the other. The notion of *class* is problematical precisely because it is the mediator between these two different notational systems; for class is population articulated according to economic function, but it is also that which permits us to translate data about machinery and the operations of production back into human and interpersonal terms.

It now becomes clear in what way the *Critique*, as different as it is from the traditional Marxist descriptions, is nonetheless profoundly consistent with the model of society proposed by Marx in *Das Kapital*: it is simply the reverse of that model, and where for various reasons Marxism has on the whole preferred the second of its two possible codes, the economic one, Sartre has here chosen to restate the entire complex of reified relationships in terms of that first and basic reality of human action and human relations. This accounts, for one thing, for the apparent discrepancy between linear historical development and the more cyclical one implied by the theory of groups. It is easier to write a history of matter than of consciousness, and the changes in

[46] *Capital*, p. 91.

the type of commodities produced and in the systems that produce them has somehow a tangible linear content that is lacking in the story of the productive power of labor and the ferocity of human antagonisms at every moment of the way. The notion of two codes also clarifies the question of basic or primary realities involved in each description; for this now becomes what I would like to call a question of rhetorical form and effect, and depends very much on the type of illusion a given description is called on to dispel. Thus the economic description clearly functions as a more basic "reality," as a demystification, when we are dealing with a point of view still entangled in the illusions of the primacy of the individual consciousness and personality, of the autonomy of spiritual life with respect to the material. The description of the *Critique* is in this sense also the demystification of a demystification: for it comes at a moment when the basic economic view has been acquired, and when consciousness, in understanding reification, is also entangled in its categories, and seems unable to go further and to dissolve in thought what it cannot yet dissolve in reality, to penetrate the deepest reality of history as the story of human powers, no matter how alienated and disguised.

In one sense, therefore, these two alternative Marxist languages, functioning as they do critically, that is, depending on the predetermined nature of the situation or context in which one or the other is to be used, must be evaluated with respect to the historical moment in which each has developed. Karl Korsch has shown the meaning of their alternation in Marx's own personal development:[47] the emphasis on the subjective factor, on history as class struggle, which is of course most evident in the *Manifesto* (1848), reflects a period of genuine revolutionary activity, in which therefore revolutionary forces were able to feel history as the result of their own praxis. The work on *Das Kapital* (1867),

[47] *Karl Marx*, pp. 115-119.

however, which strongly emphasizes the importance of economic factors and the internal evolution of the economy, corresponds to a period of reaction (the Second Empire) in which it is necessary precisely to show that revolutions do not occur until the time is ripe, but that they are also the inevitable result of the working out of internal economic contradictions.

Sartre's *Critique*, at the beginning of the 1960's, written during the Algerian revolution and appearing simultaneously with the Cuban revolution, the radicalization of the civil rights movement in the United States, the intensification of the war in Vietnam, and the worldwide development of the student movement, therefore corresponds to a new period of revolutionary ferment, and in the spirit of Marx himself offers a reworking of the economistic model in that terminology of praxis and of overt class conflict which seems now most consistent with the day-to-day lived experience of this period: it is a little like having the sound turned back on.

That Sartre should have come to his reformulation not through any initial stimulus from Marx but rather through Heidegger; that it should have been his own poetic sensitivity for the double valences of objects and of feelings about objects that provided him with the intellectual instruments with which to perform such a translation—such an eventuality is not at all surprising, particularly when we consider that Heidegger's perception itself corresponds to the commodity-structure of modern society and is a direct reflection of it.

In the long run, it is not so much the differences as the similarities between Sartre and Marx which are striking. We have shown that Sartre's starting point in the *Critique*, the idea of man as *need*, amounts to a kind of translation into concrete terms of the formula in *Being and Nothingness*, where consciousness was a lack of being, a nothing-

299

ness. But the new formula is also an application of concepts developed in the "Third Economic and Philosophic Manuscript of 1844" (the critique of Hegel's doctrine of the absolute idea), where Marx describes his point of view, in contradistinction to the mechanical materialism of the eighteenth century, as *naturalism*: meaning thereby to underline the dynamic and organic process by which man learns that he is an object precisely because he *needs* other objects to live, and thus "has his being outside himself."[48] The description corresponds almost exactly to that of *Being and Nothingness*. This new type of materialism, based on organic need, does not yet have the historical dimension enunciated in the *Theses on Feuerbach* and worked out in *The German Ideology* in 1845-1846; but *Being and Nothingness* was ahistorical in a similar fashion, providing both a larger theoretical context for the later, more specialized work and a stimulus for the working out of that historical dimension without which it would have remained incomplete. (The parallel even extends to the relationship between earlier and later works and to the "problem" of whether the later Marx remained a humanist, whether the Sartre of the *Critique* has completely broken with the existential positions of *Being and Nothingness*.)

Yet there is one essential section of *Being and Nothingness* to which we have not yet, or only fleetingly, made reference: it is that which deals with the *look*, with the trauma of the existence of the other—that contingent and yet irreparable experience that confers on me an "outside" and an objectivity, at the same time that it converts all of my actions in the world into a struggle with other people which I am not free not to enter into. For my relationship with other people is struggle in its very structure, and it is against the background of this permanent, ontological

[48] Karl Marx, *Early Writings*, ed. T. Bottomore (New York, 1964), pp. 207-209.

struggle with the other that all particular, empirical struggles arise and disappear. For it is the mere *existence* of the other that calls my existence in question in its very being and that constitutes struggle: this was the sense, as we have seen, of what Sartre calls reciprocity in the *Critique*, this charged electrical tension of a coexistence that precedes any concrete steps of antagonism or cooperation.

We have only to translate this description of interpersonal struggle onto the plane of group relations to seize the final dimension of the *Critique*. For the class struggle, in history, recapitulates the basic moments of the earlier interpersonal dialectic: each class passing from object to subject in succession, through its own look objectifying the other class, conferring on the latter an exterior, a face. The other class reacts in its turn in an attempt to recuperate this being which is beyond its reach, outside it, in the eyes and judgment of its adversary: and just as I learn myself through the mediation of other people, both from their judgments and from an attempt to parry their judgments, so each class learns to see itself because it is seen from the outside. It comes to define itself against the other, by interiorizing the other's look, and transforming what initially was experienced in shame into a sense of pride or identity (what on the level of class is known as class consciousness). Only there is a basic dissymmetry between the personal and the class experience: in my individual daily relations with other people, it would seem that there is no built-in priority of subject to object, and that I am both in succession (this impression changes, of course, when we include childhood in the history of the individual, for then it is clear that initially the child is an object for the parents felt as subject). In history, however, each rising class is initially an object for the dominant one, and learns itself in shame before it arrives at the stage of becoming a subject in turn. Thus, the bourgeoisie initially defined itself through its humiliations before the nobility; the proletariat through those suffered at the hands of the bourgeoisie. Only then does the proletariat begin to see the bourgeoisie in its turn, and to furnish the latter with yet a new image of self to live in guilt and fear.

Historically, it is this look of the oppressed which is ontologically the more fundamental one: and this is what Sartre had already tried to get across with imperfect means in *Being and Nothingness*, when he distinguished between the we-subject and the we-object. To be sure, the we-object cannot come into being until it is looked at by the we-subject: but paradoxically, the latter does not itself have any genuine being. Thus the we-subject is the cause or pretext for the emergence of the we-object; yet it finds its own identity and begins to define itself only in reaction against the latter, through a kind of defense mechanism.

Yet the look is of course not to be understood as involving actual physical presence: it is a more fundamental, implicit structure of our being, and it seems to me that the present work makes concrete a certain number of analyses which in *Being and Nothingness* still had an abstract, paradoxical air about them. Thus in discussing the de facto limits which the existence of my neighbor sets on my own freedom, Sartre had described the host of floating, objective, but implicit (and irrealizable) judgments on me which make up my life in society. It is not only the Jew who is one other people consider as a Jew:[49] I am made to submit to a great quantity of categories which strike me as being quite abstract until the concrete situation of judgment by the other from which they arise is in some existential fashion realized for me. Thus I am an American, not only in the positivistic sense of being within the United States as within a container, having American citizenship and so forth, but more particularly

---

[49] The well-known formula of Sartre's *Réflexions sur la question juive.*

because it is about *me* (as one anonymous member of a faceless, multiple, unimaginable collectivity) that foreigners think when they think about America. The label derives its ontological justification from this concrete situation of judgment, of concrete interpersonal relationship that I may never be aware I am involved in. Thus, if I never leave the country, the notion that I am an American may strike me as rather abstract, purely formal one; and it is only when I realize in my own person the hatred and suspicion, the resentment, or on the other hand the condescension or the fawning sense of complicity, with which Americans in general and America in particular are received by people of other countries, that with a kind of scandalized reaction I begin to understand the concrete situation of struggle and judgment in which I am always implicitly engaged. The sense of scandal comes, of course, from the fact that "I" am not personally responsible for what America does, and that it is unjust to condemn the guilty and the innocent alike: but this distance between my self, felt from the inside, and the judgment passed on my objective being from the outside, is what characterizes all forms of this "alienation through other people" (in the Sartrean sense), this basic struggle with the other in which we are always engaged, and in which I am always responsible, I am always guilty, if only on the grounds of my sheer existence itself.

In the context of the *Critique*, it seems to me that such analyses shed the abstract quality that they previously had (where they seemed to imply hyperorganic personal relations between countries, the "friendship" of the United States and Germany, the "hostility" between China and America) and are justified anew by the vision of history itself as perpetual struggle between others on a collective scale. The look of a distant foreigner unknown to me precisely envelops me in its judgment, inasmuch as it forms one of the numerous class and group struggles within whose context my life takes place. Now, it seems to me, we are in a little better position to evaluate that "action at distance" of the workers which Sartre described as an influence on his intellectual development and which we evoked at the beginning of this essay: this almost gravitational influence, which the workers exercise through the mere fact of their existence even before any concrete historical contact has taken place, what is it essentially but the Look itself? Those petit bourgeois intellectuals, of whom Sartre describes himself as one, were bound to react to the existence of the workers as a class because they were themselves implicitly seen and judged by that other class, because that look constituted for them an objective, external being which they had to attempt to recuperate in some fashion, either by refusing it on the grounds of their own superiority, or by assimilating it and attempting to take the point of view of the workers on themselves. But they were not free not to react to this look, and it is this politization, it seems to me, that characterizes any period in which a massive oppressed collectivity— whether workers in France or blacks in the United States— makes itself felt as a new consciousness of its oppressor, as a look in its turn, fascinating for the oppressors, attractive or terrifying by turns, in any case exercising a profound ontological magnetism: that which puts me into question in my very being, and with which, in one way or another, I must come to terms.

Now the very project of the *Critique* itself can be seen in a new light: it is Sartre's own attempt to see *himself*, to see his own class from the outside, to recuperate that external objectivity of both which is granted only through the judgment and look of the other upon them, or in other words through the concrete class antagonisms of history itself. So, in the closing pages of the *Critique*, working his way down through the layers of ideological mystification, through the substrata of fetishized cultural institutions, he attains the ultimate and determining reality of social being itself. Thus completed, his *Critique* takes its place alongside such works as Mao Tse-tung's *On Contradiction*, in which culture and logic are shown to be the reflexes of social conflict; or alongside those luminous pages in which Gramsci expresses his sense of the ultimate shaping power of social groups. Yet it works within the specificity of its own historical and cultural context; and it is within the confines of the middle-class Western world that we are thus asked to dissolve the illusions of solitude all around us, both in the present and in history as well: until what looked like a dead past reveals itself to us as a host of looks remembered, staring at us in irreparable judgment; until the abstract future becomes visible, as in *The Condemned of Altona*, as the burning judgment of some unimaginable and alien posterity; until the privacy and elbowroom of Western middle-class society in the present, the partitions of objects and the leisure time which we experience as a kind of cushioning void, as a kind of private property—until such fetishism of individual isolation itself dissolves and yields before a swarming, suffocating, intolerable feeling of human relationships and violent antagonistic struggle in all directions and at every instant. "History," said Joyce's Stephen, "is a nightmare from which I am trying to awake." But one cannot awake until one has first measured the extent and the intensity of the nightmare.

CHAPTER FIVE

TOWARDS DIALECTICAL CRITICISM

A PHENOMENOLOGICAL description of dialectical criticism? The contradiction is not so great as it might at first glance appear. The peculiar difficulty of dialectical writing lies indeed in its holistic, "totalizing" character: as though you could not say any one thing until you had first said everything; as though with each new idea you were bound to recapitulate the entire system. So it is that the attempt to do justice to the most random observation of Hegel ends up drawing the whole tangled, dripping mass of the Hegelian sequence of forms out into the light with it. So it is also that at some point or other books or essays on Marx dutifully end up as rehearsals of historical materialism as a whole. There is no content, for dialectical thought, but total content; and it is for this reason that phenomenology (like the other great contemporary philosophical systems not a discovery of new *content*, but an innovation in *form*) seems to have an answer to what would otherwise, for us, be an organizational dilemma. For phenomenology is precisely the attempt to tell not what a thought is, so much as what it feels like. It aims not at making statements about content (that being momentarily placed between parentheses), but at describing the mental operations which correspond to that content in all their temporal specificity. Its mode of proof, for the reader, consists not in logical argumentation, but rather in the shock, or the failure, of recognition.

In the preceding chapters we have given an account of contemporary work in the dialectic from a number of different points of view, the implication being that these "systems" or partial systems—Adorno on dialectical evolution

in time; Benjamin, Marcuse, and Bloch on the essentially
hermeneutic, or demystifying and at the same time restorative, nature of dialectical thinking; Lukács on the symptomatic relationship between the artistic construct and the
underlying realities of social life itself; Sartre on the disguised and undisguisable nature of those realities as class
antagonism—all ultimately complete each other, their
apparent inconsistencies dissolved in some vaster dialectical
synthesis. It is not the task of the present book to bring such
a synthesis to ordered, philosophical, *systematic* exposition:
yet, always provided we keep in mind the descriptive, phenomenological, deliberately subjective orientation of the
following pages, there would seem to be room, alongside
such local studies, for an evocation of dialectical literary
criticism, and beyond it of dialectical thinking in general,
as a form in time, as process, as a lived experience of a
peculiar and determinate structure.

It is, of course, thought to the second power: an intensification of the normal thought processes such that a renewal
of light washes over the object of their exasperation, as
though in the midst of its immediate perplexities the mind
had attempted, by willpower, by fiat, to lift itself mightily
up by its own bootstraps. Faced with the operative procedures of the nonreflective thinking mind (whether grappling with philosophical or artistic, political or scientific
problems and objects), dialectical thought tries not so much
to complete and perfect the application of such procedures
as to widen its own attention to include them in its awareness as well: it aims, in other words, not so much at solving
the particular dilemmas in question, as at converting those
problems into their own solutions on a higher level, and
making the fact and the existence of the problem itself the
starting point for new research. This is indeed the most
sensitive moment in the dialectical process: that in which
an entire complex of thought is hoisted through a kind of

inner leverage one floor higher, in which the mind, in a kind of shifting of gears, now finds itself willing to take what had been a question for an answer, standing outside its previous exertions in such a way that it reckons itself into the problem, understanding the dilemma not as a resistance of the object alone, but also as the result of a subject-pole deployed and disposed against it in a strategic fashion—in short, as the function of a determinate subject-object relationship.

There is a breathlessness about this shift from the normal object-oriented activity of the mind to such dialectical self-consciousness—something of the sickening shudder we feel in an elevator's fall or in the sudden dip in an airliner. That recalls us to our bodies much as this recalls us to our mental positions as thinkers and observers. The shock indeed is basic, and constitutive of the dialectic as such: without this transformational moment, without this initial conscious transcendence of an older, more naïve position, there can be no question of any genuinely dialectical coming to consciousness.

But precisely because dialectical thinking depends so closely on the habitual everyday mode of thought which it is called on to transcend, it can take a number of different and apparently contradictory forms. So it is that when common sense predominates and characterizes our normal everyday mental atmosphere, dialectical thinking presents itself as the perversely hairsplitting, as the overelaborate and the oversubtle, reminding us that the simple is in reality only a simplification, and that the self-evident draws its force from hosts of buried presuppositions. When, on the other hand, after the fashion of intellectuals, we begin to work our way up through a series of abstractions, each one progressively further and further away from the real itself, pervaded as we do so by an uneasy suspicion that the whole teetering construction stands as a monument not to new laws of nature, but rather to the rules of some private mental hobby, then dialectical thought comes as a brutal rupture, as a cutting of the knots that restores us suddenly to the grossest truths, to facts as unpleasantly common as common sense itself. Indeed, these two apparently antithetical effects of dialectical awareness largely correspond, as we shall see later, to the respective dialectics of Hegelianism and Marxism.

What follows is a description of a few of the most characteristic features of dialectical thought, particularly as it grapples with the specific problems of literary form. The description cannot, of course, be complete, but will try to deal with the problem of completeness; and in another sense the ever-widening nets of the exposition, in which each topic seems to recapitulate the previous one in a different context and on a higher plane, should bring us closer and closer to that ultimate object of all dialectical thought which is the concrete itself.

I. Hegelian Literary Criticism:
   The Diachronic Construct

The basic story which the dialectic has to tell is no doubt that of the dialectical *reversal*, that paradoxical turning around of a phenomenon into its opposite of which the transformation of quantity into quality is only one of the better known manifestations. It can be described as a kind of leap-frogging affair in time, in which the drawbacks of a given historical situation turn out in reality to be its secret advantages, in which what looked like built-in superiorities suddenly prove to set the most ironclad limits on its future development. It is a matter, indeed, of the reversal of limits, of the transformation from negative to positive and from positive to negative; and is basically a diachronic process.

To give a conveniently objective and external illustration,

we may recall the technological situation at the end of World War II, when both the United States and the Soviet Union were the inheritors of German research in missile development. At that time, of course, the inequality was in the field of atomic power; and it was precisely toward reducing the size of the bomb and increasing its destructiveness that American experimentation aimed. The first Soviet bombs, several years later, were still relatively cumbersome affairs. Thus, in order to deliver these large and primitive devices, Soviet technology was obliged to develop missiles capable of orbiting enormous payloads, which were then used to put the first sputniks aloft. American superiority in weaponry, however, is translated into an American lag in missile development to the degree to which the missiles had been evolved for the purpose of conveying their own relatively small atomic warheads. In further development, of course, this situation is once again reversed: the Americans, precisely because their missiles are not so powerful, find themselves forced to develop smaller and more sophisticated packages of transistorized instruments for projection aloft; while the less refined machinery of the Soviets, who are under no such pressure, transmits back relatively smaller quantities of information. And so forth. We have of course omitted a number of factors from this picture, in particular that of airpower, which would have led us back to the history of strategic bombing and thence to the opposition between a land and a sea power, and thus ultimately to the geographical, historical, and economic discrepancies between the two superpowers as a whole—which is to say that a complete picture of this particular set of dialectical reversals would ultimately have involved a reimmersion in the very element of concrete history itself.

Such a model—as abstract in its own way perhaps, as simplified and removed from the complexities of everyday social reality, as the musical illustrations of an earlier chapter—permits us to make a certain number of essential points about dialectical analysis in general. First, such analysis clearly presupposes the initial isolation of a limited group of factors from the historical totality or the historical con- tinuum: such factors here were missile development and atomic research as such. In the literary realm, however, it will become apparent that the initial choice of such key fac- tors, or dominant *categories* of the work, as we shall call them there, is a strategic moment in any dialectical criticism.

Such categories are then seen as entertaining relation- ships with each other such that an alteration in the one involves a corresponding shift in the proportions of the other as well; this is, of course, the most basic sense in which we speak of a dialectical interrelationship of phe- nomena, or, to reverse the terms, of a dialectical under- standing of such relationships. What is perhaps less often realized is the way in which such an awareness of dialec- tical relationships involves or implies a diachronic frame- work as a necessary condition of their articulation.

The example proposed above was marked by the struc- tural peculiarity of parallel sequences, which overtly called attention to each other in a point by point comparison of every stage; thus the American imbalance underlined the nature of the Soviet counterpoise, and vice versa. In most dialectical analyses this profoundly comparative character of the dialectical work is operative, as it were, under- ground, implicit only, in the form of the differential percep- tion, which, as we shall see, allows us to see what something is through the simultaneous awareness of what it is not. Thus the dialectical articulation of a phenomenon into a certain ratio of forces or categories at one and the same time implies a sense of the other logically possible disposi- tions of such categories against each other; and these other forms, which allow the full specificity of the object of study

311

to be measured, are disposed according to a sequence, which may either be a real temporal or historical continuum, or, as in Hegel, a series of possibilities working themselves out in a succession which is no less diachronic in structure for being of an ideal type only.

Indeed, it may be claimed that no matter how genuinely temporal or historical in character, such a diachronic sequence is bound to remain an abstraction, inasmuch as it is nothing but an ideal cross section of the existential density of concrete history itself—the isolation of a single plane or level of reality, where the latter is understood both as the ideal sum of all such levels and as that ultimate, unthinkable totality which can never be thus additively reconstructed through the operation of pure thought alone. Hence the final moment in the process of dialectical analysis, in which the model strains to return to that concrete element from which it initially came, to abolish itself as an illusion of autonomy, and to redissolve into history, offering as it does so some momentary glimpse of reality as a concrete whole.

Thus the dialectical model allows a given phenomenon to be perceived as a moment or single interlocking section in a single articulated process. Yet such a moment is to be distinguished from the historical *instant* itself, as the sum total of all of its moments, as the "sequence of sequences," or in Fernand Braudel's sense the massive coexistence of a host of time schemes of varying structures and varying durations. When we turn, however, to the literary realm, we find that it is never the concept of the historical here and now which offers the most stubborn resistance to dialectical thinking: there is indeed a kind of antinomy for the mind in the notion that a book "comes into being" at a fixed date, even though the same mind can deal meaningfully with the time scheme in which the work is under preparation, or with that in which it henceforth exists as a presence influential or neglected, as an existent among other existents.

Rather, it seems to me that the initial problem which a dialectical theory of literature has to face is that of the unity of the literary work itself, its existence as a complete thing, as an autonomous whole, which, indeed, resists assimilation to the totality of the historical here and now (in what sense can *Ulysses* be said to be part of the events which took place in 1922?) just as stubbornly as it refuses dissolution in some supraindividual history of forms. And no doubt our first loyalty as critics is to the wholeness of the work itself, provided it is realized that that autonomy is itself a dialectical phenomenon. For the Russian Formalists showed us that every work of art is perceived against a generic background (which may itself, to be sure, alter from moment to moment and generation to generation): it is read as work *in* a given form, or *against* a given form, in a context in which the various genres are felt to coexist at fixed distances from each other in relatively systematic complexes which can themselves form the object of study in their historical coexistence or succession.[1] It is clear, therefore, that even the self-sufficiency of the work of art varies, depending on whether it deliberately invites comparison with the whole of what already exists in the form, as with the Renaissance sonnet or the Japanese haiku, or, like *Ulysses* and *The Divine Comedy*, aims at replacing all of culture by summing it up in a single book of the world, where, however, the idea of the Book remains itself a fact of culture and an element in the generic background against which the work is perceived.

The implicit model here is of course that of Gestalt psychology, with its dialectic of form and background; but it is not the only way in which to think of the relationship between the individual whole and the totality of the other literary works, let alone the other levels of historical and

[1] See Claudio Guillén, *Literature as System* (Princeton, 1971), pp. 383-405.

313

social reality with which it may be juxtaposed. "The existing monuments," says T. S. Eliot in a well-known page, "form an ideal order among themselves, which is modified by the introduction of the new (the really new) work of art among them. The existing order is complete before the new work arrives; for order to persist after the supervention of novelty, the *whole* existing order must be, if ever so slightly, altered; and so the relations, proportions, values of each work of art toward the whole are readjusted."[2] It is of course a profoundly dialectical concept. Indeed, the rhetorical seductiveness of the passage derives in large measure from the way in which the unnamed dialectical character of the notion is passed off on the reader as a new and more dynamic way of seeing things; nor is it any longer necessary at the present time, perhaps, to take inventory of the very precise functions—both literary and ideological— which it was designed to fulfill. For us, however, for whom the word "order" no longer has the value of a fetish, the concept of a global totality is not as methodologically useful as the smaller idea of limited sequences which are modified by the addition of a new term, itself perceived against the continuum of which it is a part. Such limited sequences furnished the context or framework for literary understanding at least as long ago as the Greek tragedians; in modern times we have only to think of Richardson, Fielding, and Sterne in the English novel; Balzac, Flaubert, and Zola in the French; Baudelaire, Rimbaud, and Mallarmé in the development of modern poetry, to realize the degree to which our understanding of any one of these authors is a function of a differential perception in which his position in the sequence determines the way in which his specificity is measured. That Flaubert is *sui generis* is to say nothing; but that he is no longer Balzac, that he is not yet Zola, and this in a host of determinate ways, is to articulate the struc-

[2] T. S. Eliot, *Selected Essays* (New York, 1950), p. 5.

tures inherent in and constitutive of the novel of Flaubert. The latter is not, of course, a host of other things as well: and to spell out those determinate negations, to show how Flaubert is not the English or Russian novelist of the same period, or how he rewrites and thus negates in his own manner *Don Quixote* or *Candide*, is to enrich our knowledge of Flaubert by seeing him as a term in wholly different types of diachronic sequences. Yet the comparative or differential mode of such literary perception remains a constant: the monographic study of an individual writer—no matter how adroitly pursued—imposes an inevitable falsification through its very structure, an optical illusion of totality projected by what is in reality only an artificial isolation. That modern writers have solicited this kind of isolation, this thoroughgoing "conversion" of the critic to their works as to a kind of "world," is not an excuse for the critical procedure, but rather a phenomenon of interest to be studied in its own right.

Such sequences, and such comparisons, largely transcend traditional questions of the personal influence of one writer upon another. We are, I think, for the most part agreed to see the individual writer as the locus or working out of a certain set of techniques, as the development and exhaustion of a certain limited set of possibilities inherent in the available raw material itself. Yet the word technique is a figure of speech: we will have occasion to reconsider the essentially artisanal model of production which it implies and presupposes. What interests us at the present moment is that gesture by which an element—call it technique or structure, component, or if you will *category*—is isolated from the work in question in order to set this work in a sequential relationship with others. This is the moment, in other words, of the choice of that around which we will construct a diachronic sequence, that of which we will write the history, that which is seen as having an internal development

315

or dialectical history to tell. So it is, for instance, that we may lay stress on the importance of physical sensation in nineteenth-century poetry, beginning with some such observation on the social origins of Romantic sensibility in this respect: "In literature and art there was a crisis similar to that which occurred in morals after the Reign of Terror—a veritable crisis of the senses. People had been living in a condition of perpetual fear. When their fear was over, they abandoned themselves to the pleasures of life. Their attention was entirely engrossed in external appearances, in outward forms. The blue heaven, the splendor of sunlight, the beauty of women, sumptuous velvets, iridescent silks, the sheen of gold, the sparkle of diamonds—these were the things that filled them with delight. People lived only with the eyes, and had given up thinking."[3]

Yet to "give up thinking" is a more complex and contradictory undertaking than might at first appear. For a little closer examination shows that physical sensation—no matter how hypnotically or oppressively experienced—can never enter language in isolation. Hegel accounted for this when at the opening of the *Phenomenology* he showed how the most intense experience of the here and now emerges as the verbally abstract, as the emptiest of all genuine content. So it is that the most intense rendering of the physiological dimension is able to be registered only at the moment at which the entire sensory system sinks ominously toward oblivion: *a drowsy numbness pains/ My sense. . . .*

For taken individually the various sensations collected by the Romantics fade and wither, and what was the freshest and most vivid in them (felt against the conventional rhetoric of eighteenth-century poetry) comes across the generations to us as the very epitome of the *insipid*, a dialectical reversal in which pure sensation turns around into its own

[3] Ernest Chesneau, quoted in Plekhanov, *Fundamental Problems of Marxism* (London, 1929), pp. 74-75n.

opposite, its own absence. In this situation, it was the originality of Baudelaire to have conceived of a new way of articulating the various sensory experiences against each other:

> Il est des parfums frais comme des chairs d'enfants,
> Doux comme les hautbois, verts comme les prairies,
> —Et d'autres, corrompus, riches et triomphants,
>
> Ayant l'expansion des choses infinies,
> Comme l'ambre, le musc, le benjoin et l'encens,
> Qui chantent les transports de l'esprit et des sens.

For the point about synesthesia is that you cannot mingle the senses until they have first been clearly separated from each other, and disentangled each according to its own timbre and aroma: indeed, synesthesia is in the present context not so much a way of mingling sensations as rather of *distinguishing* them. The lines from "Correspondances" establish two simultaneous but different sets of oppositions: within the fresh, clear sensations, the various senses against each other (touch, sound, sight), each sense making the other stand out sharply by the contrast; then the larger opposition of clear sensation itself to that rich, mingled, corrupt sensory experience which is primarily odor and hallucinatory ecstasy. All of Baudelaire's work, on a thematic and ethical level, can be seen as the reduplication on ever higher planes of this initial and paradoxical mingling of contraries in order to distinguish them: dandyism, sadomasochism, blasphemy: so many attempts, on the psychological plane, to flee the insipidity of pastel, of harmonic consonance or sentimental effusion, by soiling it with its dialectical opposite. The work as a whole is generated out of a series of progressively enlarged identifications: thus the proposition, "only the spiritually vile and debased can know what purity really is," derives its force from the initial premise that the pure sensation can only be rendered through a mingling with its opposites in language.

After Baudelaire, this perceptual tension is taken as a sensation in its own right in Swinburne, with a kind of sensory monotony as a consequence. In Rimbaud the perceptual system splits apart into physical languor and debilitated yearning on the one hand, and a kind of disembodied hallucinatory phantasmagoria on the other. In Surrealism, finally, the well-nigh physiological plenitude of dream fulfillment veers into the dialectical opposite of a purely verbal and what might be called paper decoration. The diachronic sequence or construct may of course be extended to whatever dimensions are desired.

It may also be *interpreted*: and it is at this point that the relatively simplistic idea which we chose as a starting point may be corrected and more adequately grounded in concrete history. Here we might rightly begin to speak—following hints of Sartre touched on in the previous chapter—of the historically new and distinct attitude of middle-class man toward his own body and toward nature in its internal manifestation in the body itself: an attitude which serves ideologically as a weapon against feudal privilege (the superiority of blood and race), and which must then be re-adapted (in the complex fashion described by Sartre) as a defense mechanism against the new threat of the "classes laborieuses, classes dangereuses" of the nineteenth-century factory universe, but which in any case projects a new sensory mode of being-in-the-world. Here also we would replace the limited poetic phenomenon in question within the larger context of the "reduction to the body" in modern literature in general—a literary phenomenon which reflects the increasingly guilty conscience of middle-class groups after their assumption of power (but particularly after the revolt of June 1848), and the increasing anxiousness of writers to dissociate themselves from their publics as social institutions, substituting for the "signs" of social affiliation that deeper presocial reality of the physiological itself (so that the "reduction to the body" takes its place alongside Barthes' "white writing" as an attempt on the level of literary form as such to flee the guilt and complicity of being-in-society). Such an interpretation would eventually have to come to terms with the immensely influential investigations of Bachelard into the role of sensory "rêverie," correcting them theoretically on the one hand by an account of the relationship between such raw material and the inner dialectics of literary language itself, and on the other by a more genuinely historical understanding of "rêverie" as a psychic development of the middle-class world. Yet at this point the moment is at hand in which the diachronic sequence veers about under its own momentum, announcing its own ultimate abolition and its return to the concrete itself.

Such an extended illustration should serve to underline the inseparable link between what we have called the isolation of the category (the definition of the object of study, whether it be image, style, point of view, character, or those more transitory and unnamed literary phenomena which are the very substance of modern literature itself) and that articulation into a succession of alternative structural realizations which we have called the diachronic sequence or construct, and which, always implied in the very intuition of the category itself, constitutes the concrete working out of the latter by the critic. Thus these two moments stand together as the inaugural gesture of a genuinely dialectical literary criticism, of what we will call its Hegelian mode, to be distinguished later on from the specifically Marxist.

We would not, however, want to be understood as claiming that this kind of historical and dialectical articulation has never before been practiced, or only insufficiently so. On the contrary: the modern age has been marked by a proliferation of such diachronic models offering themselves under the various guises of "theories of history." We have only to think of the systems of Toynbee or Spengler, of the cultural history of Egon Friedell or Lewis Mumford, of the spectacular art syntheses of Siegfried Giedion or Malraux, of more recent novelties in the history of ideas as practiced by MacLuhan or by Michel Foucault, even of such apparently specialized sociological theses as Weber's vision of the bureaucratization of society or the well-known "inner direction/other direction" of David Riesman, of such apocalyptic visions of moral and artistic collapse as those of Yvor Winters or Wyndham Lewis—to measure the degree to which our intellectual life in general has been characterized by a ceaseless attempt to design and perfect the most streamlined model possible of the "theory of history," and then to market it. "Chacun y va," sneered Breton, "de sa petite 'observation.'" He was thinking of the novel, and the way in which the most minimal psychological "insight" has sometimes seemed to justify the elaboration of yet another novelistic "world." The multiplication of "theories of history" strikes me, however, as the symptom of an even deeper cultural illness: an attempt to outsmart the present, first of all, to think your way behind history to the point where even the present itself can be seen as a completed historical instant (as the birth of some new sensibility, the mark of some ultimate and decisive cultural mutation, at first visible only to initiates; or as the first signs of an eschatological cataclysm, if not merely the first straws in the wind of a new fashion or the first indices of a new depression); to name and label the moment you are standing in even before it reaches its ultimate consecration *sub specie aeternitatis* in the history books themselves. Such a mode of thought springs from a profound horror of time and fear of change; it is a very different kind of mental operation from the Marxist sensitivity to the present as history, which welcomes and rejoices in an ever more intense existential awareness of the historicity of life.

Indeed, it is tempting to quote against such theories of history (and against those of T. S. Eliot himself) the latter's well-known remarks on William Blake: "We have the same respect for Blake's philosophy . . . that we have for an ingenious piece of homemade furniture: we admire the man who has put it together out of the odds and ends about the house. England has produced a fair number of these resourceful Robinson Crusoes; but we are not really so remote from the Continent, or from our own past, as to be deprived of the advantages of culture if we wish them. . . . What [Blake's] genius required, and what it sadly lacked, was a framework of accepted and traditional ideas which would have prevented him from indulging in a philosophy of his own, and concentrated his attention upon the problems of the poet."[4] But it will have been clear to the reader already that from our point of view Eliot's own theological vision of history is no less "homemade" than Blake's; nor would I wish to defend Marxism in the terms suggested above, as the most suitable and all-embracing orthodoxy in which to go about our proper business as poets or literary critics—although I think that such a defense might well be made and is indeed implicit in the hermeneutic chapters of the present work. The point is rather that Marxism is not just one more theory of history, but on the contrary the "end" or abolition of theories of history as such. The fact is that from a descriptive point of view, even the most conservative "theories of history," such as those of Taine or Babbitt, or MacLuhan or Wyndham Lewis, merely offer alternate ways to "punctuate" the rise of the middle-class world itself and the various cultural and psychic metamorphoses or "coupures épistémologiques" which accompanied it. To dwell on the invention of printing or on the

[4] Eliot, *Selected Essays*, pp. 279-280.

321

rise of the nature cult or the time cult or of the "esprit classique" is only to fetishize a single moment in a total process. So it is that when we move from the "theory of history" in question to concrete history itself, we find general agreement as to the object of study itself, as to the shape of change as a whole: for as we shall see later it is a mistake to think that Marxism is simply a type of interpretation which takes the economic "sequence" as that ultimately privileged code into which the other sequences are to be translated. Rather, for Marxism the emergence of the economic, the coming into view of the infrastructure itself, is simply the sign of the approach of the concrete. The middle-class world is therefore the common object of all historical meditation, irrespective of the width or narrowness of the focus, of the generality or precision of ultimate concrete detail (that is, the lower economic reaches of reality) which is thus registered. Yet to realize that we all share a common object is only the more brutally to be brought face to face with the most painful awareness of the very sources of class judgment and ideological choice, and to find oneself inextricably "engaged" and as it were ontologically involved in that very socio-economic situation which it was one of the deeper functions of "ideology" to conceal in the first place.

The characteristic strengths and weaknesses of the "theory of history" as such may perhaps be most clearly demonstrated where the latter deliberately limits itself to a single cultural sphere or level of the superstructure. Thus it has been art history, and in particular Wölfflin's "art history without names," which has long seemed to offer a paradigm for other cultural cross sections such as the history of literary form.[5] The attractiveness of such models lies of course in the way in which they are able to work with the history and evolution of such relatively objective phe-

---

[5] See in particular Chap. IV of Arnold Hauser's *Philosophy of Art History* (New York, 1958).

nomena as artistic techniques and the raw materials of the visual arts. Media, theories of perspective, the relationship between line and color, iconography: such topics mark out a kind of lost innocence of purely formal content for which the literary critic, faced with the more ambiguous phenomena of linguistic significance and of forms in time, yearns in vain. The methodological limits of such models are equally symptomatic, for they stem in large part from those problems of "punctuation" evoked above. For what is it in the long run that is so profoundly problematical about the concept of the Baroque or of Mannerism (not to speak of the infinitely more elastic notion of the modern itself), if not the effort to locate real beginnings and endings in what can never be seized as anything but a continuity? Thus we may speak of a kind of ultimate vanity of art history which oppresses us whenever we feel too strongly that it is the art historian himself who wields a free shaping power over his historical data—raw materials which, elements of the superstructure with no inner resistance or reality of their own, are at one with his own substance.

Yet it is abundantly clear that the same process has gone on more or less unconsciously in the realm of literary criticism itself. Thus the New Critics—long thought by themselves as well as by others to be resolutely ahistorical—in reality devoted significant energies to the construction of historical paradigms: the dissociation of sensibility from Donne to Shelley, the reconquest of style and image from Swinburne to Yeats; such characteristic frameworks for analysis amount to Hegelian models of literary change, diachronic sequences of the type described above. Indeed, to the degree to which as we have already demonstrated the individual analysis inevitably projects its own diachronic framework, it could not have been otherwise. Only this model now tries to pass itself off as a theory of history in its own right, and at once the characteristic marks of pseudohistory reappear: the obsession with historical rise and decline, the never-ending search for the date of the fall and the name of the serpent. Was it Rousseau who was responsible, or his enemies the *philosophes?* The Romantics or the Positivists? Which was worse, Protestantism or the French Revolution? Such false problems arise from a misconception of what the diachronic sequence can do, but are in turn pressed into ideological service, in which an eschatological framework helps conservative politics masquerade as ethics in an ostensibly aesthetic enterprise.

Such is the structure of what we might call the diachronic version of the theory of history; yet it has a synchronic manifestation as well, in what are perhaps the most impressive and influential productions of the species: I am referring to those works which, from Taine to Spengler, and with perhaps less boundless methodological self-assurance at the present day, aim at giving an account of the total *style* of a culture and of the profound unity of each of the moments of cultural history as they succeed each other. Such a model is suggestive to the degree that it can be applied either to individual or to social reality, and can serve as a means of unifying quantities of otherwise disparate materials, of linking otherwise discontinuous levels of being. Thus Taine's notion of the "faculté maîtresse" is that which unites and informs all the diverse qualities of a given author: "a particular kind of taste and of talent, a particular mental or spiritual disposition, a particular complex of preferences and dislikes, of faculties and weaknesses, in short, a particular predominant and persistent *psychological state* which is that of its author."[6] Yet the same unity exists in a culture, so that the spirit of classicism, for instance, is that style or mode which mediates "between a hedge at Versailles, a philosophical and theological argument of Malebranche, a

---

[6] Hippolyte Taine, *Essais de critique et d'histoire* (Paris, 1887), p. ix.

prosodic rule prescribed by Boileau, a law of Colbert on mortgages, a compliment in the waiting room of the king at Marly, a statement of Bossuet about the kingship of God."[7] Such a model has of course been used to support organic theories of society or culture, yet in the present context such ideological content may be seen simply as the framework or organizational pretext for the practice of analogy in general, or for the exercise of a sensibility of what have come to be called "homologies" between the various levels of reality. And in that dialectic of identity and difference which comes into play when we increase or decrease our distance from a given moment in the past, the "morphological" preoccupations of Spengler, who aimed at finding "the language of the forms of history" and at demonstrating the unity of a cultural style as it envelops everything from engineering techniques and mathematical thinking to religious dogma and literary convention, have much justification as a propaedeutic to the study of concrete history. In the long run the most telling objection to such global analogy remains its inability to project diachrony or to operate successfully in anything but a single *instant* or vertical cross section of time. Indeed, the culture pessimism of both Taine and Spengler ultimately stems from that optical illusion of continuity projected by the mere juxtaposition in sequence of the various sealed and unrejoinable instants: in such a model, we are tempted to say, time can never run anywhere but down. So it is that, unable to identify the economic substratum of genuine historical change, Taine and Spengler find themselves reduced to evoking the latter metaphorically, in the classic images of organic decay or of disease or infection by such "false principles" as the "esprit classique."

Ultimately, however much work is permitted by all such

[7] Taine, quoted in René Wellek, *History of Criticism*, 5 vols. (New Haven, 1955-   ), IV, 37.

models, they are falsified by the misconception that their object is genuinely historical in nature. The Hegelian theoretical model which we have proposed to substitute for them distinguishes itself by that structural transparency of its diachronic sequences, which are thus clearly identified not as empirical realities but as ideal *constructs* only. For as a famous passage of *The German Ideology* reminds us, elements of the superstructure, having no genuine autonomy of their own, can have no genuine history of their own either: "We do not set out from what men say, imagine, conceive, nor from men as narrated, thought of, imagined, conceived, in order to arrive at men in the flesh. We set out from real, active men, and on the basis of their real life-process we demonstrate the development of the ideological reflexes and echoes of this life-process. The phantoms formed in the human brain are also, necessarily, sublimates [*Supplemente*] of their material life-process, which is empirically verifiable and bound to material premises. Morality, religion, metaphysics, all the rest of ideology and their corresponding forms of consciousness, thus no longer retain the semblance of independence. *They have no history, no developments*; it is rather men who, developing their material production and their material intercourse, alter, along with this their real existence, their thinking and the products of their thinking. Life is not determined by consciousness, but consciousness by life."[8]

Thus, as we have described it, the Hegelian sequence, while permitting work in time, is distinguished by that ultimate and inevitable, structurally inherent movement toward its own dissolution, in which it projects the Marxist model out of itself as its own concrete realization and fulfillment.

[8] Marx and Engels, *The German Ideology*, trans. Roy Pascal (New York, 1947), pp. 14-15. Italics mine.

II. Literary Categories: The Logic of Content

> This attitude on the part of Marx toward aesthetic values is
> clearly related 'to his discovery of commodity fetishism, as
> well as to his solution of the problem of the subjective and
> the objective in economic life. . . . While working on *Capital*
> Marx was interested in categories and forms bordering on
> the aesthetic because of their analogy to the contradictory
> vicissitudes of the categories of capitalist economy.
>
> —Mikhail Lifshitz, *The Philosophy of Art of Karl Marx*

WHAT WE have examined above in terms of a temporal or
diachronic sequence, we might also have expressed as a
contradiction between a form and its content: for the new
is to the old as latent content working its way to the surface
to displace a form henceforth obsolete. This distinction, in
which, among other things, the reader will recognize Marx's
model of revolutionary change,[9] is no doubt the central
operative mechanism of both the Hegelian and Marxist
dialectics, and in the long run the most momentous of
Hegel's conceptual innovations. For the new opposition is
to be sharply distinguished from that older idea of form
which dominates philosophical thinking from Aristotle to
Kant and for which the conjugate term is not content but
matter, inert materials, filling, the passive. Nor is the new
Hegelian duality to be seen as simply one more version of
the more primal dialectical reality of the relationship between subject and object. Rather, the distinction between
form and content is precisely that which lends the notion
of a subject-object relationship its secret dynamics, which

[9] "At a certain stage of their development the material forces of
production in society come into conflict with the existing relations
of production, or—what is but a legal expression for the same thing—
with the property relations within which they had been at work
before. From forms of development of the forces of production these
relations turn into their fetters. Then comes the period of social
revolution" (Marx, Preface to *A Contribution to the Critique of
Political Economy*, trans. N. I. Stone [Chicago, 1904], p. 12).

permits Hegel to see the various logical combinations of the latter as an emergence, as a generation out of each other, and which permits him to construct a ladder of forms out of what would remain at any point a simple empirical measurement of an existing ratio of forces. Finally, it is this dynamic mechanism in dialectical thought which accounts for what we may call the predictive value of the latter, even though, as we shall see shortly, such predictions may be said to take place only after the fact.

In the present context, what is most striking about the distinction between form and content is that despite the enormous range of phenomena to which it will be applied, the concept is essentially aesthetic in origin, for it was evolved from Hegel's studies in theology and in the history of philosophy, not to speak of art itself, or in other words from materials which belong essentially to the superstructure. This is, indeed, the secret of its enormous force in Marx's hands: for what is relatively transparent and demonstrable in the cultural realm, namely that change is essentially a function of content seeking its adequate expression in form, is precisely what is unclear in the reified world of political, social, and economic realities, where the notion that the underlying social or economic "raw material" develops according to a logic of its own comes with an explosive and liberating effect. History is a product of human labor just like the work of art itself, and obeys analogous dynamics: such is the force of this metaphorical transfer, which at the same time goes a long way toward accounting for that profound affinity between literary criticism and dialectical thinking in general which we have underlined in the thought of Lukács.

For dialectical thought may in this respect be seen as a reversal of the form-dominated, artisanally derived model developed by Aristotle: here form is regarded not as the initial pattern or mold, as that from which we start, but

328

rather as that with which we end up, as but the final articulation of the deeper logic of the content itself. "It is the nature of the content, and that alone, which lives and progresses in philosophic cognition, and at the same time it is the inner reflection of the content which posits and originates its determinations."[10] These words of Hegel on the history of philosophy are no less valid for art itself, and may serve to underscore the profound impersonality of the logic of artistic content, for which the artist is himself merely an instrument, and which works itself out through him, using the accidents of his personal life as the very element of its own formal research, developing through him, as through his predecessors and successors, according to its own intrinsic laws.

This is why our judgments on the individual work of art are ultimately social and historical in character. The adequation of content to form there realized, or not realized, or realized according to determinate proportions, is in the long run one of the most precious indices to its realization in the historical moment itself, and indeed form is itself but the working out of content in the realm of the superstructure. "The insufficiency of a work of art is not at all to be seen as the result of individual clumsiness," Hegel tells us in the *Aesthetics*, "rather, the *insufficiency of the form* derives from the *insufficiency of the content*. Thus the Chinese, Hindus, Egyptians, in their forms, images of divinity, and idols, remained formless, or subject to bad and untrue formal determinations, and unable to master true beauty, because their mythological systems, the content and thought of their art works, was indeterminate in itself or of poor determination, and not content absolute in itself. The more perfect works of art become in this sense, to that degree does their content and thought have deeper inner truth. This is, however, not only a question of the greater

[10] Quoted in Marcuse, *Reason and Revolution*, p. 121.

or lesser technical skill with which the images of nature, as they appear in external reality, have been observed and imitated. For at certain stages of the development of artistic consciousness and practice, the abandonment and distortion of the natural image is not at all the result of accidental technical incompetence and clumsiness, but rather a deliberate transformation resulting from and motivated by the content in consciousness itself. Thus there exist in this sense incomplete types of art which in technical and other respects may be wholly complete *in their own* realm, and still seem deficient in the light of the notion of art and of the ideal. Only in the highest art are idea and representation adequate to each other, so that the shape of the idea is true in and for itself because the content of the idea, which that shape expresses, is itself the true content. Related to this is what we have already indicated, namely that the idea is determined in and through itself as a concrete totality, and thus carries within itself the principle and standard of its own individuation and of the determinacy of its appearance."[11] Hegel thus subsumes intrinsic and extrinsic criticism within a single all-enveloping movement, so that we are able at one and the same time to keep faith with the work of art on its own terms (those works "complete in their own realm") and yet replace it in that larger external context in which the very formal presuppositions of the work are themselves called into question and found "deficient in the light of the notion of art and of the ideal." The latter is no longer a question of art in the narrow sense: the Hegelian Idea is here to be understood as a total life form, as the concrete mode of social life itself (or what we have referred to above as the logic of content). Thus Hegel recapitulates in this passage the essential movement of all dialectical criticism, which is to reconcile the inner and the outer, the intrinsic and the extrinsic, the existential and the

[11] *Aesthetik*, I, 81-82.

historical, to allow us to feel our way within a single determinate form or moment of history at the same time that we stand outside of it, in judgment on it as well, transcending that sterile and static opposition between formalism and a sociological or historical use of literature between which we have so often been asked to choose.

It is interesting to note in this respect that for both Hegel and Marx alike, and in spite of that reverence for Greek art which they shared, the perfect work of art, that is to say, one in which form is wholly adequate to content, cannot theoretically yet have come into being. But in Hegel's scheme of things this is so because art ultimately tends to transcend itself by becoming theology and philosophy, and abolishes itself as sensuous play as it grows increasingly nearer to that full self-consciousness which is Absolute Spirit. For Marxism, on the contrary, it is rather philosophy that abolishes itself as thought grows increasingly concrete, and the example of Lukács has shown us the degree to which art as such presents solid credentials for replacing the former discipline. But for Marxism the adequation of object to subject or of form to content can exist as an imaginative possibility only where in some way or another it has been concretely realized in social life itself, so that formal realizations, as well as formal defects, are taken as the signs of some deeper corresponding social and historical configuration which it is the task of criticism to explore.

The logic of content is *in the long run*, we have said, social and historical in character. For it is clear that to articulate the relationship between the artistic fact as such and the larger social and historical reality to which it corresponds requires a gradual enlargement of critical focus, a widening of the scope of the critic's reflection, which not every critic is prepared to effect, nor is it indeed required for every job of critical analysis. Yet to omit this enlargement, this movement from the intrinsic to the extrinsic, is itself an ideo-

331

logical act, to the degree to which it encourages belief in some ahistorical essence of art and of cultural activity in general. Thus, in a classic essay, R. H. Pearce has shown how the New Criticism was able to come to ideological terms with the historical dimension of literature by driving the latter back (I am tempted to say "repressing" it) into the notion of Language or medium, which is then as it were sealed off from the outside, so that the New Critics are able to stop their work at its boundaries while still seeming to have given a complete (and a nonhistorical) account of the work of art.[12]

For it is clear that the judgments of the New Criticism, whether they isolate examples of stylistic failure as in Crashaw or Shelley or early Yeats, or moments of stylistic density as in Dante or the Elizabethans, involve a meditation on a relationship between form and content of the kind described here. Indeed, we have already shown that the perceptions of the New Critics were differential in a dialectical sense—in that they never forgot Donne while reading Swinburne, nor indeed while reading Hardy or T. S. Eliot either—and that, implicitly or explicitly, they projected the kinds of diachronic sequences described above. Yet by eternalizing their "touchstones"—Dante, late Shakespeare, Donne—and by fetishizing language and making of it the source of a kind of ahistorical plenitude, they were able to contain their discussion of the logic of content within purely ethical limits, without being obliged to translate those ethical categories themselves into social and historical terms. Thus, despite an acute sense of what dialectical thinking will call the concrete (particularly in its verbal manifestation in lyric poetry or dramatic verse), they were unwilling to venture beyond a purely idealistic understanding of the source of such concrete language in the content

---

[12] In "Historicism Once More," in the volume of the same name (Princeton, 1970), pp. 10-13.

of the poetry, which strategic and self-imposed methodological limitations permitted them to see as a function of the
"moral" or religious attitudes of the poet.

Yet with an irony properly dialectical in character, the
ultimate price for such ideological limitations is exacted not
on the historical, but rather on the intrinsically literary level
itself. For without that profound relativism and respect for
the specificity of each concrete situation which characterizes historical thinking, the categories of the New Criticism tend to solidify and are henceforth rigidly applied to
every kind of text irrespective of its inner coherence.

For a genuinely dialectical criticism, indeed, there can be
no preestablished categories of analysis: to the degree that
each work is the end result of a kind of inner logic or development in its own content, it evolves its own categories
and dictates the specific terms of its own interpretation.
Thus dialectical criticism is at the other extreme from all
single-shot or univalent aesthetic theories which seek the
same structure in all works of art and prescribe for them a
single type of interpretive technique or a single mode of
explanation. Nor can it be reconciled with the specialized
disciplines which have been erected on such bases: thus, for
instance, from the dialectical point of view the whole concept of *stylistics* as a separate field is a profoundly contradictory one, for it implies that style, or language perceived
as style, is everywhere an essential and constitutive component of the literary work of art. Indeed, it would seem at
first glance to go without saying that all literary works are
first and foremost linguistic constructions. Yet in reality
what we call style is a relatively recent phenomenon and
comes into being along with the middle-class world itself.
It may be thought of as a consequence of the abandonment
of that classical system of education which was built around
Latin and Greek texts; for style is essentially that which in
modern middle-class culture replaces the *rhetoric* of the

333

classical period. The two categories may be most usefully distinguished through the value and role they assign to the individual personality: for rhetoric is in this sense that ensemble of techniques through which a writer or orator may achieve expressiveness or high style, conceived of as a relatively fixed class standard, as an institution in which the most diverse temperaments are able to participate. Style, on the other hand, is the very element of individuality itself, that mode through which the individual consciousness seeks to distinguish itself, to affirm its incomparable originality. Its ultimate expression is therefore that stress on the physiological uniqueness of the body and of bodily sensation which we have already seen at work as a formal category in modern poetry. Hence Roland Barthes' characterization, which goes far toward exposing the latent contradiction between the linguistic and the extralinguistic at the very heart of style as a phenomenon, insofar as the latter constitutes "something like a vertical and solitary dimension of thought. Its references are on the level of biology or of the past, rather than of history: it is the 'object' of the writer, his splendor and his prison, it is his solitude . . . its secret is a memory buried in the writer's body; the allusive virtue of style is not a phenomenon of speed as in speech, where what has not been said remains as a kind of linguistic interim, but rather a phenomenon of density, for what persists in solidity and depth beneath the style, harshly or tenderly assembled in its figures, are the fragments of a reality absolutely alien to language."[13]

It will no doubt be objected that we are playing on words, and that style as an object of research and as a literary category is not to be confused with what we have above described as the historical phenomenon of style in the modernistic sense. Yet such "wordplay," inadmissible as it may seem to the older analytical type of logical reason-

[13] Barthes, *Le Degré zéro de l'écriture*, pp. 58-59.

ing, is the very essence of the dialectical method itself: as a scandal for static rationality, its inner movement drama- tizes the irresistible link between a formal concept and that historical reality in which it originated. Thus, the abstract idea of style in general retains traces of that concrete his- torical phenomenon of style in modern times which it was first designed to express; and it is because style is a his- torical phenomenon that an absolute science of style is impossible.

We may put all this in another way by pointing out that works come into being at varying distances from the verbal, and that to say that a work is made of words is not the same as saying that "style" in the modern sense is one of its domi- nant categories. In much of the novelistic production of the nineteenth century, for instance, style is a relatively less sig- nificant element (think of the way in which we secretly modernize Dickens, for example, by thinking of him as a stylist), while the stylistic dimension of a writer such as Racine is inconsequential when compared to the rhetorical one. To define style, however, as language which delib- erately calls attention to itself, and "foregrounds" itself as a key element in the work, is to reassert, as over against stylistics, the profoundly historical nature of the phenomenon.

The most striking model of the way in which content, through its own inner logic, generates those categories in terms of which it organizes itself in a formal structure, and in terms of which it is therefore best studied, is perhaps that furnished us by Marx's economic research, where he was obliged at one and the same time to invent the appropriate categories of investigation and to justify such categories on historical grounds. Thus the opening chapter of *Das Kapi- tal*, with its establishment of the intellectual category of the commodity and its description of the relationship between the idea of the commodity and that reality of commodity

production which it both reflects and attempts to comprehend, is a classic demonstration of dialectical thinking as a
ceaseless generation and dissolution of intellectual categories. From the very beginning Marx was obliged to come
to terms with the traditional economic categories evolved
by the middle-class economists, who saw the operation of
the economy as a mechanical and ahistorical interaction of
such components as production, distribution, exchange,
consumption, wages, ground rent, property, industry, agriculture, and so forth. But the point is that at any given
moment of social and historical development these various
"components" stand in different and quite specific ratios to
each other, so that as their proportions change, the nature
of the whole process is transformed as well. Thus agriculture cannot be seen as something like a Platonic essence or
Idea: there is no fixed category such as land-ownership
which remains the same under capitalism and in precapitalist pastoral societies alike. Rather the parts are relational,
and evolve along with the evolution of the whole itself:
"The sharp line of demarcation (abstract precision) which
so clearly distinguished the trading nations of antiquity,
such as the Phoenicians and the Carthaginians, was due to
the very predominance of agriculture. Capital as trading or
money capital appears in that abstraction, where capital
does not constitute as yet the predominant element of society."[14] Thus dialectical thinking is doubly historical: not
only are the phenomena with which it works historical in
character, but it must unfreeze the very concepts with
which they have been understood, and interpret the very
immobility of the latter as historical phenomena in their
own right.

This is why a genuinely dialectical criticism must always
include a commentary on its own intellectual instruments
as part of its own working structure. Thus Plekhanov's clas-

[14] Marx, *Contribution to the Critique of Political Economy*, p. 304.

sic analysis of symbolism transcends a mere interpretation of those symbolic elements, such as the wild duck, which are structurally projected by Ibsen's work. What is significant for him is not the meaning of the individual symbols but rather the significance of the phenomenon of symbolism as such: "The history of literature shows that man has always used one or the other of these means [symbolism or realism] to transcend a particular reality. He employs the first (i.e., symbols) when he is unable to grasp the meaning of that particular reality, or when he cannot accept the conclusion to which the development of that reality leads. He resorts to symbols when he cannot solve difficult, sometimes insoluble problems; when (to use Hegel's happy expression) he is not able to utter those magic words which bring to life a picture of the future. Thus the ability to utter those magic words is a sign of power, while the inability to do so is a sign of weakness. And so in art, when an artist leans toward symbolism it is an infallible sign that his thinking—or the thinking of the class which he represents, in the sense of its social development—does not dare penetrate the reality which lies before his eyes."[15] The reader will recognize in this passage that characteristic hostility toward modernism and what we have come to call stylization, that instinctive bias toward the realistic work, which was later to be worked out only too programmatically by Lukács; he will also, perhaps, in the present context, glimpse the Hegelian origins of such a value judgment, in which the return to symbolic modes is felt to be a historical regression. Yet it is not the basic insight of Plekhanov which is at issue, but rather the transformation into a single-shot formula of what was at the time a fresh concept, evolved to do justice to the peculiar structure of a given work; such analysis is dialectical to the degree that it stresses the dynamic interaction and interdependency between symbolism and the other ele-

[15] In *Ibsen*, ed. Angel Flores (New York, 1966).

ments of the work and articulates, the way in which the overdevelopment of one element (in this case a visual object) relates vitally to the underdevelopment of others. Thus dialectical criticism replaces the older absolutes of truth or beauty with a judgment in which the insistence on the preeminence of the historical situation underlines the inseparability of strengths and weaknesses within the work of art itself or in the philosophical system, and stands as a concrete object lesson in the way in which the very strengths themselves, in all their specificity, require the existence of determinate and correlative weaknesses in order to come into being at all.

We may perhaps drive home this sense of the relativity of literary categories, of the primacy of the internal contradictions specific to the individual work itself, by reexamining the present enterprise in their light. For it is clear that up to this point our description has been essentially undialectical to the degree to which it has taken dialectical thought as its *object* only, and has failed to underscore its own self-consciousness as thought to the second power. That this is the case may be judged from the dominant category of the present essay, which is that of the *example*: for only where thought is imperfectly realized is it necessary to offer examples as such. The latter are always the mark of abstraction or distance from the thought process: they are additive and analytical, whereas in genuine dialectical thinking the whole process would be implicit in any given object. Here, on the contrary, concrete thinking has been torn asunder, into two wholly separate operations: on the one hand, not genuine thinking, but presentation of a *method*, and on the other not the attachment to a genuine object, but only a series of *examples* of objects. Yet the very essence of dialectical thinking lay in the inseparability of thought from content or from the object itself. This was the burden of Hegel's Preface to the *Phenomenology*, where he

denies that one can characterize philosophy from the outside, or speak about it genuinely in any other way but
through the actual practice of philosophy itself: "the demand for such explanations [i.e., external statements about
the philosophic process, presentations of its aim and
methods, illustrations and examples, etc.], as also the attempts to satisfy this demand, very easily pass for the essential business philosophy has to undertake. Where could the
inmost truth of a philosophic work be found better expressed than in its purposes and results? and in what way
could these be more definitely known than through their
distinction from what is produced during the same period
by others working in the same field? If, however, such procedure is to pass for more than the beginning of knowledge,
if it is to pass for actually knowing, then we must, in point
of fact, look on it as a device for avoiding the real business
at hand, an attempt to combine the appearance of being in
earnest and taking trouble about the subject with an actual
neglect of the subject altogether. For the real subject-mat-
ter is not exhausted in its purpose, but in working the
matter out; nor is the mere result attained the concrete
whole itself, but the result along with the process of arriving at it. The purpose by itself is a lifeless universal, just as
the general drift is a mere activity in a certain direction,
which is still without its concrete realization; and the naked
result is the corpse of a system which has left its guiding
tendency behind it."[16]

Thus the only genuinely concrete presentation of dialectical criticism is the practice of such criticism itself,
which from the descent into a given object ultimately works
its way through to literature itself. So that it is only with our
example of the *example* that our presentation is raised to a
higher dialectical plane and attains a more adequate con-

[16] Hegel, *Phenomenology of Mind*, trans. J. B. Baillie (London,
1949), pp. 68-69.

sciousness of its own activity, through commentary on its own commentary reaching out for a glimpse of what a genuinely concrete criticism might be.

III. TAUTOLOGY AS THE MEDIATION BETWEEN FORM AND CONTENT

THUS dialectical thought is in its very structure self-consciousness and may be described as the attempt to think about a given object on one level, and at the same time to observe our own thought processes as we do so: or to use a more scientific figure, to reckon the position of the observer into the experiment itself. In this light, the difference between the Hegelian and the Marxist dialectics can be defined in terms of the type of self-consciousness involved. For Hegel this is a relatively logical one, and involves a sense of the interrelationship of such purely intellectual categories as subject and object, quality and quantity, limitation and infinity, and so forth; here the thinker comes to understand the way in which his own determinate thought processes, and indeed the very forms of the problems from which he sets forth, limit the results of his thinking. For the Marxist dialectic, on the other hand, the self-consciousness aimed at is the awareness of the thinker's position in society and in history itself, and of the limits imposed on this awareness by his class position—in short of the ideological and situational nature of all thought and of the initial invention of the problems themselves. Thus, it is clear that these two forms of the dialectic in no way contradict each other, even though their precise relationship remains to be worked out.

Yet self-consciousness does not mean introspection, and dialectical thinking is by no means a personal thought, but rather a way in which a certain type of material lifts itself to awareness, not only as the object of our thought, but also as a set of mental operations proposed by the intrinsic nature of that particular object. Dialectical thinking is therefore not only thought to the second power, thought about preexisting thought, but also the latter's fulfillment, its realization and abolition in a sense yet to be described. For to the degree to which it places the older mental operation or problem-solving in a new and larger context, it converts the problem itself into a solution, no longer attempting to solve the dilemma head on, according to its own terms, but rather coming to understand the dilemma itself as the mark of the profound contradictions latent in the very mode of posing the problem. Thus, faced with obscure poetry, the naïve reader attempts at once to *interpret*, to resolve the immediate difficulties back into the transparency of rational thought; whereas for a dialectically trained reader, it is the obscurity itself which is the object of his reading, and its specific quality and structure that which he attempts to define and to compare with other forms of verbal opacity. Thus our thought no longer takes official problems at face value, but walks behind the screen to assess the very origin of the subject-object relationship in the first place. But this type of self-consciousness, which phenomenology defined as the *epoche* or the putting between parentheses, receives its own dialectical evaluation through its place in the historical process.

Thus at its extreme limit thought tends somehow to unravel itself, and it is this more than anything else that justifies the description of dialectical thought as tautological—tautological in the ontological sense, as part of a dawning realization of the profound tautology of all thought. What is meant goes deeper than mere logical tautology, even though the basic temporal form is the same: there, where a proposition had seemed to link two separate, independent entities, they suddenly turn out to have been the same thing all along, and the very act of thinking dissolves away. Here the identity is not that between two words or two concepts, but rather between subject and object itself, between the process of thinking and the very reality on which it is exercised, which it attempts to apprehend. Nondialectical thought establishes an initial separation, an initial dualism, naïvely imagining itself to be a subjectivity at work upon an objectivity wholly different and distinct from itself. Dialectical thinking comes as an enlargement upon and an abolition of this initial dualism, for it realizes that it is itself the source of that external objectivity it had imagined to be something separate; and this must now be understood in a twofold way, both in the sense of the Hegelian "objective idealism," in which all experience is a function of a subject-object structure of a determinate kind, and in the Marxist sense in which the external world is the product of human labor and human history so completely that the human producer is himself the product of that history.

It was precisely this dependency of thought on its own content or object which was responsible for that dialectical "wordplay" or punning glimpsed at work in the preceding section and indeed profoundly characteristic of dialectical thinking in general. Thus the reader of such an essay as Adorno's "Society" may too rapidly conclude that the writer has unjustifiably mingled two different types of considerations, two wholly different objects of research—that he frequently, and indeed deliberately, confuses social theory or the history of the various *concepts* of society with sociology or the empirical study of the various existing societies themselves. And it is certainly true that Adorno's is an incessant shifting of reference back and forth between the two levels: for as we have already seen above, he aims precisely at demonstrating that the difficulties inherent in the *concept* of society (insofar as it can be thought of neither as a hyperorganism nor an empirical object in the world) result not from imperfect theorization, which greater ingenuity or more accurate data might be expected to rectify, but rather from the objective condition of society itself as a real object, undefinable at any point and yet omnipresent, whose control over individuals is reflected in the very contradictions of the idea itself: "while the notion of society may not be deduced from any individual facts, nor on the other hand be apprehended as an individual fact itself, there is nonetheless no social fact which is not determined by society as a whole."[17]

There is, no doubt, something scandalous for analytical thought in this notion that not only the theories, but the very problems and categories of thought themselves—whether they be such entities as money, violence, society, style, or point of view—are themselves in constant historical change and have no fixed and objective reality. Yet even the physical sciences themselves are beginning to take into account the profoundly disturbing possibility that the very laws underlying the universe may be in a state of evolution, so that the very concept of physical law, of a fixed and changeless order of nature, is called into question.[18]

The most recent logical analyses of historical thought and historical propositions have confirmed this notion of its tautological structure. Michael Scriven, for instance, has shown how all apparent explanations in historiography, whether they claim to establish laws or merely causes, turn out in reality to be simply "truisms" in disguise: they are, in other words, already presupposed to begin with in the initial phenomenon to be accounted for, and what we took to be explanation was nothing more than an articulation of that initial "postulate," as in geometry, an analysis reducing it to its various implied propositions. Yet in a sense,

---

[17] Adorno, "Society," *Salmagundi*, Nos. 10-11 (Fall 1969-Winter 1970), p. 145.

[18] See Stephen Toulmin and June Goodfield, *The Discovery of Time* (New York, 1965). This is, incidentally, a dialectic of nature rather different from that proposed by Engels.

this circularity was already present in the explanations of the physical sciences as well: "When scientists were asked to explain the variations in apparent brightness of the orbiting second-stage rocket that launched the first of our artificial satellites, they replied that it was due to its axial rotation and its asymmetry. This explanation, perhaps illustrated by moving a pencil through the air while turning it, was perfectly adequate even for newsmen. Yet it contains no laws. . . . It is perfectly true that the apparent brightness of the rocket varies because a varying number of photons is passing into the retina of the observer; but this would also be true if the rocket were symmetrical and being illuminated by a light source of variable brightness, etc., and our interest lies in having one of these states *of the particular object* of enquiry selected out for us as the explanation, i.e., in being told whether it is the shape and motion of the rocket or the varying illumination of it that is responsible for what we see."[19] The explanation, in other words, is inherent in the initial description of the event, just as the geometrical theorem is inherent in the initial definition. Understanding in history does not, therefore, derive from the combination of two wholly different items, such as a law and its manifestation, or the premises of a syllogism, but rather simply from the enlargement of the description of the basic event itself, and the rearticulation of its parts into cause and effect, or problem and explanation. Such understanding is therefore something on the order of a form moving in time, but as a separate thought process it collapses into tautology when we become aware of the real nature of the mental operation performed.

Thus, to return to an illustration from an earlier chapter, the Gironde no doubt represented the interests of a particular mercantile class in Bordeaux, and their activities acquire

[19] *Theories of History*, ed. Patrick Gardiner (Glencoe, 1959), pp. 445, 447.

a kind of transparency for the mind when so understood. Yet the idea that the event in question (the Gironde itself) and its explanation (the class to which they belong) are related as an effect to a cause is in the long run not a very coherent one. If we examine our own mental operations carefully, we find that we have begun with a fairly limited vision of the Gironde (the various parliamentary personalities, the anecdotal material, their official political philosophies and speeches, their program), which is then abruptly expanded to include the social experience of their place of origin, their pasts, their family connections, and so forth. The only way the latter could take on the function of an *explanation* would be if it were understood to be an implicit negation of such senseless propositions as: the Gironde were peasants, the Gironde were nineteenth-century liberals, the Gironde were Austrian aristocrats, etc. That the Gironde were what they were is therefore a truism, and in the long run our understanding of history dissolves back into the operation of the law of noncontradiction, into the ultimate realization that all events carry their own logic, their own "interpretations," within themselves: an interpretation which we then articulate into a logical succession.

In the realm of the history of ideas, this illusion of causality is stronger because in the course of time the concrete situations have vanished, while the ideas have remained behind all by themselves. The original relationship between thought and its object was not an external but an internal one, and the best dialectical analyses show not so much that external social reality *causes* a particular type of thought, as that it imposes basic inner limitations upon it, in an almost a priori fashion. This was, of course, the thesis of Lukàcs' *History and Class Consciousness* on a very abstract level: that the social situation of the bourgeoisie set a priori limits to its speculative thought, or, to use our own terminology, that the forms of middle-class thought are dependent on the deep inner logic of the content of middle-class life. Thus Herbert Marcuse shows how the ideological distortions of Hegel's system (the Absolute Idea, the political conservatism, the idealistic basis of the system in general) are at one with the content of his social and historical situation. They are not external defects, but are rather part and parcel of Hegel's recognition of the nature of social reality at that particular moment of development: "He gives the state the supreme position because he sees the inevitable effects of the antagonisms within modern society. The competing individual interests are incapable of generating a system that would guarantee the continuance of the whole, hence an incontrovertible authority must be imposed on them . . . the rational order that Hegel is here discussing . . . now indicates for him the furthest limits within which this society can be reasonable without being negated in principle. He holds up the revolutionary terror of 1793 as brutal warning that the existing order must be protected with all available means."[20] Thus Hegel's "conservatism" is also a recognition of the moral anarchy inherent in capitalism. His defense of the Prussian state results from his inability, at his particular moment in history, to see clearly any form of genuine social change and reorganization which is not simply the explosion of the Terror. The only concrete correction of Hegel's system is therefore the passage of time, the development of the socio-economic situation beyond those limits, which is to say that the only adequate critique of Hegel is the philosophy of Marx. Thus philosophical thinking, if pursued far enough, turns into historical thinking, and the understanding of abstract thought ultimately resolves itself back into an awareness of the content of that thought, which is to say, of the basic historical situation in which it took place.

[20] Marcuse, *Reason and Revolution*, pp. 175, 177.

When we come to our own time, however, this notion of the internal limits of thought becomes at once more drastic in its implications. It takes the form of a leap between two discontinuous zones of being, the inner and the outer, the psychological and the sociological, the qualitative, lived reality of individual experience, and the quantitative, external, collective conditions of existence. The shock of such a leap is that of external judgment, of finding oneself uprooted from one's own mind, now looking back inside the monad with the eyes of others, or of history: we have already described Sartre's *Critique* as the deliberate realization of such a process. Yet if we examine Sartre's earlier philosophy (taking it as an illustration of one of the most thoroughgoing descriptions of existence from the *inside*, and the most thoroughgoing methodological defense of such a description as well), we find that it is possible at one and the same time to recognize our own experience in such a description and to admit Marcuse's argument that what are there offered as the ontological structure of the existence of consciousness in the world, and of its concrete relationships to other people, are no more than forms of historical alienation, with their characteristic language of possession and reification.[21] Yet with such an analysis, where the ontological turns out to be the historical in disguise, it is not just Sartre's system, but we ourselves who are in a sense turned inside out like a glove, obliged to see ourselves from the outside in larger terms, and to recognize the familiar inner conditions of our experience as the very structure of alienation itself. Such an operation is far more complex than the conventional critique of philosophical positions on their own terms: an example of the latter would be the way in which Merleau-Ponty, positing too radical a separation of subject from object in the initial pre-

[21] See Marcuse, "Existentialismus," *Kultur und Gesellschaft*, II, 49-84.

suppositions of *Being and Nothingness*, reconstructs the system of the latter on a new and for him more adequate experiential basis in the *Phenomenology of Perception*. The Marcuse essay, on the other hand, no longer seeks to distinguish between the true and the false elements in Sartre's thought, but rather to isolate and to identify that concrete historical experience or situation to which Sartre's system as a conceptual whole corresponds: this type of dialectical critique therefore involves a leap from the purely conceptual to the historical level, from idea to that corresponding lived experience which is then "judged" insofar as it is put in historical perspective for us. This is, indeed, the hermeneutic dimension of dialectical thinking, which is called upon to restore to the abstract cultural fact, isolated on the level of the superstructure, its concrete context or situation; the latter has, of course, vanished when we have to do with cultural objects from the past. But when we have to do with products of contemporary culture, this concrete situation becomes the object of repression to the degree that we wish to ignore the socio-economic situation in which we are really involved. Thus such dialectical judgments enable us to realize a momentary synthesis of the inside and the outside, of intrinsic and extrinsic, of existence and history: but it is a synthesis which we pay for by an objective historical judgment on ourselves.

In the purely literary realm, this is nowhere so strikingly evident as in precisely that literary form which takes history for its object, namely in the historical novel itself. Here if anywhere the primacy of the logic of the raw material over the form is absolute, and the process through which the contradictions of the historical object are transformed into the contradictions of the form can be observed openly, as in a laboratory experiment. This is the substance of a remarkable letter from Adorno to Thomas Mann on the subject of Mann's novella *The Black Swan (Die Betrogene)*:

"The figure of Ken, if I'm not mistaken, bears all the earmarks of an American from the forties or fifties rather than from the decade after the *First* World War; you are yourself obviously far more keenly aware of this than I am. Now one might claim [such transposition] as the legitimate freedom of artistic creation, and maintain that requirements of chronological accuracy must be subordinate to the latter, even where it is a question of precision in characterization. Yet I wonder if such a self-evident argument really has much force. If you place a work in the twenties and have it unfold after the First rather than the Second World War, you have your own good reasons for doing so—the most obvious being that an existence such as that of Frau von Tümmler is inconceivable today; and on some deeper level this is tied in with an attempt to put distance between us and such immediate reality, to transform it magically into an earlier moment in history, at precisely that period whose patina *Krull* also rendered. Yet when one begins to transpose decades in this fashion, one becomes involved in obligations not unlike those set by the opening bars of a musical composition, from whose *desiderata* one is not free until the final notes, which reestablish the balance. I'm not talking about some obligation to an external fidelity in the temporal palette, but rather of the obligation to illuminate the images conjured up by art with a historical lighting as well, one which for the obvious immanent-aesthetic reasons can scarcely dispense with using those first, rather external, attributes also. For unless I'm mistaken, one finds oneself here in that paradoxical situation in which the evocation of such images, or in other words the genuine magic of the work of art itself, is more fully achieved to the degree to which it is composed of authentic materials. One might almost think that the suffusion of the work with subjectivity stands not at all—as our traditional formation might make us think—in simple opposition to that precept of realism

that sounds throughout your work, but rather that spiritualization, the world of the imago, is achieved in proportion
to the exactness with which one remains true to the historical, and this in character types also. . . . At the moment,
it strikes me that this precision is by way of being penance
for the sin under which all artistic fiction labors, trying to
cure itself by means of exactness in fantasy."[22]

Yet if everything in the historical moment coheres, then
ultimately the historical novel itself must dissolve as a form,
for in its gradual straining for the concrete totality it bursts
the existential limits of art itself. The emergence of the historical novel was itself only a symptom of the increasing
historicism of the novel in general, and in our own time it
is generally agreed that all novels are historical, in that in
keeping faith with the present their object is just as profoundly historical as any moment from the distant past. The
implication is that the novel of the present has become as
contradictory as the historical novel, and as impossible to
realize; and indeed, over and above the displacement of the
novel by journalism and sociology, the formal crisis of the
novel today has its roots in the historical situation, which
seems too complex for presentation in a narrative model.
This is how Simone de Beauvoir in *The Mandarins* describes the dilemma of her character Henri Perron, as he
tries to do justice to the historical content of the postwar
period: "He spread his notes in front of him—almost a hundred pages. It was good to have put them away for a
month; now he would be able to reread them with a fresh
eye. He plunged into them joyfully, happy to rediscover
memories and impressions formed into careful and smooth-
flowing sentences. But after a while he began to worry.
What was he going to do with all this stuff? These scrib-
blings had neither head nor tail, even though they did have

[22] T. W. Adorno, "Aus einem Brief über *Die Betrogene* an Thomas
Mann," *Akzente*, II, No. 3 (1955), 286-287.

something in common—a certain feeling, a climate, the climate of the prewar era. And that suddenly bothered him. He had thought vaguely, 'I shall try to give the flavor of my life.' As if such a thing were a perfume, labeled, trademark-registered, always the same year after year. But the things he had to say about traveling, for example, were all in terms of a young man of twenty-five, the young man he had been in 1935; they had nothing at all to do with what he had experienced in Portugal [after the liberation of Paris]. The story of his affair with Paula was equally dated; neither Lambert, nor Vincent, nor any of the boys he knew would have any similar reactions today. And besides, with five years of living under the German occupation behind her, a young woman of twenty-seven would be very different from Paula. There was one solution: deliberately to place the book around 1935. But he had no desire to write a 'period' novel, recreating a world that no longer was. On the contrary, what he hoped for in jotting down those lines was to throw himself live and whole onto paper. Well then, he would have to write the story in the present, transposing the characters and events. 'Transpose—what an annoying word! what a stupid word!' he said to himself. 'It's preposterous, the liberties one takes with the characters in a novel. They're transported from one century to the next, pulled out of one country and pushed into another, the present of one person is glued to the past of a second. And all of it is larded with personal fantasies. If you look closely enough, every character in a novel is a monster, and all art consists in preventing the reader from looking too closely. . . .' "[23] No doubt an American account of this abolition of art, this abdication of the storytelling gesture in guilt before its own fictionality, would find more room for the role of the advertising system in the distortion of events by

[23] Simone de Beauvoir, *The Mandarins*, trans. L. M. Friedman (New York, 1956), pp. 131-132.

a kind of omnipresent false consciousness; it would also, as we shall see shortly, link narrative difficulties with a determinate configuration in the political structure, with the unique structure of the present historical moment itself. Yet Simone de Beauvoir here underlines the threat to the artistic process itself of a temporal experience ever more strongly marked by historicity and dominated by an increasingly urgent political awareness. The gravity of the evocation is by no means diminished if we add that it is precisely in novelistic form that she does so, and that it is thus in some sense dialectically that the novel regenerates itself out of its own impossibility, taking the latter as the content of narration renewed.

Thus in the long run the tautological movement which we have described within the work of art, in which from a certain elevation intrinsically formal considerations suddenly dissolve into problems of content, is reproduced outside the work in the relationship between the content and its historical context. It is a forgotten truism to say that forms such as the epic, the costume tragedy, the epistolary novel are inherently dependent for their existence on possibilities in their content, or in other words on the structure of the social experience which they use as raw material and from which they spring as artifacts. Hegel's is still perhaps the most exhaustive description of the way in which, with a transformation in concrete social life, the whole system of the arts is abruptly displaced, and the practice of whole forms falls into oblivion: such is for him, for instance, the passing of the epic world, with its organization of life as a totality of experience, and the coming into existence of that world of middle-class individualism which he calls the "world of prose," where "the individual human being must repeatedly, in order to preserve his own individuality, make himself a means for other people, serve their limited ends, and transform them into means in order to satisfy his own

narrow interests. The individual, therefore, as he appears
in this world of daily life and of prose, does not draw his
principle of activity from himself as a totality, is not comprehensible in himself, but only in relationship to other people. For he finds himself dependent on external influences,
laws, political structures, domestic relationships which preceded him and to which he must yield, whether he has been
able to interiorize them or not. Furthermore, the individual
subject is no totality for other people, but appears from
their point of view only in the context of their own immediate and isolated interests in his actions, wishes and opinions.
What immediately interests people is only the relationship
to their own aims and intentions.—Even the greatest actions
and undertakings to which a collectivity can rouse itself
prove in this area of relative appearances to be little more
than a multitude of individual efforts. . . . [Thus] in this
realm the individual is no longer able to maintain that appearance of autonomous and complete vitality and freedom
which is the very foundation of the notion of beauty. It is
true that neither system nor a totality of activities are lacking in the immediate human reality [of the world of prose]
and in the undertakings and institutions of the latter; yet
that whole is but an aggregate of individualities, its occupations and activities are split and fragmented into innumerable parts, so that only tiny particles of the whole fall to the
various individuals. . . . This is the prose of the world, as it
appears both to our own consciousness and to that of other
people, a finite world, one of mutability, of relativization,
a world under the rule of a necessity which the individual
is unable to escape. For the individual being is caught in a
contradiction in which he sees himself as a sealed unity,
while being all the while wholly dependent on other people,
and the struggle to resolve this contradiction lasts as long
as the attempt and as long as the battle lasts."[24] Hegel thus

[24] *Aesthetik*, I, 150-152.

distinguishes the structural peculiarity of capitalism in terms of the dilemma it poses as potential content for the work of art: to constitute a collective totality which fails to have any existential equivalent in individual experience, to determine individual reality while remaining structurally inaccessible to the categories of the latter's understanding or image-making power.

From our present methodological point of view, however, this description may serve to illustrate that moment which mediates between literary criticism and sociology, in which the former begins to pass over insensibly into the latter under its own momentum: for the key terms of such a description—totality and individuality—are common both to the analysis of concrete social life and to that of the work of art, so that with a slight enlargement of the historical focus what seemed a statement about the work of art proves to retain its validity in the social and historical dimension. What is implied here, in other words, is the notion that at a certain level of concreteness the *thing itself*—or what we will later call its existential reality—may be formulated in any one of a number of alternate codes, may be rearticulated in any one of a number of different dimensions: as literary structure, as the lived truth of a determinate social organization, as a certain type of subject-object relationship, as a certain distance of language from its object, as a determinate mode of specialization or of the division of labor, as an implied relationship between classes. This is truly the place of the concrete, in which alone we may mediate between one level and another of reality, and translate technical analysis of the idea into its truth in the lived reality of social history. It is clearly the most urgent task of a genuinely dialectical criticism to regain, on the occasion of a given work of art, this ultimate reality to which it corresponds; and we will return at the end of the present work to a fuller examination of the implications of such a view for literary method.

Yet we cannot leave behind the subject of the transition from form to content without adding that what holds true for the form of the work of art itself also holds for the categories of literary criticism: they too are profoundly dependent on a situation of a changing and historical character, and we cannot illustrate this better than by reference to the concept of the point of view as it has been presented in an influential and characteristic work of American criticism, Wayne Booth's *Rhetoric of Fiction*. Booth's position, in the spirit of neo-Aristotelian criticism, is that the novel must never be understood as a statement about realities, but rather as a structure of illusions designed to produce certain effects (just as sentences themselves were designed to do within the narrower confines of traditional "rhetoric"). Thus, although he is of course post-Jamesian and deeply influenced by James' formulation of the concept of point of view, he remains profoundly ambivalent about the ultimate implications of the Jamesian doctrine. For with all James' attention to construction and method, his teaching ultimately aimed at a kind of novelistic *truth*: point of view is for him the basic category of novelistic practice not so much because of the illusions and effects it permits the novelist to achieve, but rather because it corresponds to our lived experience, in which we always remain in situation, seeing life from the relatively restricted vision of our own monad. This idea, in Booth's opinion, is pernicious on two counts, which in the long run amount to the same thing: first, the mechanical application of point of view tends to ruin subjects which a nineteenth-century omniscient narrator would have been able to handle to far greater effect (Fitzgerald's uncertainty in the two versions of *Tender is the Night* may here serve as the *locus classicus*). Second, pure point of view ushers in a kind of total relativism, in which we are obliged to accept any narrator on his own terms, and which results in the destruction of all absolute values and standards of judgment, and consequently, of the very source of literary effects as well.

For Booth's book is a defense of the omniscient narrator, the implied author or reliable commentator, who unobtrusively but strategically makes his presence between reader and characters felt in such a way that the former is provided with the standards by which to judge the latter appropriately. The implied author is of course not the real author either, but rather the absolute embodiment of positive cultural values: "when we read [*Emma*] we accept ['Jane Austen,' the dramatized author] as representing everything we admire most. She is as generous and wise as Knightley; in fact, she is a shade more penetrating in her judgment. She is as subtle and witty as Emma would like to think herself. Without being sentimental she is in favor of tenderness. She is able to put an adequate but not excessive value on wealth and rank. She recognizes a fool when she sees one, but unlike Emma she knows that it is both immoral and foolish to be rude to fools. She is, in short, a perfect human being, within the concept of perfection established by the book she writes; she even recognizes that human perfection of the kind *she* exemplifies is not quite attainable in real life. The process of her domination is of course circular; her character establishes the values for us according to which her character is then found to be perfect. . . . It is a choice of the moral, not merely the technical, angle from which the story is to be told."[25]

In the absence of such a figure, and of such absolute standards of moral judgment, the modern novel for Booth ends up in a relativistic subjectivism, the ultimate symbol

[25] Wayne Booth, *The Rhetoric of Fiction* (Chicago, 1961), pp. 264-265.

of which he finds in the nihilism of Céline. The modern concept of irony was of course just such a rudderless absence of value, a gratuitous ambiguity turning on itself and hypostasized as a value in its own right; and it is one of the great merits of Booth's work to have taken the hammer to those plaster idols of modern criticism which are irony and point of view.

Yet the return to the omniscient narrator is in the long run no more attractive as a "solution" for the contemporary novelist than is the scarcely veiled defense of middle-class ethical norms and values for the contemporary reader. Both recommendations mark the basically ahistorical approach of the critic, who does not seem to have grasped the irreversibility of literary history any more than he has understood the way in which in our time the political has taken precedence over the ethical in the old-fashioned sense of the word. The fact is that the implied or reliable narrator described by Booth is possible only in a situation of relative class homogeneity, and indeed reflects a basic community of values shared by a fairly restricted class of readers: and such a situation is not brought back into the world by fiat. Céline's nihilism, on the other hand, and modern subjectivistic relativism in general, reflect an increasing atomization of middle-class society, a fragmentation and decay of the larger social units and institutions. Indeed, it would not be difficult to show this process at work in the development of the novel as a form from Henry James on. Such a demonstration would bring out the relationship between point of view as a literary technique and monadic isolation as a social fact; it would find confirmation in the creation of artificial totalities (such as Gide's concept of the *roman* as a kind of additive sum of the various *récits* of individual existences) and in the premium placed on epistemology as a theme and on the irony of reality and appearance in a relativistic universe, an irony of which Pirandello is the dramatist, Conrad and Ford the novelists, and Fernando Pessoa, perhaps, the poet laureate.

This is the point at which the tautological paradox intervenes: for surely it is paradoxical to speak of point of view as a historical phenomenon when *all* stories and anecdotes, from earliest times, have of necessity involved the choice of a narrative viewpoint of one kind or another? This is, however, precisely the point. To the degree that point of view as a category reflects the historical situation of the middle classes in modern times, it is an unsuitable concept for dealing with historically different forms, and cannot without a contradiction in terms be applied to such works as medieval narrative or folk epic. I will go even further and say that in the same way the solution to the dilemma described by Booth can itself be conceived only as a result of social and historical change, and would imply the transcendence of individualistic point of view in general by more genuinely collective forms, by new modes of narration which correspond formally to the realities of a postindividual world; and indeed the beginnings of such new forms may be seen everywhere in modern literature.

Thus the ultimate value of Booth's work is that of the conservative position in general: useful as diagnosis, and as a means of disengaging everything that is problematical in the existing state of things, its practical recommendations turn out to be nothing but regression and sterile nostalgia for the past. Indeed, the very attempt to think through a noncontradictory, universally valid (and thereby ahistorical, nondialectical) reformulation of the concept of point of view is itself historically symptomatic. Mr. Booth has thus something in common with the object of his criticism: for James also attempted to arrive at the universal laws governing the proper composition of the novel in general, and showed as little awareness of the historically conditioned nature of form. The difference is that James in do-

358

ing so reflected his moment in history, whereas Mr. Booth does not.

IV. IDEALISM, REALISM, MATERIALISM

> All good Marxists ought, *ex officio*, to constitute a "Société des amis matérialistes de la dialectique hegelienne."
>
> —Lenin

So it is that the vexed question of historical determinism slowly comes into view before us, even in what seemed to be a purely literary context. It is no doubt a false problem, to the degree to which it amounts to a covert application of the model of the physical sciences to history: for there is no common denominator between the unique events of the latter and laboratory experiments which one is able to *repeat*. There can be no concept of law, in other words, or scientific prediction, unless one is able to see the elements involved in succeeding experiments as being the *same*; but in history the hypothesis of identical or recurrent factors in different events is possible only at the price of increasing generalization, a movement away from the unique historical fact which permits us to see similarities as from over a great distance.

This is the kind of generalizing movement which is responsible for such statements as those of Plekhanov, in his well-known essay "The Role of the Individual in History": "Owing to the specific qualities of their minds and characters, influential individuals can change the *individual features of events and some of their particular consequences*, but they cannot change their general *trend*, which is determined by other forces."[26] It is not hard to object philosophically to such a statement, whether from the empiricist point of view of professional historians or from the existential position of a Sartre; yet it certainly corresponds to a

[26] *Theories of History*, ed. Gardiner, pp. 159-160.

common-sense feeling about the past and deserves a little closer examination.

For one thing, if there is anything that distinguishes history as such from other modes or objects of study, it would seem to be precisely this indeterminacy of distance, which permits us to change focus and to see the same event anew, either close up, from a relatively documentary viewpoint, or else from across a longer range in which it comes before us as the mere detail of a larger movement or pattern. Historical understanding is a process of *specification*, said Michelet: but it would seem more accurate to include both movements in the description, and to see such understanding as a constant process of *rectifying* the received images we already have of historical events, specifying them, no doubt, correcting them with a mass of detail when the images are vague, yet on the other hand moving away, and replacing them in larger contexts when we have become so absorbed in the empirical complexity of an event as to have forgotten that it can also have a meaning. If historical truth, as opposed to historical accuracy, can be said to have any validity as a philosophical concept, it is hard to see how it could be formulated in any other way than as just such a process of determinate negation.

Such is the context in which Plekhanov's claim may be justified as a statement about history. When we come, however, to the intention behind it, it becomes clear that Plekhanov is evoking not so much determinism as the historical *necessity* of events. It is perhaps more a question of a feeling than of a concept; and I am tempted to say that the feeling of necessity or historical inevitability is simply the emotion characteristic of historical understanding as such, that feeling which accompanies the mental process by which, through that movement of specification or rectification which we have described, we now as for the first time suddenly comprehend a historical event, which is to say

that we understand for the first time how it had to happen
that way and no other. The notion of historical necessity is
therefore something like a historical trope, the very temporal figure of the process of historical understanding, and
presupposes an ever closer approximation of the concrete,
an ever greater enlargement of the context of the historical
meditation, such that the alternative feeling of chance is not
so much disproven as it is rendered inconceivable and
meaningless.

The concept of historical necessity or inevitability is
therefore operative exclusively *after the fact*; and this characteristic of Marxism as a conceptual operation has been
insufficiently understood and has significant implications.
They are, no doubt, implications of a primarily philosophical or historical nature, and concern literature directly
only in the way in which they exclude literary prescription
of the socialist-realist type. Yet to the degree that the
method proposed in the present work represents a coordination of Hegelian and Marxist conceptual operations, it is
necessary to sketch out, however briefly, a justification
against the attacks upon Hegelian "idealism" which have
often been made in the name of orthodox Marxism; and
such a justification is implied in the concept of Marxism as
a *critical* philosophy.

For the attempt to predict is but one of the symptoms of
a failure to think in a situational way; and as a mode of
philosophical thought, we may say that Marxism itself
operates primarily after the fact with respect to other philosophical positions. It is in this sense also, then, that Marxism
may be seen as the "end" of philosophy, in that in its very
structure it refuses system, or what amounts to the same
thing, metaphysical content. The latter results from a hypostasis of the mental processes, an attempt to hold something aside from the concrete operation of the mind upon
its determinate object, something which can then be treated

in absolute fashion, as the universally valid. And no doubt, to the degree to which it is painful to remain in situation and to eschew system or dogma, the emotional motivation behind the metaphysical impulse is self-evident.

It is this critical structure of dialectical thought, this anti-systematic thrust, which makes its formulation such a complicated matter. For if Marxism as a mental operation is to be characterized as a kind of inner "permanent revolution," then it is clear that every systematic presentation of it falsifies it in the moment in which it freezes over into a system. This is indeed the profound formal objection to such otherwise estimable summaries of Marxism as those of Bukharin: the notion of a "scientific socialism" encourages the misconception that Marxism is an objective and systematic body of ideas rather than a form moving in time, and thereby contributes to the transformation into one more ideology of that which was in its very structure a refusal of all ideology as such.

Initially, however, it is certain that those who understood Marxism as a critical philosophy had in mind its emergence from and consequent repudiation of the Hegelian system and the Hegelian metaphysics. In reaction, they insist on historical materialism as a method, and it is instructive to see such incongruously associated philosophers as Benedetto Croce and Karl Korsch reach much the same conclusions in this context. Thus Croce retained from his Marxist period the conclusion that historical materialism was "neither a new *a priori* notion of the philosophy of history, nor a new method of historical thought; it must be simply a *canon* of historical interpretation. This canon recommends that attention be directed to the so-called economic basis of society, in order that the forms and mutations of the latter may be better understood. The concept canon ought not to raise difficulty, especially when it is remembered that *it*

362

implies no anticipation of results, but only an aid in seeking for them; and is entirely of empirical origin."[27]

Croce, of course, speaks as a non-Marxist, and the terminology of Karl Korsch will perhaps be more familiar: "Even where Marx departs from that purely critical position, he does not lay down any general propositions as to the essential nature of all society but merely describes the particular conditions and developmental tendencies inherent in the historical form of contemporary bourgeois society. The critical principle of Marx's *social science* was during the subsequent development of Marxism converted into a general *social philosophy*. From this first misconception, it was only a step further to the idea that the historical and economic science of Marx must be based on the broader foundation not only of a social philosophy but even of an all-comprehensive 'materialistic philosophy' embracing both nature and society, or a general philosophical interpretation of the universe. Thus the definitely scientific forms which the real kernel of the philosophical materialism of the 18th century had assumed in the historical materialism of Marx were ultimately carried back to what Marx himself had once unmistakably repudiated as 'the philosophical phrases of the Materialists about matter.' "[28]

Actually, the similarity between Croce's and Korsch's positions ceases to be quite so surprising when one remembers that in this case both idealist and materialist set out from a basic denial of the relationship between Marx and Hegel: Croce because he is himself a Hegelian and not a Marxist, Korsch because he believes that genuine Marxism involves the thoroughgoing eradication of Hegelian dialectical elements, which for him are still speculative.

[27] Benedetto Croce, *Historical Materialism and the Economics of Karl Marx*, trans. C. M. Meredith (New York, 1966), pp. 77-78.
[28] Korsch, *Karl Marx*, p. 168.

Yet paradoxically enough, the ultimate justification for considering the dialectic as a critical rather than a speculative instrument comes from Hegel himself, who describes it thus in a famous page of the Preface to the *Philosophy of Law*: "A word on preaching about how the world should be. For that, philosophy always arrives too late.· As the *thought* of the world, it only makes its appearance after actuality has finished its process of development and is over. What the conception teaches, history also shows to be necessary. Only in the maturation of actuality does the ideal appear to confront the real. Then the ideal reconstructs this world for itself in the form of an intellectual realm comprehending it in its substance. When philosophy paints its grey in grey then the form of life has grown old, and this grey in grey is not capable of rejuvenating it, merely of understanding it. The owl of Minerva only begins its flight when the twilight falls."[29] Hegel's notion of the Absolute Idea, of that "Sunday of life" when history stops, is clearly the ultimate working out of the contradiction present in this passage, of which Marx's work is an explicit correction. One is reminded a little of Freud's earliest conception of the psychoanalytic process, in which, he thought, the patient would suspend his life and his most essential decisions in order to work out his problems in a relatively closed experimental situation, returning to life after the completion of the cure. As soon, however, as one is able to feel one's own thought as a historical action on equal terms with the objects studied, as soon as one is able to reckon one's own position as an observer into the critical thinking in process, then the Hegelian contradiction is overcome, and one no longer has to posit an end to history in order for historical thought to take place. In the apprehension of all events, mental or otherwise, as profoundly historical and situational in char-

[29] Quoted in Frank Manuel, *The Prophets of Paris* (Cambridge, Mass., 1962), pp. 298-299.

acter, Marx's thought represents an advance over that of Hegel, who reserved a single position outside of history for the philosopher of history himself, and was to that extent unable to grasp the notion of being-in-situation in its most paradoxical dimensions.

It is therefore this particular aspect of Hegel's philosophy which is rejected by Marxism, and not the content of that philosophy as a whole. Yet Croce and Korsch are far from being the only thinkers to feel that Hegel's "idealism" is irreconcilable with Marx's "materialism," and we would do well to examine the relationship of these two positions at this point.

Insofar as Marxism is a critical rather than a systematic philosophy, however, we would expect the materialism of Marx to be not a coherent position in itself but rather a correction of other positions—a rectification in dialectical fashion of some preexisting phenomenon, rather than a doctrine of a positivistic variety existing in its own right. This is to say that we cannot really understand Marx's materialism until we understand that which it is directed *against*, that which it is designed to *correct*;[30] and it is worth pointing

[30] Compare also Sidney Hook, *Towards the Understanding of Karl Marx* (New York, 1933): "Marx came to critical self-consciousness by settling accounts with the varied intellectual traditions and attitudes of his day. . . . None of his works can therefore be understood without a comprehension of the opposing positions to which he makes explicit or implicit reference. Against the idealism of Bruno Bauer and his Young-Hegelian associates, Marx presents the argument for materialism. Against the passive materialism of Feuerbach, Marx defends the principles of activity and reciprocity which were central to Hegel's dialectic. Against the fatalism of both absolute idealism and 'vulgar' (reductive) mechanism, Marx proclaims that human beings make their own history. As opposed to the revolutionists of the phrase, however, he adds that history is not made out of whole cloth but under definite, limiting conditions. . . . The critics who made so much of Marx's contradictory positions never made an attempt to find a point of view from which these alleged contradictions turned out to be applications of the same principles and purposes to different historical situations" (pp. 65-67). Hook's

out that the materialistic dialectic has not one basic philosophical enemy but two, and that besides *idealism*, philosophical *realism* (in the classic sense of Aristotle or Thomas Aquinas) furnishes the other prototype of nondialectical thought, with its common-sense epistemology of the adequation of the concept to external reality, its mechanical and "objective" distinction between subject and object. We cannot, in other words, fully understand the relationship between Marx and Hegel unless we see that there are in reality three basic positions involved; so that although Marx rejects the idealistic spirit of Hegel's dialectic, he is at one with Hegel in repudiating the essentially analytical, antidialectical thinking of philosophical realism as such. The whole problem therefore turns on the relative structures of these two alternatives to the Marxist dialectic, and ultimately resolves itself into the social and historical, or in other words ideological, functions of realism and idealism respectively. The question becomes one of deciding which of these two philosophical attitudes is to be understood as the principal ideological instrument of the middle classes, which of them is the source of that mystification which then becomes the object of the specifically Marxist critique.

Thus formulated, it seems to me that the question contains its own answer, and that if the word idealism is to retain any kind of precise philosophical content, it is preposterous to claim that Hegelian idealism could in any way constitute the dominant ideology of the Western middle classes. Breton, in the *First Manifesto of Surrealism*, offers a particularly striking evocation of the relative thrust of its twin adversaries: "It becomes necessary to open the *dossier* of the realistic attitude, after that of the materialistic. The latter, besides being more poetic, implies on the part of man a monstrous form of pride, no doubt, but not some new and

---

later work, *From Hegel to Marx* (Ann Arbor, 1962), is a valuable presentation of just those historical and philosophical situations.

more complete degradation. We may best understand it as a happy reaction against some of the more ludicrous tendencies of spiritualism. It is, lastly, not incompatible with a certain nobility of thought. In contrast, the realistic attitude from Saint Thomas to Anatole France, inspired by positivism, seems to me utterly antagonistic to any kind of upward intellectual or moral impulse. I loathe it, for that combination of mediocrity, resentment, and base conceit which makes it up."[31] Materialism is in other words a reaction against religion, whereas realism is primarily a reaction against *enthusiasm,* or in more general terms against speculation itself, against any intellectual transcendence of the empirical present itself.

We may therefore conclude that the materialistic strategy of Marxism grows more pronounced whenever the ideology of the dominant classes takes on a religious or spiritualistic form, whenever religion is the principal weapon in the struggle against change and social revolution; and no doubt there are still areas in the Western countries, not to speak of the Third World, in which this is still the case.

But on the whole it must be said that for the essentially feudal and reactionary world view of religion, with its doctrine of hierarchy, submission to suffering, and insistence on the primacy of the spiritual, more indigenous middle-class thought patterns have been substituted which have proved equally capable of holding the line. For the dominant ideology of the Western countries is clearly that Anglo-American empirical realism for which all dialectical thinking represents a threat, and whose mission is essentially to serve as a check on social consciousness: allowing legal and ethical answers to be given to economic questions, substituting the language of political equality for that of economic inequality and considerations about freedom for doubts about capitalism itself. The method of such thinking,

[31] *Manifestes du surréalisme,* p. 9.

in its various forms and guises, consists in separating reality
into airtight compartments, carefully distinguishing the political from the economic, the legal from the political, the
sociological from the historical, so that the full implications
of any given problem can never come into view; and in
limiting all statements to the discrete and the immediately
verifiable, in order to rule out any speculative and
totalizing thought which might lead to a vision of social
life as a whole. I might add that when in the opening chapter of the *Anti-Duehring* Engels attacks "metaphysical"
thinking, it is precisely empiricist thought of the tradition
of Bacon and Locke, rather than the school of German
idealism, that he has in mind.[32]

If therefore *this* is what is meant by that idealism which
it is the task of historical materialism to refute, then we will
have to find another name for idealism of the Hegelian and
Germanic variety, whose ideological distortions are of another type altogether. For it is clear that for Marxism
Anglo-American empiricism is a class ideology, while the
idealism of the Hegelian variety presents distortions of a
more psychological kind. The illusions of Hegelian idealism
are not so much the result of social and political mystification as they are of that permanent danger of unconscious
egocentrism that hangs over the human mind at all times.
This optical illusion of our own centrality is an inevitable
and recurrent fact of our conscious life, a structural delu-
sion which is projected by the contradiction between
thought as a universalizing process and the nature of the
mind as an individual existent. Yet this "idealism," as a perpetual temptation, is part and parcel of our very being and
strikes "idealist" and "materialist" alike, for it is nothing
more than the forgetfulness of our own position as observers. In such a situation prephilosophical naïveté and dog-

[32] Friedrich Engels, *Herr Eugen Duehring's Revolution in Science*
(New York, 1966), pp. 27-29.

matism meet, for both come to stare at their own concepts as though they were things; yet at the other end of the philosophical spectrum Hegel's ingenious and sophisticated solution to the dilemma is no less wrong, positing in Absolute Spirit, as we have seen, a term in which somehow universality and the existence of the individual consciousness are reconciled. It is the psychological function of the materialistic doctrine to rebuke such illusions, in its hygienic downgrading of the pretensions of spirit as such and of the individual mind's claim to universality, in its regrounding of our beings and our bodies in the physical and sociohistorical universe.

A characteristic complex of images marks the development of this theme throughout the works of Marx and Engels: that of ocular inversion as a figure for the seeming autonomy and self-sufficiency of the intellectual and cultural realm. "If in all ideology," they tell us in a famous passage of *The German Ideology*, "men and their circumstances appear upside down as in a *camera obscura*, this phenomenon arises just as much from their historical lifeprocess as the inversion of objects on the retina does from their physical life-process."[33] The figure is paradoxical to the degree to which in it a socially conditioned and historically determined mystification is described in terms of a permanent natural process: at this stage both class ideology and that inherent and more natural tendency of consciousness toward a kind of unconscious idealism are still identified.

It is through this same image that the whole complex relationship of Marx to idealizing tendencies in Hegel is evoked in the well-known remarks from the Preface to the second edition of *Das Kapital*: "The mystification which dialectic suffers in Hegel's hands by no means prevents him from being the first to present its general form of working

[33] *The German Ideology*, p. 14.

369

in a comprehensive and conscious manner. With him it is standing on its head. It must be turned right side up again, if you would discover the rational kernel within the mystical shell."[34] The image is, however, not that of a man standing on his head, but rather that of a whole world reversed and inverted as on the retina of the eye.

What has less often been realized is that the image has its origin in Hegel himself, in that chapter of the *Phenomenology of Spirit* that deals with "Force and Understanding," that is to say, with the scientific interpretation of the sensible world. For Hegel, indeed, the evolution from sensory perception of the external world to a scientific investigation of its inner laws is characterized by the creation of an "inverted world" which is precisely the realm of physical law itself. Scientific thinking, in other words, involves the projection of elements from the "real" or sensory universe into that suprasensible realm "inside" or "beyond" phenomena which is the place of abstract natural law in general, and constitutes thereby a kind of optical inversion of the empirical world of which it is at once the reflection and the explanation. But for Hegel such consciousness, scientific though it may be, is naïve insofar as the scientist thinks of that inverted world as a reality in its own right, insofar as he imagines that laws exist somehow "within" the objects of the world and fails to achieve consciousness of his own mind as the very origin of such theoretical models or constructs.

It was the achievement of Marx and Engels to have transferred this analysis of the self-perpetuation of theory, of that inner momentum through which the process of abstraction tends to substitute itself for its object in reality, to the domain of our everyday understanding of the social and cultural world in which we are involved. The concept of the fetishism of commodities is of course the definitive formu-

[34] *Capital*, p. 25.

lation of this perceptual opacity as it is determined by the structure of our own historical society. But it is Engels who in his old age returns to the imagery of inversion to work out its fullest implications for a theory of culture: "Economic, political and other reflections are just like those in the human eye: they pass through a condensing lens and therefore appear upside down, standing on their heads. Only the nervous apparatus which would put them on their feet again for presentation to us is lacking. The money-market man sees the movement of industry and of the world market only in the inverted reflection of the money and stock market, and so effect becomes cause to him. . . . Where there is division of labor on a social scale, there the separate labor processes become independent of each other. In the last instance production is the decisive factor. But as soon as trade in products becomes independent of production proper it follows a movement of its own, which, while governed as a whole by that of production, still in particulars and within this general dependence again follows laws of its own inherent in the nature of this new factor; this movement has phases of its own and in its turn reacts on the movement of production. . . . The reflection of economic relations as legal principles is necessarily also a topsy-turvy one: it goes on without the person who is acting being conscious of it; the jurist imagines he is operating with a priori propositions, whereas they are really only economic reflexes, so everything is upside down. And it seems to me obvious that this inversion, which, so long as it remains unrecognized, forms what we call *ideological outlook*, reacts in its turn upon the economic basis and may, within certain limits, modify it."[35] In the long run, therefore, what we have called the idealizing tendency inherent in abstract thought reflects the establishment of the various specialized

[35] Letter to Conrad Schmidt, 27 October 1890 (Basic Writings, ed. Feuer, pp. 400-401, 404). The whole letter is of the greatest interest.

disciplines, or in other words the division of labor itself; it is because thought has become a specialized domain, and the property of specialists, that it tends thus to hypostasize itself. In this sense the anti-idealistic thrust of Marxism simply aims at breaking the spell of the "inverted world" of conceptual thought. The dialectic is designed to eject us from this illusory order, to project us in spite of ourselves out of our concepts into the world of genuine realities to which those concepts were supposed to apply. We cannot, of course, ever really get outside our own subjectivities: to think so is the illusion of positivism; but, every time they begin to freeze over, to spring us outside our own hardened ideas into a new and more vivid apprehension of reality itself is the task of genuine dialectical thinking.

Such thought is therefore essentially process: it never attains some ultimate place of systematic truth in which it can henceforth rest, because it is as it were dialectically linked to untruth, to that mystification of which it is the determinate negation and against which it is perpetually forced to reclaim a fitful apprehension of reality, itself perpetually in danger of losing contact with the real in its turn.[36] In the context of our present description, which limited itself to an account of the dialectic as a mental operation, dialectical thinking thus proves to be a moment in which thought rectifies itself, in which the mind, suddenly drawing back and including itself in its new and widened apprehension, doubly restores and *regrounds* its earlier notions in a new glimpse of reality: first, through a coming to consciousness of the way in which our conceptual instruments themselves determine the shape and limits of the results arrived at (the Hegelian dialectic); and thereafter,

---

[36] Georges Gurvitch has named his own, analogous concept of the dialectic "dialectical hyperempiricism" (see *Dialectique et sociologie* [Paris, 1962]). He considers, however, that Marxism is itself another such "dogmatic philosophy of history" which genuine dialectical thinking is called on to "correct."

in that second and more concrete movement of reflection which is the specifically Marxist form, in a consciousness of ourselves as at once the product and the producer of history, and of the profoundly historical character of our socio-economic situation as it informs both solutions and the problems which gave rise to them equally.

If now, to revive a distinction of an earlier chapter, we take a point of view not so much *philosophical* as *hermeneutic*, it becomes possible to see much in modern thought as a kind of unconscious movement and striving toward this ultimate dialectical position. Thus, I am tempted to see even that profound formalism of all the great schools of modern philosophy (whether those of pragmatism or phenomenology, logical positivism, existentialism, or structuralism) as an attempt to dispense with the baggage of system or metaphysical content: such an attempt, pursued to its ultimate consequences, veers about, in a kind of dialectical reversal, into what we may in the present context call the "absolute formalism" of Marxism itself, whose unique concept of dialectical and historical self-consciousness allows it to square the circle and to hold the absolute wholly within the utter relativity of the individual consciousness or the individual observer. To take another aspect of dialectical thinking, I am inclined to understand such paradoxical and self-implicating concepts as Sartrean authenticity, with its perpetual correction of a perpetually reforming *mauvaise foi*; but also Wittgenstein's "therapeutic positivism" (Ferrater Mora); Nietzsche's genealogies; indeed the very Freudian analytical situation itself; as relatively specialized and distorted versions of what we have here described as dialectical self-consciousness. To go even further afield, it seems to me that even such aesthetic concepts as the *ostranenie* or "making-strange" of Russian Formalism (as well as its American version, "make it new"), indeed the profound drive everywhere in modern art toward a renewal of our perception of the world, are but manifestations, in aesthetic form and on the aesthetic level, of the movement of dialectical consciousness as an assault on our conventionalized life patterns, a whole battery of shocks administered to our routine vision of things, an implicit critique and restructuration of our habitual consciousness. What distinguishes such concepts *philosophically* from genuine dialectical thinking is of course their failure to account for the initial numbness of our perception in the first place, their inability to furnish a sufficiently historical explanation for that ontological deficiency which they can only understand in ethical and aesthetic terms. Yet such intellectual distortion, such structural repression of an essential element in the situation, is amply accounted for by the Marxist theory of ideology, which posits a kind of resistance or *mauvaise foi* that grows ever stronger as we draw closer and closer to that truth of the socio-economic which, were it realized in all its transparency, would immediately obligate us to praxis.

Hegel's *Logic* stands as the supreme monument to the transformation of a system of fixed concepts into that fluidity of process from which they ultimately came, their return and reimmersion in the very shaping and unshaping power of mind to which their rigidity as absolute law blinded us. In the same way, one might imagine a dialectical *Rhetoric*, in which the various mental operations are understood not absolutely, but as moments and figures, tropes, syntactical paradigms, of our relationship to the real itself, as, altering irrevocably in time, it nonetheless obeys a logic that like the logic of language can never be fully distinguished from its object. Such a fancy would be useful, I think, to the degree to which it might suggest the profound vocation of dialectical thinking to reopen the approaches to time and to history itself, and to reconstruct a truth in process upon the ruins of a never-ending ideological formation.

V. MARXISM VERSUS SOCIOLOGY: THE REGROUNDING OF THE WORK

IN THIS light, it becomes clear that even what we have called a Hegelian literary criticism includes an essentially critical, negative, rectifying moment, one which forces upon us an abrupt self-consciousness with respect to our own critical instruments and literary categories. When we turn now to a properly Marxist literary criticism, it will be through a similar epistemological shock that we will be able to identify its presence: for such a shock is constitutive of and inseparable from dialectical thinking, as the mark of an abrupt shift to a higher level of consciousness, to a larger context of being.

The absence of such shock is indeed the telltale symptom of the nondialectical character of much of what passes for Marxist criticism. For the sorting out of literary history into the classic periodization—primitive accumulation, triumph of middle-class revolution, age of imperialism—described by Marxist economic theory remains a static enterprise, whether practiced by Christopher Caudwell or under the more sophisticated guise of Lucien Goldmann's "homologies." To read the former is indeed to acquire the gradual impression of a figure named Poetry, which, not unlike the Orlando of Virginia Woolf, alters its shape in the course of its successive adventures down through the ages of modern history. The secret vice of such parallelisms, and the all-informing flaw of vulgar Marxism as such, may be traced to a misconception of the so-called economic level itself: for to the degree that the economic schema is diachronic, and purports to furnish a continuous model of economic development over a long period, to that degree it is itself an ideal and indeed often an unconsciously idealistic construct. To the economic sequence applies everything we have shown about the characteristically Hegelian operation of creating

375

an artificial model of continuity in order intellectually to grasp the otherwise inconceivable reality of diachrony as such. Thus it is only an apparent paradox to claim that in the sequence feudalism-capitalism-socialism Marxist economic theory projects an essentially Hegelian model. And if this is so, then it is equally clear that the positing of homologies between the various levels of reality, between cultural and ideological history, the evolution of political institutions, and ultimately the development of the economy itself can never be anything but a more complex version of those static cultural models discussed in connection with Taine and Spengler in an earlier section, and serving more as a propaedeutic to the concrete than as its genuine realization.

For the apprehension of the concrete, the characteristic gesture of a genuinely Marxist literary criticism, takes place in the realm of the *synchronic*, and it is at this point that the problem of the distinction between the Marxist conceptual operation and that of sociological criticism in general poses itself most acutely. For the sociological approach also implies the juxtaposition of a given literary or cultural fact with some more fundamental "ground" in the realities of a given society or culture; and like Marxist thinking also, sociology frequently expresses itself in terms of groups or social classes. Thus the problem of a sociological literary criticism poses itself most insistently in the context of what we have in the preceding chapter called the *subjective* dimension of Marxism, that is, that alternative code or language of which Marxism disposes to express and reformulate the ambiguous reality of economic institutions in terms of class.

We may perhaps suggest the essentials of the problem in the context of the particularly rich literature about Jansenism in recent French criticism, whose most significant achievements are Paul Bénichou's *Les Morales du grand siècle,* Henri Lefèbvre's *Pascal,* and Lucien Goldmann's *Dieu caché.* In particular Lefèbvre's study, one of the first (1949) and still one of the most striking realizations of French Marxism in the critical domain, replaces the question of the class affiliation of Jansenism squarely within a detailed and suggestive evocation of the historical period itself, with all its contradictory tendencies and archaic survivals: already such a reconstruction of the concrete context of Pascal's work is tantamount to a kind of regrounding of it in the infrastructure. It is a question, perhaps, of something both a little more and a little less than that historical background with which literature is so often supplied, and which is at the same time felt to be something extraneous or extrinsic to the most genuine and formal literary analysis. For the latter, indeed, the work is to its context as a piece of furniture is to its setting; and at the best there can come into play between the two terms, the object and the background, an exchange of stylistic affinities, the practice of that stylistic or cultural analogy of which we have spoken above.

But for a Marxist criticism, the work is precisely not complete in itself but is handed down to us as a kind of gesture or verbal thrust incomprehensible unless we are able to understand the situation in which the gesture was first made, and the interlocutors to whom it was a reply. This is to say that for Marxism, the passage from the literary to the socio-economic or to the historical is not the passage from one specialized discipline to another, but rather the movement from specialization to the concrete itself. We have already shown that for Marx political economy is not just one type of research among others, it is rather that on which the others are founded, and its artificial subdivision in our time into the various branches of the social sciences, its fragmentation into sociology, economics, history, political science, and anthropology, is already an implied commentary on its subversiveness as a unified mode of apprehending social life. When, therefore, the Marxist study of literature appears to shift gears from the literary to the socio-economic, when Engels' commentary on Ibsen turns into a disquisition on the differences between the German and Norwegian petite bourgeoisie ("The Norwegian peasant has never known serfdom, and this fact gives an altogether different background to the whole development of the country, as it did in Castile. The Norwegian petty bourgeois is the son of a free peasant and for this reason he is a *man* compared to the miserable German philistine");[37] when Henri Lefèbvre prefaces his examination of Rabelais with a lengthy essay on the state of the peasantry in the sixteenth century, the progressive nature of the crown, and the evolution of the legal structure of marriage and of women's property rights; when, indeed, lesser Marxist criticism seems obligated to a kind of ritual gesture of the schematic economic or class background sketch—this is to be understood, not as the introduction of material which could have been dispensed with had the historians taught it properly (although I believe it is true that the historians do not generally provide us with these materials in an adequate way), but rather as an enlargement structurally inherent in such criticism, as an intrinsic and indispensable moment in Marxist literary criticism seen as a *form* of understanding.

Thus we do not replace a discussion of Pascal by a discussion of some other thing when we resituate his work within the larger social context of a Jansenism seen as the oppositional ideology of the *noblesse de robe*: rather, we thus restore to it its concrete richness as a complex, contradictory, polyvalent historical act. The pessimism of the Jansenistic world view thus becomes something a little more historical in content than a simple metaphysical option. It now proves

[37] *Ibsen*, ed. Flores, pp. 23-24.

to be the renunciation of life by men whose class has missed its historical opportunity, caught between the rebellious nobility and the crown with its new middle-class bureaucracy, facing the blank wall of an "end" of history in its fate as an influential and relatively independent social group. Or perhaps it would be more fitting to say that in such an analysis, the metaphysical option itself recovers something of its concrete character as a total human response to a historical situation; and it is of course Lucien Goldmann who has gone the farthest in articulating the relationship of the tragic sense of Pascal and of Racine to the religious refusal of the world by the "extremists" in the Port-Royal group, and thus ultimately to the sense of failure of the *noblesse de robe* as a class.

Yet paradoxically, the most vigorous and suggestive model of a Marxist correlation between class and ideology is furnished by Paul Bénichou, who deliberately leaves aside the semiobligatory excursions into the economic and social history of the period and restricts his discussion to the level of the history of ideas. Indeed, he appeals as a precursor to none other than Sainte-Beuve himself, who had already formulated thus the thesis of a class origin of Jansenism: "Port Royal was the religious enterprise of the middle-class aristocracy in France."[38] Yet the contrast between this essentially *sociological* observation and Bénichou's own practice is revealing and instructive: for Bénichou shows us in some detail that the philosophical, artistic, and religious practice of Port Royal is always to be understood in a double sense, not only as a coherent system or world view in its own right, but also as an offensive arm against its class enemies and particularly against the heroic feudal ethic as it is embodied, for example, in Corneille. Indeed, this second or offensive aim is the informing motive behind the construction of the system as such, which only

[38] Paul Bénichou, *Les Morales du grand siècle* (Paris, 1948), p. 114.

comes down to us as a kind of metaphysical vision because we are no longer aware of the concrete context in which it was first and foremost an act. Thus the return in Jansenism to a renewed sense of sin and of self-loathing ("le moi est haïssable") is at one with that strategic and aggressive operation which Bénichou calls the "demolition of the hero." The Other—feudal grandee with all his ostentatious dramatization of a profound inner sense of caste and worth —is drawn into the annihilation of the Self and obliterated with it in its own ruin.

Such an analysis differs from the purely sociological kind in that it describes not simply the affiliation between a doctrine and a class but also the functional role of that doctrine in *class struggle*. It is an often-taught and often-forgotten lesson that ideology is designed to promote the human dignity and clear conscience of a given class at the same time that it discredits their adversaries; indeed, these two operations are one and the same, and as a cultural or intellectual object ideology may be defined as just such a reversible structure, a complex of ideas which appears either systematic or functional depending on the side from which it is approached. Thus, the feudal code of "honor" discredits those classes unable to defend themselves (or in Marc Bloch's formulation, too poor to own a horse); the Protestant work ethic holds up the idleness and conspicuous waste of the nobility to shame; the nineteenth-century notion of middle-class "distinction," as we have seen in the previous chapter, separates middle classes from workers in their way of living their own body. We may therefore say that what distinguishes the Marxist from the sociological notion of class is that, for the former, class is precisely a *differential* concept, that each class is at once a way of relating to and of refusing the others. Whatever its philosophical presuppositions, the sociological view is *formally* wrong to the degree that it allows us to think of the individual classes in a kind of isolation from each other, with the almost physical separation of social groups in city or countryside, or as "cultures" somehow self-developing and independent from each other: for the notion of the isolated class or social group is just as surely a hypostasis as the notion of the solitary individual in eighteenth-century philosophy. In history also there are no substances tranquilly persevering in their own essence, but rather a relationality and struggle of every instant, in which the class is no more free than the individual not to be engaged. So it is that each class implies the existence of all the others in its very being, for it defines itself against them and survives and perpetuates itself only insofar as it succeeds in humilating its adversaries. Thus, to use the convenient but of course very abstract tripartite formula, the bourgeois defines himself as a nonnoble and a nonworker at the same time, or better still, as an antinoble and an antiworker all in one. And with such a relational concept of class, the criterion of a genuinely Marxist analysis is given also: it will necessarily imply the shock of demystification in its very structure, it will always in one way or another presuppose a movement from an apparently systematic and intellectually coherent, self-contained surface to that historical situation behind it, in terms of which the ideological product under examination suddenly proves to have had a functional and strategic value as a weapon of a determinate kind in a concrete and local struggle. The truth of such an analysis may, then, be measured by the degree to which this translation has been realized, by the completeness with which the cultural fact has been reexpressed in terms of the code of the life and death struggle of groups.

Thus, to use the well-known terminology, the work of art or the cultural fact certainly reflects something, but what it reflects is not so much the class in itself as some autonomous cultural configuration, as rather the situation of that class, or, in short, class conflict. To put it this way, however, is to become aware that the model proposed allows for a fairly wide range of possibilities in the mode of reflection itself. Within the analyses of Jansenism described above, for instance, there would seem to be an essential difference between the way in which, for Goldmann, Jansenism as a philosophy "reflects" its tragic social situation and Bénichou's concept of it as a deliberate, if desperate, ideological strategy. This disparity may be most usefully understood, it seems to me, not as an empirical difference in interpretation but as a shift or rearrangement within the model itself: as the substitution, for a relatively passive conception of the way in which "reflection" takes place, of a relatively active one where the ingenuity and creative power of the writer or ideologue are more strongly insisted on. Such a shift is essentially a function of historical distance itself, of the focus on historical events: from far away, cultural objects seem to reflect their situation or infrastructure in a relatively passive way, and this is neither true nor false but rather simply the formal implication of the medium itself. As we move closer and closer to such phenomena, on the other hand, the individual actors begin to emerge and we grow oppressively aware of the unique existential situations in which each of their acts springs into being; in such a focus, close up, classes are no longer even visible, and we find ourselves slowly being forced to the conclusion that if the notion of reflection is to mean anything at all, it must at least be reformulated in such a way that it is the individual writer who *makes himself* over into an instrument for such reflection. But, of course, this formulation also is simply a function of our distance from history, or rather, of our too great proximity to it.

So it is that for Sartre Flaubert's work can be said to reflect the social contradictions of his period, but on condition that we understand it to do so on the mode of attempting to resolve, in the imaginary, what is socially irreconcilable. We have already seen how for Sartre class affiliation is not given, but rather learned through the mediation of the family in childhood, and as it were reinvented as though for the first time. In the case of Flaubert, however, such affiliation is problematical: the bourgeois is for him the object of a repugnance of very much the same order as self-loathing. Hence the work itself, which Sartre shows to be an imaginary synthesis between Voltairean irony and religious devotion. These two terms correspond on the level of Flaubert's childhood experience to the dispositions of his father and mother, and beyond them, in the larger world of social class, to the ideology of a rising bourgeoisie still only a generation or two away from the soil, on the one hand, and on the other to that of the petty nobility from which the mother came. Thus, even the formal level of Flaubert's work reflects an impossible attempt to combine these two irreconcilables; and the work becomes a kind of emblematic transfer of concrete social phenomena into the characteristic mode of being of literature itself, where they are embodied in that peculiar Flaubertian combination of a religion of art and a corrosive social pessimism, of a formal unction and a kind of revulsion in the content, ennui being so to speak the empty passage of time in an attitude of prayer for someone who does not believe and cannot pray.

We find a similar view of art as imaginary resolution, this time to be sure in the context of a primitive or preclass society, in the remarkable pages consecrated by Lévi-Strauss to the peculiar decorative art of the Caduveo Indians. On the formal or purely stylistic level he sees the specificity of this art as a kind of dialectical interaction between symmetry and asymmetry, "a complex situation corresponding to two contradictory forms of duality, which results in a compromise realized by a secondary opposition between the ideal axis of the object and that of the figure it represents." This purely formal structure Lévi-Strauss now reads as a reflection of the contradictions within the social organization of the Caduveos, which discloses an uneasy hesitation between binary and ternary institutions. Thus an abstract formal pattern proves to have been the attempt to "solve" a real social contradiction on an imaginary mode: "since they were unable to come to consciousness [of this contradiction] and to live it, they began to dream it."[39]

At this point, no doubt, the problem arises of the more generally representative character of such imaginary solutions: or in other words, and particularly for a sophisticated and individualistic art, of the discrepancy between a sociology of the artist, with his individual psychology and situation, and that of his *public*. The apparent dilemma can however be avoided if with Sidney Hook we reformulate it in terms of the "distinction between the *origin* of any cultural fact and its *acceptance*. In art, for example, all sorts of stylistic variations or mutants appear in any period. The social and political environment acts as a *selective* agency upon them."[40] Indeed, in the present context we are tempted to see such a shift from consideration of the writer to consideration of his public as the key moment of a dialectical reversal in which, with a whirring of gears, our model readjusts from an *active* to a *passive* conception of the way in which art reflects its social ground. What is here lost in the way of attention to the artistic process itself as an act may be regained in the precision with which, in such works as Sartre's *What Is Literature?*, the class uses of artistic form are described. And with respect to the work itself, I am tempted to see this active-passive axis as roughly coinciding with a general shift from considerations of form to

[39] Claude Lévi-Strauss, *Tristes tropiques* (Paris, 1955), pp. 199, 203.
[40] *Towards an Understanding of Karl Marx*, p. 160.

considerations of content: or rather—since the range of possibilities is here to be considered a continuum in which an increasingly detailed or increasingly general inspection of the phenomenon slowly causes a dialectical reversal in the manner in which it is described—as the translation of what were before expressed as formal phenomena into what now proves to be the terminology of content. Thus Flaubert "solves" a contradiction through formal innovation, while it is the pessimism of Jansenism that expresses the hopelessness of the cause of the *noblesse de robe*. Yet, refocusing these phenomena in a different way, one would no doubt be able to describe the formal specificity of Pascal's work as a symbolic act in its own right, just as one would be able to correlate the emotional content of Flaubert's novels with the social and political climate of France after the failure of the Revolution of 1848.

At the same time, the hypothesis of "imaginary" solutions brings forward a new and somewhat different set of problems which we have not yet directly touched on and which have nonetheless been paramount for Marxist literary criticism in the past. For if the *noblesse de robe* failed to make its revolution, if there exist social contradictions which are structurally insoluble, at the same time we must remember the fact of successful revolutions as well, and make a place for an art which might be prophetic rather than fantasy-oriented, one which might portend genuine solutions underway rather than projecting formal substitutes for impossible ones. The Marxist concept of class, in other words, involves a diachronic dimension as well as the synchronic, differential one we have emphasized up to this point: a class is defined no less by its place in the historical process, by its participation in a given and determinate stage in historical evolution, than by its antagonistic relationship to the other classes contemporaneous with it. This temporal destiny of a class is, however, measured not so much from without, on some external graph or chart of the overall course of economic history, as rather from within, in a kind of rising or falling internal temperature, as a confident feeling of open possibilities and of riding with the flood tide of historical opportunity or a kind of morose turning back upon the self, a sense of stagnation and futility, of the closing of doors, of deteriorating talents and wasted energies. This altered mood of a class as it passes from the great days of its rise to those of its decline Marxism now characterizes by the well-known political language of *progressive* or *reactionary*.

Such expansion or contraction of historical limits has of course the most momentous consequences for artistic production, both in content and in form; and it seems to me that Plekhanov's classic statement, in *Art and Social Life*, is no less true today than when it was written: "The tendency of artists, and of those who have a lively interest in art, toward art for art's sake, arises when they are in hopeless disaccord with the social environment in which they live. Nor is this all. The example of the Russian 'men of the sixties' who firmly believed in the approaching triumph of reason, and the example also of [the Jacobin painter Jacques Louis] David and his friends, who were no less firmly of the same opinion, show us that the so-called utilitarian view of art, that is to say, the inclination to attribute to works of art the significance of judgment on the phenomena of life, and its constant accompaniment of glad readiness to participate in social struggles, arises and becomes stronger wherever a mutual sympathy exists between individuals more or less actively interested in artistic creation and some considerable part of society."[41] For the most part, no doubt, Marxist critics have discussed this renewal of the sources of artistic production in collective life as one form or another of *realism*; and have tended to associate the

[41] Plekhanov, *Art and Social Life*, trans. A. Rothstein (London, 1953), p. 177.

arts of the various rising classes of the past (with chief
emphasis, of course, on the great middle-class realism of the
eighteenth and nineteenth centuries, but with references to
the naturalistic rejuvenation of Egyptian art under Ikhna-
ton, to the archetypal stylistic evolution of classical Athens,
to the rise of Gothic art and to the Renaissance as well) in
a kind of cyclical revival of which the latest manifestation
was seen as socialist realism. We will be less inclined to
dwell on the inherent difficulties of the concept of realism,
however, if we understand that it has for the most part involved a focus on the content of art rather than essentially
formal phenomena. When the problem of realism is posed
in a formal way, as we have seen in our discussion of
Lukács, criteria of representationality and verisimilitude
tend to be replaced by others of a wholly different kind, by
such formal judgments as are implied in the concepts of totality and the concrete, and of narration versus description.

Yet Plekhanov's discussion of the eighteenth-century
drame bourgeois already showed that the relationship of
art to a rising class did not have to be analyzed in the simplistic terms of realistic content. The historical and artistic
phenomenon under analysis is indeed the paradoxical fact
that as the French middle classes drew closer to their moment of truth, the realistic and sentimental drama in prose
which had seemed in the 1750's to be their most characteristic production, and of which Diderot was the theoretician,
fell into disfavor before the renewed popularity of the
heroic costume drama, with its origins in the taste of an
upper-class public. In the long run, of course, this apparent
revival turned out to have heralded the birth of an art
movement which *was* essentially middle class: that of neoclassicism, to which the costume paintings of David are a
monument. Yet Plekhanov's analysis is a shrewd one, and—
using a model not unlike that of Bénichou for Jansenism—
regrounds what is now an essentially *stylistic* phenomenon

387

in the concrete situation of class antagonism: "bourgeois drama," he tells us, "was born of the *opposition* temper of the French bourgeoisie and was no longer of any use in expressing its *revolutionary* aspirations."[42] The *drame bourgeois*, in other words, helped the middle classes to an awareness of themselves as a class distinct from the others, a class with its own life-style, ideology, and self-respect; yet when that class felt strong enough to enter in direct and aggressive confrontation with the nobility, it needed to draw on the more stimulating images of the Roman Republic, of Brutus and the great tribunes, of the heroic gestures of classical antiquity.

Such an analysis might, of course, be completed with Sartre's discussion of the Roman masquerade of the Gironde, outlined in the previous chapter; for it is clear enough that the appeal to costume drama involves an element of self-mystification just as much as an element of praxis. Yet in our present context such a modulation in historical judgment has a rather different theoretical significance: it emphasizes the essential *relativity* of the class descriptions we have been using, of the assessment of the rising or declining destinies of a class, of its progressive or reactionary characteristics. For the eighteenth-century middle classes are from our point of view *both* progressive and reactionary, in that they represent the rising fortunes of a class nonetheless in the long run historically doomed. And they are both these things at once: that heroic and universalizing ideology which was theirs may be seen at one and the same time as a part of the patrimony of mankind as a whole, with its logic of political liberation which has remained active in the Third World of our own day, and as an example of special class pleading. We are thus reconfirmed in our impression that our relationship to a historical fact is not a fixed, static one, but rather one that constantly

[42] *Art and Social Life*, p. 151.

expands and contracts according to a dialectical readjustment of our own distance and of the point of view we take on our own situation. We may thus understand such judgments not as a series of mutually exclusive positions, in which we decide once and for all whether Jansenism was progressive (because of what it was against) or reactionary (because of what it was for), but rather as positions along a kind of sliding scale that spans the twin polemic extremes of complete refusal and complete identification, in such a way that a work or movement can be relocated at a relatively more negative or relatively more positive position along the continuum.

A Marxist class analysis therefore proves to involve two distinct axes of judgment, depending on whether we stress the nature of the relationship between the cultural object and the class which it "reflects" or whether we focus on the historic destiny of the class itself. We may then articulate the possibilities inherent in such a model as follows:

	NEGATIVE: (reactionary)	POSITIVE: (progressive)
PASSIVE REFLECTION: (content)	Jansenism (ideology)	Realism (political consciousness)
ACTIVE RESOLUTION: (form)	Flaubert, Caduveo art (artistic formalisms)	David's paintings (open or prophetic form?)

Such a chart is however worse than misleading unless it is clearly understood that under the right circumstances, the same cultural fact may be seen as occupying *any* of these positions, or, indeed, as accomplishing a rotation through all of the available positions in succession. Thus the novels of Balzac, normally understood as a "realism" in the sense indicated above, may be seen as reflecting the reactionary ideology of a dying class, as evolving what are essentially personal and formal wish-fulfillments out of his own per-

sonal situation, or as anticipating, through the complex interpersonal structure of *La Comédie humaine,* some new
postindividualistic collective formal organization. In much
the same way, I believe that it would not be difficult to
articulate Lenin's various assessments of Tolstoy—reactionary and progressive alike, both a religious ideologue and
a revolutionary prophet—according to some such combina-
tional scheme. What this implies is that such apparent
contradictions in judgment are in reality to be seen as
variations on a common model, rather than as "opinions"
which we are called upon to adopt or to repudiate. History
is indeed precisely this obligation to multiply the horizons
in which the object is maintained, to multiply the perspectives from which it is seen; and I believe that to see differing judgments or evaluations in this fashion is not to speak
out for some theoretical objectivity or neutrality, but rather
to replace us at the very source of value itself and of such
structural permutation, and to translate apparently literary
disagreements back into the ultimate reality of conflicting
groups in the historical world.

Such is the form taken by Marxist literary or cultural
criticism insofar as it seeks to reunite its object with the
reality of class as such, insofar as it sees in its object a relatively transparent form of class practice. But what of the
reality, rather than the illusion, of fetishization? What happens when we consider the work not so much as a relatively
disguised relationship but rather as a form of density in its
own right, as something produced, as consciousness quite
deliberately reified? When we recall, in short, the two possible codes or languages of a Marxist analysis, we may begin to suspect that everything we have hitherto described
in terms of class may also be developed in a quite different
way, and indeed with quite different, although no less revealing, results.

Here we have evidently to do with a setting of the work

in contact with economic, rather than social, reality: the coordinates of such analysis will therefore no longer be those of ideological formation, but rather of the forms of commodity production. Yet any thoroughgoing description of an object qua object has an obligation to come to terms in one way or another with the Aristotelian four causes—formal, material, efficient, and final—as an inventory of the various points of view from which an object may be understood: "in one of these we mean the substance, i.e., the essence (for the 'why' is reducible finally to the definition, and the ultimate 'why' is a cause and principle); in another the matter or substratum, in a third the source of the change, and in a fourth the cause opposed to this, the purpose and the good (for this is the end of all generation and change)."[43] But Aristotle's model derives from the world of artisanal production and handicraft; it projects a process in which an agent, imitating a given pattern, forms a certain material in order to create an object which then has some determinate use, such as a cooking pot, an article of clothing, a piece of jewelry, or a spear. It is clear that to the degree that the work of art is itself just such a handmade product, there is a preestablished harmony between the Aristotelian model and the aesthetic object which (among other things) it has been called upon to illuminate.

Such preestablished harmony is likely to hold for the process of perception as well as for that of the making of the object. We have already touched on Heidegger's essential doctrine of the priority of objects-in-use over objects-in-rest: so it is that the dominant category of substance through which we view the outside world is itself conditioned and governed by the types and the structure of the practical objects or implements which surround us. Yet Heidegger's model derives from a peasant world, in which

---

[43] Aristotle, *Metaphysics*, I, 3 (*Basic Works*, ed. Richard McKeon [New York, 1941], p. 693); and see also *Physics*, II, 3 (pp. 240-241).

the cup and the plow, the axe and the staff mold the natural world that comes into sight behind them.

A Marxist criticism must therefore readapt the insights of these two models—the insistence on the making process and the priority of the instruments or objects characteristic of the environment—to the modern world of the industrial production of consumers' goods. Following Heidegger's formula, it will stress the way in which the commodity form conditions all more contemplative and theoretical perceptions of objects, including of course the aesthetic mode of perception. And in a world in which exchange value takes precedence over use value (such is, essentially, the definition of a commodity) it is not surprising that the making of works of art should also be governed by this dominant structure, which reaches down to influence everything in our daily world, our relationships with other people just as much as our relationships with objects. Thus the Aristotelian model, based on a simpler world in which use value was predominant, requires a complete overhaul and readjustment if it is to do justice to the structural mystifications of the advertising universe. We would therefore expect a profound modification and expansion in the Aristotelian final cause, as well as in the formal one. Moreover, to the degree that the paradigm of modern creation has become factory and institutional work rather than the skills of the individual craftsman, we would expect to think henceforth in *collective* rather than in *individual* terms, so that the efficient cause refracts into a class of workmen before an established process, and implies the class for which they work as well. So it is that an adequate vision of the Aristotelian model for the realities of capitalism would see the work of art as a *product* rather than as a made object; it would deal not only with the mode of production, but also with those of distribution and consumption. It would imply study of the consumer as well as of the producer, and

392

might even, indeed, find itself touching on the problems of supply and of the sources of raw materials.

Such a regrounding of the work of art in the world of commodities would first be understood in as literal a fashion as possible. For it is a sobering and salutary experience for professional intellectuals to be reminded that the objects of their study and manipulation have a whole material infrastructure as well, which has traditionally been the realm of the sociology of literature. The investigations thereby implied—of the publishing industry and its gradual economic concentration, of the literary market, of the role of the older forms of distribution as well as the newer media —are external to literature only in the sense that the public world is external to private life. Yet since in America private middle-class consumption has increasingly been replaced by that of the university system, which seems destined to play as crucial a role in the culture of postindustrial capitalism as did the monastery for medieval times, it seems appropriate to quote as an example of such analysis one of the most characteristic pages of the late C. Wright Mills on the commodity structure of academic intellectual life: "The *producer* is the man who creates ideas, first sets them forth, possibly tests them, or at any rate makes them available in writing to those portions of the market capable of understanding them. Among producers there are individual entrepreneurs—still the predominant type—and corporation executives in research institutions of various kinds who are in fact administrators over production units. Then there are the *wholesalers*, who while they do not produce ideas do distribute them in textbooks to other academic men, who in turn sell them directly to student consumers. In so far as men teach, and only teach, they are *retailers* of ideas and materials, the better of them being serviced by original producers, the lesser, by wholesalers. All academic men, regardless of type, are also *consumers* of the products of others, of producers and wholesalers through books, and of retailers to some extent through personal conversation on local markets. But it is possible for some to specialize in consumption: these become great *comprehenders*, rather than *users*, of books, and they are great on bibliographies."[44]

Such a passage may serve as a transition from a relatively external consideration of the literary infrastructure—a kind of mechanical materialism, so to speak, on the level of literary criticism—to the relatively more internal questions of literary consumption. For what we consume is always to a certain extent an *idea* rather than a material thing: this is the very essence of the distinction between use and exchange values, that the object no longer exists primarily to satisfy a need, understood by analogy with the needs of the body, but rather as a kind of abstract and emblematic value in which we can no longer clearly distinguish between need-satisfaction and artificial stimuli. We may measure the distance between these two states, the relatively natural precapitalist relationship to objects and our own, by attention to the whole notion of aesthetic *pleasure*. For Aristotle, the emotional satisfaction of tragedy is easily divided into its functional components of pity and fear, which attach to the fate witnessed and thereby purge individual and community alike of their own social and existential anxiety. Such a final cause of tragedy is therefore able to serve a so-

---

[44] C. Wright Mills, *White Collar* (New York, 1956), p. 132. A survey of the more traditional, non-Marxist sociology of literature would want to take note of Q. D. Leavis, *Fiction and the Reading Public* (New York, 1965); of the research of Ian Watt and Pierre Bourdieu; of Robert Escarpit, *Sociologie de la littérature* (Paris, 1964) and *The Book Revolution* (London, 1966); as well as the useful *Hauptrichtungen der Literatursoziologie und ihre Methoden* of Hans Norbert Fügen (Bonn, 1964). But it is worth observing how in the context of MacLuhanism or of Derrida's *De la grammatologie* (Paris, 1967) all of those hitherto extrinsic questions of public and of physical book production now find themselves, as in Eric A. Havelock's remarkable *Preface to Plato* (Oxford, 1963), drawn back inside the work itself and interiorized, being now seen as aspects of the work's thematics or inner structure.

cial function in its very nature. In contrast, pleasure under capitalism is simply the sign of the consumption of an object: it is thus relatively extraneous to the object's structure or use, since it can attach to any kind of object, and is at the same time gratuitous to the degree that it serves no collective function beyond that of encouraging further consumption and making the system operate at top capacity.

At this point, then, we begin to glimpse what is the profound vocation of the work of art in a commodity society: *not* to be a commodity, *not* to be consumed, to be *unpleasurable* in the commodity sense. And we may now return to Adorno's musical analyses as perhaps the most fully worked out application of this principle, which constitutes, indeed, the most genuinely Marxist part of his work, in contrast to an otherwise relatively Hegelian practice. For in the present context, it becomes clear that the history of musical development which Adorno has given us, and which serves as the framework and vital situation for the twin dramas of Schoenberg and Stravinsky, is none other than the struggle between music and the commodity form itself. That new and quickened evolutionary logic which enters musical history around the time of the French Revolution is but an emanation of capitalism itself—yet capitalism not as some parallel evolution on the level of the economic system, not as homology, but rather at work *within* the musical material, as the intrinsic distortion of it by the commodity form, which draws the various musical elements, theme, instrumentation, harmony, indeed the length of development and the overall form itself, into its orbit. This is what explains the simplified, prepackaged, and easily consumed leitmotifs of Wagner, what accounts for the prodigious energy with which Schoenberg attempted to stem the dissolution of the work into easy melody and to restore some of the earlier total organization of the work, with its henceforth intolerable demands on the attention and powers of concentration of the consumer; this is what accounts for the innovations of Stravinsky as well, who, remaining within the commodity universe, evolves the newest production techniques to restore a little of the emotional shock for his easily jaded public, with its increasingly rapid exhaustion of new products.

If it should prove possible to do for the literary work what Adorno has thus done for musical analysis, then we should find ourselves in the presence of a kind of "intrinsic" Marxist criticism, a kind of Marxist philology or systematic investigation of the inner, social forms of art in general. Such a discipline would demand the prolongation of the various kinds of local critical studies (themselves already enlarged to the more adequate dimensions of the Hegelian model described above) to the point where, intersecting either with the realities of class or those of commodity production, they find themselves once more regrounded in concrete social history. We cannot, of course, make the kind of systematic inventory of such local studies which the old-fashioned aesthetics (and indeed such newer "systems" as the Wellek and Warren *Theory of Literature*) claimed to have achieved: such systematizing is ruled out by the priority of history itself, which alone dictates the dominant categories and configurations of the works that, ever new, rise from out of its own perpetual renewal.

Yet such regrounding may be observed at work in the observations of Plekhanov and Lukács on symbolism, for instance, which may essentially be thought of as laying the foundations for a Marxist theory of the *image*. A slightly different formulation of the same phenomenon may be found in Sartre's theory of the "imaginary" as well, which he sees as a reorganization of the object in such a way that it is withdrawn from the time of praxis, as a transformation of an *act* into a *gesture*.[45] Such analyses have in common a

[45] See my "Three Methods," in *Modern French Criticism*.

situational and historicizing logic: they do not imply a structure of the image which holds for all time and in all situations, but rather see the specific literary phenomenon as something which draws attention to its own peculiar structural characteristics, which identifies itself as a process of *symbolizing*, which is conscious of itself as "irrealizing" the world.

In much the same way, if we have shown above that a general science of stylistics is a contradiction in terms, then at least we may for style in modern times project something like a Marxist stylistics, in which the art-sentence itself, as it has been so variously cultivated and practiced in modern times from Flaubert to Hemingway, may be seen alternatively as a type of work or mode of production, and as a type of commodity as well. For nowhere, perhaps, is the peculiar influence of the commodity structure greater than in that ambiguous reality which is language, and which can be consumed as a rich object just as easily as it can attempt to efface itself in that socially motivated transparency which Barthes has called "white writing." In modern literature, indeed, the production of the sentence becomes itself a new kind of event *within* the work, and generates a whole new kind of form.

In the same spirit, a Marxist theory of plot might be elaborated: indeed, Lukács has already gone a long way toward doing so. Yet for such a theory, the restrictions indicated above would hold in even stronger measure: for insofar as in the narrative work plot is the very ground of the concrete itself, there can be no independent analysis of it. It simply coincides with the work itself, as do the functional "descriptions" which normally supply the bulk of what are analyzed as "images." Plot becomes susceptible of analysis only to the degree that it somehow attracts attention to itself as something to be consumed in its own right, as something "foregrounded," standing out in relief from the work as a whole.

Thus the *well-made* plot is certainly a distinct literary and historical phenomenon, which has significant things to show us both about how contemporaries saw the social life in which they participated and how they wanted to see it. But plot in general has nothing of the kind to show, because it is a mere hypostasis.

So it is with the other elements of the work as well, and in particular with a theory of characters, which would no doubt find itself developing most closely in connection with an analysis of the prevalance of otherness as a category and a judgment in the concrete social life of a period; it would also have something to say about the way in which the very presentation of the other is for the novelist a sign of his acquisition of *knowledge* about his society and about reality. At the same time, as with the other kinds of studies sketched out above, such a theory would be an intermittent one, recognizing that the omnipresence of "characters" in literary works is not the same as the dominance of the literary character as a category; and this is no doubt the moment to say something about one of the most familiar kinds of Marxist critical practice, which has to do precisely with character as such.

For many readers, indeed, this, in which character is interpreted as typical of social class or as representative of a given class position, will have been the classical form of the Marxist approach to literature. Was it not the typicality of his characters which attracted Marx and Engels to Balzac? And has not the concept of the typical remained a fetish of Marxist criticism down to our own time? The vices of such criticism have of course often been pointed out, the gravest of them being that such schematic notions of class are a priori ones which end up being able to take no more out of the work of art than they originally put into it in the first place. Such a method is most properly described as an allegorical one; and to say so is only to show the way in which any genuinely dialectical criticism must ultimately turn about and question the sources of its own instruments as well. For it is clear that class consciousness itself—in those societies in which it exists as an existential fact—is an allegorical mode of thought to the degree to which for it individuals are seen as types and manifestations of the social groups to which they belong. Thus a work such as Zola's *Pot-Bouille*, in which the various levels of the apartment house correspond to the various social classes, from the wealthy inhabitants of the first floor all the way up to the maids and workers in the garret, is allegorical because class consciousness still functions structurally within the society as such: it is carried within as a kind of map or chart of society as a whole, as a differential feeling whereby I locate myself with respect to the other classes.

The profound value of such social "typicality" for the production of literature itself may be negatively assessed by considering the situation of the United States today, where it no longer exists. For if there is something unique in the American class situation, it has to do with a kind of overflowing of national limits in such a way that the older national experience, a microcosm in which the truth of the individual coincides with the socio-economic structure, is no longer available. In the age of American imperialism, indeed, as has often been pointed out, we have our lower classes *outside* the national borders: even our working classes are as a bourgeoisie to the alien peasantry or proletariat of the Third World.[46] American literature has there-

[46] "Taking the entire globe, if North America and Western Europe can be called the 'cities of the world,' then Asia, African, and Latin America constitute the 'rural areas of the world.' Since World War II, the proletarian revolutionary movement has for various reasons been temporarily held back in the North American and West European capitalist countries, while the people's revolutionary movement in Asia, Africa, and Latin America has been growing vigorously. In a sense, the contemporary world revolution also presents a picture of the encirclement of cities by the rural area . . ." (Lin Piao, "Long

fore become problematical, not to say impossible, because if it limits itself to the traditional language and form of a national literature it misses the basic truths about itself, while if it attempts to tell those truths it abolishes itself as literature.

If the allegorical interpretation of character seems more convincing when applied to a single *persona* than to a whole array of characters as in a Chekhov play, then I believe this is because the latter merely offers itself as a homology between a set of characters and a set of classes, whereas the former involves in the best of cases something like the shock of a genuine enlargement or regrounding, that brutal passage from some inner "truth of existence" to the external world of history that we have seen as the most essential feature of Marxism as a mental operation. So it is that when, in one of the most famous of all Marxist analyses, Lukács interprets the story of *Death in Venice* in political terms, he seems to have reversed the very inner logic of the work itself, whose subject is indeed the breakthrough of the unconscious itself, with its characteristic welling up of the repressed and of the symbolically invested into Aschenbach's conscious mind. The shock involved in the notion that the fate of the biographer of Frederick the Great is emblematic of the disintegration of Prussia itself, with its mixture of the repressive-authoritarian and the decadent— an interpretation which won the endorsement of Thomas Mann himself—is an essential structural component of Marxist analysis, and is designed to turn the reader, as well as the work, inside out. Yet Thomas Mann is essentially an allegorical writer, so that even this interpretation ultimately finds its justification within the historic structure of the work itself.

Live the Victory of the People's War!"; speech of 3 September 1965, quoted in *Monthly Review*, XVII, No. 6 [November 1965], pp. 5-6).

VI. MARXISM AND INNER FORM

> Ich bin wenigstens überzeugt, dass die Schönheit nur die
> Form einer Form ist, und dass das, was man ihren Stoff
> nennt, schlechterdings ein geformter Stoff sein muss.
>
> —Schiller, *Kallias-Briefe*

THE preceding description of dialectical criticism as critical
rather than systematic, as an operation of rectification, of
an almost ontological restitution, should not be understood
as precluding some more unified critical approach. It
should, however, be kept in mind that in proposing one
such approach, the pages which follow have become more
speculative than descriptive, and that there are certainly
alternative ways of coordinating the essentials of a Marxist
criticism. In particular, if the emphasis on class is not
strong, this is because the class model has never been
worked out as satisfactorily as it should be for American
social reality with its racial and ethnic groupings. The task
is all the more urgent today, in the context of that new and
unparalleled global class situation alluded to above.

The concept of an "inner form," as it was developed by
Goethe and Wilhelm von Humboldt out of Plotinus, recommends itself to us in several ways. It is, first of all, a *hermeneutic* concept, that is, it does not imply a truth of a positivistic kind somehow timelessly associated with its object,
like the laws of the natural sciences; rather, it emphasizes
the operation of interpretation itself, as it moves in time
from outer to inner form as from one moment to another in
a dialectical process. Thus the critic is recalled to his own
procedures, as a form unfolding in time but also reflecting
his own concrete social and historical situation.

Moreover, its model of an ordered sequence of levels
within the work (or, what amounts to the same thing, of a
consecutive series of moments in the interpretive process)
corresponds particularly well to a number of key joints or

transitions which we have described above. The overall movement of a Marxist criticism is, of course, just such a passage from a surface to an underlying reality, from an apparently autonomous object to a vaster ground of which this object proves a part or articulation. Yet we have seen that such a movement can take a number of different forms: in one, as in a kind of *Vexierbild*, an apparently systematic ideology is abruptly refocused into a class polemic. In another, Humboldt's essentially linguistic distinction between the external forms of a language and its inner capacity for meaning is more closely followed, and the work of art, always in one sense an external object produced for a public, is seen from within to be a kind of commodity as well, reflecting either directly or through the force of its negation the state of commodity production in its historical period.

Such interpretation may be incomplete but it can scarcely be described as arbitrary: indeed, I believe it can be said that the only philosophically coherent alternative to such an interpretation out of the social substance is one organized on a religious or theological basis, of which Northrop Frye's system is only the most recent example. We may therefore define religion as that set of imaginary propositions which must be believed to be true if the theoretical consequences of Marxism are to be avoided.

In the long run, however, there is no need to justify the socio-economic "translation" which Marxism sees as the ultimate explanatory code for literary and cultural phenomena. Such justification is already implicit in the dialectical notion of the relationship between form and content, which as we noted above is something quite different from the older Aristotelian notion of form and matter. For the essential characteristic of literary raw material or latent content is precisely that it never really is initially formless, never (unlike the unshaped substances of the other arts) initially contingent, but is rather already meaningful from the outset, being neither more nor less than the very components of our concrete social life itself: words, thoughts, objects, desires, people, places, activities. The work of art does not confer meaning on these elements, but rather transforms their initial meanings into some new and heightened construction of meaning; for that very reason neither the creation nor the interpretation of the work can ever be an arbitrary process. (I do not mean to imply by this that the work necessarily has to be realistic, but only that any stylization or abstraction in its form must ultimately express some profound inner logic in its content, and is itself ultimately dependent for its existence on the structures of the social raw materials themselves.)

This is, I believe, the "materialistic kernel" of Schiller's remark, which serves as the epigraph of this section: "As far as I am concerned, I am convinced that beauty is only the form of a form, and that what is ordinarily called its content must necessarily be thought of as content already formed." Indeed, the first methodological consequence of the dialectical notion of form and content is that, depending on the progress of the interpretive work and the stage at which it has arrived, either term can be translated into the other: thus every layer of content proves, as Schiller implies, to the but a form in disguise. But we have seen above that it is just as true to say that form is really only the projection of content and of the inner logic of the latter. In fact, this essential distinction is useful only on condition that it ultimately reabolish itself in the ambiguity of the artistic substance itself, which can be seen alternately as either all content or all form.

What we have called interpretation is therefore a misnomer: content does not need to be treated or interpreted, precisely because it is essentially and immediately meaningful in itself, meaningful as gestures in situation are meaningful, or sentences in a conversation. Content is already concrete, in that it is essentially social and historical experience, and we may say of our own interpretive or hermeneutic work what the sculptor said of his stone, that it sufficed to remove all extraneous portions for the statue to appear, already latent in the marble block. Thus the process of criticism is not so much an interpretation of content as it is a revealing of it, a laying bare, a restoration of the original message, the original experience, beneath the distortions of the various kinds of censorship that have been at work upon it; and this revelation takes the form of an explanation of why the content was so distorted and is thus inseparable from a description of the mechanisms of this censorship itself.

And since I will speak of Susan Sontag shortly, let me take as a demonstration of this process her remarkable essay on science fiction, "The Imagination of Disaster," in which she reconstructs the basic paradigm of the science fiction movie, seeing in it an expression of "the deepest anxieties about contemporary existence . . . about physical disaster, the prospect of universal mutilation and even annihilation . . . [but more particularly] about the condition of the individual psyche."[47] All of this is so, and her essay provides a thorough working through of the materials of science fiction *taken on its own terms*. But what if those terms were themselves but a disguise, but the "manifest content" that served to distract us from some more basic satisfaction at work in the form?

For beneath the surface diversion of these entertainments, beneath the surface preoccupation of our minds as we watch them, introspection reveals a secondary motivation quite different from the one described above. For one thing, these works, particularly during the period of their heyday after the war and in the 1950's, rather openly express the mystique of the scientist: and by that I refer not

[47] *Against Interpretation*, p. 220.

so much to external prestige or social function as rather to a kind of collective folk-dream about the life-style of the scientist himself: he doesn't do *real* work (yet power is his and social status as well), his remuneration is not monetary or at the very least money seems no object, there is something fascinating about his laboratory (the home workshop magnified to institutional dimensions, a combination of factory and clinic), about the way he works nights (he isn't bound by routine or the eight-hour day), his very intellectual operations themselves are caricatures of what the non-intellectual imagines brainwork and book-knowledge to be. There is, moreover, the suggestion of a return to older modes of work organization: to the more personal and psychologically satisfying world of the guilds, in which the older scientist is the master and the younger one the apprentice, in which the daughter of the older man becomes naturally enough the symbol of the transfer of functions. And so forth: these traits may be indefinitely enumerated and elaborated. What I want to convey is that ultimately none of this has anything to do with science itself, but is rather a distorted reflection of our own feelings and dreams about *work* alienated and nonalienated: it is a wish-fulfillment that takes as its object a vision of ideal or what Marcuse would call "libidinally gratifying" work. But it is of course a wish-fulfillment of a peculiar type, and it is this structure that it is important to analyze.

For we do not have to do here with the kind of direct and open psychic identification and wish-fulfillment that might be illustrated (for the subject matter of scientists) by the works of a C. P. Snow, for instance. Rather, this is a symbolic gratification that wishes to conceal its own presence: thus the identification with the scientist is not here the mainspring of the plot, but rather its precondition only, and it is as though, in a rather Kantian way, symbolic gratification attached itself not to the events of the story but to that

405

framework (the universe of science, the splitting of the atom, the astronomer's gaze into outer space) without which the story could not have come into being in the first place. In this perspective all the cataclysmic violence of the science fiction narrative—the toppling buildings, the state of siege, the monsters rising out of Tokyo bay—is nothing but a pretext, serving both to divert the mind from its deepest operations and fantasies, and to motivate those fantasies as well.

No doubt we could go on and show that alongside this fantasy about work, there is present yet another kind which deals with collective life and which uses the cosmic emergencies of science fiction as a way of reliving a kind of wartime togetherness and morale: the drawing together of the survivors of planetary catastrophe is thus itself merely a distorted dream of a more humane collectivity and social organization. In this sense, the surface violence of the work is doubly motivated, for it can now be seen as a breaking through the routine boredom of middle-class life; while in either event, the violence in the disguise may be understood as the expression of rage at the nonrealization of the unconscious fantasies thus aroused.

The inner form of such an apparently negative and anxiety-ridden type of work is therefore a positive fantasy, one which we have expressed in the language of work satisfaction. The terms in which we describe this inner form or *Erlebnis* are however less important than the movement itself, by which we reemerge into that *place of the concrete* which has been described in a previous section as the mediation between private and public, between individual and socio-economic realities, between the existential and history itself. The task of a dialectical criticism is not indeed to *relate* these two dimensions: they always are related, both in our own life experience and in any genuine work of art. Rather, such criticism is called upon to articulate the work and its content in such a way that this relationship stands revealed, and is once more visible.

For we have to do with a relationship of identity which nonetheless requires a complete translation from one set of terms into the other: the two dimensions are one, and indeed the propaedeutic value of art lies in the way in which it permits us to grasp the essentially historical and social value of what we had otherwise taken to be a question of individual experience. Yet this is done by shifting levels or points of view, by moving from the experience to its ground or concrete situation, as from a form to a content or from a content to a form. The terms in which the socio-economic dimension of experience are described are however by no means limited to those of work, as the production of value and the transformation of the world. Indeed the essential content of such experience can never be determined in advance, and varies from the most substantial kinds of grappling with the world to the smallest and most minute specialized perceptions. Such authenticity is indeed more easily described in a negative way, as being that which escapes the emptiness of routine existence, or of some dull marking time: it is therefore that which restores us to some fitful contact with genuine experience, and the form which such contact takes is at one with the historical possibilities of the socio-economic organization itself.

Yet the terminology of work satisfaction is useful because it fulfills one function for which any other description of such inner form must account in one way or another: it explains the *censorship* of the work itself, it makes us understand why such an impulse had to be disguised in order to come to artistic satisfaction in the first place. For, particularly in middle-class society, the fact of work and of production—the very key to genuine historical thinking—is also a secret as carefully concealed as anything else in our culture. This is indeed the very meaning of the commodity

407

as a form, to obliterate the signs of work on the product in order to make it easier for us to forget the class structure which is its organizational framework. It would indeed be surprising if such an occultation of work did not leave its mark upon artistic production as well, both in the form and in the content, as Adorno shows us: "Works of art owe their existence to the social division of labor, to the separation of mental and physical work. In such a situation, however, they appear under the guise of independent existence; for their medium is not that of pure and autonomous spirit, but rather that of a spirit which having become object now claims to have surmounted the opposition between the two. Such contradiction obliges the work of art to conceal the fact that it is itself a human construction: its very pretension to meaning, and indeed that of human existence in general along with it, is the more convincingly maintained the less anything in it reminds us of its character as a product, and of the fact that it owes its own existence to spirit as to something outside itself. Art which can no longer in good conscience put up with this deception—its innermost principle—has already dissolved the only element in which it can realize itself. . . . And if the autonomy of art in general is unthinkable without this concealment of work, the latter nonetheless becomes problematical, itself now a program, in late capitalism, under the domination of the exchange value and the increasing contradictions of such domination."[48] There is thus given within the very concept of work —either in the form of the division of labor in general or in the more specialized types of production characteristic of capitalism—the principle of a censorship of the work process itself, of a repression of the traces of labor on the product.

When we turn now from popular culture to the more sophisticated artifacts of official literature, we find that the

---

[48] *Versuch über Wagner*, p. 88.

fact of artistic *elaboration* adds a new complexity to the structure of the work without essentially altering the model we have given. In particular, art-literature can be said to reckon the whole value of its own creation itself into the process, so that the inner form of literary works, at least in modern times, can be said to have as their subject either production as such or *literary* production as well—both being in any case distinct from the ostensible or manifest content of the work.

Thus it is a mistake to think, for instance, that the books of Hemingway deal essentially with such things as courage, love, and death; in reality, their deepest subject is simply the writing of a certain type of sentence, the practice of a determinate style. This is indeed the most "concrete" experience in Hemingway, yet to understand its relationship to the other, more dramatic experiences we must reformulate our notion of inner form after the more complex model of a *hierarchy of motivations*, in which the various elements of the work are ordered at various levels from the surface, and serve so to speak as pretexts each for the existence of a deeper one, so that in the long run everything in the work exists in order to bring to expression that deepest level of the work which is the concrete itself; or, reversing the model after the fashion of the Prague School, to *foreground* the work's most essential content.[49]

Thus the enormous influence of Hemingway as a kind of life model would seem to derive first from a kind of ethical content, not a "philosophy of life" so much as an instinctive and intransigent refusal of what suddenly turns out to have ceased to be real living. "It isn't fun any more": such is the

---

[49] This is perhaps the moment to say that I do not regard Formalism—either Czech or Russian—as being at all irreconcilable with Marxism: indeed, I think of the analysis of Hemingway that follows as being essentially a Formalist one; but will reserve a fuller discussion of the Formalist literary model, as well as of structuralism, for another place.

irrevocable boundary line between euphoria and ill humor, between real life and a kind of failure to live which exasperates and poisons the existence of the hero and everyone else around him. Such are the two poles of Hemingway's creation: those incomparable moments of plenitude in nature on the one hand, and on the other, bitching and sudden moods, sudden fits of envy or temper. Both are present indeed almost emblematically in those luminous opening pages of *Across the River and Into the Trees*, where the sullen boatman comes before Colonel Cantwell as the very harbinger of death itself. It is not too much to say that this opposition corresponds to a more general one between life among things and life with other people, between nature and society; indeed, Hemingway often said so himself: "People were always the limiters of happiness except for the very few who were as good as spring itself."[50]

Yet this, which would seem to be first and foremost a life experience, is in reality merely a projection of the style itself. Hemingway's great discovery was that there was possible a kind of return to the very sources of verbal productivity if you forgot about words entirely and merely concentrated on prearranging the objects that the words were supposed to describe. So the following, which has always struck me as being the very prototype of the Hemingway sentence: "From Smith's back door Liz could see ore barges way out in the lake going toward Boyne City. When she looked at them they didn't seem to be moving at all but if she went in and dried some more dishes and then came out again they would be out of sight beyond the point."[51] Something is left out: both the actual movement itself and that full style or *parole pleine* which would have somehow "rendered" it; and Hemingway has spoken in other connec-

[50] *A Moveable Feast* (New York, 1964), p. 49.
[51] "Up in Michigan," in *The First Forty-Nine Stories* (London, 1962), p. 80.

tions as well of the importance of omission as a literary procedure.[52] Yet in the portrayals of ill humor something is omitted also: the space between the remarks, as it were, and it is this prearrangement, now practiced on human material, which gives the Hemingway dialogue its electrical effect. Thus one is wrong to say that Hemingway began by wishing to express or convey certain basic experiences; rather, he began by wishing to write a certain type of sentence, a kind of neutral *compte rendu* of external displacements, and very quickly he found that such a sentence could do two kinds of things well: register movement in the external world, and suggest the tension and fitful resentment between people which is intermittently expressed in their spoken comment.

So we return to our initial contention that what really happens in a Hemingway novel, the most essential event, the dominant category of experience for both writer and reader alike, is the process of writing; and this is perhaps clearest in a simpler work like the *Green Hills of Africa*, where the shooting of the animal in the content is but the pretext for the *description* of the shooting in the form. The reader is not so much interested in observing the kill as he is in whether Hemingway's language will be able to rise to the occasion: "A little beyond there a flock of guineas quick-legged across the road running steady-headed with the motion of trotters. As I jumped from the car and sprinted after them they rocketed up, their legs tucked close beneath them, heavy-bodied, short wings drumming, cackling, to go over the trees ahead. I dropped two that thumped hard when they fell and as they lay, wings beating, Abdullah cut

[52] See, for instance, *Death in the Afternoon* (New York, 1932), p. 192: "If a writer of prose knows enough about what he is writing about he may omit things that he knows and the reader, if the writer is writing truly enough, will have a feeling of those things as strongly as though the writer had stated them." And see also *A Moveable Feast*, p. 75.

their heads off so they would be legal eating."[53] The real "pursuit" involved is thus the pursuit of the sentence itself.

From this central point in Hemingway's creation all the rest can be deduced: the experience of sentence-production is the form taken in Hemingway's world by nonalienated work. Writing, now conceived as a *skill*, is then assimilated to the other skills of hunting and bullfighting, of fishing and warfare, which project a total image of man's active and all-absorbing technical participation in the outside world. Such an ideology of technique clearly reflects the more general American work situation, where, in the context of the open frontier and the blurring of class structure, the American male is conventionally evaluated according to the number of different jobs he has had, and skills he possesses. The Hemingway cult of *machismo* is just this attempt to come to terms with the great industrial transformation of America after World War I: it satisfies the Protestant work ethic at the same time that it glorifies leisure; it reconciles the deepest and most life-giving impulses toward wholeness with a status quo in which only sports allow you to feel alive and undamaged.

As for the human environment of Hemingway's books, expatriation is itself a kind of device or pretext for them. For the immense and complex fabric of American social reality itself is clearly inaccessible to the careful and selective type of sentence which he practices: so it is useful to have to do with a reality thinned out, the reality of foreign cultures and of foreign languages, where the individual beings come before us not in the density of a concrete social situation in which we also are involved, but rather with the cleanness of objects which can be verbally circumscribed. And when at the end of his life the world began to change, and the Cuban Revolution made a retreat back within the borders of the United States in order, it does not seem too

[53] *The Green Hills of Africa* (New York, 1935), pp. 35-36.

412

farfetched to speculate that it was the resistance of such American reality, which as a writer he had never practiced, that brought him to stylistic impotence and ultimate suicide.

If this suggests something of the way in which a Marxist criticism would reconstruct the inner form of a literary work, as both disguise and revelation of the concrete, it remains for us to say a word about the implications of such a theory for judgment or literary evaluations as they are currently practiced. For to claim that the task of the critic is to reveal this censored dimension of the work implies precisely that, at least in art as it is practiced today, in the society in which it is practiced, the surface of the work is a kind of mystification in its structure. This is the point, in other words, at which a Marxist criticism must once again come to terms with modernism in the arts, and I have already implied that the antimodernism of a Lukács (and of the more traditional Soviet critics) is at least partly a matter of taste and of cultural conditioning.

Nonetheless it seems to me that something more must be said in the face of such articulate defenses of modernism as Susan Sontag's "new sensibility" or Ihab Hassan's *Literature of Silence*. These theories reflect a coherent culture with which we are all familiar: John Cage's music, Andy Warhol's movies, novels by Burroughs, plays by Beckett, Godard, camp, Norman O. Brown, psychedelic experiences; and no critique can have any binding force which does not begin by submitting to the fascination of all these things as stylizations of reality.

It should be pointed out, however, that this new modernism differs from the older, classical one of the turn of the century in at least one very essential way: that older modernism was in its essence profoundly antisocial, and reckoned with the instinctive hostility of the middle-class public of which it stood as a negation and a refusal. What characterizes the new modernism is however precisely that it is

413

popular: maybe not in small mid-Western towns, but in the dominant world of fashion and the mass media. That can only mean, to my mind, that there has come to be something socially useful about such art from the point of view of the existing socio-economic structure; or something deeply suspect about it, if your point of view is a revolutionary one.

Yet, it will be said, such art *expresses* American reality; and there, indeed, the ambiguity lies. Insofar as we are Americans, none of us can fail to react to such things as pop art which admirably express the tangible and material realities, the specificity of that American life which is ours. It should be clear, therefore, that a critique of the new modernism cannot be an external but only an internal affair, that it is part and parcel of an increasing self-consciousness (in the heightened, dialectical sense we have given to that term), and that it involves a judgment on ourselves fully as much as a judgment on the works of art to which we react. The ambiguity, in other words, is as much in the revolutionary's own position as it is in the art object: insofar as he is himself a product of the society he condemns, his revolutionary attitude is bound to presuppose a negation of himself, an initial subjective dissociation that has to precede the objective, political one. This is why the drama of the new art involves a more complicated cast of characters than the older struggle between the philistine and the modernist: these two, in the persons of the consumer and of the art salesman and stager of happenings, have begun to merge, and to them may be added a third character, in the form of the revolutionary unhappy consciousness we have described, which in our culture finds it increasingly difficult to distinguish between real and imaginary negation, or indeed between imaginary negation and the promotion of the positive itself.

The most telling criticism of the ideology of the new

sensibility or the new mysticism still remains the comment of Marx on Hegel's notion of religion in the *Economic and Philosophic Manuscripts of 1844*. For just as the spokesmen for the new modernism claim that it *expresses* our society, so Hegel showed that religion was an expression of the human spirit, its *objectification*, with all the ambiguous hesitation between embodiment and alienation which that word implies. Thus, Hegel's system "implies that self-conscious man, insofar as he has recognized and superseded the spiritual world (or the universal spiritual mode of existence of his world) then confirms it again in this alienated form and presents it as his true existence; he reestablishes it and claims to *be at home in his other being*. Thus, for example, after superseding religion, when he has recognized religion as a product of self-alienation, he then finds a confirmation of himself in *religion as religion*. . . . Thus reason is at home in unreason as such. Man, who has recognized that he leads an alienated life in law, politics, etc., leads his true human life in this alienated life as such."[54] So it is that from the recognition of a work of art as a disguised expression and an alienation of reality, to making your peace with the very necessity of such disguises and such alienation, it is but a step.

In this situation the function of literary criticism grows clear. Even if ours is a critical age, it does not seem to me very becoming in critics to exalt their activity to the level of literary creation, as is loosely done in France today. It is more honest and more dialectical to point out that the scope and relevance of criticism varies with the historical and ideological moment itself. Thus, it has been said that literary criticism was a privileged instrument in the struggle against nineteenth-century despotism (particularly in Czarist Russia), because it was the only way one could smuggle ideas and covert political commentary past the censor. This

[54] Marx, *Early Writings*, ed. Bottomore, p. 210.

is now to be understood, not in an external, but in an inner and allegorical sense. The works of culture come to us as signs in an all-but-forgotten code, as symptoms of diseases no longer even recognized as such, as fragments of a totality we have long since lost the organs to see. In the older culture, the kinds of works which a Lukács called realistic, were essentially those which carried their own interpretation built into them, which were at one and the same time fact and commentary on the fact. Now the two are once again sundered from each other, and the literary fact, like the other objects that make up our social reality, cries out for commentary, for interpretation, for decipherment, for diagnosis. It appeals to the other disciplines in vain: Anglo-American philosophy has long since been shorn of its dangerous speculative capacities, and as for political science, it suffices only to think of its distance from the great political and Utopian theories of the past to realize to what degree thought asphyxiates in our culture, with its absolute inability to imagine anything other than what is. It therefore falls to literary criticism to continue to compare the inside and the outside, existence and history, to continue to pass judgment on the abstract quality of life in the present, and to keep alive the idea of a concrete future. May it prove equal to the task!

BIBLIOGRAPHY

Adams, H. P. *Karl Marx in His Early Writings*. New York: Russell and Russell, 1965.

Adorno, T. W. *Aesthetische Theorie*. Frankfurt: Suhrkamp Verlag, 1970.

―――. "Aus einem Brief über *Die Betrogene* an Thomas Mann." *Akzente*, II, No. 3 (March 1953), 284-287.

―――. *Drei Studien zu Hegel*. Frankfurt: Suhrkamp Verlag, 1957.

―――. *Moments musicaux*. Frankfurt: Suhrkamp Verlag, 1964.

―――. *Negative Dialektik*. Frankfurt: Suhrkamp Verlag, 1966.

―――. *Noten zu Literatur*. 3 vols. Frankfurt: Suhrkamp Verlag, 1958-1965.

―――. *Philosophie der neuen Musik*. Frankfurt: Europäische Verlagsanstalt, 1958.

―――. *Prisms*. Translated by S. and S. Weber. London: Spearman, 1967.

―――. "Society." *Salmagundi*, Nos. 10-11 (Fall 1969-Winter 1970), pp. 144-153.

Baron, Samuel H. *Plekhanov: The Father of Russian Marxism*. Stanford: Stanford University Press, 1963.

Baxandall, Lee. *Marxism and Aesthetics: An Annotated Bibliography*. New York: Humanities Press, 1968.

―――. "Marxism and Aesthetics: A Critique of the Contribution of George Plekhanov." *Journal of Aesthetics and Art Criticism*, XXV, No. 3 (Spring 1967), 267-279.

Bénichou, Paul. *Les Morales du grand siècle*. Paris: Gallimard, 1948.

Benjamin, Walter. *Briefe*. Edited by G. Scholem and T. W. Adorno. 2 vols. Frankfurt: Suhrkamp Verlag, 1966.

417

BIBLIOGRAPHY

Benjamin, Walter. *Illuminations*. Edited and with an introduction by Hannah Arendt. Translated by H. Zohn. New York: Harcourt Brace, 1968.

———. *Schriften*. Edited by T. W. Adorno and Gretel Adorno. 2 vols. Frankfurt: Suhrkamp Verlag, 1955.

———. *Versuche über Brecht*. Edited and with a Nachwort by Rolf Tiedemann. Frankfurt: Suhrkamp Verlag, 1966.

Benseler, Frank, ed. *Georg Lukács zum 80sten Geburtstag*. Neuwied: Luchterhand, 1965.

Bloch, Ernst. *Geist der Utopie*. Frankfurt: Suhrkamp Verlag, 1964.

———. *Das Prinzip Hoffnung*. Frankfurt: Suhrkamp Verlag, 1959.

———. *Spuren*. Frankfurt: Suhrkamp Verlag, 1960.

———. *Thomas Münzer als Theologe der Revolution*. Frankfurt: Suhrkamp Verlag, 1962.

———. *Tübinger Einleitung in die Philosophie*. 2 vols. Frankfurt: Suhrkamp Verlag, 1963-1964.

———. *Verfremdungen*. 2 vols. Frankfurt: Suhrkamp Verlag, 1963- .

Breton, André. *Les Manifestes du surréalisme*. Paris: Gallimard, 1969.

Burnier, M.-A. *Les Existentialistes et la politique*. Paris: Gallimard, 1966.

Caudwell, Christopher. *Illusion and Reality*. New York: Russell and Russell, 1955.

Chiodi, Pietro. *Sartre e il marxismo*. Milan: Feltrinelli, 1965.

Clecak, Peter. *Marxism and American Literary Criticism*. Ann Arbor, Michigan: University Microfilms, 1964.

Cooper, D. G. and Laing, R. D. *Reason and Violence*. London: Tavestock, 1964.

Croce, Benedetto. *Historical Materialism and the Economics of Karl Marx*. Translated by C. M. Meredith. New York: Russell and Russell, 1966.

418

Danto, Arthur C. *The Analytical Philosophy of History.* Cambridge, Eng.: Cambridge University Press, 1965.

Della Volpe, Galvano. *Critica del gusto.* Milan: Feltrinelli, 1964.

Demetz, Peter. *Marx, Engels and the Poets.* Chicago: University of Chicago Press, 1967.

Desan, Wilfrid. *The Marxism of Jean-Paul Sartre.* New York: Doubleday, 1965.

Engels, Friedrich. *Herr Eugen Duehring's Revolution in Science.* Translated by E. Burns. New York: International, 1966.

Erickson, Robert. *The Structure of Music: A Listener's Guide.* New York: Noonday, 1955.

Fischer, Ernst. *Art against Ideology.* Translated by Anna Bostock. London: Penguin Books, 1969.

———. *Dichtung und Deutung.* Vienna: Globus, 1953.

———. *The Necessity of Art.* Translated by Anna Bostock. London: Penguin Books, 1963.

Flores, Angel, ed. and trans. *Ibsen.* New York: Haskell House, 1966.

Gallie, W. B. *Philosophy and the Historical Understanding.* New York: Schocken Books, 1968.

Gardiner, Patrick, ed. *Theories of History.* Glencoe: Free Press, 1959.

Goldmann, Lucien. *Le Dieu caché.* Paris: Gallimard, 1955.

———. *Pour une sociologie du roman.* Paris: Gallimard, 1964.

———. *Recherches dialectiques.* Paris: Gallimard, 1959.

Gramsci, Antonio. *Lettere dal carcere.* Turin: Einaudi, 1965.

Guérin, Daniel. *La Lutte de classes sous la première République.* 2 vols. Paris: Gallimard, 1946.

Hauser, Arnold. *The Philosophy of Art History.* New York: Alfred A. Knopf, 1959.

———. *The Social History of Art.* New York: Alfred A. Knopf, 1951.

BIBLIOGRAPHY

Hegel, G.W.F. *Aesthetik.* 2 vols. Frankfurt: Europäische Verlagsanstalt, 1955.

———. *The Phenomenology of Mind.* Translated by J. B. Baillie. London: Allen and Unwin, 1949.

Heissenbüttel, Helmut. "Vom Zeugnis des Fortlebens in Briefen." *Merkur,* XXI, No. 3 (March 1967), 232-244.

Holz, Hans Heinz; Kofler, Leo; and Abendroth, Wolfgang. *Gespräche mit Georg Lukács.* Hamburg: Rowohlt, 1967.

Hook, Sidney. *From Hegel to Marx.* New York: Humanities Press, 1958.

———. *Towards an Understanding of Karl Marx.* New York: John Day, 1933.

Horkheimer, Max, ed. *Zeugnisse: T. W. Adorno zum 60sten Geburtstag.* Frankfurt: Suhrkamp Verlag, 1963.

Hyman, Stanley Edgar. *The Armed Vision.* New York: Alfred A. Knopf, 1948.

Hyppolite, Jean. *Études sur Marx et Hegel.* Paris: Rivière, 1955.

Kerry, S. S. *Schiller's Writings on Aesthetics.* Manchester, Eng.: Manchester University Press, 1961.

Korsch, Karl. *Karl Marx.* New York: Russell and Russell, 1963.

———. *Marxismus und Philosophie.* Frankfurt: Europäische Verlagsanstalt, 1966.

Kraft, Werner. "Walter Benjamin hinter seinen Briefen." *Merkur,* XXI, No. 3 (March 1967), 226-232.

Labriola, Antonio. *Essays on the Materialist Conception of History.* New York: Monthly Review Press, 1966.

Lapassade, Georges. "Sartre et Rousseau." *Etudes philosophiques,* XVII, No. 4 (Winter 1962), 511-517.

Lefèbvre, Henri. *Pascal.* 2 vols. Paris: Nagel, 1949-1954.

———. *Rabelais.* Paris: Editeurs français réunis, 1955.

Lenin, V. I. *O literature i iskusstve.* Moscow: Khudozhestvennaya literatura, 1967.

Lévi-Strauss, Claude. *La Pensée sauvage.* Paris: Plon, 1962.
————. *Tristes tropiques.* Paris: Plon, 1955.
Lichtheim, George. *George Lukács.* New York: Viking, 1970.
————. "Sartre, Marxism and History." *History and Theory,* III, No. 2 (1963-1964), 222-246.
Lieber, Hans-Joachim, and Ludz, Peter. "Zur Situation der Marxforschung." *Kölner Zeitschrift für Soziologie u. Sozialforschung.* X (1958), 446-499.
Lifshitz, Mikhail. *The Philosophy of Art of Karl Marx.* Translated by R. B. Winn. New York: Critics Group, 1938.
Lukács, Georg. *Aesthetik.* 2 vols. Neuwied: Luchterhand, 1962.
————. *Balzac und der französische Realismus.* Berlin: Aufbau Verlag, 1953.
————. *Deutsche Realisten des neunzehnten Jahrhunderts.* Berlin: Aufbau Verlag, 1956.
————. *Essays on Thomas Mann.* Translated by Edith Bone. New York: Grosset and Dunlap, 1964.
————. *Goethe und seine Zeit.* Berlin: Aufbau Verlag, 1955.
————. *Histoire et conscience de classe.* Translated by K. Axelos. Paris: Editions de minuit, 1960.
————. *The Historical Novel.* Translated by H. and S. Mitchell. London: Merlin, 1962.
————. *Probleme der Aesthetik.* Neuwied: Luchterhand, 1969.
————. *Probleme des Realismus.* Berlin: Aufbau Verlag, 1955.
————. *Schriften zur Literatursoziologie.* Edited by P. Ludz. Neuwied: Luchterhand, 1961.
————. *Studies in European Realism.* Translated by Edith Bone. New York: Grosset and Dunlap, 1964.
————. *Die Theorie des Romans.* Neuwied: Luchterhand, 1962.

BIBLIOGRAPHY

Lukács, Georg. *Wider den missverstandenen Realismus.* Hamburg: Claasen, 1958.

Macheray, Pierre. *Pour une théorie de la production littéraire.* Paris: Maspéro, 1970.

Mann, Thomas. *Doktor Faustus.* Frankfurt: Fischer Verlag, 1947.

Mao Tse-tung. "On Contradiction." In *Selected Works,* II, 13-53. 5 vols. New York: International, 1954-1962.

Marcuse, Herbert. *Eros and Civilization.* New York: Random House, 1955.

————. *An Essay on Liberation.* Boston: Beacon Press, 1969.

————. *Kultur und Gesellschaft.* 2 vols. Frankfurt: Suhrkamp Verlag, 1965.

————. *Negations.* Boston: Beacon Press, 1968.

————. *One-Dimensional Man.* Boston: Beacon Press, 1964.

————. *Reason and Revolution.* Boston: Beacon Press, 1960.

————. "Repressive Tolerance." In Wolff, R. P.; Moore, Barrington, Jr.; and Marcuse, Herbert, *A Critique of Pure Tolerance.* Boston: Beacon Press, 1965.

Marx, Karl. *Capital.* Vol. I. Translated by S. Moore and E. Aveling. New York: Kerr, 1906.

————. *A Contribution to the Critique of Political Economy.* Translated by N. I. Stone. Chicago: Kerr, 1904.

————. *Early Writings.* Edited and translated by T. B. Bottomore. New York: McGraw-Hill, 1964.

Marx, Karl, and Engels, Friedrich. *Basic Writings on Politics and Philosophy.* Edited by L. S. Feuer. New York: Doubleday, 1959.

————. *The German Ideology.* Translated by R. Pascal. New York: International, 1947.

————. *Über Kunst und Literatur.* Berlin: Aufbau Verlag, 1953.

Maslow, Vera. "Lukács' Man-Centered Aesthetics." *Philosophy and Phenomenological Research*, XXVII (1967), 542-552.

Mayer, Hans. *Von Lessing bis Thomas Mann*. Pfullingen: Neske, 1959.

————. *Zur deutschen Klassik und Romantik*. Pfullingen: Neske, 1963.

Merleau-Ponty, Maurice. *Les Aventures de la dialectique*. Paris: Gallimard, 1955.

Moore, Stanley. *Three Tactics: The Background in Marx*. New York: Monthly Review Press, 1963.

Morawski, Stefan. "The Aesthetic Views of Marx and Engels." *Journal of Aesthetics and Art Criticism*, Vol. XXVIII, No. 3 (Spring, 1970), pp. 301-314.

————. "Lenin as a Literary Theorist." *Science and Society*, XXIX, No. 1 (Winter 1965), 2-25.

————. "Mimesis—Lukács' Universal Principle." *Science and Society*, XXXIII, No. 1 (Winter 1968), 26-38.

Morpurgo-Tagliabue, Guido. *L'Esthétique contemporaine*. Milan: Marzorati, 1960.

Parkinson, G.H.R., ed. *Georg Lukács: The Man, His Work and His Ideas*. London: Wiedenfeld and Nicolson, 1970.

Plekhanov, G. V. *Art and Social Life*. Translated by A. Rothstein. London: Lawrence and Wishart, 1953.

————. *Fundamental Problems of Marxism*. Translated by E. and C. Paul. Edinburgh: Lawrence and Wishart, 1929.

Ricoeur, Paul. *De l'interprétation: essai sur Freud*. Paris: Seuil, 1965.

Sartre, Jean-Paul. "Les Communistes et la paix." *Situations*, VI. 7 vols. Paris: Gallimard, 1947- .

————. "La Conscience de classe chez Flaubert." *Temps modernes*, Nos. 240-241 (May-June 1966), pp. 1921-1951, 2113-2153.

BIBLIOGRAPHY

Sartre, Jean-Paul. *Critique de la raison dialectique.* Vol. I. Paris: Gallimard, 1960- .

———. "Flaubert: du poète à l'artiste." *Temps modernes,* Nos. 243-245 (August-October 1966), pp. 197-253, 423-481, 598-674.

———. "Marxisme et revolution." *Situations,* III.

———. "Qu'est-ce que la littérature?" *Situations,* II.

———. *Search for a Method.* Translated by Hazel Barnes. New York: Random House, 1968.

Schiller, Friedrich. *On the Aesthetic Education of Man.* Edited and translated by E. M. Wilkinson and L. A. Willoughby. Oxford, Eng.: Clarendon Press, 1967.

———. *Philosophische Schriften.* Basel: Birkhäuser, 1946.

Staël-Holstein, Germaine de. *De la littérature considérée dans ses rapports avec les institutions sociales.* 2 vols. Geneva: Droz, 1959.

Taine, Hippolyte. *Essais de critique et d'histoire.* Paris: Hachette, 1887.

"Walter Benjamin." *Times Literary Supplement,* 22 August 1968.

Williams, Raymond. *Culture and Society 1780/1950.* New York: Harper and Row, 1958.

Zitta, Victor. *Georg Lukács' Marxism: Alienation, Dialectics and Revolution.* The Hague: Martinus Nijhoff, 1964.

424

INDEX